St Thomas Aquinas
(1225–1274)

Pioneers in Economics

Series Editor: Mark Blaug

> Professor Emeritus, University of London
> Consultant Professor, University of Buckingham
> Visiting Professor, University of Exeter

This important new series presents critical appraisals of influential economists from the 17th century to the present day. It focuses in particular on those economists who were influential in their own time and whose work has had an impact – often inadequately recognized – on the evolution and development of economic thought. The series will be indispensable for a clear understanding of the origin and development of economic ideas and the role played by the leading protagonists of the past.

A full list of published and future titles in this series is printed at the end of this volume.

St Thomas Aquinas (1225–1274)

Edited by

Mark Blaug

Professor Emeritus,
University of London

An Elgar Reference Collection

Published by
Edward Elgar Publishing Limited
Gower House
Croft Road
Aldershot
Hants GU11 3HR
England

Bx
1795
.E27
57
1991

Edward Elgar Publishing Company
Old Post Road
Brookfield
Vermont 05036
USA

British Library Cataloguing in Publication Data
St Thomas Aquinas (1225–1274). – (Pioneers in economics,
   3).
   1. Italy. Economics, history
   I. Blaug, Mark *1927*– II. Series
   330.092

Library of Congress Cataloguing in Publication Data
St Thomas Aquinas (1225–1274)/edited by Mark Blaug.
      p. cm. – (Pioneers in economics series: v. 3) (An Elgar
reference collection)
      Includes bibliographical references and index.
      1. Economics–Religious aspects–Catholic Church–History of
doctrines–Middle Ages, 600–1500–Sources. 2. Right of property.
3. Prices. 4. Usury–Religious aspects–Catholic Church–History of
doctrines–Middle Ages, 600–1500–Sources. 5. Catholic Church–
Doctrines–History–Sources. I. Blaug, Mark. II. Series.
III. Series: An Elgar reference collection.
BX1795.E27S7 1991
338.5′2–dc20   90–26845
                                                                                        CIP

ISBN 1 85278 465 2

Printed in Great Britain by Galliard (Printers) Ltd, Great Yarmouth

Contents

Acknowledgements   vii
Introduction   ix

1. B. W. Dempsey (1935), 'Just Price in a Functional Economy', *American Economic Review*, **25**, September, 471–86   1
2. E. A. J. Johnson (1938), 'Just Price in an Unjust World', *International Journal of Ethics*, **48**, January, 165–81   17
3. R. de Roover (1951), 'Monopoly Theory Prior to Adam Smith: A Revision', *Quarterly Journal of Economics*, **65**, November, 492–524   34
4. R. de Roover (1955), 'Scholastic Economics: Survival and Lasting Influence from the Sixteenth Century to Adam Smith', *Quarterly Journal of Economics*, **69** (2), May, 161–90   67
5. R. de Roover (1958), 'The Concept of the Just Price Theory and Economic Policy', *Journal of Economic History*, **18**, December, 418–34   97
6. J. J. Spengler (1964), 'Economic Thought of Islam: Ibn Khaldun', *Comparative Studies in Society and History*, **6**, April, 268–306   114
7. S. Hollander (1965), 'On the Interpretation of the Just Price', *Kyklos*, **18** (4), 615–34   153
8. J. Melitz (1971), 'Some Further Reassessment of the Scholastic Doctrine of Usury', *Kyklos*, **24** (3), 473–92   173
9. J. D. C. Boulakia (1971), 'Ibn Khaldun: A Fourteenth-Century Economist', *Journal of Political Economy*, **79** (5), September–October, 1105–18   193
10. G. W. Wilson (1975), 'The Economics of the Just Price', *HOPE*, **7** (1), Spring, 56–74   207
11. S. T. Worland (1977), 'Justum Pretium: One More Round in an "Endless Series"', *HOPE*, **9** (4), Winter, 504–21   226
12. L. Haddad (1977), 'A Fourteenth-Century Theory of Economic Growth and Development', *Kyklos*, **30** (2), 195–213   244
13. D. D. Friedman (1980), 'In Defense of Thomas Aquinas and the Just Price', *HOPE*, **12** (2), Summer, 234–42   263
14. O. Langholm (1982), 'Economic Freedom in Scholastic Thought', *HOPE*, **14** (2), Summer, 260–83   272

Name Index   297

Acknowledgements

The editor and publishers wish to thank the following who have kindly given permission for the use of copyright material.

American Economic Association for article: B. W. Dempsey (1935), 'Just Price in a Functional Economy', *American Economic Review*, **25**, 471–86.

Cambridge University Press for article: R. de Roover (1958), 'The Concept of the Just Price Theory and Economic Policy', *Journal of Economic History*, **18**, 418–34.

Duke University Press for articles: G. W. Wilson (1975), 'The Economics of the Just Price', *History of Political Economy*, **7** (1), 56–74; S. T. Worland (1977), 'Justum Pretium: One More Round in an "Endless Series"', *History of Political Economy*, **9** (4), 504–21; D. D. Friedman (1980), 'In Defense of Thomas Aquinas and the Just Price', *History of Political Economy*, **12** (2) 234–42; O. Langholm (1982), 'Economic Freedom in Scholastic Thought', *History of Political Economy*, **14** (2), 260–83.

John Wiley & Sons Inc. for articles: R. de Roover (1951), 'Monopoly Theory Prior to Adam Smith: A Revision', *Quarterly Journal of Economics*, **65**, 492–524; R. de Roover (1955), 'Scholastic Economics: Survival and Lasting Influence from the Sixteenth Century to Adam Smith', *Quarterly Journal of Economics*, **69** (2), 161–90.

Kyklos for articles: S. Hollander (1965), 'On the Interpretation of the Just Price', *Kyklos*, **18** (4), 615–34; J. Melitz (1971), 'Some Further Reassessment of the Scholastic Doctrine of Usury', *Kyklos*, **24** (3), 473–92; L. Haddad, 'A Fourteenth-Century Theory of Economic Growth and Development', *Kyklos*, **30** (2), 195–213.

University of Chicago Press for articles: J. D. C. Boulakia (1971), 'Ibn Khaldun: A Fourteenth-Century Economist', *Journal of Political Economy*, **79** (5), 1105–18; E. A. J. Johnson (1938), 'Just Price in an Unjust World', *International Journal of Ethics*, **48**, 165–81.

Every effort has been made to trace all the copyright holders but if any have been inadvertently overlooked the publishers will be pleased to make the necessary arrangement at the first opportunity.

In addition the publishers wish to thank the Library of London School of Economics and Political Science and the Librarian and Staff at The Alfred Marshall Library, Cambridge University for their assistance in obtaining these articles.

Introduction

Thomas Aquinas is generally acknowledged to be the greatest theologian of the Middle Ages and his masterpiece, *Summa Theologica,* provides a complete and authoritative statement of medieval economic thought that has remained the official Catholic view right up to the present time. He was born near the city of Naples and joined the Dominican order at an early age, eventually becoming a pupil of Albertus Magnus (1206–80). He travelled widely throughout his career, teaching at such famous medical centres of learning as Paris, Orvieto, Rome, Naples and Cologne. Aristotle's *Politics* was translated into Latin about 1250, hard on the heels of a Latin translation of his *Nicomachean Ethics.* St Thomas steeped himself for years in the writings of Aristotle and large parts of the *Summa* consist in fact of commentaries on Aristotle's writings on private property, trade, money, exchange, and interest.

For St Thomas economic reasoning is always treated as part and parcel of moral philosophy and jurisprudence. For him economic activity necessarily raises the question of appropriate standards in dealings between citizens and so is an aspect of the inquiry into justice. The category of justice which St Thomas found most relevant to economic life is Aristotle's third form of justice, namely, commutative justice and much of his analysis of price, money and interest takes the form of asking what in each case are the requirements of commutative justice.

St Thomas' *Summa* provides, incidentally, a perfect example of 'scholasticism', the accepted method of analysing social and political questions for almost 500 years. First a particular question is posed and then the question is interpreted from a variety of viewpoints, showing with the aid of copious citations of authorities, that every one of these interpretations has been held by someone, somewhere. Then an answer to the question is presented and again contrary views and counter-examples are criticized in great detail with ample quotations.

St Thomas had a decisive influence on economic thought in at least three broad areas: the theory of private property; the theory of the just price; and the doctrine of usury.

Traditional Christian doctrine which was still accepted in the 12th century, ascribed the origin of private property to human sin. Nature, so the Fathers of the Church had taught, gives all goods in common to all men and the ideal community is one in which no-one calls anything his own. However, Aristotle had written a spirited defence of private property in terms of its necessity for the orderly conduct of human society. St Thomas strove to reconcile Aristotle and the traditional texts but on all important points he came down decisively on the side of Aristotle. To demonstrate the triumph of arguments advanced by St Thomas, we need only mention that the Franciscan order, which adhered strictly to the traditional view that private property was inherently sinful, was sternly rebuked by Pope John XXII in 1322, at which time the Pope declared heretical the doctrine that Christ and his disciples chose deliberately to follow a life of absolute poverty.

St Thomas' discussion of the just price in the *Summa* appears as an answer to the question: 'Whether a man may lawfully sell a thing for more than it is worth?' that worth or value of a good is its 'just price'? The nearest that St Thomas comes to telling us what are the determinants of a just price is that a just price equals 'cost to the seller'; however, his discussion of what is to be included in 'cost to the seller' left a great deal to argument. Since he linked his theory of the just price with the Aristotelian theory of justice in exchange, the interpretation of his analysis has aroused almost as much debate as Aristotle's concept of commutative justice. In the first half of the 19th century everyone read him as endorsing a labour theory of value but after 1870 he was interpreted as endorsing the utility theory of value – a perfect example of reading into past texts whatever ideas prevail at the time. Be that as it may St Thomas' discussion of the concept of the just price was pregnant with suggestions of theories of value to come.

That brings us to usury, the biggest single problem in medieval social theory. Usury was forbidden by the New Testament, by patristic writings, and by the newly discovered authority of Aristotle who left no doubt that money was barren in yielding no usufruct that alone would justify the charge of interest. St Thomas argued that usury is a sin because it involves a charge for a 'consumptible', a good which can be used only by being consumed, in contrast to a non-consumptible like a farm for which a rent can be charged because its use yields a usufruct. However, he allowed a number of exceptions, indeed so many as to almost subvert the very doctrine he was advocating. Thus, *damnum emergens* (damage suffered) was said to be a legitimate ground for a compensating payment and this damage was even allowed to be psychic rather than pecuniary. Similarly, the risk of *mora* (default) constituted a reason for charging something like interest in the form of a penalty contracted in advance that would be forfeited if the debtor defaulted on the loan. Finally, *periculum sortis* (risk) was allowed in a partnership agreement where losses had to be shared with someone else. However, St Thomas never allowed *lucrum cessans* (forgone gain) to serve as a reason for a compensating interest payment. That loophole in the medieval prohibition on usury crept in after his time as the prohibition was gradually whittled down in the 14th, 15th and 16th centuries.

St Thomas' great contribution to economic thought, as to theology, moral philosophy and politics, lies in his emphasis on ratiocination, on the Greek ideal of accepting nothing unless good reasons can be given for it. He has justly been called the 'Christian Aristotle'.

Note

Several paragraphs in this Introduction were borrowed from my *Great Economists Before Keynes* (Wheatsheaf Books, 1986).

[1]

JUST PRICE IN A FUNCTIONAL ECONOMY

The current recrudescence of corporate economy bestows importance on historical analogies hitherto neglected. Medieval economy combined a corporate and functional concept of economic society with political ideals close kin to American constitutional principles. But at present, very incorrect notions of just price, widely accepted, preclude an objective examination of medieval economic theory by American economists. Just price is here examined in its historical sources, the Roman law and the writings of Augustine; development is then traced by quotation from the leading medieval thinkers. Just price thus appears as an integral part of a consistent social philosophy and properly applied as a workable general principle.

I

When the record of economic history is viewed in its full length, that lack of a system which we call the system of individualism is seen to be a recent episode. Historically speaking, only the last century and a half have endeavored to live an economic life without organization or control; and even within that century and a half, individualism has never held the field uncontested. Since the war, as is perfectly evident, the nineteenth century individualistic mood has been replaced by a powerful twentieth century trend toward a corporate economy. Moreover, the economists of the English-speaking world who do not like the Hegelian outlook of Stalin, Mussolini and Hitler, face this world of facts under a severe handicap with the postulates of their own system challenged on various scores.

In all the years of economic activity, and all the types of economic organization before and since the brief day of liberalism, one only attempted to combine the ideas that "all men are by nature equal";[1] that the state is for man and not man for the state;[2] and that there is a measure and a limit and a norm for government interference with individual effort.[3] When we are being pushed into a corporate economy, an historical example of a system that could maintain those three objectives is worthy of consideration. Any economy based on such theory, however faulty in practice, can in our present situation be profitably studied. From this emphasis on principle, it should be clear that we shall not describe the archaic external trappings of medieval economic life, upon which undue emphasis has been placed by enthusiasts and critics alike. The question is one of radical economic principles, not of gargoyles or stained glass windows.

Yet the American economist does not consider the medieval system of economic thought a fruitful field of study. The reason is that he approaches the subject with a fundamental misconception; at the mere mention of just price or objective value, the matter is closed. Regardless of practical considerations, a concern for objective truth would alone justify a re-examination of basic medieval economic concepts. There are few subjects in the field of

[1] Thomas Aquinas, *Summa Theologica*, 2a 2ae quaestio 104, ad 5um.
[2] Thomas Aquinas, *De Regimine Principum* (De Regno) Lib. 3, cap. ii.
[3] Thomas Aquinas, *Summa Contra Gentiles*, Lib. 3, cap. 71.

social science upon which misinformation can be more readily obtained. Scholastic philosophy has recently enjoyed a renascence, both in development as neo-scholasticism, and in historically accurate studies. That the fruit of these studies has not penetrated into the economic world is evident from the fact that it was possible, as late as 1928, to reprint pages 90-96 of Dr. Lewis H. Haney's *History of Economic Thought,* with the statement among others that:

The general notion appears to have been that value is absolute, and objective, and independent of price.[4]

Nor can much be said for Dr. James Westfall Thompson's summary save that it is in harmony with the tall gratuities found elsewhere in his volume. Relying on a second-hand quotation from Thomas Aquinas, through an unidentified Miss Davidson, Dr. Thompson commits himself to the unequivocal position that:

The Church's concept of value was something absolute and apart from value in use and value in exchange, something independent of supply and demand, something intrinsic and fixed.[5]

Even so carefully objective an investigator as Dr. Norman S. B. Gras is able to remark of medieval economics rather complacently:

It was assumed that there was such a thing as an objective value, something inherent in the object rather than in the minds of the buyer and seller. We now have had enough experience and have made enough examination of the problem, of course, to know that no such value ever existed.[6]

Medieval schoolmen are frequently criticized for their lack of scientific method, though Hugo Grotius felt that:

Whenever they are found to agree on moral questions they can scarcely be wrong, they who are so keen in discovering the flaws in each other's arguments.[7]

But whatever may be said for the methods of the schoolmen, one can scarcely approve of the critical technique of the writers cited above or indeed of most writers in English on this subject. In such case, it behooves us to let the schoolmen speak for themselves, and thus to remove the principal misconception which has prevented modern writers from seeing in realistic perspective the medieval organic economy which is the only historical analogy which can now be of service to us. Our present purpose is to look the bogey of just price squarely in the eye, and thus to clear the air. Around

[4] Haney, *op. cit.,* p. 90.

[5] Thompson, *Economic and Social History of the Middle Ages,* New York, 1928, pp. 697-698.

[6] Gras, "Economic Rationalism in the Late Middle Ages," *Speculum,* viii, 3, July, 1933, p. 305.

[7] Grotius, *De Jure Belli et Pacis,* reproduction of the edition of 1646, Washington, 1916, pages unnumbered (17).

the correct conception of just price, we shall then seek to sketch some of the leading principles of scholastic economic organization. The space devoted to the question of price is objectively disproportionate but the disproportion is necessary under the circumstances.

II

The scholastic moralist in questions of right and justice founds his general principles on the natural law. The principles of the natural law, however, are in many matters not sufficiently detailed to offer solutions for concrete cases. For this reason, schoolmen have always conceded to the civil law a competence in determining the scope of certain rights, if not in constituting the rights themselves. For example, the right of acquisition by prescription is founded upon natural law, but it is for the civil law to determine after what period of time a title by prescription becomes valid. Acquisition by accession, by the finding of treasure, the determination of the formalities which are required for a binding contract, are other matters which, though grounded in the natural law, may in a specific instance receive their final determination from the civil law. Not only is this true in general, but the moralist also regarded the statement of the natural law as contained in Roman law and, in particular, in the Justinian Code as very satisfactory in many respects. Thomas Aquinas devotes a whole special article to the corroboration of Ulpian's definition of justice set down in the first sentence of the *Institutes*,[8] a definition which had already been accepted, probably from legal sources by Ambrose,[9] and by Augustine.[10] Later when specialists in moral theology would separate the treatise *De Jure et Justitia* from dogmatic tracts and commentaries, the sequence and structure of the treatise would follow that of the Code very closely.

The Justinian Code discusses the Falcidian law[11] "which required that there remain entire to each heir a fourth part of his hereditary portion. But this law regarded only those estates unduly burdened with legatees."[12] The law itself sought to settle a prolonged legal dispute which lies outside our present purpose. But what is to our present purpose is the commentary of the legist Paul in the *Digests*. Question has arisen concerning the manner of the computation of this one-fourth portion.

The prices of things function not according to the whim or utility of individuals, but according to the common estimate. A man who has a son whom he would ransom for a very large sum is not richer by that amount. Nor does he who possesses another man's son possess the sum for which he could sell him to his father; nor is that amount to be expected when he sells him.

---

[8] Aquinas, *Summa Theologica*, 2a 2ae, Quaestio 58, art. 1.
[9] Ambrose, *De Officiis Ministrorum*, Lib. I, c. 24, Migne PL., vol. 16, p. 57.
[10] Augustine, *De Civitate Dei*, Lib. XIX, c. 21, CSEL (CV), vol. 40:2, p. 409.
[11] *Corpus Iuris Civilis*, Krueger-Mommsen ed., Berlin, 1928, Institutes, xxii, p. 25.
[12] P. Vidal, S.J., *Institutiones Iuris Romani*, Prati, 1915, p. 594.

In the present circumstances he is evaluated as a man and not as somebody's son. . . . Time and place, however, bring about some variation in price. Oil will not be evaluated the same in Rome as in Spain, nor, since here as well prices are not constituted by momentary influences, nor by occasional scarcity, will it be evaluated the same in times of prolonged sterility as in times of abundant harvest.[13]

"Even after the extinction of the Western Empire in the year 476, the Roman law did not cease to have force. First of all, the clergy settled among the various German peoples were not hindered from using the Roman law in their own affairs even when these affairs were secular."[14] The case with reference to which this price doctrine occurs in the code was that of the settlement of inheritances. From very early times, the administration of wills and similar questions of the "orphans' courts" were under ecclesiastical jurisdiction.[15] Later scholastic writers of the highest authority refer specifically and approvingly to this passage in substantiation of their doctrine of just price and the theory of prices underlying it.[16]

In view therefore of the place held by the Roman law in the schoolmen's discussion of right and justice, in view of the close connection of ecclesiastical and civil law on the precise point involved, in view of the general preeminence of Roman law in the training of the clergy, and in view of subsequent specific quotation by weighty authorities of the same tradition, the commentary of Paul on the Falcidian law can scarcely be denied a place among the influences forming medieval price and value theory. And that influence was certainly not in the direction of an objective and absolute value and price.

III

Aurelius Augustinus, bishop of Hippo Regius in Africa, saint, Father and Doctor of the Church, would by some be placed outside the scholastic tradition because of his platonist leanings. Yet so great was his influence upon all subsequent western thought, especially in the domain of psychology and epistemology, that the distinction would do violence to historical sequence in spite of the truth it seeks to emphasize. In the theory of value his influence is great as elsewhere.

There is, however, a different value set upon each thing proportionate to its use. Wherefore we set a greater value upon some insentient objects than we do upon some sentient objects. So much so in fact, that were it within our

---

[13] *Op. cit.*, Ad Legem Falcidiam, *Digests*, xxxv, 2, 63, p. 556.

[14] F. X. Wernz, S.J., *Ius Decretalium*, Prati, 1913, vol. i, Pars 2a, tit. xi, no. 10, p. 346.

[15] Wernz, *op. cit.*, vol. v, Pars 2a, tit. IX, no. 2, p. 221. Blackstone, *Commentary on the Laws of England*, Philadelphia, 1860, Book III, ch. 7. nos. 5-6 (pp. 95-103), vol. 2, p. 72 sq.

[16] Luis Molina, S.J. (d. 1600), *De Jure et Justitia*, Antwerp, 1615, Tomus II, Disp. 348, sec. 4, p. 166. Joannis Cardinalis de Lugo, S.J. (d. 1660), *Disputationes Scholasticae et Morales*, Paris, 1869, vol. vii, Disp. 26, no. 38, p. 273.

power we should like to remove these living things from the order of nature, either because we do not know what place they hold in the scheme of nature, or, even if we did know, because we value these living things less than our own convenience. Who does not prefer to have bread in the house rather than mice, or money rather than fleas? But why be surprised since in the value set upon men themselves, whose nature is certainly of paramount dignity, very frequently a horse is held more dear than a slave, or a jewel more precious than a maid servant. Since every man has the power of forming his own mind as he wishes, there is very little agreement between the choice of a man who through necessity stands in real need of an object, and of one who hankers after a thing merely for pleasure.[17]

This passage resounds through centuries of writing by scholastics and is found either in direct quotation or in paraphrase in almost every important treatment of the subject. Aquinas gives the substance of it;[18] Scotus refers to it specifically;[19] and its influence is clear in Antoninus of Florence,[20] in Bernardine of Sienna,[21] in the great Dominican moralist, Dominic Soto,[22] and Cardinal de Lugo[23] among others. This is a decidedly imposing array of scholastic authorities who accept, approve and adapt the quotation from Augustine. And that analysis of Augustine's can in no sense be interpreted as setting up an objective and absolute standard of value.

And yet Augustine could say that "to wish to buy cheap and sell dear is a vice." He narrates the story of an actor who promised on a certain day to reveal to the members of his audience:

. . . what they had in their hearts and what they all wanted, and a large crowd assembled on the appointed day, silent and expectant, to whom he is said to have announced, "You wish to buy cheap and sell dear." That actor, either from self-examination or from experience of others, came to the conclusion that to wish to buy cheap and sell dear was common to all men. . . . As a matter of fact, it is a vice. . . . I myself know a man to whom the sale of a book was offered; he saw that the seller was unaware of its real price and for that reason was asking very little for it. And yet he gave the seller, ignorant as he was, the just price which was far greater. . . . We have known people from humanitarian motives to have sold cheaply to their fellow citizens grain for which they had paid a high price.[24]

The inability to reconcile these apparently contradictory points of view— namely, that there is a powerful subjective element in our evaluations, and yet that there is a just price which is independent of my subjective judg-

  [17] Augustine, *De Civitate Dei*, Book XI, cap. 16, CSEL (CV), vol. 40, p. 535.
  [18] Aquinas, *Summa Theologica*, 2a 2ae quaestio 77, art. 2, ad 3um.
  [19] Joannis Duns Scoti *Opera Omnia*, Paris, 1894, vol. 18, "Quaestiones in Quartum Librum Sententiarum," Dist. XV, quaestio 2a, n. 14.
  [20] Antonini *Summa Theologica*, Verona, 1740, Lib. II, tit. 1, cap. 16, no. 3.
  [21] Bernardine of Sienna, *Quadragesimale de Evangelio Aeterno*, Venice, 1745, Serm. 35, a. 1, c. 1.
  [22] Dominic Soto, *De Jure et Justitia*, Lyons, 1558, Lib. 1, cap. 6, q. 2, a. 3.
  [23] de Lugo, *op. cit.*, sec. 4, no. 42.
  [24] Augustini, *Opera Omnia*, St. Maur's ed., Paris, 1841, vol. 8, *De Trinitate*, Liber XIII, cap. 3, sec. 6, cols. 1017-1018.

ments, seems to be the reason why modern writers of ability and authority are led to make statements concerning scholastic price and value theory which are at variance with the truth to the point of being bizarre. How scholastic writers themselves effected this reconciliation, we shall seek to show by quotation as we proceed. But it may now be observed in general that the resultant of a large number of personal judgments, the community estimate, though partly subjective in origin, and partly objective, insofar as it is based on a consideration of the actual physical qualities of the object for sale, is for me in practice wholly objective. The matter is analogous to a political election; my vote may have gone for Mr. Hoover; the community estimate went for Mr. Roosevelt. Though my subjective choice was one of the factors determining the election, the ultimate outcome, Mr. Roosevelt's presidency, is for me a wholly objective consideration. Similarly, my estimate of the worth of an object to me will be one of the factors determining the community estimate which will determine the just price. Yet that just price, resultant of many objective and subjective forces, once determined is for me a wholly objective fact.

IV

The Dark Ages, if there were any such, offer us little new on price and value save the work of the canonists properly so-called who lie beyond the scope of this present writing. The next writer of importance to whom we turn is Albertus Magnus (1193-1280), a Suabian of the noble family of Bollstadt, teacher at Paris and Cologne, bishop of Ratisbon and founder of the theological tradition of the Dominican order. Albert, though one of the few writers who quotes neither the commentary of Paulus, nor the famed passage of Augustine, is on his own grounds an advocate of just price. He is commenting on the *Ethics* of Aristotle:

There is accordingly always a just mean between gain and loss. This mean is preserved when in a voluntary contract the antecedent situation is equivalent to the consequent, that is to say, before and after the contract. A couch, for example, prior to the contract had a value of five; if one received five for it, the situation consequent to the contract is equal to that which was antecedent. No one can complain that he has been in any way injured thereby.[25]

Such exchange, however, does not take place through an equality of the things exchanged but rather according to the value of one thing in relative proportion to the value of the other with due regard for the need which is the cause of the transaction.[26]

This "need" of which Albert speaks includes not only my personal need of this particular object but also and more significantly the need which all

[25] B. Alberti Magni, *Opera Omnia*, Paris, 1891, vol. vii, *In Librum V Ethicorum*, Tract. 2, cap. 7, no. 30.
[26] *Ibid.*, cap. 9, no. 31.

men have of living in society and of exchanging with one another the products of their labor, if human life is to be carried out on a level in any way
proportionate to human capacity and dignity. My need is included, to be
sure, but the principles of justice involved derive from the general nature
of human needs in society, as the writer proceeds to show in the continuation of the passage cited above.

According to this analysis, the carpenter ought to receive the product of the
tanner and in turn pay the tanner that which according to a just exchange
is his. . . . And when this equality is not preserved, the community is not
maintained, for labor and expense are not repaid. For all would, indeed, be
destroyed if he who makes a contract for so much goods of such a kind, does
not receive a similar quality and quantity. For the state cannot be built up of
one type of workers alone. Properly, therefore, these things are exchanged
not absolutely but with a certain comparison to their value according to use
and need. Otherwise, there would be no exchange.[27]

To this end, money was invented, that community life might be facilitated
and preserved through just contracts which through the device of money are
made both easier and more just:

Wherefore all exchangeable goods are properly priced in money and thus there
will always be exchange. . . . While there is exchange, there is also a community.
Now money equals all exchangeable goods just as the unit of a ruler by addition and subtraction equals all things ruled. We have just said that without
an exchange of products there will be no community life. But community
life cannot be unless the products are reduced to proportionate equality. . . .
And this is the reason why the first and primary measure of all exchangeable
goods (money, to wit) was of necessity invented.[28]

Lest his doctrine be misunderstood, Albert is careful to explain how what
he says fits in with the traditional scholastic doctrine of immutable essences
and final values with reference to a last end. Time has shown the wisdom
and need of the warning.

. . . In a certain way, natural objects are immutable, as for example, with
regard to those first principles by which man is ordained for the good and
the true, for these are imprinted on humankind and do not change. However,
the use of these things when applied in practice varies with many customs and
institutions. Thus, although with the gods every just thing is precisely so and
in absolutely no degree otherwise, for with the gods nothing suffers change,
with us, however, an object is by nature in a certain sense changeable, for
whatever is human is changeable, and as this is the case, so there is in human
justice an element that is of nature and an element that is not.[29]

These citations manifest an intimate connection in the writer's mind between just price and social organization. Because men must live in community, because life can be sustained only by mutual exchange of products

[27] *Ibid.*, cap. 9, no. 31.
[28] *Ibid.*, cap. 10, no. 36.
[29] *Ibid.*, Tract. 3, cap. 1, no. 49.

for the subvention of mutual needs, the contracts arising from these exchanges must be equitable. And if they must be fundamentally equitable, the expression of that basic equity in money must be a just price. The process, as a whole, is radically a social phenomenon arising from man's need for life in society, and his inability adequately and congruously to develop his personality alone; "the commonwealth cannot be built up of one type of workers alone." Albert is talking not only of a division of labor but more particularly of the organic interrelation arising from this specialization of function. Because exchange is socially necessary, money is socially necessary, and because both money and exchange are designed to serve the development of persons in community, the quantitative determination of price is necessarily social. Prices must be equitable because all of the functional groups are necessary to each other and live in mutual interdependence. By fair exchange manifested in a fair price, is progress made and the commonwealth maintained.

Had Albertus Magnus no greater claim to distinction than his part in the intellectual formation of Thomas Aquinas (1225-1274), it should be enough. Master and pupil are both Doctors of the Church, and the works of Thomas are rightly regarded as an epitome of medieval thought. Before we turn to the question as to whether Thomas thought that value and price were exclusively objective, it is necessary to consider briefly the structure of the society in which these transactions would take place.

That human societal relations are natural and, therefore, both normal and normative is axiomatic in the work of Thomas Aquinas as indeed in all scholasticism. The principle of Aristotle, "Man is by nature a social animal,"[30] is cited almost every time a social topic is discussed. Out of the innumerable places in Thomas's vast works that touch upon social analysis, we limit ourselves to a few which indicate in what manner he regarded society, economic society included, as organic.

Economic need is one of the most powerful motive forces impelling to social organization, in the mind of Aquinas as well as in that of Albert.

"Man is naturally a social animal." This is evident from the fact that one man does not suffice for himself if he lives alone because the things are few in which nature makes adequate provision for man, since she gave him reason by means of which to provide himself with all the necessities of life such as food, clothes, and so forth, for the production of which one man is not enough. Wherefore man has a natural inclination to social life.[31]

In a totally different connection, and in a different work, after an introduction which is almost *verbatim* with the above, Aquinas continues:

Just as one man has various members by which he functions in various capacities, all ordered to supply any need, since all functions cannot be supplied by

[30] Aristotle, *Nichomacean Ethics*, Book I, c. 7.
[31] Aquinas, *Summa contra Gentiles*, Book III, c. 85.

one member, so the eye sees for the whole body and the foot carries the whole body. Likewise, in what pertains to all mankind, one man is not able to do all the things which are needed in a society, and, accordingly, different people properly work at different tasks.

But since in Thomas's thought, order and liberty when properly conceived are not exclusive notions but complementary ones, he explains:

This diversity of men in different functions, happens, in the first place, by divine providence which has so distributed the types of men that nothing necessary for life will ever be found wanting. But this also comes about from natural influences by which different men have different inclinations for this function of that manner of life.[32]

The thought is also developed by an analogy from the animal world, the division of labor in the bee-hive.

For, as many things are needed for man's livelihood for which one man is not sufficient for himself, it is necessary that different things be done by different men, that some, for instance, should cultivate the land, that some build houses, and so forth.[33]

All of which may thus be summarized:

In civic relationships, all men who belong to the same community are regarded as one body, and the whole community as one man.[34]

A division of labor, therefore, is fundamental in Aquinas's idea of social organization and progress:

For the welfare of human society, many things are necessary; divers offices are done better and more expeditiously by divers persons than by men singly.[35]

But, though there be a division of labor, competition as a ruling principle is far from his mind. Scholastic economic organization is pre-eminently one of non-competing groups.

In the temporal commonwealth, peace departs because the individual citizens seek only their own good. . . . Rather through diversity of function and status is the peace of temporal commonwealths promoted inasmuch as thereby there are many who participate in public affairs.[36]

When there is combined with this organic concept of economic society, the scholastic doctrine on private property, which cannot be here elaborated, we achieve a conclusion which sounds odd to modern ears.

All particular goods which men procure are ordained for the common good as for their end.[37]

[32] Aquinas, *Quaestiones Quodlibetales,* Quodlibetum 7um, quaestio 7, art. xvii, ad corpus.
[33] Aquinas, *Summa contra Gentiles,* Book III, c. 134.
[34] Aquinas, *Summa Theologica,* 1a 2ae, quaestio 81, art. 1, ad corpus.
[35] Aquinas, *Summa Theologica,* 2a 2ae, quaestio 40, art. 2, resp.
[36] Aquinas, *Summa Theologica,* 2a 2ae, quaestio 183, art. 2, ad 3um.
[37] Aquinas, *De Regimine Principum,* Book I, c. 15.

And we come also to that fundamental notion of the basic community of goods which the institution of private property is to promote and not impede.

And, therefore, the division and appropriation of goods that proceeds from human law cannot come in the way of man's need of being relieved out of such goods. . . . To use the property of another, taking it secretly in a case of extreme need, cannot, properly speaking, be characterized as theft.[38]

In the economic society of which Thomas had practical experience, these diverse functions and various tasks and offices and duties of which he speaks were carried out not by isolated individuals but by well-defined *universitates* and *corpora,* gilds, in other words, each of which was an organ of the state for fulfilling some requisite of community life. Thomas was no advocate of the modern "monolithic" state, ruled with high hand from above. Association took place naturally on many levels.

Since there are various grades and orders in these communities, the highest is that of the commonwealth which is ordained to procure by itself a sufficiency of goods for human life.[39]

Thus, though the state has a proper regulatory office, these lesser associations should be left to carry out their organic functions freely within the limits of justice.

The optimum in any government is that things should be provided for according to their own measure for in this does the justice of an administration consist. Accordingly it would be against the principle of human government if men were to be prevented by the governor of the commonwealth from carrying out their own functions, unless perchance for a brief time because of some emergency.[40]

From this brief sketch, of necessity inadequate,[41] we wish to point out those factors in Thomas's analysis which bear on our present problem. The state is a natural society within which flourish many lesser coördinate societies, each enjoying within its own sphere an ordinate autonomy, all, however, designed through coöperation to serve the interests of the persons who compose the state, and all attaining these ends through an observance of justice which regulates those acts of men which concern a second person.

With these observations in mind, what Thomas has to say on the subject of just price becomes more intelligible. On the origins of money and ex-

[38] Aquinas, *Summa Theologica,* 2a 2ae, quaestio 66, art. 7.

[39] Aquinas, *In Libros Politicorum,* prologus.

[40] Aquinas, *Summa contra Gentiles,* Book III, c. 71.

[41] Among the many writings on the political thought of Thomas Aquinas few compendious statements will be found to excel the work of Dr. Clare Q. Riedl of Marquette University, "The Social Theory of Thomas Aquinas" in *Philosophy of Society,* Philadelphia, 1934. For a scholastic interpretation of general modern "value" theory see, *Philosophy of Value* by Leo R. Ward, of the University of Notre Dame, New York, 1930.

change, he comments approvingly upon the words of Aristotle,[42] but a fuller discussion is given elsewhere.

To the end that exchange be just, as many shoes should be exchanged for a house, or for a man's food, as the labor and expense of the builder or farmer is greater than that of the tanner because, if this be not observed there will be no exchange, nor will men share their goods with one another. . . . This one thing which measures all other things is, in truth, the need which embraces all exchangeable goods insofar as all things are referred to human needs. *For things are not valued according to the dignity of their natures,* otherwise a mouse which is a sentient thing would have a higher price than a pearl which is an inanimate thing. This is manifest because, if men had no needs, there would be no exchange. . . . In other words, insofar as the farmer, whose function is the provision of food, is more necessary than the tanner whose function is the provision of shoes, by that amount in numerical proportion must the work of the tanner exceed that of the farmer so that many shoes are exchanged for one measure of grain. . . . Moreover, it is true that money also suffers the same as anything else. . . . That is to say that it has not always the same value but ought, nevertheless, to be so instituted that it have greater permanency in the same value than other things.[43]

If, however, this reciprocity is absent, there will be no equality of the things exchanged, and thus men are no longer able to dwell together. . . . All the crafts would be destroyed if each would not receive an amount proportionate to that which he produced.[44]

In the light of these considerations of the natural and all-inclusive mutual interdependence of men, of the close articulation of all parts of the community for the maintenance and progress of all, and of the necessary observance of justice if these ends are to be obtained, the jejune remarks of Thomas in the passage usually cited from his works in this connection, acquire a fuller meaning.

Buying and selling were instituted for the common good of both parties since each needs the products of the other and vice versa as is evident from the Philosopher. But what was introduced for the common utility ought not to bear harder on one party than on the other, and therefore, the contract between them should rest upon an equality of thing to thing. The quantity of a thing which comes into human use is measured by the price given, for which purpose money was invented, as said. Therefore, if the price exceeds the quantity of the value of the article, or the article exceeds the price, the equality of justice will be destroyed. And, therefore, to sell a thing dearer or to buy it cheaper than it is worth, is, in itself, unjust and illicit. . . . The just price of things, however, is not determined to a precise point but consists in a certain estimate. . . . The price of an article is changed according to difference in location, time, or risk to which one is exposed in carrying it from one place to another or in causing it to be carried. Neither purchase nor sale according to this principle is unjust.[45]

[42] Aquinas, *In Primum Librum Politicorum*, lect. 7.
[43] Aquinas, *In Decem Libros Ethicorum*, Liber V, lect. 9 (italics inserted).
[44] *Ibid.*, lect. 8.
[45] Aquinas, *Summa Theologica*, 2a 2ae, quaestio 77.

Elaborate demonstration that scholastic writers are not concerned with an absolute, immobile, intrinsic value should, in the light of the quotations given, be quite superfluous; for "things are not valued according to the dignity of their natures." Value rests upon a kind of estimate, not of the buyer and seller alone, but of the whole community. This is true because man is social by nature and for him production and progress are possible only in association. That society which arises through this association is a commonwealth in the fullest sense of the word, and will flourish only when all its parts are sound. By the production of a useful commodity, man makes his contribution to the commonweal for which contribution he expects a reciprocal support. Because social relations are governed by justice, (which we do not here prove, but assume as axiomatic in scholasticism, or in any other civilized philosophy) the exchange must take place according to the community's estimate of the social utility of the two products because the producer who expects sustenance from society in return for his labor, by performing his function in the social organism, has earned his right to a just return. The factors which will normally determine the community estimate of social utility are labor, cost of materials, risk and carriage charges.

V

There remains, for the sake of completeness, to consider the writings of a few other thinkers who each in his day enjoyed great authority and who, though accepting without qualification the traditional scholastic position, extended it in one or other minor point arising from the circumstances of his own time. John Duns Scotus, for example, Aquinas's much younger contemporary (1265-1308) and the principal ornament of the Order of St. Francis in the field of speculative thought, extends or makes explicit several principles. After citing the two quotations from Augustine and setting down general principles substantially the same as those of Aquinas, Scotus continues:

Beyond the rules which have been given above as to what is just and what is not, I add two. The first is that such an exchange be useful to the community, and the second, that such a person shall receive in the exchange recompense according to his diligence, prudence, trouble, and risk. . . . This second rule follows because every man who serves the community in an honest function ought to live by his work. But such a one as transports or stores goods is of honest and useful service to the community, and should, therefore, live by his work. And, moreover, one can sell his effort and care for a just price. But great industry is required of one who transports goods from one country to another inasmuch as he must investigate the resources and needs of the country. Therefore, may he take a price corresponding to his labor beyond the necessary support for himself and those of his establishment employed according to his requirements, and thirdly, something beyond this corresponding to his risk. For if he is a transporter or custodian of goods (*e.g.*, in a warehouse), he does this at his own risk and for this risk he is in all conscience entitled to some recompense. And this is especially true if, now and then, through no fault of his own in such a service to the community he suffers a loss; for a merchant engaged in transport now and then loses a ship laden with fine wares, and the custodian occasionally loses in an accidental fire, the valuable goods which he stores for the use of the commonwealth.

It is evident from these two conditions requisite in just business how some are called business men in a vituperative sense, those to wit who neither transport, nor store, nor by their own industry better a salable article, nor guarantee the worth of some object for sale to one who lacks the necessary knowledge of it. These people who buy only to sell immediately, under none of the above conditions ought to be crushed by the community and exiled. Such persons are called by the French *regratiers* because they prevent the unhampered exchange of those who wish to buy or make an economic exchange, and as a result, they render a salable and usable article dearer to the buyer than it should be, and dearer to the seller. Thus the contract is defective on both sides.[46]

The emphasis given to cost factors on the supply side by Scotus caused certain sixteenth century scholastics to object to his theory as they understood it.[47] The version of the theory which they took they promptly riddled with objections very similar to those which the Austrian School brought against the classical cost analysis. Not even in this sense would the scholastic moralists tolerate an objective theory of economic value. However, as the commentator on Scotus justly remarks, "They object in vain, for the Doctor assigns justice and the causes thereof to the nature of the object . . . and the common estimate."

The increasing mercantile activity of the Italian cities brought new moral problems to the desk of Antoninus, saint, archbishop of Florence, and a moral theologian of great repute (1389-1459). Antoninus was not loath to recognize changed conditions and to apply the old principles to the new facts, and for this reason some have regarded his ideas as involving new principles. We shall here note merely that his approach is substantially that of Albertus Magnus two centuries before.

Many unsupportable statements have been made concerning the medieval attitude toward trade; the neat summary of Antoninus will bear repeating.

The notion of business implies nothing vicious in its nature or contrary to reason. Therefore, it should be ordered to any honest and necessary purpose and is so rendered lawful, as for example, when a business man orders his moderate gain which he seeks to the end that he and his family may be decently provided for according to their condition, and that he may also assist the poor. Nor is condemnation possible when he undertakes a business as a public service lest necessary things be wanting to the state, and seeks gain therefrom, not as an end, but in remuneration for his labor observing all other due considerations which we mention. But if he places his final purpose in gain, seeking only to increase wealth enormously and to keep it for himself, his attitude is to be condemned.[48]

[46] Scotus, *op. cit.*, nn. 21-22.
[47] Soto, *op. cit.*, Book VI, quaestio 2, art. 3; Molina, *op. cit.*, Disp. 348; de Lugo, *op. cit.*, Disp. 26, sec. 4, no. 41.
[48] Sancti Antonini, Archiepiscopi Florentini, O.P., *Summa Theologica*, Verona, 1740,

So close is the resemblance of the doctrine of Antoninus to that of his predecessors, that the first sections consisting of paraphrase and quotation from Aristotle and Aquinas may be omitted. We begin where he, paraphrasing Augustine, and accepting Scotus's conclusions, proceeds to develop them.

The value of an article rests on a three-fold consideration, (1) its intrinsic qualities, (2) its scarcity, and, (3) the desire which it arouses in us.

The intrinsic qualities of a thing are known from the way in which, due to its inherent properties, it is more effective for our use. Thus, good wheaten bread has greater value for us than barley bread, and a powerful horse has greater value for traveling than an ass.

Secondly, the value of a salable object is judged according to its scarcity, that is, things which are found rarely or with difficulty are more necessary in proportion as, because of their scarcity, we feel a greater need of them and there is less opportunity of owning and using them. According to this principle, grain is worth more in time of famine and scarcity than at a time when there is plenty for all. . . .

Thirdly, a salable object is judged from its pleasant effect upon us, that is, according to the degree in which it pleases our fancy to own and use such an object. Thus no small part of the value of salable objects arises from the pleasure of the will taking greater or less satisfaction in the use of this thing or that. One horse is more pleasing to one person than to another, and an ornament pleases this person more than that.

The third thing to be considered regarding the value of an object is that we can hardly ever determine it except conjecturally and with probability, and this not at a mathematical point but within a certain range respecting times, places, and persons. . . . With regard to the second principle division, namely, that there is an appropriate range within the limits of which prices may vary, it should be observed that this may be known in three ways; from law, from custom, and from practical judgment. First of all, from the law—*extra De empt. et vend., Cum Dilecti.*[49] This same proper range is known also in a second way. For as Scotus says in his commentary referred to above, experience shows clearly enough that the matter is ordinarily left to those making the exchange so that, having due regard for each other's wants, they judge themselves to give and receive equivalents. . . . Thus a certain real gift or concession commonly accompanies contracts. It is therefore probable enough that when the contracting parties are mutually satisfied, they wish to concede something to each other as long as they do not too grossly depart from perfect justice.

This same appropriate range of price is known, in the third place, from practical judgment. For practical judgment dictates that when a thing, which in itself is worth ten, is as dear to the owner as though worth twelve, if I propose to own it, I must give not only the ten but as much as it is worth to him according to his desire of retaining it.[50] One reason why things are worth

---

vol. 4, Pars 2a, Tit. 1us, c. 16, n. 2, col. 250. For an interesting comparison see Mill, Ashley ed., Bk. I, ch. 7, sec. 3, p. 106.

[49] This reference is given as written by Antoninus. The passage will be found in *Decretalium Gregorii IX*, Lib. III, tit. XVII, De Emptione et Venditione, cap. III, Alexander III, Attrebatensi Episcopo, *Corpus Juris Canonici*, Editio Lipsiensis 2a, Leipzig, 1922, p. 518.

[50] Antoninus, *op. cit.*, col. 255.

more or less is the shortage or abundance of money among the townspeople. When they have money, they buy and then things sell dearer, but when those who have power in the community need money, things are bought and sold for less.[51]

We observe here that with the passage of time and with the expansion of Europe's economic outlook, the just price analysis was not changed but developed. In Antoninus, accepting and building upon his early medieval predecessors, we find a doctrine of value based upon three factors: (1) intrinsic qualities, which are the foundation of value in any system save that of the hopeless idealist; (2) scarcity, which, as explained by Antoninus following Scotus, includes the element of cost; and (3) the subjective influence óf these objective qualities, (*complacibilitas*). Finally, some hint is given that money is becoming an independent factor in the process of translating value into price. These elements are, and must be the leading components in any value theory. Whatever may have been the source of the prevailing opinion that medieval value theory was inherent, fixed, absolute, objective, independent of supply and demand, that source was not the writings of the men who are the acknowledged spokesmen for medieval intellectual life.

VI

Scholastic writers demanded a just price because purchase and sale is a social transaction and social transactions are governed by justice. Purchase and sale is a social transaction because man is social by nature, and only through exchange is he able to provide himself with congruous sustenance. Man is a person with the right and obligation to develop and perfect his personality. But this he can do only in society. The two societies in which he invariably seeks and finds the proper medium for development are the family and the state, which are for this reason called natural societies. Among the functions of the state, one of the principal is the procuring of economic prosperity for its members, yet, for this purpose the state is not directly equipped. Men, ever social in tendency, in this as in everything else, lean naturally toward association for the more efficient fulfillment of their material needs, and the state achieves its purpose by fostering, protecting, or, if need be, restraining these associations. Functional associations of this sort are not absolutely indispensable to social life as are the family and the state but they are requisite for a healthy commonwealth for which reason they are called quasi-natural societies. They stand lower than the family and the state but above the purely conventional society like a joint stock corporation or a club.

The achievement of prosperity is patently a coöperative enterprise to which each producer brings his labor as his means of production and his

[51] Antoninus, *ibid.*, col. 186.

title to subsistence. For the protection of that right and the improvement of those powers, it is natural that man should associate with all, owners or workers, who function in the same industry where each makes his contribution, whence each receives his sustenance. Such associations are the economic organs of the body politic; they are the vertical girders furnishing structural balance in the social edifice along with the horizontal, geographical, political framework. The exchange of the increased product made possible by the diversification of function must take place at a fair price, else the commonwealth will suffer. In an organism, the diminution of function in one organ means a diminution of function in all. When society permits transactions at other than just prices, it is cutting off its nose to spite its face, or is enacting the ancient pantomime of the hands that would not feed the lazy stomach.[52]

In such an organization of society, the tension of class conflict, which is unnatural and philosophically as well as practically inhuman, is relieved because men, on a basis of what they are, stand united according to what they do, not divided according to what they have or have not. There is achieved, not a sterile and futile socialization of goods, but a natural and fruitful socialization of men.

BERNARD W. DEMPSEY

Saint Louis University

[52] The application of scholastic principles to modern economy will be found in the five volume work of Heinrich Pesch, S.J., *Lehrbuch der National Ökonomie*, Freiburg, 1907. Pesch was a pupil of Adolph Wagner, and Spann rates his work as "the most comprehensive economic treatise in the German language."

[2]

JUST PRICE IN AN UNJUST WORLD

E. A. J. JOHNSON

I

IN SPITE of its wonder-working power, the radio has one serious shortcoming. However distressed he may be, the listener cannot challenge or heckle the speaker. He can only turn off an offending argument, even though he feels a strong moral duty to rebuke the pundit whose electrically magnified words spread abroad ambiguous doctrines based on careless reasoning. Particularly during the period preceding the national election—but actually for the last three or four years—I have listened with enforced, although perhaps foolish patience, to a persuasive doctrine which has formed a very real part of the Rooseveltian political creed. That doctrine is one of just price, although it is designated more often as a "fair" price or "fair" wages. I propose to examine this doctrine in a general way and to raise questions about the possible meanings which this alluring doctrine can have in a political democracy using machine technology in the business of production and characterized by pluralistic interests which defy classification. Although I have been and still am extremely sympathetic toward the Roosevelt administration, I have not yet reached that state of hero worship which saps the critical faculties so completely that adoration replaces appraisal. Jove may be Jove, but even so he needs watching.

The doctrine of a just price, which Mr. Roosevelt has chosen to enunciate, cherish, and promote, has a venerable past. In patristic literature it was given classic statement by Augustine "I know a man who, when a manuscript was offered him for purchase, and he saw that the seller was ignorant of its value, gave the man the just price though he did not expect it."[1]

[1] *Opera omnia* (Paris, 1841) Vol. VIII (xiii. 3).

Unfortunately the learned Bishop of Hippo gave no explanation of the exact process whereby his honest buyer determined how much he should pay for the manuscript. He merely paid the just price; that is all we know. And the moral, of course, was that every good Christian should do likewise. Augustine's admonition that ethical standards should be observed in buying and selling was of course not new. Aristotle, for example, in the *Nicomachean Ethics* had insisted that just exchange must equate the persons who were parties thereto: "When people get as a result of exchange exactly what they had at the beginning, neither more nor less, they are said to have what belongs to them and to be neither losers nor gainers."[2]

Whatever its origin, the concept of just price has exhibited remarkable powers of survival; yet in the course of its long life it has suffered strange vicissitudes. From Augustine in the fourth century to Antinino in the fifteenth century, the doctrine of just price exhibited increasing vitality, and in this millennium it came to be defined in a satisfactory functional sense. My first task is to clarify this early meaning of just price.

II

Although careless historians of the history of economic thought have labeled the patristic and scholastic concept of just price as a quaint notion which presumed that every commodity which entered into exchange had an objective value—inherent, intrinsic, and immutable—closer inspection of Christian literature and more consideration of contemporaneous institutional development indicate beyond peradventure that the just price doctrine of the Universal church was essentially functional in nature.[3] Building on the teachings of the jurist Paulus, the patristic and scholastic writers admitted that subjective elements influenced the prices that sellers would take and buy-

---

[2] Welldon's translation (London, 1927), p. 149.

[3] E.g., Bernard W. Dempsey, "Just Price in a Functional Economy," *American Economic Review*, XXV (1935), 471–86.

ers would give. Out of a sizeable number of individual subjective decisions, however, a "common estimate" of value would
emerge which would cancel out disparate personal judgments
and tend presumably to establish a value commensurate with
the objective qualities of exchanged commodities. The same
process, subjective in origin but objective as a group phenomenon, would also measure the value of services. The translation
of this value-determining process from goods to personal services may be illustrated by the writings of Albertus Magnus in
the thirteenth century:

> the carpenter ought to receive the product of the tanner and in turn
> pay the tanner that which according to a just exchange is his . . . . when
> this equality is not preserved, the community is not maintained, for labor
> and expense are not repaid . . . . the state cannot be built up of one type
> of workers alone. Properly, therefore, these things are exchanged not
> absolutely but with a certain comparison to their value according to use
> and need. Otherwise there would be no exchange.[4]

It should be noticed that this Aristotelian-flavored argument
proceeds to establish an intimate connection between just price
and social organization (by means of just occupational remuneration). The just price of goods must necessarily yield adequate income to the practitioner of any craft to cover his "labor
and expense"; fair wages must be fair in the sense of sufficient
to permit persons to carry on those occupations which are necessary to well-ordered social life. Just price has been transformed
from Augustine's moral precept to a principle of medieval
economics; it has become a social device whereby an adequate
number of persons is presumably allocated to each calling and
maintained therein.

The fusion of Christian teachings with Aristotelian philosophy, which Albertus Magnus began, was more fully achieved by
Thomas Aquinas. Like his great teacher, Aquinas envisaged a
functional society bound together by just price. "One man,"
said Thomas, "is not able to do all the things which are needed

[4] *Opera omnia* (Paris, 1891), Vol. VII (Cap. 9, No. 31).

in a society, and, accordingly, different people properly work at different tasks." The causes for the socially necessary occupational division of labor were both natural and providential. Disparate natural abilities provided therefore the necessary elements of a functional society. Only through "diversity of function," said Thomas, is the "peace of temporal commonwealths" promoted.

Exchange provides the mechanism for achieving social functionalism, but it can only do so if it is just. Blending a cost doctrine with a concept of social utility, Aquinas concludes that occupational remuneration must compensate the "labor and expense" of production, although this necessary return will vary with the social importance of each particular employment.

Insofar as the farmer, whose function is the provision of food, is more necessary than the tanner whose function is the provision of shoes, by that amount in numerical proportion must the work of the tanner exceed that of the farmer so that many shoes are exchanged for one measure of grain.[5]

Clearly then the social calculus must take priority over absolute occupational costs, for otherwise the presumed scale of balanced output would be distorted to the advantage of particular groups; and "If this reciprocity is absent . . . . men are no longer able to dwell together."

By incorporating into this theory of occupational stratification, the "common estimate" which had formed a part of the theory of just price since the patristic period, Thomas succeeds in finding an institutional scheme of things wherein just price as a functional device might be realized. The "common estimate" sanctioned status, and hence if the income received by all members of a given class were adequate for the maintenance of appropriate status, justice would presumably be guaranteed. The institutional expression of the Thomistic theory of fair incomes would therefore be a society composed of noncompeting economic groups, each content with its status, and therefore

[5] *In decem libros ethicorum* v. 9.

JUST PRICE IN AN UNJUST WORLD   169

refraining from business practices designed to make it possible for the members thereof to transcend the socially approved standards of life appropriate to their respective status. Within each group all members would be presumably equal, although between groups inequalities were to be expected as the normal consequence of the absence of interstatus competition.

The resulting stratification was defended by means of a theory of social classes which found scriptural justification in the doctrine of stewardship. Built around the parable of the talents, it re-emphasized function as a mandatory Christian duty. Each person was responsible to his Creator for the dutiful employment of his talents. The test of stewardship was fidelity: modest utilization of a few talents was in God's sight as praiseworthy as more splendid achievements appropriate to the possessors of more bountiful talents.

The extent to which this doctrinal enchainment merely rationalized a stratified society and defended that type of social organization presents a very difficult problem. Fortunately it is not necessary for my purposes to attempt much of an answer. The scholastic theory did fit reasonably well with social reality (which is more than can be said for the economics of perfect competition in a society characterized by imperfect competition or monopoly). The scholastic social theorists most certainly did formulate their concept of just price in terms of contemporaneous social structure, and thought they found in a theory of reciprocal demand the nexus whereby the elements of economic society were theoretically integrated.

At any rate, the medieval concept of "just price" can appropriately be regarded as inseparable from a theory of "fair income," and "fair income," in turn, had reference to a functional stratification of society. The social policy which this theory indicated was therefore necessarily conservative: it demanded that government and public opinion should (*a*) keep the members of one social class from transcending the appropriate limits of their class and (*b*) guarantee that the members of each social class should obtain income appropriate to their status.

It is not necessary for my purposes to discuss the nice refinements which were incorporated in the medieval theory of just price. I can, therefore, gloss over the exact arguments whereby compensation for risk was permissible, or the neat distinctions drawn between what was and what was not usury. I must not, however, fail to re-emphasize the essentially conservative nature of medieval just-price teachings. That which "common estimate" had shown necessary should be preserved, and public authority should therefore be vigilant lest the presumably "good" occupational stratification be jeopardized by self-seeking business practices.

The contemporaneous fear of competition illustrates this attitude, and a seventeenth-century German writer, Johann Becher,[6] has given us a partial terminology which helps to describe this lingering distrust of competition, which the early modern era inherited from the medieval age. The approved form of medieval business organization was *oligopoly*[7]—the conduct of an occupation by a limited number of technically competent persons. This is the basic economic concept underlying guild organization—a concept quite imperfectly realized institutionally. The rewards accorded to each oligopoly should provide suitable subsistence, and the restraints on output which an oligopoly could impose would presumably give it adequate leverage to insure income for its members appropriate to status. Oligopoly was the Aristotelian mean, the extremes of which were *monopoly* and *polypoly*. Monopoly constituted an enemy of a well-conducted commonwealth because by its unrestrained price policies it was able to threaten the necessary subsistence of every occupational group which required its products. Similarly polypoly (unrestrained competition) was presumed to set in

[6] See Eli F. Heckscher, *Mercantilism* (2 vols., London, 1935) I, 271–76.

[7] Heckscher has appropriately added this word to Becher's "monopoly" and "polypoly."

JUST PRICE IN AN UNJUST WORLD 171

motion such limitless competition that adequate subsistence
would be lost to all. Of the two evils, polypoly seems to have
been regarded as the more cancerous. For whereas monopoly
could be destroyed by the majesty of government, polypoly
could not be as easily cured. Once begun, a process of unrestrained competition would, it was feared, destroy the whole
functional stratification, which was the product of centuries of
social wisdom.

All this engaging social theory is plausible enough except for
one detail. Just how was the "fair standard of living" for each
oligopoly to be determined? Burke's view that there is more
wisdom in institutions than in men, gives us the only sensible
answer. For by more complex processes than medieval scholars
could have traced, custom had accorded levels of income to
particular occupational groups. I do not consider it grossly inaccurate to describe medieval just price in action as the maintenance of time-sanctioned and customary incomes. The difficulty with this view is that it strips the *justum pretium* of most
of its normative content and makes it essentially descriptive and
taxonomical. And so the early concept of just price reveals
itself as a disciplinary hybrid which had, nevertheless, the virtue of reasonably simple, practical application. It could be
applied if one accepted the *status quo* as functionally satisfactory.

III

It is a commonplace of intellectual history that the medieval
definition of just price was slowly abandoned and that in its
place there emerged the comforting doctrine of the economic
harmonies. New kinds of economic activity bring new social
theories. Thomas Wilson's *Discourse upon Usurie*,[8] proving, as
he thought, that the usurer was the cause of all social distress,
fell on unwilling ears. Gerard de Malynes's ceaseless effort to
restore the office of the Royal Exchanger so that foreign exchange would be sold at its just price (*par pro pari*) brought

[8] London, 1584.

only ridicule and an insistence that "there is no use of remedies where there is no disease."[9] In Massachusetts Bay, Rev. John Cotton did succeed in convincing the Deputies to fine a certain Robert Keaine £200 because he had violated the rules of just price—rules which Cotton set forth on a lecture day with Thomistic completeness.[10] That single episode tells the story of just price in its scholastic meaning in Massachusetts. "Those good orders," wrote William Hubbard sorrowfully, "were not of long continuance, but did expire with the first and golden age in the new world."[11] So it was elsewhere. The social order based on noncompeting oligopoly was progressively undermined by the amoral competitive forces of early capitalism (polypoly), and as business individualism and competition became dominant, a new reality was rationalized by the theory of economic harmonies.

Nevertheless, the break was more apparent than real. The affinity of the thirteenth and the eighteenth centuries has been made abundantly clear by Carl Becker in his *Heavenly City of the Eighteenth Century Philosophers*. The "natural price" of the classical economists was invested with the normative qualities of just price. The social consequence of this allegedly benevolent natural justice of the price-making process was, however, so tremendous, and the evangelical religious awakening which paralleled the growth of early capitalism so influential, that the natural benevolence of laissez faire was not given a chance to reveal its Cartesian blessings. Hours of labor and working conditions became the first objects of legislation, although it was inescapable that this form of intervention with free enterprise would ultimately lead to direct interference with wages and profits. When a demand for "decent" working conditions has been succeeded by a demand for "decent" wages, one is again

---

[9] See E. A. J. Johnson, *Predecessors of Adam Smith* (New York, 1937), chap. iii.

[10] See E. A. J. Johnson, *American Economic Thought in the Seventeenth Century* (London, 1932), pp. 123–27.

[11] *Ibid.*, p. 127.

JUST PRICE IN AN UNJUST WORLD 173

called upon to define "fair wages." Unfortunately there is no longer a nice theory of reciprocally socially necessary oligopolies to explain the meaning of "fair." What meaning can "fair" have in a capitalist society? The Sophist's argument that justice is the interest of the stronger may be superficially adequate for trade-union organizers. Similarly, wages which will permit laborers to enjoy more of the good things of life may be a sufficient answer for the friends of the poor or for those who are distressed by the sight of suffering and hardship. Unfortunately, neither definition can be depended upon as a guide to really intelligent social policy. The former, if it be accepted as a goal of policy, may conceivably generate new social problems of unmanageable proportions, while the latter may prove that hell as usual is paved with very good intentions.

IV

After seventy-five years or more of humorous references to "just price," the nineteenth-century legislators and judges began to experiment with "a fair return on a fair valuation." From the great number of books and articles written about a "fair return" I can find out everything except the meaning of this attractive expression. Reading between the lines, however, I divine that a fair return is intended to approximate what would have been obtained if all the benevolent forces of an eighteenth-century natural order had been realized. It is apparently an attempt to achieve by law the never beheld "normal competitive price" of classical and neoclassical economics. The inference is seemingly that the "substitution of corporations for individuals" or the acceptance of "natural monopolies" has rendered inoperative the natural benevolence of free enterprise. Although no historical period, to my knowledge, can be found in which these normal competitive prices were either wholly normal or purely competitive, the common law is invoked to provide rules derived from the customs of a time when competition was presumably free and prices were "fair."

I do not wish to plunge into a discussion of the valuation of public utilities. About this esoteric puzzle I am very ignorant. I do, however, see that fair return is, like just price, partly a functional concept. Necessary investments, presumably, will not be made in regulated industries unless yields comparable to those obtainable in unregulated business areas are forthcoming. Apparently we are back again to Albertus Magnus' compensation for "labor and expense" except that there are no differentials. In terms of the modern jargon of economics, unless the governmentally permitted demand-price for capital in regulated industries is as high as the competitively determined demand-price for capital in all other industries, funds will not flow to regulated industries, and society will suffer in a functional sense exactly as medieval society would have suffered if shoemakers had not received enough to cover their "labor and expense." Conversely, if returns in natural monopolies are not regulated by the state, all users of public utility services will suffer injustices. But if you ask why rates which yield more than a fair return are unjust, the answer is given in terms of classical economics, not in terms of any positive injury to the consumer (although injury can be inferred easily enough from the diminution of consumer's choice and hence you derive an answer in terms of hedonism). The usual answer, then, is that competition is absent, and hence the normative justice which would otherwise be dispensed is not forthcoming. In other words, the conditions for generating the justice of the economic harmonies are wanting, and hence a regulated price, ostensibly the equal of what would have been attained by natural-law-economics, must be determined by law.

Stripped of all technical details, then, the "fair return" version of just price attempts theoretically to reinstitute a good natural competitive order. It defines fairness to the investor in terms of opportunity costs. Outside of the regulated indus-

JUST PRICE IN AN UNJUST WORLD 175

tries, the rational investor has presumably other opportunities for investment, hence the permissible return from regulated industries must be no less if injustice to investors is to be avoided. This concept of opportunity cost is strictly of the Smith-Ricardian variety. It merges interest and profits in some unknown way and allows a net return, let us say, of 7 per cent. The bulk of actual investments, however, have probably been made by bondholders who accept $4\frac{1}{2}$ to 5 per cent, by preferred stockholders who get perhaps 6 per cent, making it possible for common stockholders "to trade on the equity" and get perhaps 15 per cent. By generalizing investment motives (or rather by the fiction of the capitalist-entrepreneur) an eighteenth-century doctrine of necessary reward can become the basis for Hopson high finance.

To the users of the services of regulated industries, "fair" means apparently less than would have been paid had natural monopolies remained unregulated. This assumption (for it is, after all, only an assumption) is defended in terms of a theory of social efficiency, which postulates that competition in an area of natural monopoly would lead to a waste of resources (two telephone companies with duplicate equipment). To permit monopoly (if debarred by regulation from oppressing the public) is therefore "good," and "good" must mean that careful husbanding of resources is socially wise. But there is subjoined to this conservation of resources argument another concept of social efficiency which postulates that better public service will result from monopoly than from competitive public utilities, and in this doctrine the medieval fear of polypoly is resurrected in a commodity income sense, except that the opposite of the socially undesirable polypoly is regulated monopoly.

There is another element in the "fair return" version of just price which essays to be dynamic. How shall the benefits of managerial efficiency be shared? In a corporately organized public utility should all the benefits flow to the stockholders, or should the consumers also participate? In some cases a sliding scale has been adopted by virtue of which reductions in rates are to go hand in hand with increased dividends to stockholders. The underlying assumptions must be either that stockholders do not need all of the reward, or that they do not deserve it. The first involves defining the supply price of managerial ability; the second involves some theory of the social causation of managerial or technical progress.

V

Before the "fair return" version of just price had been formulated, another variety• of just price was advanced by the trade-unionists. The history of the various efforts to define a "living wage," a "fair wage," or a "social wage" would carry me far afield. The only thing that I see is that these concepts are bound on a lower extremity by the idea of a minimum wage, and on the upper by all that a tightly organized, closed-union can get. Early fair wage clauses (like those adopted in Belgium in 1855) were based on the presumed natural justice of a system of free private enterprise; wages for calculating public contracts were to equal those currently paid by reputable employers. The early New Zealand wage legislation, designed to eliminate "sweating," accepted wages in some competitive areas as satisfactory, in others as unsatisfactory, and required that the wage rates in the satisfactory areas be used as models for the statutory minimum wages in the unsatisfactory areas. For the most part, however, the modern attempts at defining fair wages have been less certain. No normal general rate of wages underlies the Continental or the feeble American minimum wage laws. They recognize distressed areas, differences in bargaining power, and differing supplies of particular types of labor. Three allegedly theoretical criteria have come to be recognized (involving as I see it three different ideas of justice): a wage should be either a "living wage," a "fair wage," or a "wage which industry can bear."

All reasonably accurate definitions must be drawn from non-

JUST PRICE IN AN UNJUST WORLD 177

American experience. Let us start with a "living wage." How is it determined? In Australia the dominant argument has been that it should be uniform (except for adjustments for "family allowances," which in turn are apparently based on either or both of two assumptions: that the national income will not allow each worker to support an average-sized family, and/or that the average-sized family is unrealistic). The uniform rate is conceived in terms of a minimum amount of subsistence for livelihood regarded as a minimum by prevailing conventional standards (a Thomistic "common estimate" I suppose), and except where two races exist side by side as in South Africa (where there are presumably two decent standards) an egalitarian practice is serviceable for dispensing minimum justice. The humanitarian aspects of the minimum wage are unambiguous, the functional aspects much less. To my knowledge (I may easily be wrong) the minimum wage, unlike the trade-union doctrine of high wages, has not been defended on a theory of consumption. But there has been a persistent argument that a minimum wage can be the functional device for putting parasitic industries to death. This argument refuses to sanction cheap goods if they are produced by cheap labor. The idea of justice must be that consumers have no right to goods produced under conditions which do not grant subsistence to producers; "labor and expense" have not been covered.

The "fair wage" doctrine (and I now use "fair" in a technical sense) postulates that work of equal skill, difficulty, or unpleasantness should be equally compensated. This doctrine agrees with classical wage theory in its ideals,[12] but denies that the ideal can or will be realized without social intervention. What Adam Smith thought would emerge naturally, the advocates of a "fair wage" insist must be attained socially. The idea of justice which underlies is, nevertheless, of the eighteenth-century variety. Equal real costs should be compensated by equal remuneration. Since no common denominator can be found

[12] E.g., *Wealth of Nations* (Cannan ed.), I, 102–13.

which measures real costs, and since offsetting satisfactions (for example, the prestige derived from certain employment) cannot be measured either, the "fair wage" doctrine, in spite of its theoretical balancing of exertions and rewards, must become arbitrary in practice.

"A wage which industry can bear" apparently means a wage as high as possible without destroying the incentives of business men. Here is a clear functional concept, based squarely on a theory of proportionality which assumes that the productivity of the factors can be measured. Each factor deserves exactly what it produces. There is infused, however, a dynamic aspect in the allegation that, because of the unequal size and unequal efficiency of the firms which make up an industry, the productivity of labor must be defined in relation to the most efficient firms. Underlying this insistence is the presumption that productivity so defined would, by raising contractual wages, compel less efficient enterprises to rearrange their factors and to increase managerial efficiency until they reach a parity with the "best" firms. Justice (in the sense of a right to what is produced) would then be joined with a minimum of economic inefficiency.

VI

I now turn to a wholly different variety of modern just price teachings: the just monetary unit. That falling prices cause injustice to debtors and rising prices cause injustice to creditors is a very, very old complaint; that a just money unit can be devised which will guarantee justice for all is a relatively modern belief. Until index numbers were used for measuring price-level changes, no convenient mathematical demonstration of the injustice of price changes could be made. The techniques employed and the controversies about methods need not detain us; only the underlying theory need be considered.

Fisher's phrases, "a stabilized dollar" or "a compensated dollar," involved no appraisal; the modern term "an honest dollar," however, is the antithesis of an unjust dollar. The "dishonest" dollar is held to be the cause of unjust prices.

JUST PRICE IN AN UNJUST WORLD 179

Fisher always (as far as I can remember) considered prices in a gold standard regime unjust when they did not square with expectation. A bondholder, for example, expected to receive a certain goods equivalent of his interest money; if prices rose, he received less. A debtor expected to pay a certain goods equivalent in principal money; if prices fell, he paid more. A wage earner expected to realize a certain commodity income for his labor; if prices rose faster than his wages, he received less. Justice in this sense must then be the realization over a time period of an anticipated goods outlay or goods income. Back of this lies, of course, the maintenance of equitable relations between persons. The fortuitous gains of the lucky allegedly represent the fortuitous losses of the unlucky. The blame, however, falls on a money system, not on malicious persons (except where price changes are deliberately caused by groups of persons who expect to profit thereby).

The justice which an "honest dollar" would occasion boils down to a certainty that incomes expected through time will purchase similar quantities of goods, and that a succession of outlays distributed through time will occasion the sacrifice of equal quantities of goods. The essence of this kind of justice is certainty as to the quantity of goods receivable or payable. Yet if one speculates about the possible functional consequences of a stabilized dollar, it is easy to imagine cases where a great deal of injustice might result. Assume farmers to be 25 per cent of a nation's population. Suppose a drought reduces all crop yields to one-half normal yield. The annual crop being halved, agricultural prices rise, let us say, 40 per cent. The rise in farm products raises the index number of wholesale prices, let us say, 10 per cent. The price stabilization board raises the gold content of the dollar 10 per cent. What corrective justice is dispensed? The only thing that indisputably occurs is that gold miners will now get 10 per cent less for newly mined gold. Yet the purpose of the revision of the gold content of the dollar was to prevent all prices from rising. Suppose this statistical result is reached. If it is reached, it can only be because some particular prices fall (since by assumption agricultural prices have, because of the drought, risen considerably). Marginal firms will now lose money, marginal laborers will not produce enough to cover their wages, and deficits for some firms and unemployment for some laborers may be the functional consequences of a quest for index number stability. Meantime the rise of farm prices will be somewhat reduced. Conceivably, a 40 per cent increase in prices was needed to cover costs. Suppose farm prices sag back to a net rise of only 20 per cent. Will a decrease in general wholesale prices by 10 per cent compensate the absolute decrease in farm incomes? The puzzle simply cannot be solved. Modern society is made up of thousands of occupational groups (each containing a heterogeneity of enterprises) for which the process of holding an index number of wholesale prices constant cannot conceivably guarantee justice (even when defined as contractual certainty). Such are the problems which center about the concept of price-level justice. The "compensated dollar" is no Pythagorean coin. One side is simple and beautiful in design; the other is vague, confused, and indecipherable.

VII

"Ideas have a pedigree which, if realized, would often embarrass their exponents." These words of R. H. Tawney[13] seem peculiarly applicable to the Roosevelt administration which has frankly set about to make our complex economy more just. But can such a program be truly intelligent unless some consistent, functional meaning of a just economy is formulated? I raise this question in all modesty; I do not know the answer. I do have great doubts about the appropriateness of talking about "fairness" when our concepts of economic justice are such weird hybrids. What is meant, for example, by a "fair" price for agricultural commodities? The Roosevelt administration at one time thought the prices that prevailed in 1926 were "fair"; at another time 1913 prices were so designated. This is appar-

---

[13] *Religion and the Rise of Capitalism* (New York, 1926), p. 18.

JUST PRICE IN AN UNJUST WORLD 181

ently price-level justice with all its limitations. Yet when the statistical argument is abandoned in favor of a comfortable living definition, we are apparently back to a medieval concept of society. When the securities legislation was advocated, however, the principles of justice were drawn from the rules of an eighteenth-century natural order. All corporations that issue securities are now required to make available exact financial information, so that each presumably rational investor can exercise true powers of choice. Justice will here be reached by the exercise of reason. But in the establishment of fair earnings for public utilities, the wisdom of the economic harmonies is no longer trusted. Publicly owned and operated hydroelectric plants should rather supply a yardstick; in other words, state socialism should determine what rates are just by means primarily technical. Prices which cover costs are presumably fair, but the costs of no existing plants can be trusted. "Fair wages" are even more ambiguous in definition: they seemingly blend in unknown proportions the sophistic trade-union definition of justice with a medieval status-functional concept.

This catholicity may be wise, but still an economic system is a functional organism. In onerous occupations, short hours of labor at high hourly wage-rates are undoubtedly just in terms of a real cost calculus. Are they equally just in a functional sense if they occasion no corresponding increase in productivity; if they decrease employment and saddle society with a group of chronically unemployed? Conversely, a fair return upon investment calculated, let us say, on original investment is just in terms of a Lockean theory of property. Yet may it not be essentially unjust in a functional sense if it gives *rentiers* a return in perpetuity thereby allowing them to claim a share of the national commodity income without exertion?

"The separation of ethics and economics," wrote E. J. Cohn in the 1880's, "is simply a huge mistake." Few persons would today disagree. Just how ethical criteria are to be applied in matters economic, unfortunately, is not a simple matter.

NEW YORK UNIVERSITY

[3]

MONOPOLY THEORY PRIOR TO ADAM SMITH:
A REVISION

By RAYMOND DE ROOVER

First, I put downe for a Maxime that all Monapolies have bin condemned by all politique men and in all well governed Comonweales, as a cause of all dearth and scarcetie in the same, contrarie to the nature and kinde of all Societies, which first growe into Townes and Cities to lie in safetie and to leve in plentie and cheapnes. — *A Discourse of Corporations* (1587–89?).

I. Introduction, 492. — II. The monopoly theory of the Doctors, 495. — III. Monopoly theory and economic policy, 501. — IV. Post-Scholastic monopoly theories, 508. — V. Conclusions, 522.

I. INTRODUCTION

A leading economist in this country recently asserted that Adam Smith "let off the first thunderous broadside" in the attack on monopoly.[1] While the merits of Adam Smith are great, indeed, it would be a mistake to believe that the science of political economy begins with the *Wealth of Nations*. Adam Smith was by no means a pioneer but a voracious reader and a master in the difficult art of synthesis.[2] He used not only the materials contained in the technical treatises of the French physiocrats and the English mercantilists but also the ideas and concepts scattered throughout the great books, philosophical, historical and legal, which are the common heritage of western civilization. It is, therefore, not surprising that Adam Smith's monopoly theory, far from being original, can be traced back to Aristotle's *Politics*.

Apparently, it is in this work that the Greek philosopher coined the word "monopoly" or μονοπωλία from μόνος, which means "one," and πωλεῖν, which means "to sell." The word is used for the first time in the paragraph where Aristotle tells the delightful story of the philosopher Thales, who, annoyed at being taunted for his poverty, decided to prove that philosophers, too, could make a fortune, if only they cared to apply their wits to the solution of practical business problems.[3] Foreseeing a bumper crop of olives, on the basis of astronomic observations, he leased all the oil presses available on the Isle of Chios and around Miletus on the coast of Asia Minor. Having

1. K. E. Boulding, "In Defense of Monopoly," this *Journal*, LIX (1944), 524.

2. See, in particular, the pertinent remarks of Alexander Gray, *The Development of Economic Doctrine* (London, 1937), p. 122.

3. Aristotle, *Politics*, I, iv, 5.

MONOPOLY THEORY PRIOR TO ADAM SMITH 493

thus acquired control of the local supply, he let out the presses at harvest time with a huge profit. Aristotle adds that, in his time, to secure a monopoly had already become a universal principle of business and that some states raised revenue by granting exclusive rights on the sale of marketable commodities.

From the Greek, the word "monopoly" or *monopolium* was introduced into Latin, retaining the same meaning. However, it remained a neologism as late as the reign of Emperor Tiberius who, in a speech to the Senate, apologized for using it for want of a better term.[4] Later, Pliny the Elder reports that nothing was a subject of more frequent legislation than illegal monopolies.[5]

It is well known that the Romans did not excel in speculative science and it is, therefore, not astonishing that they did not develop the rudiments of economics which are found in the writings of the Greeks. On the other hand, the Romans, being expert administrators, made a major contribution in developing the body of Roman law, codified in the time of Justinian. Monopolies are not overlooked. An edict of Diocletian, promulgated in 301, had decreed the death penalty for any attempt to bring about artificial scarcity of commodities, especially victuals. This stringent enactment was probably repealed upon Diocletian's abdication in 305, but this repeal did not affect the leading principle of Roman law that all monopolies and conspiracies to raise prices were illegal.[6] This principle is embodied in the Codex, which outlaws all monopolies and illicit pacts among merchants, artificers, or operators of the baths.[7]

The real foundations of price theory in general, and of monopoly in particular, should, however, not be sought among the Greeks and the Romans, but in the learned treatises, which the Doctors of the scholastic school devoted to the important subject of social ethics. Unfortunately, these writings have been systematically ignored by professional economists. It is true that the current textbooks on the history of economic thought mention the price theories of Thomas Aquinas and the monetary theories of Oresme, but from there they jump to the mercantilists, entirely overlooking that Aquinas was the founder of a school and that his doctrines were further elaborated and refined by his followers.[8]

---

4. Suetonius, *De vita caesarum. Tiberius*, III, 71.
5. Pliny, *Naturalis historia*, VIII, 56, §135.
6. Roman Piotrowski, *Cartels and Trusts; Their Origin and Historical Development* (London, 1933), pp. 107 ff.
7. *Corpus juris civilis, codex*, IV, 59.
8. Some of the standard textbooks, such as Gide and Rist, Heimann, and Scott, omit the subject altogether and start with the English mercantilists or the French physiocrats. With respect to early and foreign economic doctrines,

494　　　*QUARTERLY JOURNAL OF ECONOMICS*

The causes of this neglect are manifold. One may be Protestant prejudice against scholastic philosophy.[9] Another is that the economic doctrines of the Doctors are buried in ponderous Latin treatises, which have discouraged the most courageous investigators. Still another cause of this contempt for early economics is traceable to the prevailing tendency among sociologists and economists to over-emphasize recent developments and to disparage the past. As a result of this trend, the belief has spread that Adam Smith is the founder of a new science and that there is little merit in the writings of his predecessors. And, finally, it must be admitted that there is in English no good book available on the subject. The essay of Father George O'Brien on mediaeval economics is naturally apologetic and, moreover, deficient in economic analysis and critical sense.[1] The most erudite book is still the two-volume work of Wilhelm Endemann, but it is in German; it overstresses the importance of the usury doctrine and is now partly out of date, since it was written some seventy years ago.[2] A reliable and more recent book is that of Edmund Schreiber, also in German, on the economic doctrines of Aquinas and his school.[3] Unfortunately, it does not show the influence of scholastic economics on the subsequent evolution of economic thought.

In this respect, it should be pointed out, that, contrary to common belief, scholastic economics is by no means the economic doctrine of the Middle Ages. As a matter of fact, the great works on scholastic economics, such as those of Luis Molina and Leonardus Lessius, did not appear until the sixteenth and seventeenth centuries.[4] Moreover, we should not forget that human knowledge grows by accretion;

a useful guide is still Luigi Cossa, *An Introduction to the Study of Political Economy* (London, 1893). There are earlier editions with a different text.

9. To be fair and impartial, it should perhaps be added that the Catholic scholars have missed a golden opportunity to emphasize the importance of the contributions made by eminent members of their own Church. The latest failure in this regard is Joseph F. Flubacher, *The Concept of Ethics in the History of Economics* (New York: Vantage Press, 1950). All in all, in this book, less than twenty pages are devoted to the great Catholic thinkers of the Middle Ages, and the moralists and jurists of the 16th and 17th centuries are simply ignored.

1. *An Essay on Mediaeval Economic Teaching* (London, 1920).

2. *Studien in der romanisch-kanonistischen Wirtschafts- und Rechtslehre bis gegen Ende des 17. Jahrhunderts* (2 vols., Berlin, 1874–1883).

3. *Die volkswirtschaftlichen Anschauungen der Scholastik seit Thomas v. Aquin* (Jena, 1913).

4. Luis Molina (1535–1600) was a Spanish Jesuit. His work, *De justitia et jure*, was first published in 1593 and was so esteemed that it ran into several editions. Leonardus Lessius, or de Leys (1554–1623), was born in Brecht (Belgium). He also entered the Society of Jesus and taught theology at the University of Louvain. His major work bears the same title as that of Molina and is also extant in several editions.

scholastic thought, by influencing such men as Grotius, Pufendorf, and Galiani, left its stamp on all later writings, including those of Adam Smith.[5] Whether the last was conscious of this influence does not matter at all: it is present in his work, and that is the essential point. Perhaps we ought to become more aware of the problems of continuity and filiation in dealing with the evolution of economic ideas.

In passing judgment on early writers, we are confronted with a major difficulty in that their method of approach is so entirely different from analytical procedure today. Differences in terminology are another source of trouble, because certain words either were not used at all, like "competition," for example, or were used in an entirely different meaning, like the expression "free trade." Other expressions, such as "common estimation," used constantly in old treatises, have fallen completely into disuse. Unless one is extremely careful about the definition of terms, there is always the danger of misreading and misinterpreting the texts.

II. THE MONOPOLY THEORY OF THE DOCTORS

The scholastic Doctors approached economic problems from an ethical and legal point of view. Their primary concern was with social justice. They were much less concerned with the operation of the economic system: this was undoubtedly the great weakness of their method of analysis. In accordance with the doctrine of St. Thomas Aquinas, the Doctors distinguished between distributive and commutative justice. The first dealt with the place of the individual within the social order and was not based on the principle of equality.[6] On the contrary, it was based on the premise that each person was entitled to a share of the goods of this world according to his station in life. Distributive justice, then, regulated the distribution of wealth and income. According to Aquinas — followed by all the

5. Hugo Grotius, or de Groot (1583–1645), was a famous Dutch jurist. Much valuable economic theory is included in his treatise, *De jure belli ac pacis, libri tres.* The same applies to the treatise, *De jure naturae et gentium, libri octo,* by Baron Samuel von Pufendorf (1622–1694), a German jurist and philosopher. Both treatises, with an English translation, have been republished recently by the Carnegie Endowment for International Peace. Ferdinando Galiani (1728–87) was a Neapolitan *abbé,* whose wit made him very popular in the Parisian salons. He wrote on money and on the corn trade. Abbé Galiani has a name in French and Italian literature as well as in economics. He has been praised for developing a value theory based on utility and scarcity, but this was good scholastic economics! All the works of Abbé Galiani show traces of his theological training.

6. Thomas Aquinas (1226–1274), *Summa theologica,* II, ii, quest. 61, art. 1. I have used the English translation prepared under the auspices of the Dominican Order.

496   QUARTERLY JOURNAL OF ECONOMICS

Doctors — the basis of this distribution depended upon the social structure and could vary from one society to another. Commutative justice, on the other hand, dealt with the relations between individuals and was based on the principle of absolute equality, since justice required that the thing delivered be the equivalent of the thing received. Consequently, the exchange of goods, as in buying and selling, was within the province of commutative justice. Hence, the latter applied to the theory of value and price.[7]

It is impossible to give here an exhaustive discussion of the price theory evolved by the Doctors. It centered around the concept of the just price. What was the just price? A bewildering variety of answers have been given to this question, but it seems clear to me that the just price was nothing more mysterious than the competitive price, with this important qualification: the Doctors never questioned the right of the public authorities to set and regulate prices.[8] In the absence of regulation, however, the just price was the one set by common estimation, that is by the free valuation of buyers and sellers, or, in other words, by the interplay of the forces of demand and supply.[9] By some of the Doctors, this price was called the natural price as opposed to the legal price fixed by public authority. In any case, contrary to a widespread belief, the just price was not necessarily based on the cost of production.[1]

7. *Ibid.*, art. 2.

8. Thomas Aquinas gives no precise definition, but it may be inferred from the examples given that he has in mind the market price (*Summa*, II, ii, quest. 77, art. 3, objection 4). This interpretation agrees with that of Armando Sapori, "Il giusto prezzo nella dottrina di san Tommaso e nella pratica del suo tempo," *Studi di storia economica medievale* (2nd ed., Florence, 1946), pp. 203 ff. The best definition which I have found is that of Lessius, *De justitia et jure*, libr. 2, cap. 21, dub. 2, §7: "The just price is either that which is fixed by public authority in consideration of the common good or that which is determined by the estimation of the community" (*Respondeo, Justum Pretium, censeri, quod vel a potestate publica ob bonum commune est taxatum, vel communi hominum aestimatione determinatum*).

9. Everything depends, of course, on the definition of "common estimation" as a synonym of market valuation. The correctness of this definition is confirmed by a passage of Tommaso Buoninsegni, O. P., *Trattato de' traffichi giusti e ordinari* (Venice, 1591), cap. VI, §1, fols. 14ᵛ–15ʳ. From his description, it appears that the "common estimation" is the result of the process of price determination in a free market. According to Father Buoninsegni, there was general agreement on this subject among the Doctors — theologians as well as jurists. From my acquaintance with other texts, there is no reason to doubt his word.

1. This belief is shared, among others, by Sir William J. Ashley, *An Introduction to English Economic History and Theory* (4th ed., London, 1919), I, 138. However, it is in contradiction with the treatises of the Doctors. According to Henry of Ghent (*c.* 1217–1293), the Solemn Doctor, "a commodity is worth as much as it is commonly sold for in the market place" (*prout communiter venditur in foro*). This text is quoted by O'Brien, *op. cit.*, p. 110 n. Besides Henry of

MONOPOLY THEORY PRIOR TO ADAM SMITH   497

Briefly, if there was no legal or fixed price, the natural or competitive price was the just price. This doctrine was incipient in the writings of Thomas Aquinas, but it was first clearly formulated by one of his students, Aegidius Lessinus, who stated that "a thing is justly worth what it can be sold for without fraud."[2] The words "without fraud" should be interpreted to mean "without cunning devices, in a competitive market."[3] The famous Buridan (1300–1358), rector of the University of Paris in 1327, went even further and stated that prices should be set with reference to the utility and needs of the entire community and not by taking advantage of an individual's urgent desire to buy or to sell.[4] From these premises, the Doctors drew the inescapable conclusion that price discrimination and monopoly were both evil practices.[5]

Throughout the Middle Ages, monopolies, therefore, were regarded with universal reprobation.[6] Clearly such practices were iniquitous on all counts. For one thing, by enhancing the price, monopolists sold something for more than it was worth, which was against the idea of equality underlying commutative justice. In the second place, exploitation in whatever form was against the precept of charity and brotherly love. And, thirdly, monopolies were injuri-

---

Ghent, the market price was considered just by the following Doctors: Richard Middletown (fl. 1300), Aegidius Lessinus, Buridan, Johannes Nider (1380–1438), San Bernardino of Siena, and San Antonino of Florence (Schreiber, *op. cit.*, pp. 140–142, 163–164, 187, 208, 218). According to the last, the cost of production enters into consideration only in so far as it affects the supply. This theory is not only correct, but up to date. In his *Instrucion de mercaderes* (Medina del Campo, 1544, fol. 30ʳ), Dr. Saravia de la Calle declares that "the just price is determined by the abundance or the lack of goods, merchants, or moneys . . . and not by cost, labor or risk." (*Porque el justo precio nasce de la abundancia o falta de mercaderias, de mercaderes y dineros . . . y no de las costas, trabajos y peligros.*) And Buoninsegni (*Trattato de' traffichi giusti e ordinari*, 1591, fol. 15ʳ) declares that "a thing is worth as much as it can commonly be sold for" (*che tanto vale la cosa, quando si pu vendere communemente*). He adds that prices rise and fall in response to the scarcity or abundance of the commodities. From a Catholic point of view, the orthodoxy of the authors quoted is beyond question. And, further, I should like to point out that the Doctors did not disagree on such a fundamental point.

2. Text quoted by Amintore Fanfani, *Le origini dello spirito capitalistico in Italia* (Pubblicazioni della Università cattolica del Sacro Cuore, serie terza, scienze sociali, v. XII, Milan, 1933), p. 12.

3. This interpretation conforms to the definition of "fraud" given by Luys de Alcala, O.F.M., *Tractado de los prestamos que passan entre mercaderes y tractantes* . . . (Toledo, 1546), fol. 5ᵛ.

4. Schreiber, *op. cit.*, p. 184.

5. According to San Bernardino of Siena, O.F.M., a merchant ought to sell to all at the same price and not charge one customer more than another (Fanfani, *op. cit.*, p. 110).

6. O'Brien, *op. cit.*, pp. 124 f.

ous to the commonweal, because monopolists not only increased prices, but also withheld supplies from the market and thus created artificial scarcity. The dictum was: *Monopolium est injustum et rei publicae injuriosum.*[7]

In accordance with canon law, monopoly profits were considered as *turpe lucrum* or ill-gotten gains.[8] Like usury, they were subject to restitution, under the penalty of eternal damnation. The only difference consisted in the fact that usury was, in principle, repayable to the aggrieved party or to his heirs. Monopoly profits, on the other hand, were usually made by exploiting the public, that is, the anonymous crowd. *In incertis*, since the persons wronged were unknown, restitution could be made in the form of alms to the poor, gifts to charities, bequests to hospitals, and other pious works.[9] There are countless examples of restitution of usury and ill-gotten gains in mediaeval wills, so that there can be no doubt that the code of social ethics was actually enforced by the Church, chiefly *in foro conscientiae*, that is, through the sacrament of confession.[1]

Thomas Aquinas (1226–1274) deals with monopoly only by implication, since a monopolist is not an honest trader, but one who pursues an excessive gain to the detriment of the public.[2] One of the first to attack monopoly specifically was apparently Nicole Oresme (*c.* 1320–1382). In his famous treatise on money, he denounces any monopoly on the necessities of life, even if it is public and designed to raise revenue for the Crown.[3] The treatise, as a whole, is an indictment of debasement as a tyrannical abuse by the prince of his regalia or monopoly on coinage.

In the fifteenth century, the attack does not abate. San Anto-

7. Joseph A. Schumpeter, "Science and Ideology," *The American Economic Review*, XXXIX (1949), 357. Cf. Endemann, *Studien*, II, 59.

8. *Corpus juris canonici*, Decr. II, c. xiv, qu. 4, c. 9. The text of this canon seems to be the same as that of a capitulary of Charlemagne promulgated in 802. Piotrowski, *Cartels and Trusts*, p. 131.

9. T. P. McLaughlin, "The Teachings of the Canonists on Usury," *Mediaeval Studies*, I (1939), 125: "Restitution in all cases of *turpe lucrum* is to be made, not to the buyers, but to the poor." Cf. Thomas Aquinas, II, ii, qu. 62, art. 5, obj. 3.

1. Typical examples are given by Fanfani, *op. cit.*, p. 51. One should also consult the interesting article of Benjamin N. Nelson, "The Usurer and the Merchant Prince: Italian Businessmen and the Ecclesiastical Law of Restitution, 1100–1550," *The Tasks of Economic History*, suppl. to *Journal of Economic History*, VII (1947), 104–122, esp. 112 ff.

2. Thomas Aquinas, II, ii, qu. 77, art. 4. See also the comments of Cardinal Cajetan (Thomas de Vio) quoted by Fanfani, *op. cit.*, p. 123.

3. *Traictié de la première invention des monnoies*, ed. M. L. Wolowski (Paris, 1864), chap. 10, pp. xxx ff.

MONOPOLY THEORY PRIOR TO ADAM SMITH 499

nino (1389–1459), archbishop of Florence, fiercely inveighs against the formation of any temporary rings or more permanent cartels for the purpose of securing larger profits and higher prices. Such combinations ought not to be tolerated by the State, especially not if they involve victuals or other necessities and thus place an excessive burden on the poor.[4] The same note is struck by San Bernardino of Siena (1380–1444), a popular preacher and a coeval of the archbishop of Florence, San Antonino. To him, as to others, the word "monopoly" has a broad meaning and applies to the control of the supply of a commodity by a few as well as by one person.[5] The same is true of later moralists.

According to Molina (1535–1600), the term "monopoly" covers all pacts by which merchants set a maximum price above which they refuse to buy or a minimum price below which they agree not to sell. The term even covers agreements according to which one artificer will not finish a job begun by another.[6] In short, the Doctors gave to "monopoly" an extensive meaning which included oligopoly, monopsony, and even restrictive labor practices, which we think are weapons developed by our modern trade unions, but which, in fact, were already known to the mediaeval guilds.

Since it is impossible to study all the Doctors, one by one, it may be well to confine ourselves to one typical example of their analysis and to examine in some detail what Leonardus Lessius, or de Leys, has to say on the subject of monopoly. Lessius (1554–1623) is a rather late moralist, since his treatise did not appear until the beginning of the seventeenth century.[7] By that time, however, scholastic economics had reached its zenith in elaboration and refinement; hence, we are dealing with a fully developed doctrine.

After giving the usual definition, Lessius distinguishes four kinds of monopoly: (1) that in which sellers "conspire" (*conspirant*) to set a minimum price; (2) that which is granted by a privilege of the prince; (3) that which consists in cornering the market by buying

4. Bede Jarrett, O. P., *San Antonino and Mediaeval Economics* (St. Louis, 1914), pp. 69 f.

5. San Bernardino, *Istruzioni morali al traffico e all'usura* (Venice, 1771), istr. 1, cap. 3, §5, pp. 21 f.

6. Molina, *Justitia et jure*, tract. II, disp. 345, §2.

7. Lessius, *De justitia et jure caeterisque virtutibus cardinalibus*, libri IV (Paris, 1606), lib. 2, cap. 21, dub. 20, pp. 270 ff. There is an article on Lessius by the Belgian economist Victor Brants, "L'économie politique et sociale dans les écrits de L. Lessius (1554–1623)," *Revue d'histoire ecclésiastique*, XIII (1912), 73–89 and 302–318. I do not agree with the commentator, who contends that Lessius condemned competition as well as monopoly.

up the available supply and by refusing to sell until the price has risen; and (4) that which consists in impeding the importation of a commodity by others. For example, the Portuguese used force and attacked Arab vessels in the Indian Ocean to prevent spices from reaching Alexandria and thence Venice.

With regard to the first of those practices, Lessius remarks that monopolists who make price agreements sin against charity in any case, but also against justice, if they fix a price higher than the one that would be set by common estimation in the absence of fraud or conspiracy. In other words, there is exploitation whenever the price charged by monopolists or oligopolists is above the competitive price. According to Lessius, commutative justice is also violated in cases of monopsony — although he does not use this word — when buyers get together to lower the price of the goods or services offered to them. With respect to exclusive privileges conceded by a prince, one should consider whether or not the grant is for the public good. If it applies to necessities, the prince ought to be extremely careful to keep the price low but, if trifles or luxuries are involved, he may have good cause to make them expensive and to restrict consumption. In the opinion of Lessius, practices three and four are doubtless contrary to justice and, because they create dearth, harmful to the common weal. Thus, monopoly became a public offense which was punishable *in foro externo*, that is, by the courts.

Lessius was a theologian, but the jurists adopted much the same point of view. For example, de Damhoudere (1507–1581), the renowned Flemish criminologist, propounds the theory that merchants may legitimately earn enough to live from their business, but that they must adhere to the market price (*pris du marché publicq*).[8] Only in times of dearth are the authorities allowed to fix a reasonable price for victuals and other necessities, so that the poor would not die from starvation. Probably de Damhoudere, if he were living today, would, in case of national emergency, have approved wholeheartedly of price controls, food rationing, priorities, and the allocation of scarce supplies.

As for monopoly, it is a crime which is forbidden by the laws of many states, but which, de Damhoudere complains, remains often unpunished. It is committed not only by merchants, but also by artificers and craftsmen who enter into collusion not to work except at the rate which they have established themselves and which is often exorbitant and exceeds the wage paid in neighboring towns.

8. Joost de Damhoudere, docteur ès Droitz, *Practique judiciaire ès causes criminelles* (Antwerp, 1564), fols. 169^r–170^v.

III. MONOPOLY THEORY AND ECONOMIC POLICY

It would be a grievous mistake in historical interpretation to assume that the theories of the Doctors did not affect economic policy or influence legislation. For example, a French ordinance of 1519, regulating the rates chargeable by innkeepers, states that the latter, driven by avarice and cupidity, had endangered the salvation of their souls by overcharging their customers "in disregard of all honesty and of commutative justice."[9] So the government decided to be kind and to save the souls of the French innkeepers by reducing their prices to a more reasonable level. For us, the significant fact is the reference to commutative justice in a piece of legislation.

England, around 1600, affords an even better example of the persistent grip of scholastic ideas on the minds of legislators. As is well known, the question of monopolies was being hotly debated in the House of Commons. The tempest eventually calmed down after enactment of the Statute of Monopolies (1624). What interests us is to ascertain which theory inspired the arguments used in the debate. A perusal of the Journals of the House of Commons leaves no doubt as to the source of inspiration. In the debate of 1601, for example, one learned speaker gave an etymology of "monopoly" which is wrong, but which must have been taken from a mediaeval treatise, since I have found the same in San Bernardino of Siena.[1] Secretary Robert Cecil made a distinction between *forum conscientiae* and *forum judicii*, no doubt a scholastic reminiscence.[2] Nearly all speakers pointed out that monopolies were a "restraint of freedom" and that they were oppressive to the public and hurtful to the commonwealth, an observation which the Doctors had made long ago.[3] When the Statute of Monopolies was finally passed, the old and venerable principle of restitution was written into the law, and the persons aggrieved were given a claim against monopolists at common law.[4] All this is not surprising: the legal and social doctrine of the Doctors

9. *Recueil général des anciennes lois françaises*, eds. Isambert, Decrusy et Armet, Vol. XII (Paris, 1828), p. 168, No. 72.

1. This error was made by Mr. Spicer, member for Warwick, who derived the word "monopoly" from *monos* (one) and *polio* (city). Sir Simonds D'Ewes, *A complete Journal of the Votes, Speeches, and Debates of the House of Lords and the House of Commons* (London, 1693), p. 644. Cf. San Bernardino, *Istruzioni*, I, cap. iii, §5.

2. D'Ewes, *op. cit.*, p. 653.

3. The expression "restraint of trade" is used as early as 1604. The text of the debates is easily accessible in *Tudor Economic Documents*, eds. R. H. Tawney and Eileen Power (London, 1924), II, 269–92, and in *English Economic History, Select Documents*, eds. A. E. Bland, P. A. Brown, R. H. Tawney (London, 1915), p. 443.

4. 21 James I, c. 3 (1623–24). Text available in *Select Documents*, pp. 465 ff.

was still taught in all the universities, including Oxford and Cambridge, where Sir Francis Bacon, Sir Robert Cecil and other members of Parliament had received their formal training.

It has been asserted that the canonists considered free competition as the root of all evil.[5] Such a contention agrees neither with the texts nor with the facts. It is in a class with the error of those who draw an idyllic picture of the mediaeval guild system as a panacea against all the ills of rationalism and unrestricted competition.[6] The truth is rather different. The policy of mediaeval authorities was not always consistent, but its purpose was often to enforce and maintain competition. This is especially true of the towns in their relation with the country; their main concern was to provide their population with an adequate supply of goods, especially victuals, at as low prices as possible. Professor Eli F. Heckscher has called this policy "the policy of provision."[7] In order to achieve their aim, most towns, if not all, had open markets where the peasants from the neighborhood were expected to bring their produce and to sell it directly to the consumer at prices determined by competitive bidding among buyers as well as sellers.[8] Any attempt to engross, to regrate, or to forestall was punishable by the pillory, banishment, or confiscation, not only in England but everywhere.[9]

As for the guilds, they were often accused of abusing their regulatory and supervisory functions in order to engage in monopolistic practices.[1] Complaints of this sort were especially loud and frequent in France. As early as 1283, the jurist Beaumanoir vituperates

5. August Oncken, *Geschichte der Nationalökonomie* (Leipzig, 1902), I, 135: "Die Kanonisten umgekehrt erblickten in der freien Konkurrenz die Wurzel alles Ubels, die Ursache aller Ungleichheit und riefen daher nach einer unumschränkten Intervention der öffentlichen Gewalten." I have not found any support for such a statement: even today, Catholic moralists, true to tradition, consider free competition necessary and disapprove only of abuses arising from unfair and unbridled competition. See Albert Muller, S.J., *La morale et la vie des affaires* (Tournai, 1951), pp. 140 f.

6. This point of view is represented, among others, by Amintore Fanfani, *Cattolicesimo e Protestantesimo nella formazione storica del Capitalismo* (Milan, 1934), pp. 34 f. After the fall of fascism, the author became minister of Labor in the de Gasperi cabinet.

7. *Mercantilism* (London, 1935), II, 80 ff.

8. This aspect of the question has been studied by Vernon A. Mund, *Open Markets, an Essential of Free Enterprise* (New York, 1948), pp. 13 ff. I do not always agree with the point of view of this author, but his book is the fruit of extensive research and contains valuable material not available elsewhere.

9. For a definition of these terms, see *ibid.*, pp. 43 ff.

1. In theory, the guilds were supposed to prevent unfair practices, to supervise quality, to make apprenticeship rules, etc., but not to put monopolistic restrictions on trade. Humanity being what it is, the practice was often different.

against the monopolizing tendencies of the craft guilds.[2] In 1339, shipmasters were forbidden by an ordinance of the king, Philip VI, to form *harelles* or seditious associations for the purpose of improving their bargaining position.[3] In 1500, under Louis XII, the Parlement of Paris censured the officials of the guilds for combining to raise the price of their services or merchandise at the expense of the public. The complaints were repeated under Francis I, Charles IX, and Henry III.[4] As is known, the famous Jean Bodin (1520–1596) was the first to attribute the rise in prices during the sixteenth century to the influx of precious metals pouring into Europe from the New World. What is less known, is that he listed monopolies second as the principal cause of dearth.[5] According to Bodin, illicit combinations were often disguised under the cloak of religious fraternities.

Our anti-trust laws are not the first of their kind. Throughout the Middle Ages and the sixteenth century, legislation was passed to bring business practice into conformity with the teachings of the Church and the code of social ethics developed by the theologians and the jurists. It is true that mediaeval statutes often remained a dead letter and that the abyss between enactment and enforcement was rarely bridged. Nevertheless, when the opportunity arose or when complaints grew too loud, the authorities might unexpectedly awake from their slumbers and display a sudden zeal for the enforcement of a long forgotten statute. As long as the law was on the books, wrongdoers were never safe: infringement could always lead them to the pillory, if not to the gallows. In one respect, anti-monopoly legislation had a pernicious effect: it was scarcely ever applied to the big merchants, but it was frequently misused to catch the small fry guilty of organizing workmen into brotherhoods.

In the Middle Ages, the statutes of most Italian city-states contained provisions forbidding "conspiracies," coalitions, and other combinations for the purpose of increasing the prices of commodities.[6] Even the guilds themselves incorporated such prohibitions in their statutes, for example, the Florentine merchant guild or Arte di

2. Emile Coornaert, *Les corporations en France avant 1789* (3rd ed., Paris, 1941), p. 69.
3. "Harelle," Charles du Cange, *Glossarium.*
4. Coornaert, *op. cit.*, p. 119.
5. Jean-Yves Le Branchu, *Ecrits notables sur la monnaie (XVIe siècle) de Copernic à Davanzati* (Paris, 1934), I, 84, 94–95.
6. A list of the statutes is given by Alessandro Lattes, *Il diritto commerciale nella legislazione statutaria delle città italiane* (Milan, 1884), p. 140, and notes on pp. 145–46. The word "conspiracy" is actually used in a Pisan statute (Sapori, "Il giusto prezzo," *op. cit.*, pp. 216 f.).

Calimala.[7] On the other hand, the same statutes often contained regulations whereby the workers or artificers subject to the guild's jurisdiction were threatened with blacklisting (*divieto*), if they dared to assemble in "conventicles" or to form "leagues" or brotherhoods.[8] In 1345, a Florentine woolcarder, named Ciuto Brandini, was arrested and even executed for attempting to organize some sort of labor union.[9] Naturally, it was to the interest of the masters to maintain, at all costs, competition in the labor market.

Beyond the Alps, the anti-monopoly movement did not gain momentum until the sixteenth century, when international cartels, such as the copper, alum, and spice cartels, aroused a storm of protests. In Germany, the first important act of legislation was a resolution of the Diet of Trier-Cologne in 1512. Attempts at enforcement by the attorney of the Empire (*Fiskal*) caused the Augsburg magnates some worries, but, in the end, produced little in the way of tangible results. The Emperor Charles V depended too much on the credit of the principal offenders (the Fuggers) to allow the charges to be pressed.[1] Moreover, the high-German business magnates had an exceedingly clever and influential counsel in the person of Dr. Conrad Peutinger (1465–1547), who was closely related to two of the leading merchant families, the Höchstetters and the Welsers.

Peutinger has often been regarded as opposed to the economic ethics of the Middle Ages and as favoring concessions to capitalist monopolies and cartels.[2] As it stands, this statement, it seems to me, is somewhat of an exaggeration. In my opinion, it is based on a misinterpretation of his *Concilium*, or *Gutachten*, of 1530, in which he

7. Statuto dell'Arte di Calimala (1332), lib. II, rubr. 35. I have used the text published by Paolo Emiliani-Giudici, *Storia dei Municipi italiani* (Florence, 1851), Part IV.

8. Statuto dell'Arte di Calimala (1332), lib. II, rubr. 6. The statutes of the Wool and Silk guilds contain similar provisions. Niccolò Rodolico, *La democrazia fiorentina nel suo tramonto, 1378–1382* (Bologna, 1905), pp. 54, 114. Cf. Gaetano Salvemini, *Magnati e popolani in Firenze dal 1280 al 1295* (Florence, 1899), p. 36.

9. Rodolico, *op. cit.*, p. 119. Cf. Ferdinand Schevill, *History of Florence* (New York, 1936), pp. 265 f.

1. More details are given in Jakob Strieder, *Studien zur Geschichte kapitalistischer Organisationsformen* (Munich, 1925), pp. 53–92. Cf. A. Kluckhohn, "Zur Geschichte der Handelsgesellschaften und Monopole im Zeitalter der Reformation," *Historische Aufsätze dem Andenken an Georg Waitz gewidmet* (Hanover, 1886), pp. 666–704. I am indebted to Professor Adolph Lowe for this reference.

2. Jakob Strieder, "Peutinger, Konrad," *Encyclopaedia of the Social Sciences*. The same point of view is taken by Mary Catherine Welborn, "An Intellectual Father of Modern Business," *Bulletin of the Business Historical Society*, XIII (1939), 20–22.

MONOPOLY THEORY PRIOR TO ADAM SMITH   505

took up the defense of the great Augsburg mercantile and banking houses.[3]

Since Peutinger was steeped in the knowledge of Roman law, he did not ignore that monopoly was a crime according to the *Codex*. As a matter of fact, he fully admits this point in several of his writings; his line of argument is not that monopoly was legal or justifiable, but that the great Augsburg firms were not guilty of illegal practices. To make his point, Peutinger places a strict interpretation on article IV, 59, of the Codex and contends that it applies only to the necessities of life (*res viles*), such as grain or wine, and not to luxury articles, such as spices or silks, in which the Fuggers and other large companies were dealing. In his *Concilium* of 1530, he argues at great length that, even with regard to these commodities, they did not control the supply and were unable to set prices according to their fancy.

It is true that Peutinger defends the freedom of the pricing process. He protests that it is unfair to blame merchants if they sell at the best price which they are able to secure. Sometimes they may be favored by luck, but if the market goes down, they stand to lose. Contrary to the general belief, I do not see anything in this statement that is in disagreement with the economic ethics of the Middle Ages: the Doctors take the same attitude. One might ask, however, whether the high-German houses really refrained from manipulating prices, but this is raising a question of fact and not of theory.

It is also true that Peutinger secured legislation which was favorable to big business. The resolution of the German Diet of 1512 threatened monopolists with confiscation of all their property, which, incidentally, was going beyond the requirements of canon law. Peutinger, however, persuaded the Emperor to issue the edict of March 10, 1525, which overruled the Diet by defining monopoly more strictly and by reducing the penalty to the confiscation of excess profits. This penalty was in agreement with the principle of restitution found in canon law. Peutinger went further; he saw to it that even this milder ordinance became ineffective. Due to his influence, the cognizance of monopoly cases was transferred from the imperial jurisdiction to the local courts. Of course, Peutinger knew very well that the City of Augsburg would never start proceedings against its leading citizens. By using legal tricks, he thus made sure that the anti-monopoly edicts remained a dead letter.

3. Parts of this *Concilium* have been published by P. Hecker, "Ein Gutachten Conrad Peutingers in Sachen der Handelsgesellschaften," *Zeitschrift des Historischen Vereins für Schwaben und Neuburg*, II (1875), 188–216. The best study, however, is that by Erich König, *Peutingerstudien*, "Studien und Darstellungen aus dem Gebiete der Geschichte," IX (Freiburg in Breisgau, 1914).

506   *QUARTERLY JOURNAL OF ECONOMICS*

It would be a mistake to attach too much importance to Peutinger's pronouncements. They represent only the opinion of a legal counsel who used every possible argument and legal technicality to keep his clients out of trouble. Today lawyers do the same when they try to convince the Supreme Court that the policies of this or that large corporation are not infringements of the anti-trust laws. In short, Peutinger was a brilliant lawyer, but this is a far cry from saluting him as an intellectual father of modern business or as one of the founders of economic individualism.

In France, the most important ordinance was that of 1539 by which Francis I forbade merchants to enter into secret price agreements to the detriment of the Crown and of public interest (*la chose publique*). Another ordinance of the same year was aimed at the monopolistic practices of the guilds. But the evil did not cease. As late as 1676, Louis XIV promulgated an edict against profiteering and engrossing by rings concealed as legitimate business organizations (*sociétez*).[4]

In the sixteenth century, the powerful international cartels all had factors in Antwerp, the great emporium of the time.[5] In principle, any agreement smacking of monopoly was illegal in the Low Countries, as elsewhere; moreover, monopolies were explicitly forbidden by the ordinances, especially by the *placard* of October 4, 1540.[6] In practice, it was soon proved that the international cartels were above the law. Nevertheless, pressure of public opinion from time to time forced the government to take action. In 1525, members of the spice cartel were arrested but were soon released, when they threatened to divert the trade to foreign parts.[7] In dealing with the alum cartel, the authorities once or twice resorted to the expedient of confiscating all the local stocks and selling them at a reasonable price. But the cartel threatened to retaliate and to halt shipments to the Low Countries. Finally, the Brussels government, to protect as much as possible the interests of its subjects, came to terms and concluded an

4. Piotrowski, *Cartels and Trusts*, p. 187.
5. These combines were not temporary rings but real cartels based on written agreements containing price arrangements, fixing quotas, and providing penalties in case of non-observance of the contract.
6. *Recueil des anciennes ordonnances de la Belgique (Ordonnances des Pays-Bas sous le règne de Charles-Quint, 1506–1555)*, eds. Ch. Laurent, J. Lameere and H. Simont, IV (Brussels, 1907), 234.
7. One of them, Diego Mendez, was a *marano* or converted Jew. He was accused of practicing Judaism, but as no evidence was found, only charges of monopoly were retained. J. A. Goris, *Etude sur les colonies marchandes méridionales à Anvers de 1488 à 1567* (Louvain, 1925), pp. 194 ff.

MONOPOLY THEORY PRIOR TO ADAM SMITH   507

agreement limiting the price which the alum cartel was allowed to charge.[8]

Later on, economic and political developments caused the decline of Antwerp and the gradual disappearance of the great international cartels until they were revived in recent times. Trust busting was even less successful in the past than it is in the present. I know of no historical instance where a government succeeded in breaking up a strong cartel and in restoring competition.

In England, the activities of the Antwerp monopolists created much ill-feeling, and Sir Thomas Gresham in his letters and reports advocated an economic policy designed to free his country from their control. He also accused the Antwerp merchant-bankers of rigging the money market, although it must be said in all fairness that Sir Thomas himself tried to do the same thing and to manipulate the exchange rate of the pound sterling.[9] In England, however, public opinion did not really become aroused until the end of the sixteenth century when the Crown began to grant patents for the sale or manufacture of all sorts of commodities from playing cards to salt and saltpeter.[1] After a struggle of thirty years, the issue was finally settled by Parliament enacting the Statute of Monopolies, as we have already stated in another connection. This statute was effective in suppressing the royal patents, but it still allowed the grant of patents for fourteen years to new inventions, and, more important, it stopped at the trading companies, did not touch the East India Company, and left the guilds and municipal corporations in the undisturbed possession of their privileges.

From a legal point of view, the discussion in Parliament brought out the fact that monopolies were illegal at common law. When, in 1601, the House of Commons wanted to pass a bill prohibiting monopolies, Sir Francis Bacon, speaking on behalf of the Crown, opposed such a move on the grounds "that a bill which is only expository, to expound the Common Law, doth enact nothing."[2] And Sir Edward Coke wrote: "All monopolies are against the Magna Charta because they are against the Liberty and Freedom of the Subject."[3]

8. "Stukken rakende de aluin-, saltpeter- en zouthandel hier te lande in de eerste helft der XVI. eeuw," *Het archief*, II (Middelburg, 1844?), 265–272.

9. R. de Roover, *Gresham on Foreign Exchange* (Cambridge, Mass.: Harvard University Press, 1949), pp. 259 ff.

1. As a speaker in Parliament listed salt, but forgot saltpeter, another cried out: "Do not forget to add 'peter' to the salt." On these monopolies, consult William H. Price, *The English Patents of Monopoly* (Harvard Economic Studies, No. I, Cambridge, Mass., 1906).

2. *Journal of Elizabeth's Parliaments*, ed. D'Ewes, p. 648.

3. Sir Edward Coke, *The Second Part of the Institutes of the Laws of England* (London, 1681), p. 47.

From an economic point of view, the debate on monopolies gave rise to a war of pamphlets in which the early mercantilists fought to defend their vested interests. Wheeler and Misselden took up the defense of the Merchant Adventurers, Mun wrote a reply to the attacks on the East India Company, and Malynes continued to indict the bankers as the source of all monopolies. The quarrel became the more vehement as it fanned the flames of another controversy about the control of foreign exchange and the desirability of a favorable balance of trade.

IV. Post-Scholastic Monopoly Theories

The Reformation did not bring about a sudden change in social ideals. On the contrary. Martin Luther, for example, is quite mediaeval in his concepts and, in his writings, he does not mince his words in upholding the just price and in decrying usury and monopolies.[4] Even in England, there was no sudden break, and scholastic doctrines continued to exert considerable influence until well into the seventeenth century. This is particularly true of such writers as William Ames,[5] Philippus Caesar,[6] Thomas Rogers,[7] Dr. Thomas Wilson,[8] and even the celebrated Richard Baxter,[9] whose writings, according to Max Weber, are typical manifestations of the contamination of Protestant ethics by the spirit of capitalism![1] But the truth is that these Anglican and Puritan divines, despite their Reformatory zeal, were frequently preaching the traditional Catholic

4. Especially in his tract, *Vom Kauffshandlung und Wucher* (Wittenberg, 1524). Cf. Piotrowski, *Cartels and Trusts*, pp. 216–17.

5. William Ames (1576–1633) was a Protestant theologian and casuist, who wrote a book entitled *De conscientiae ejus jure et casibus* (London, 1632). For a summary of his doctrine, see Joseph Dorfman, *The Economic Mind in American Civilization* (1606–1865), I (New York: The Viking Press, 1946), pp. 12–13. Professor Dorfman states that "on both the 'just price' and usury, the Puritans were clearly attuned to the commercial needs of the times." In my opinion, they followed the traditional pattern, especially in the matter of price, and their approach to economic problems was entirely scholastic.

6. Philippus Caesar, probably a brother of Sir Julius Caesar, the lawyer, wrote, in Latin, a book on usury, which was translated by Thomas Rogers under the title, *A General Discourse against the Damnable Sect of Usurers* (London, 1578).

7. Thomas Rogers (d. 1616) was an Anglican who wrote chiefly on religious matters.

8. Thomas Wilson (c. 1525–1581) published in 1572 a *Discourse upon Usury*, republished in 1925 (New York: Harcourt, Brace) with a historical introduction by R. H. Tawney.

9. Richard Baxter (1615–1691) was a non-conformist preacher whose sermons drew huge audiences. He poured out so many books that it is impossible to list them here.

1. Max Weber, *The Protestant Ethic and the Spirit of Capitalism*, trans. Talcott Parsons (New York, 1930), pp. 155 ff.

MONOPOLY THEORY PRIOR TO ADAM SMITH   509

doctrine. Far from relaxing the rules, some of them, and this is the case of Dr. Thomas Wilson, were even stricter on certain points than the most orthodox theologians.[2]

In the matter of just price, there was little, if any, change. In accordance with tradition, Thomas Rogers, for example, in 1578 defined the just price as the one "whiche is either appointed by indifferent and wise men in aucthoritie or paied according to the common estimation of the thyng at such tyme as the bargaine is made."[3] On the subject of monopolies, he takes the usual view that they are extortions and that it is illicit if a seller "makes other men to paie extremely for his ware."[4] Baxter, in the next century, continues to expound the same principles.[5] For both authors common estimation is equivalent to the market price. Contrary to prevailing opinion, there is, consequently, no departure whatsoever from the norms formulated long before by mediaeval scholasticism.

From England, Puritan and Congregational divines brought the doctrine of the just price to the shores of America. It is expounded by the Reverend John Cotton who, following tradition, identifies just price with current price. In Massachusetts and Connecticut, it was an accepted principle of law that to make a monopoly of any trade was against the public good and the liberty of the people. Why would it be otherwise, since the theologians and the leading laymen derived their knowledge of economic principles from theological treatises, like that of Ames, and from the standard works of Jean Bodin, Hugo Grotius, and Gerard de Malynes?[6]

It may not be surprising that the Protestant divines continued to preach the Christian ethics first developed by the Universal Church. What is more surprising is that scholasticism left its stamp on English mercantilism. The fact has been noted and emphasized by Professor Heckscher.[7]

The early mercantilists, especially, were preoccupied with preserving the ideal of economic liberty. Restrictions were only to be imposed — as the lesser of two evils — in order to prevent the overthrow of a trade. Among the writers prior to, and including, Mun, there is not a single one who unreservedly defends monopoly. Scho-

2. R. de Roover, *Gresham*, p. 106.
3. *A Godlie Treatice concerning the lawful use of Ritches* (London, 1578), fol. 7ᵛ. In this quotation, "indifferent" means "impartial." Rogers also states that consideration must be given to the scarcity or plenty of things.
4. *Ibid.*, fol. 8ʳ.
5. The pertinent texts are quoted *verbatim* by H. M. Robertson, *Aspects of the Rise of Economic Individualism* (Cambridge, 1935), p. 17.
6. Dorfman, *op. cit.*, I, 41, 47–50.
7. *Mercantilism*, II, 277.

lastic tradition was still too strong.[8] Even Wheeler, in taking the defense of the Merchant Adventurers, denied vigorously that this company was in any way a monopoly and argued strenuously that its purpose was only to maintain what would be called today fair standards of competition.[9] The same is true of Mun. He does not defend the East India Company purely on the ground of business considerations, and he fails to call attention to the fact that the risks were so great that, without a charter granting exclusive privileges, it would have been impossible to attract the necessary capital.[1] Instead, he cautiously avoids the issue. Reading his *Discourse of Trade*, one almost gets the impression that the East India Company must have been a philanthropic society dedicated to such humanitarian projects as the training of mariners, the relief of unemployment, the support of preachers, and in general to the welfare of the commonwealth. About the ticklish subject of monopoly, not an iota.

Other mercantilists are less reticent and generously furnish a definition.[2] The wording varies a little from one author to another, but the gist is the same. As with the Doctors, the definition is generally so worded that it includes oligopoly, because "the name of monopoly, though taken originally for personal unity, yet is fitly extended to all improportionable paucity of the sellers in regard of the ware which is sold."[3]

One of the best definitions is that given by Edward Misselden. It reads:

> Monopoly is a kinde of commerce, in buying, selling, changing or bartering usurped by a few and sometimes but by one person, and forestalled

8. R. de Roover, *Gresham*, p. 284.

9. John Wheeler, *A Treatise of Commerce*, ed. George B. Hotchkiss (New York, 1931), pp. 363, 426–36; Middelburg, 1601, pp. 51, 142–52. The good faith of Wheeler is seriously open to question. His tract is a piece of clever propaganda. For example, his definition of monopoly is so worded that it is susceptible of strict interpretation only, and does not include oligopoly. Then he contends that the definition does not apply to the Merchant Adventurers and that they are not a monopoly. In the strict sense of the term, they were not. However, had Wheeler given a broader definition, it would have been more difficult to prove that it did not apply to Merchant Adventurers and that the charges of oligopoly levelled against them were entirely unfounded.

1. On similar grounds, Luis Molina had justified the monopoly of the East India trade by the King of Portugal. The text is in Strieder, *Studien*, pp. 90–91. Even Adam Smith justifies the granting of a temporary monopoly under those circumstances (*The Wealth of Nations*, Book V, chap. 1, part III, art. 1, §2: For facilitating particular branches of Commerce).

2. "A Discourse of Corporations, 1587–89?," *Tudor Economic Documents*, III, 266; Wheeler, *Treatise*, Hotchkiss ed., pp. 73, 427 and Middelburg ed., p. 143 and *T. E. D.*, III, 299; Gerard de Malynes, *The Maintenance of Free Trade* (London, 1622), p. 69; *Cambium Regis or the Office of His Majestie's Exchange Royall* (London, 1628), p. A3.

3. *English Economic History, Select Documents*, p. 446.

MONOPOLY THEORY PRIOR TO ADAM SMITH 511

from all others, to the gaine of the monopolist and the detriment of other men. The parts then of a monopoly are twaine: the restraint of the liberty of commerce to some one or a few; and the setting of the price at the pleasure of the monopolian to his private benefit and the prejudice of the publique. Upon which two hinges every monopoly turneth.[4]

One must admit that it would be difficult to be more complete. The principal point is that monopoly was a "restraint of freedom," since, by definition, the monopolists or the oligopolists were the only dealers and could exclude all others from the exercise of a trade.

Nothing is likely to create more confusion than misunderstanding about the meaning of words. In the history of economic thought, misunderstandings of this kind have repeatedly led to misinterpretations. One should not forget that a language does not remain static: new words are added, others become obsolete, and still others change their meaning or acquire a new connotation. Moreover, changes in terminology often correspond to change in habits of thought. Thus it happens that the word "competition" was never used by the mercantilists. In its economic signification, it probably does not antedate the eighteenth century.[5] Prior to that time, it does not occur. To designate competition, the mercantilists used the expression "freedom of trade" or "free trade." Consequently, in their parlance, "freedom of trade" was not the opposite of protectionism — which was not yet an issue — and had nothing to do with the absence of trade barriers between countries. "Freedom of trade" was the antithesis of "restraint of trade" and of monopoly.[6] The accent,

4. Edward Misselden, *Free Trade or the Meanes to Make Trade Florish* (London, 1622), p. 57.

5. In support of my interpretation, I should like to quote the following declaration made to the House of Commons in 1604: "All free subjects are born inheritable, as to their land, so also to the free exercise of their industry in those trades, whereto they apply themselves and whereby they are to live. Merchandize being the chief and richest of all other, and of greater extent and importance than all the rest, it is against the natural right and liberty of the subjects of England to restrain it into the hands of some few, as now it is." *Engl. Econ. Hist.*, *Select Documents*, pp. 443–44 and *Journals of the House of Commons*, I, 218. R. H. Tawney (*Religion and the Rise of Capitalism*, London: Pelican Books, 1938, pp. 166–67), places on this text a different interpretation, but he assumes that there was a change in outlook on this matter between the Middle Ages and the sixteenth century. I question such a view very much. The statement belongs to the mercantilist period only because it insists that trade is more important than agriculture or industry.

6. Adam Smith uses the word "competition," but always preceded by the article and not yet as an abstract concept (*Wealth of Nations*, Book I, chap. 7, Modern Libr. ed., p. 56). But he continues to use the expression "perfect liberty" to designate what would be called today "perfect competition" (see chaps. 7 and 10, pp. 56, 62, 99). However, "competition" in a modern sense is used earlier by Sir James Steuart, whose treatise appeared in 1767 (*An Inquiry into the Principles of Political Oeconomy*, Vol. I, p. 200).

instead of being on rivalry, as in "competition," was on the freedom of ingress into a profession or a trade and, more than that, on the absence of all hindrances to traffic.[7]

Such a way of thinking is quite understandable in an age of privileges and restrictions. To receive the freedom of a guild, for example, meant to become a member and to acquire consequently the right or freedom to practice a given trade. The tract of Edward Misselden, entitled *Free Trade or the Meanes to Make Trade Florish*, was not, as one may suppose, an attack on protectionism, but a plea in favor of the preservation of competition — as understood by the author. As a matter of fact, Misselden was the spokesman of the Merchant Adventurers and wanted to prove that this company had been unjustly accused of monopolistic practices. Its purpose was to regulate trade, and Misselden spent much of his eloquence in trying to convince his readers that regulation or "government in trade" was necessary to avoid unfair competition or "disorderly trade."[8] In other words, he argued along the same lines as many business men today, who contend that quotas and other devices are necessary to avoid the disastrous results of cutthroat competition. Whether Misselden was right or wrong is not the point. I simply want to show that the problem is not new.

Since we are on the subject, it may be well to point out that the French word *concurrence* is not much older than competition, its English equivalent. Apparently, in the seventeenth century, *concurrence* had not yet acquired the special meaning which economists now give to it.[9] At that time, the expression used was *liberté du commerce* or simply *liberté*.[1] Even Colbert paid lip service to the principle of competition and wrote to his *intendants* that "la liberté est l'âme du commerce," although, as is well known, he attempted to revive trade by multiplying monopolies.[2] Presumably, Montes-

7. It had the same meaning in colonial America (Dorfman, *Economic Mind*, I, 50). What is more startling, "free trade" is still used with this meaning by Adam Smith (*Wealth of Nations*, Book V, chap. 1, part 3, art. 1, §2, Mod. Libr. ed., p. 712), although he uses "freedom of trade" in a more modern sense in his chapter on restraints of trade.

8. The same point of view is taken by Henry Parker, *Of a Free Trade. A Discourse Seriously Recommending to Our Nation the Wonderfull Benefits of Trade, Especially of a Rightly Governed and Ordered Trade* (London, 1648). Cf. Dorfman, *Economic Mind*, I, 8.

9. Alwin Kuhn, *Die französische Handelssprache im 17. Jahrhundert* (Leipziger romanistische Studien, Sprachwissenschaftliche Reihe, Heft 1, Leipzig, 1931), p. 79. *Concurrence* occurs in one text of 1648, but not quite in an economic sense. The reference is "to the competition" of English and Dutch drapery. *En concurrence avec* ("in competition with") was common usage.

1. *Ibid.*, p. 207.

2. Heckscher, *Mercantilism*, II, 274.

MONOPOLY THEORY PRIOR TO ADAM SMITH 513

quieu (1689–1755) is one of the first to use the word "competition" in the modern sense when he writes: "C'est la *concurrence* qui met un *prix juste* aux marchandises et qui établit les vrais rapports entre elles."[3] The juxtaposition of *concurrence* and *prix juste* is significant: scholasticism had not lost its hold, even on Montesquieu.

Misselden's definition is not original with him. He himself gives as his source Althusius, or Johann Althaus (1557–1638), syndic of Emden from 1604 until his death. For a while the Merchant Adventurers kept their mart in that town, a circumstance that explains why Althusius' writings were known to Misselden. Probably the two men met in an official capacity, or possibly on a more friendly basis. Althusius is by no means a second-rate figure: Professor Friedrich of Harvard would rank him with Machiavelli, Bodin, Grotius, and Hobbes, as one of the five foremost political thinkers of the period from 1500 to 1650.[4] Althusius may be termed an Aristotelian whose sources of inspiration were the Bible, Roman law, classical philosophy and history, and contemporary political controversy.[5] He also quotes from the mediaeval canonists and civilians. His major work is a treatise on government, entitled *Politica Methodice Digesta*. The later and revised editions of this work take on, more and more, a practical tinge, the result of his experience as an administrator.

On monopoly, Althusius has much more than Misselden leads us to suppose. Besides the definition which the latter reproduces in an English translation, there is a long description of sundry monopolistic practices.[6] Althusius is even less favorable to monopoly than the scholastics, and he reveals himself as a staunch defender of "free trade" and even of individual bargaining and freedom of contract.[7] In Althusius' opinion, there is only one case in which monopoly is justifiable: in a national emergency, it may be imposed by the State

3. *Esprit des lois* (first published in 1748), Book XX, chap. 9. In the next chapter, however, Montesquieu uses the more common expression *liberté du commerce*, which is placed in contraposition to the *privilèges exclusifs* granted to a trading company.

4. Johannes Althusius (Althaus), *Politica Methodice Digesta*, ed. Carl Joachim Friedrich (Harvard Political Classics, Vol. II; Cambridge, Mass., 1932), p. xv. The authoritative study on Althusius is that of Otto von Gierke, *Johannes Althusius und die Entwicklung der naturlichen Staatstheorien* (1st ed., Breslau, 1902; 4th ed., 1929).

5. Althusius, *op. cit.*, p. xx. Cf. George R. Sabine, *A History of Political Theory* (New York, 1937), p. 417.

6. *Politica Methodice Digesta*, cap. XXXII, §20–25, pp. 306–308 (Friedrich ed.).

7. However, he admits that public authorities have the right to set prices taking into consideration all attending circumstances (*ibid.*, cap. XXXII, §15, p. 305).

in order to provide revenue, if it is impossible to raise enough by taxation or other means, or if communications are disrupted by enemy action. In all other cases, public and private monopolies are illicit. Althusius gives three reasons. First, it would be tyrannical for the supply of the necessities of life to depend upon the whim or the discretion of a few, and, furthermore, to create dearth by restrictions on trade is against charity. Secondly, free commercial intercourse is a principle of public law which gives every one the right, in any legitimate way, to barter, to buy and sell, to acquire and alienate. And, finally, commerce has been justly introduced so that men from all parts may exchange what is necessary for their subsistence. To take away this right, is it not like robbing them of life itself?

According to Althusius, monopoly can be perpetrated in many ways, and he proceeds to give an impressive list of nineteen different restraints. They fall into three categories: (1) commercial, (2) industrial, and (3) political. The abuses laid at the door of merchants include chiefly practices which may be labelled as engrossing, forestalling, and regrating, and which were designed to prevent the operation of free competition in an open market. In most cases, this aim is achieved by means of illicit agreements, secret pacts, or conspiracies; these are the words used by Althusius.

More interesting, since other authors remain vague on the subject, are the details which he gives about the monopolistic practices of the guilds. Thus he considers as monopolistic any guild rules restricting membership. Such are, for example, those by which artificers agree that they will not teach their art except to their sons or grandsons, or that they will require apprentices to pay excessive entrance fees or to serve an exceedingly long time before becoming masters. In the same class are regulations which provide that nobody will be admitted as member of a guild unless he is from a certain family or from a certain town.

Another abuse of the guild system is when bakers, taverners, innkeepers, and the like connive to make rules for their own benefit, but to the detriment of the common weal. If he were living today, Althusius would not be in favor of labor unions. This phrase is not used by him, but he disapproves of artificers agreeing together that they will not hire themselves out unless they receive the minimum wage set by themselves. Wages are not the only issue; freedom of hiring or firing is another. The workers in the building trades are censured for making agreements that no one of them will accept a job already started or contracted by a fellow-worker. Apparently, even

MONOPOLY THEORY PRIOR TO ADAM SMITH   515

strikes are not modern phenomena. Althusius, at any rate, regards it as a monopoly for craftsmen or journeymen to band together and refuse to work for the citizenry of any city or town, presumably in order to obtain better wages. In my opinion, it would be wrong to attribute Althusius' economic individualism to his Calvinism.[8] Let us not forget that in mediaeval Florence, long before the Reformation, it was a capital offense to organize a labor union, let alone a strike.

In the political field, Althusius condemns any class legislation as apt to foment strife, as, for example, when one group attempts to obtain the enactment of a statute advantageous to itself but harmful to other groups. In short, lobbies, too, are monopolies. Political power is also abused when no one is permitted to grind at any mill other than that of the lord. Evidently, Althusius has no use for oppressive feudal customs.

One form of monopoly described by him is rather amusing: it is that of any soothsayers or fortune-tellers who collect large sums of money from people who consult them before they embark upon a business venture.[9] That such a practice was still prevalent at the time of Althusius, I doubt very much. It must be a practice reported in a classical work: Althusius, like other learned men of his time, had the pedantic habit of quoting from Greek or Latin whenever there was the least opportunity.

On the whole, Althusius does not make much of a contribution. On the matter of monopolies, as on other subjects, he is more outspoken than profound.[1] His approach to the problem is entirely legal: there is the same lack of economic analysis, the same dogmatism, and the same reliance upon authority, as in scholastic works. Perhaps the only difference is that Althusius was more specific in his criticism. His attitude reflects the growing impatience with the narrow, restrictive, and particularistic tactics of the guilds; it was a sign of the times.[2] A comparison, perhaps, is not out of order: for the same reasons which moved Althusius, there is today a disposition in certain quarters to extend the application of the anti-trust laws to

8. According to Professor Friedrich, Althusius was the political theorist of Calvinism *par excellence*.
9. I have never found any mention of it in the numerous mediaeval business records that I have examined.
1. Sabine, *op. cit.*, p. 417.
2. The same trend is observable in Catholic countries. At Liége, one Mathias de Grati, in 1676, complains that the town is full of monopolies, and yet this detestable crime goes unpunished. J. Lejeune, "Religion, morale et capitalisme dans la société liégeoise du XVIIᵉ siècle," *Revue belge de philologie et d'histoire*, XXII (1943), 117.

the monopolistic restraints of labor unions, especially in the building trades, already singled out by him more than three centuries ago.[3]

Althusius was a German, a Calvinist, and a political theorist. But the same doctrines with regard to monopoly were professed by Giovanni Domenico Peri, who was an Italian, a Catholic, and a practical man. Instead of a treatise on the art of government, he wrote a popular handbook on business, that contains a valuable description of the so-called fairs of Besançon, which were actually held in Piacenza and Novi, in Peri's time. These fairs were the international clearing house of the time, that is, during the period between the decline of Antwerp and the rise of Amsterdam to the rank of the world's financial center, and were dominated by the all-powerful Genoese bankers.

For Peri, as for Althusius, as for the Doctors before them, monopoly is the sum of all perversity and may be practiced by one or a few who buy or sell at an unjust price in the hope of illicit gain.[4] One of the main characteristics of monopoly, Peri insists, is that of being a conspiracy. Merchants are not the only ones who may be guilty, but also artificers who contrive to exact more than the just wage, that is, the current or the opportunity wage.[5] One of the worst forms of monopoly is that committed by bankers who, by their manoeuvers, manipulate the exchange rates in order to create artificial stringency in the money market.[6] As a matter of fact, such manoeuvers had been formally condemned by Pope Pius V in 1571.[7] Another reprehensible fraud is when dealers drive prices up by spreading false rumors that ships bringing supplies have been wrecked, delayed by bad weather, or seized by pirates.[8] On the whole, there is nothing in Peri that deviates in the least from the traditional teachings of the Doctors. In another connection — the legitimacy of certain exchange

3. Corwin Edwards, "Public Policy toward Restraints of Trade by Labor Unions: an Economic Appraisal," *American Economic Review, Supplement*, XXII (1942), 432–448, esp. 440.

4. Giovanni Domenico Peri, *Il Negotiante* (rev. ed., Venice, 1707), Part III, cap. xx, pp. 74–75. The date of the first edition is 1638.

5. It is impossible to discuss here the just wage. As evidence, I should like to refer to the passages from Cardinal Juan de Lugo (1583–1660) quoted by J. Brodrick, S.J., *The Economic Morals of the Jesuits* (London, 1934), pp. 89–90.

6. At that time, "exchange-dealer" and "banker" were synonymous expressions, and the credit system, because of the usury prohibition, was tied to foreign exchange.

7. R. de Roover, *Gresham*, p. 164.

8. This was common practice even in as large a center as Venice. Market fluctuations were very sensitive to news. Pierre Sardella, *Nouvelles et spéculations à Venise au début du XVIe siècle* (Cahiers des Annales, No. 1, Paris, 1948), pp. 27, 81.

transactions — Peri does not question their principles, either; he argues only that they do not apply to certain specific business practices.

In the course of the seventeenth century, criticism was more and more directed at the collective monopolies of the guilds and the exclusive privileges of the trading companies. The Dutch writer, Pieter de la Court (1618–1685) — his real name was van den Hove — especially represents this new trend.[9] Because of his liberalism, he was hailed in the nineteenth century as the greatest of the early Dutch economists.[1] De la Court's main work, however, is nothing more than a political pamphlet which contains a passionate plea for freedom in matters of religion and for freedom of trade and of occupation (*vrijheid van negotie en van nering*). The main argument is that select or "closed" (*beslotene*) guilds and companies, because they were in the secure possession of exclusive rights, promoted inefficiency, blocked any innovations, and discouraged initiative.[2] Their restrictions were all the more dangerous because Holland's prosperity, which depended upon the exportation of the products of its fisheries and manufactures, was already threatened by foreign competition and discriminatory duties. In particular, de la Court deems it a mistaken policy to disregard the tastes of foreign customers and to expect them to buy, not what they wanted, but what the guilds, in their wisdom, permitted their members to produce. Such a presupposition, according to de la Court, is simply ridiculous (*bespottelijk*), and one can hardly disagree with him if his diagnosis is correct. Another of his

---

9. His major work is entitled *Aenwysing der heilsame politike gronden en maximen van de Republike van Holland en West-Vriesland* (Leyden-Rotterdam, 1669). An earlier edition, under the title *Interest van Holland* (Amsterdam, 1662), gives only the initials V.D.H. as a clue to the author's name. In the preface of the *Aenwysing*, de la Court claims that the earlier edition was published without his knowledge or permission. This imperfect edition was translated into French, English and German. The English edition bears the title: *The True Interest and Political Maxims of the Republick of Holland and West Friesland* (London, 1702). It gives as author, John de Witt, the leader of the Dutch republican party, who was assassinated by supporters of the House of Orange, but this is a deliberate error. Pieter de la Court is the author of another tract, *'t Welvaren der Stad Leiden, anno 1659*, which remained in manuscript until 1845 when the most important sections were printed. It was not published completely until 1911 (ed. Felix Driessen).

1. Etienne Laspeyres, "Mittheilungen aus Pieter de la Court's Schriften, ein Beitrag zur Geschichte der niederländischen Nationalöconomie des 17. Jahrhunderts," *Zeitschrift für die gesamte Staatswissenschaft*, XVIII (1862), 330; O. van Rees, *Geschiedenis der Staathuishoudkunde in Nederland tot het einde der achttiende eeuw* (Utrecht, 1865), I, 362; Cossa, *Introduction*, p. 219.

2. *Aenwysing*, Part I, chap. 16, p. 72.

criticisms is that the high prices charged by the guilds were a tax imposed upon the consumer.[3]

With regard to the Dutch East India Company, he contends that its administration was wasteful and inefficient, because of unmanageable size, lack of control, corruption among its personnel, and excessive salaries:[4] all abuses which, according to Adam Smith, were the scourge of chartered companies.[5] The Dutch East India Company was also accused of restricting the supply of raw silk and spices when, thereby, it could increase its profits.[6] Finally, de la Court complains of the expense incurred by maintaining military establishments in the colonies and fears that the Dutch Republic might lose its vital European trade, because, in order to preserve the far less important East India trade, it had become entangled in recurrent commercial wars with foreign powers.[7] Nevertheless, Pieter de la Court does not advocate the abolition of the East India Company, but demands only that it be required to enlarge and "open" its trade to all Hollanders.[8]

On the whole, the writings of de la Court are tracts in favor of an economic policy designed to improve Holland's competitive position by removing internal restrictions. No attempt is made to give an analysis of price determination, although there is an accurate description of monopolistic practices.[9] In contrast with Scholastic writers, de la Court condemns monopoly for reasons of inefficiency and not on the basis of moral principles or a just-price theory. This was a new approach to the problem.

3. *Ibid.*, Part I, chap. 20, p. 89.
4. *Ibid.*, Part I, chap. 16, p. 74. The English edition uses the expression "vast and consequently unmanageable designs" (*The True Interest*, p. 73). The Dutch original uses the words *niet wel beheerbaren omslag*. *Omslag* is best translatable as "volume of business," hence "size."
5. *The Wealth of Nations*, Book IV, chap. 7 ("Of Colonies"), part 3, and Book 5, chap. 2 (pp. 557 ff. and 771 ff. of Mod. Libr. ed.)
6. *Aenwysing*, Part I, chap. 19, p. 86.
7. *Aenwysing*, Part I, chap. 7, pp. 32–34. The statement corresponds to the facts. All Dutch economic historians now agree that the East India trade, although spectacular, was far less important than the Baltic and other trades. In the seventeenth century, the East India trade was never more than ten per cent of the total.
8. *Aenwysing*, Part I, chap. 7, p. 32.
9. Dutch economics in the age of mercantilism has been very much neglected. The only study is that of Etienne Laspeyres and it dates from 1863 (*Geschichte der volkswirtschaftlichen Anschauungen der Niederländer und ihrer Litteratur zur Zeit der Republik*, Preisschriften gekrönt und herausgegeben von der Fürstlich Jablonowski'schen Gesellschaft, Vol. XI (Leipzig, 1863). Laspeyres lists several eighteenth-century doctoral dissertations on monopoly and free trade (competition), manuscripts preserved in the Municipal Library of Amsterdam. Whether they contain anything of value, I do not know.

MONOPOLY THEORY PRIOR TO ADAM SMITH   519

From the theoretical point of view, a more significant author is the German cameralist, Johann Joachim Becher (1635–1682).[1] He was a man of no mean attainments, proficient in many arts, and yet he was what the French call *un génie raté* or what we may call a crank. Despite his vast learning, his proposals were often far from sound. Besides being a physician and a pseudo-scientist, he was a typical projector, whose fertile imagination devised all kinds of schemes for social reform and economic improvement. During his lifetime, he moved from one German court to another, offering his recipes for the cure of individual and social ailments. In Austria, he tried to find gold by washing the sands of the Danube. Probably because several of his projects miscarried, he eventually fell into disgrace and was compelled to seek refuge in England, where he died.[2]

Becher, the son of a Lutheran minister, was still strongly influenced by the venerable Aristotelian tradition.[3] In connection with our topic, he made a minor contribution in proposing a new terminology for various kinds of market situations: monopolium, propolium, and polypolium. Monopolium has the familiar meaning and refers to any situation in which the supply of a commodity is controlled either by one individual or collectively by a corporation, such as a guild.[4] Propolium appears to be the same as *Fürkauf*, or forestalling in English.[5] By polypolium, Becher means that there are a great many sellers.[6] Perhaps his concept can best be described as unrestricted competition.

According to Becher, all three "polia" are detrimental to society, because they distort the equilibrium which should exist between population and means of subsistence. Monopoly is bad, since it leads to

1. I am grateful to Professor Emil Kauder, of the University of Wyoming, for calling my attention to Becher, whom I had overlooked in the first draft of this article.

2. Emil Kauder, "Johann Joachim Becher als Wirtschafts- und Sozialpolitiker," *Schmoller's Jahrbuch für Gesetzgebung, Verwaltung und Volkswirtschaft im Deutschen Reiche*, XLVIII (1924), 811–841, esp. p. 814. Cf. Louise Sommer, *Die österreichischen Kameralisten in dogmengeschichtlicher Darstellung*, II (Vienna, 1925), 49–63; Kurt Zielenziger, *Die alten deutschen Kameralisten*, Vol. II of *Beiträge zur Geschichte der Nationalökonomie* (Jena, 1914), pp. 235 ff.; Albion Small, *The Cameralists, the Pioneers of German Social Polity* (Chicago, 1909), pp. 107 ff.

3. Kauder, *op. cit.*, p. 819.

4. Johann Joachim Becher, *Politische Discurs von den eigentlichen Ursachen des Auff- und Abnehmens der Stadt, Länder und Republicken . . . Von dem Monopolio, Polypolio und Propolio* (Frankfort-on-the-Main, 1672), Part II, chap. 2, pp. 110 ff.

5. *Discurs*, Part II, chap. 21, p. 206.

6. *Ibid.*, Part II, chap. 2, p. 111.

an undesirable concentration of wealth, is responsible for high prices, and reduces the opportunities for employment.[7] Polypolium, the opposite of monopolium, is equally bad: when a trade is overcrowded, it ceases to afford a decent livelihood. The guilds had been originally created to prevent this evil, but they abused their power and became monopolistic organizations.[8] Still, Becher does not suggest that they be abolished, but they should be placed under strict government supervision.

To redress social and economic maladjustments, Becher relies on government action. He distrusts the individual and puts his faith in the state.[9] The chief aim of economic policy, he contends, should be to maintain a proper balance between human resources and employment opportunities.[1] As remedies against the evils resulting from monopolium and propolium, Becher recommends the creation of public granaries, public workhouses, and market-halls, or commodity exchanges.[2] With regard to the first, Becher expected to kill two birds with one stone. The public warehouses, or granaries, would be used to store the oversupply of grain and other produce in years of plenty and the stocks thus accumulated would be sold at a reasonable price in years of crop failure. Thus Becher hoped to stabilize the price of grain, which, in his time, was subject to violent fluctuations in response to good or bad harvests. In other words, he anticipated in some ways the ever-normal-granary program. Becher's anti-monopoly program also called for the encouragement of manufactures, the erection of banks, and the appointment of market supervisors.

As Becher was also a supporter of autarchy, one can see why his system based on government regulation and paternalism would appeal to the enlightened despots of the eighteenth century. Some of his more practical suggestions were actually carried out. Even his project for an ever-normal granary found practical application in the *Magazinpolitik* initiated by Frederick William I, King of Prussia (1713–1740), and developed by his son and successor, Frederick the Great (1740–1786).[3] Becher's terminology is not used today.

---

7. Sommer, *op. cit.*, pp. 49 ff.

8. *Discurs*, Part II, chap. 2, pp. 113–114, 119. Polypolium also enables the manufacturers to keep their workers in constant poverty and toil.

9. Kauder, *op. cit.*, p. 829.

1. *Discurs*, Part II, chap. 2, p. 115.

2. *Ibid.*, Part II, chap. 25, pp. 236 ff.

3. Wilhelm Naudé and Gustav Schmoller, *Getreidehandelspolitik*, Vol. II, *Die Getreidehandelspolitik und Kriegsmagazinverwaltung Brandenburg-Preussens bis 1740* (Acta Borussica, ed. G. Schmoller, Berlin, 1901), pp. 91–92, 271–334.

MONOPOLY THEORY PRIOR TO ADAM SMITH 521

However, it was adopted in Germany by later authors of the eighteenth century.[4]

Although Becher considerably modified the scholastic views, his work exerted little influence outside of Germany. Elsewhere, the traditional doctrines still lingered on, especially in the handbooks on commerce of the eighteenth century.[5] One even finds them in the work of the English mercantilist, Sir James Steuart (1712–1780),[6] and, what is more surprising, in the *Encyclopédie* of Diderot. The latter calls monopoly "un trafic odieux et illicite" and states that it is illegal by virtue of the ordinances of Francis I and subsequent regulations.[7] According to Savary des Bruslons, a particularly dangerous kind of monopoly is that obtained by deceit or trickery from a well-meaning sovereign, because it evades the law with the acquiescence of the legislator himself.[8] Postlethwayt in his *Universal Dictionary of Commerce* also has an article on monopoly. It gives the English point of view: monopolies granted by the King are null and void, but not those established by act of Parliament.[9] The text of the definition given is word for word the same as that of Malynes in his *Lex Mercatoria*, a century earlier.

It is improbable that Adam Smith went back to the ponderous treatises of the Doctors, that he was acquainted with the work of Althusius or of Becher, or that he attached much importance to the brief articles in Postlethwayt's *Dictionary* or in Diderot's *Encyclopédie*. How, then, were the mediaeval doctrines transmitted to Adam Smith? In my opinion, the connecting link is in the writings of Hugo Grotius (1583–1645) and Samuel Pufendorf (1622–94). At least, there is evidence. Adam Smith refers to both authors in the *Wealth of Nations* and we know that he had copies of their books in his library.[1] Grotius and Pufendorf each has a chapter on value and price. Both chapters bear all the earmarks of scholastic influence and accordingly stress the fact that utility and scarcity are the two

4. Carl Günther Ludovici (1707–1778), *Grundriss eines vollständigen Kaufmanns-Systems* (Stuttgart, 1932, reprint of 2nd ed., 1778), p. 251, §496.

5. For example, Antonio Maria Triulzi, *Bilanzio de' pesi e mesure* (Venice, 1766), p. 190.

6. *An Inquiry into the Principles of Political Oeconomy* (1767), I, 200. Sir James does not even overlook the penalty of restitution.

7. "Monopole," *Encyclopédie ou Dictionnaire raisonné des sciences, des arts et des métiers* (Geneva, 1778), XXII, 161.

8. "Monopole," Jacques Savary des Bruslons, *Dictionnaire universel du commerce* (Paris, 1723).

9. Malachi Postlethwayt, "Monopolies," *The Universal Dictionary of Trade and Commerce* (London, 1755), II, 290.

1. James Bonar, *A Catalogue of the Library of Adam Smith* (2nd ed., London, 1932), pp. 78, 151.

sources of value. Pufendorf's analysis is the more acute. Although Adam Smith must have read those chapters, it is regrettable that he made no better use of them.[2] Instead, he became entangled in the contradiction between "value in use" and "value in exchange," a paradox which had been solved more felicitously by some of the Doctors.

To both Grotius and Pufendorf, monopoly theory is only an appendix to their theory on the just price. Pufendorf still clings to the principle that the just price is either the legal price or the natural or market price.[3] Monopoly is an anomaly. According to Grotius, it is contrary to natural law. Only those monopolies are excepted that are permitted by the sovereign power for a just cause and with a fixed price, or that are established by private persons, "if only with a fair price."[4] In all other cases, monopolies are illegal, and the monopolists are bound to make good the loss. Pufendorf has the peculiar notion that "a monopoly in the proper sense cannot be established by private citizens, because it has the force of a privilege."[5] Private citizens, therefore, can only carry on spurious monopolies which are generally maintained "by clandestine frauds and conspiracies."

V. Conclusions

This study is only what the French call *une mise au point*. It is based on a preliminary investigation and it does not pretend to exhaust the subject. Its aim is simply to correct some misconceptions and to dispel some prejudices. On the topic of value and price, the contributions of the Schoolmen and their successors, the casuists and the jurists, up to the eighteenth century have been far greater than those of the mercantilists. The economists have overlooked a current of thought which runs parallel to mercantilism and connects Adam Smith directly with the mediaeval Doctors.

In the field of economics, the scholastic doctrines do not mature and receive their final formulation until the seventeenth century. Later authors, such as Grotius and Pufendorf, added little or nothing; they only passed on the legacy which they had received from the great thinkers of the preceding age.

2. Moreover, this material was used by Francis Hutcheson, Adam Smith's teacher and predecessor in the chair of Moral Philosophy at Glasgow College, for the preparation of his lectures. Cossa, *Introduction*, p. 251.

3. *De jure naturae et gentium, libri octo* (Oxford: Clarendon Press, 1934), Book V, chap. 1, §8; Vol. II, pp. 665–686.

4. *De jure belli ac pacis, libri tres* (Oxford: Clarendon Press, 1925), Book II, chap. 12, §16; II, 353; I, 233–234.

5. *De jure naturae*, Book V, chap. 6, §7; II, 739.

MONOPOLY THEORY PRIOR TO ADAM SMITH   523

On some crucial points, the theory of the Schoolmen is sometimes equal to that of Adam Smith and sometimes even superior. Monopoly is a good example. Adam Smith states that monopolists keep the market constantly understocked, that is, limit the supply, in order to sell their commodities above the natural price, or cost of production. He then goes on: "the price of monopoly is upon every occasion the highest which can be got."[6] This latter statement is ambiguous, since it neglects the elasticity of demand. The Doctors do not fall into the same error. They say that the monopolist can set the price at his pleasure (which is correct in so far as he can regulate the price by regulating the supply) and that this price will normally be above the level of the just, or competitive, price (which is also correct, since the monopolist seeks to increase the price at the expense of the consumers). The Doctors do not carry their analysis further and do not explain how the monopoly price is determined, assuming that the monopolist tries to maximize his profits. As is known, this problem was finally solved by Augustin Cournot. With regard to the limitation of supply, the Doctors remain a little bit vague, although they state repeatedly that monopolists restrain trade and create artificial scarcity. One should not expect to find the rigor of analysis to which we are accustomed.

This investigation fully confirms what Schumpeter has said on the subject: the economists and moralists from Aristotle to Adam Smith were consistent in their condemnation of monopoly.[7] There is hardly a dissenting voice. Perhaps there was some reason for this attitude: the advantages of large-scale production were practically nil prior to the introduction of machinery. Most monopolies were the effect of collusion, which was favored either by the guild system or by the small extent of the market. Or else they were common in branches of trade dominated by regulated or joint-stock companies. Reread Adam Smith: his blast against monopolies is aimed at the exclusive privileges, first, of the guilds or corporations and, next, of the regulated and joint-stock companies.[8] It may be trite, but I wish to remind the reader that the *Wealth of Nations* was written before the Industrial Revolution had made much headway. Conditions in 1776 were closer to those existing in the sixteenth century than to those existing today.

In view of the fact that the anti-trust laws declare illegal any

6. *Wealth of Nations*, Book I, chap. 7 (Mod. Libr. ed., p. 61).
7. Schumpeter, "Science and Ideology," *op. cit.*, p. 357.
8. Especially Book I, chap. 10, part II, and Book V, chap. 1, part III, art. 1, §2 (Modern Libr. ed., pp. 118 ff., 690 ff).

"conspiracies in restraint of trade," I wish to stress that such a concept is very old. In connection with monopoly, the word "conspiracy" occurs again and again, both in the text of statutes and in the treatises of moralists and jurists, from the Middle Ages down to Adam Smith. The latter, we should not forget, was a professor of Moral Philosophy.

This study is based on the premise that the just price was either the legal price or the market price. If this is so — and the texts leave no room for doubt — it follows that both a black-market price and a monopoly price must be unjust.[9] This was also the conclusion of the Doctors. Why have their theories been misinterpreted? Part of the explanation is that modern scholars have been misled by an antiquated terminology, by an unfamiliar method of analysis, and by their own prejudices.[1] As a result, the Doctors have not received a fair deal. Their theory of value and price, especially, deserves reconsideration: it is much closer to modern theory than one may suspect.

RAYMOND DE ROOVER.

WELLS COLLEGE

9. I use the expression "black-market price" only for want of a more satisfactory term. Of course, it was never used by the Doctors. According to them, the legal price was definite; any price deviating from it was *ipso facto* unjust.

1. Since this article was completed, I have had the privilege of glancing at the manuscript of the late Professor Schumpeter's *magnum opus* on the history of economic analysis. Professor Schumpeter does not repeat any of the old errors, and his interpretation of just price corresponds to mine. I am grateful to Dr. Elizabeth Boody Schumpeter for permitting me to examine the typescript of her husband's forthcoming book.

[4]

THE

QUARTERLY JOURNAL
OF ECONOMICS

| Vol. LXIX | May, 1955 | No. 2 |

SCHOLASTIC ECONOMICS:
SURVIVAL AND LASTING INFLUENCE
FROM THE SIXTEENTH CENTURY TO ADAM SMITH

By Raymond de Roover

I. Introduction: the medieval contribution, 161. — II. The school of Salamanca, 167. — III. The demise of scholastic economics, 171. — IV. Scholasticism and mercantilism: a contrast, 177. — V. Conclusions, 185.

I. Introduction: The Medieval Contribution

Shortly before the end of the nineteenth century, Luigi Cossa deplored the fact that there existed no work on scholastic economics "without some underlying bias towards systematic refutation or extravagant apology."[1] Despite Cossa's own efforts to amend this situation, there has been very little improvement in recent years, and scholastic economics has remained a field which is so neglected or so poorly cultivated that, in the opinion of most economists, it hardly deserves serious consideration. As a result, most of the standard textbooks on the history of economic thought — if they do not omit the subject altogether and start with the physiocrats — devote little space to what they call "medieval" economics. After some trite comments on Thomas Aquinas, they greet Oresme (c. 1330–1382) from a distance and then hasten on to Thomas Mun and the theory of the balance of trade. Usually, the treatment is not only superficial but replete with errors which could have been avoided by going to the sources instead of repeating clichés.[2]

1. Luigi Cossa, *An Introduction to the Study of Political Economy* (London, 1893), p. 141. Although this book is not analytical, it is still extremely useful for its bibliographical and other accurate information.

2. A laudable exception is the book of Edgar Salin, *Geschichte der Volkswirtschaftslehre* (4th ed.; Berne, 1951). Another is, of course, the great work of Joseph A. Schumpeter, *History of Economic Analysis* (New York, 1954). As this article was written independent of Schumpeter — in fact, the manuscript was sent to this *Journal* before his book appeared — no references to his *History* have been

162   *QUARTERLY JOURNAL OF ECONOMICS*

As has already been pointed out in this *Journal*, the current textbooks entirely overlook the fact "that Aquinas was the founder of a school and that his doctrines were further elaborated and refined by his followers."[3] It should be added that these followers continued far beyond the Middle Ages until well into the seventeenth century. Moreover, some of their important economic doctrines were taken over, with only slight modifications, by the philosophers of natural law, such as Hugo Grotius (1583–1645) and Samuel Pufendorf (1622–94), who were still Aristotelians, even if they were opposed to scholasticism.

Since the later scholastic writers built on the foundations laid by their predecessors, it appears necessary to say a few words about the method used by the medieval Schoolmen and about their economic contributions of a technical nature. The author assumes that their contributions in a broader sense are known, in spite of the limited treatment accorded the subject in most histories of economic thought.

No more than the authors of antiquity, did the medieval Schoolmen consider political economy as an independent discipline, but as an appendix to ethics and law.[4] This situation still persisted in the eighteenth century when Adam Smith took charge of the chair of Moral Philosophy at Glasgow College. The courses of his predecessor, Francis Hutcheson (1694–1746), and his contemporary at Edinburgh, Adam Ferguson (1723–1816), are available in print. According to these sources, the contents of a course in Moral Philosophy in the eighteenth century and in Presbyterian Scotland still corresponded, by and large, to the description of the subject matter given in the thirteenth century by Thomas Aquinas in his *Comments on the Ethics of Aristotle*.[5] Economics, in the modern sense, occupied a very subordinate position and was still viewed as an ethical and legal matter involving the application of natural law to civil contracts.

What the Doctors in the Middle Ages were really interested in was to determine the rules of justice governing social relations. Following Aquinas, they distinguished two kinds of justice: distribu-

added. The reader may be interested in comparing this essay with Schumpeter's remarks and conclusions. He will find a different treatment of the subject, but fundamental agreement on various points.

3. R. de Roover, "Monopoly Theory prior to Adam Smith: a Revision," this *Journal* (Nov. 1951), p. 493.

4. I avoid using the term "economics" here, because in the Middle Ages it still retained the same meaning as in antiquity and referred to household management.

5. Thomas Aquinas, *In X libros ethicorum ad Nicomachum*, I, 1.

SCHOLASTIC ECONOMICS 163

tive justice, which regulated the distribution of wealth and income, according to the place of the individual in society, and commutative justice, which applied to the reciprocal dealings between individuals, that is, to the exchange of goods and services.[6]   In other words, economic matters pertained to justice, not to charity, as can be readily ascertained by merely running through the table of contents of Aquinas' *Summa theologica*.

In dealing with questions of justice, the Doctors unavoidably hit upon economic matters and were forced to consider them.   At first their investigation was limited to the just price and usury, but it soon branched out to involve a host of other questions, including the just wage, debasement (inflation), justice in taxation, public debts, monopoly, foreign exchange, partnerships, and all the contracts that might involve any taint of usury.

The medieval mind was legalistic and, under the influence of Roman law, a great deal of importance was attached to the form of contracts.   The principal problem was always to determine whether a contract was licit or illicit.   This emphasis tended to narrow the scope of economics to the study of the legal nature of contracts and their ethical implications, a tendency which reflects itself even in the title and the arrangement of scholastic treatises.   One will be sure to find economic matters discussed — along with other topics, of course — in any treatise on moral theology bearing as title *De contractibus* (Concerning Contracts) or *De justitia et jure* (Concerning Justice and Law).   Almost invariably economic subjects are also touched upon in guides for confessors, though the exposition in works of this type is likely to be less systematic and analytical and more casuistic.   As a matter of fact, the word "casuistry" derives from the concern of the late scholastic writers with cases of conscience.

Thomas Aquinas (1226–1274) had given a place to economics in his universal scheme: it was ruled by justice and grounded on private property and exchange.   In any case, the pursuit of material welfare was not to be regarded as an end in itself, but as a means to achieve the *summum bonum* of salvation.[7]   These fundamental principles were never questioned by his followers, but practical necessities soon spurred them to elaborate his rather sketchy analysis on usury and price.   The first who refined it considerably was John Buridan (1300–1358), a pupil of William of Ockham and a rector of the Univer-

6. *Idem, Summa theologica*, II, ii, quaest. 61, arts. 1 and 2.
7. *Ibid.*, II, ii, qu. 55, art. 6, and *Summa contra Gentiles*, III, c. 30.   Cf. Aristotle, *Nicomachean Ethics*, I, 5 and 8.

sity of Paris. He insisted on the point that value was measured by human wants: not by those of a single individual, but by those of the entire community (*rei venalis mensura est communis indigentia humana*).[8] He made it clear, also, that he considered the market price as the just price. Buridan's analysis even anticipates the modern concept of a consumer scale of preferences, since he states that the person who exchanges a horse for money would not have done so, if he had not preferred money to a horse.

After Buridan, the next writer of importance was the Florentine jurist and diplomat, Messer Lorenzo di Antonio Ridolfi (1360–1442), who in 1403 wrote a treatise on usury.[9] It contains the first detailed discussion of foreign exchange. Of course, he deals with the subject from the scholastic point of view, which is radically different from the later mercantilist or balance-of-trade approach.[1] The question raised by Ridolfi is whether exchange dealings are lawful or involve usury.

Lorenzo Ridolfi was followed by the famous preacher, San Bernardino of Siena (1380–1444), whom Professor Edgar Salin considers as one of the most notable economists of all times.[2] As sources of value, he lists three factors: utility (*virtuositas*), scarcity (*raritas*), and pleasurableness (*complacibilitas*). He also mentions that goods may be more or less gratifying, according to the intensity of our desire to possess and to use them. Without stretching these statements too far, it seems to me that San Bernardino had undoubtedly a psychological theory of value and even some inkling of varying degrees of utility. According to him, the just price is determined by "the estimation made in common by all the citizens of a community" (*æstimatio a communitatibus civilibus facta communiter*). In my opinion, this is clearly the competitive price in a free market. The correctness of this interpretation is beyond question, since Bernardino

8. Edmund Schreiber, *Die volkswirtschaftlichen Anschauungen der Scholastik seit Thomas von Aquin* (Jena, 1913), pp. 178–86.

9. *Tractatus de usuris et materiae montis* (1st ed.; Pavia, 1490); republished in Vol. VII of the *Tractatus universi juris* (Venice, 1583), fols. 15r–50r.

1. R. de Roover, *Gresham on Foreign Exchange; an Essay on Early English Mercantilism* (Cambridge, Mass.: Harvard University Press, 1949), pp. 173–80, and *L'évolution de la lettre de change, XIVe–XVIIIe siècles* (Paris: Armand Colin, 1953), pp. 51, 58–60, 127–29.

2. *Op. cit.*, p. 45. There are two recent monographs on the economics of San Bernardino: Franz Josef Hünermann, *Die wirtschafts-ethischen Predigten des hl. Bernardin von Siena* (Münster, 1939) and Alberto E. Trugenberger, *San Bernardino da Siena, Considerazioni sullo sviluppo dell'etica economica cristiana nel primo Rinascimento* (Berne, 1951). The sermons of Bernardino of Siena dealing with economics are in his collection, *De Evangelio Aeterno*, Nos. 32 to 42.

is outspoken in his condemnation of monopolistic practices, that is, of "fraudulent and pernicious agreements" by which merchants drive up prices in order to increase their profits. Finally, San Bernardino states that the "difficulty" of producing a good makes it scarcer and more valuable. Does he imply that the cost of production determines price by affecting the supply? An interesting point is that "difficulty," instead of supply, appears in the lectures of Francis Hutcheson, Adam Smith's teacher, as a price-determining factor. The concept is not used in *The Wealth of Nations*, but it reappears in Ricardo's *Principles of Economics* (chap. 20) where it is said that value depends upon the difficulty or facility of production, which is apparently synonymous with more or less labor. In his *Logic of Political Economy*, Thomas De Quincey (1785–1859), trying to improve upon Ricardo, recognizes two sources of value: utility and difficulty of attainment. His discussion is quoted at length and with approval by John Stuart Mill in his *Principles of Political Economy* (Book III, chap. 2, §1). These observations lead to two conclusions. First, the persistent use of the same terminology points to a continued tradition. Second, it seems that this part of value analysis made little, if any, progress from the time of San Bernardino to John Stuart Mill. On the contrary, it might even be argued that the latter's analysis is inferior, because it is less explicit on the point that difficulty creates scarcity.

Although San Bernardino, like the other Schoolmen, regards money as sterile, he contradicts himself elsewhere when he admits that it acquires a seminal quality by becoming "capital."[3] By capital, he does not mean the principal of a debt, but money invested in a business venture.[4] The same contradiction is found in Thomas Aquinas, who, in one passage, affirms that money is barren and, in another, compares it to seed which, if put into the soil, will sprout and produce a crop.[5]

San Bernardino also mentions *cambium* and government debts, but a better discussion of these topics is found in the writings of his contemporary, San Antonino (1389–1459), Archbishop of Florence.[6]

3. Ernest Nys, "The Economic Theories of the Middle Ages," *Researches in the History of Economics* (London, 1899), p. 164.

4. In this meaning, the word "capital" is already used in notarial and business records from the twelfth century onward. Numerous examples occur in the cartulary of Giovanni Scriba, or John the Scribe, which contains acts dating from 1154 to 1164 (*Il cartolare di Giovanni Scriba*, ed. Mario Chiaudano, Turin, 1935).

5. *Summa theologica*, II, ii, qu. 61, art. 3. Elsewhere (qu. 78, art. 1), quoting Aristotle, Aquinas states that money was invented mainly to serve as a medium of exchange.

6. On San Bernardino and San Antonino, see also Amintore Fanfani, *Le origini dello spirito capitalistico in Italia* (Milan, 1933), pp. 106–19.

Although not a very original thinker, San Antonino wrote with ease and was well versed in the extant canonistic and theological literature. His works contain an excellent summary of the controversy, then raging, about the lawfulness of interest-bearing shares in the public debt. With regard to value and price, he takes over the theory of San Bernardino without modification; yet he has often received undeserved credit as the first to mention utility.[7]

The last of the important economic writers of the Middle Ages is Thomas de Vio (1468–1524), better known as Cardinal Cajetan.[8] His work in the field of economics includes three brief treatises: one on usury, another on *cambium*, and a third on the *Montes Pietatis*, which he bitterly opposed. The most remarkable of the three treatises is perhaps the one on *cambium*, in which he shows himself well-informed on banking practices. In conformity with scholastic dialectics, he defines *cambium* as a *permutatio*, one of the nominate contracts found in Roman law, and not as a *mutuum*. Thus he justified real exchange provided that the place difference be observed, that is, that the bill of exchange be issued in one place and payable in another. Dry exchange, a practice without analogy in modern business, is proscribed because it is a faked exchange transaction violating this rule.[9]

This brief and incomplete survey omits the minor Schoolmen, some of whom are not without interest. The authors discussed are all men of singular merit, justly famous for their achievements, not merely in economics but chiefly outside this field.

A grave shortcoming of the medieval as well as the later Schoolmen is their overemphasis of the usury question. The space devoted to it in scholastic treatises has given the mistaken impression that it was regarded as all important. Sir William Ashley even asserts that "the prohibition of usury was clearly the centre of the canonist doctrine."[1] This is untrue. As stated above, the Schoolmen considered equity in distribution and exchange as the central problem in eco-

7. On the economic doctrines of San Antonino, there are the following studies, none of outstanding quality: Carl Ilgner, *Die volkswirtschaftlichen Anschauungen Antonins von Florenz* (Paderborn, 1904); Bede Jarrett, *San Antonino and Mediaeval Economics* (St. Louis, 1914); and August Pfister, *Die Wirtschaftsethik Antonin's von Florenz (1389–1459)* (Fribourg, Switzerland, 1946).

8. *De Monte Pietatis* (1498), *De cambiis* (1499), *De usura* (1500); republished recently in *Scripta philosophica, opuscula oeconomico-socialia*, ed. P. P. Zammit (Rome, 1934).

9. R. de Roover, "What is Dry Exchange? A Contribution to the Study of English Mercantilism," *Journal of Political Economy*, LII (1944), 250–66.

1. *An Introduction to English Economic History and Theory*, Vol. I, Part 2 (9th impression, London, 1920), p. 395. Cf. *ibid.*, p. 382.

nomics. The usury question was a side issue, but concern with it was allowed to crowd out nearly everything else.[2]

II. THE SCHOOL OF SALAMANCA

By many authors, Gabriel Biel (c. 1435–1495), professor at the University of Tübingen, is considered the last of the Schoolmen. Actually, scholasticism did not die with him; on the contrary, it received a new lease on life in the sixteenth century. This regeneration was the work of the school founded by Francisco de Vitoria (1480–1546), who, from 1526 to 1544, taught at Salamanca — in this period, the queen of the Spanish universities. As a matter of fact, the term "the school of Salamanca" is often applied to the body of his students, his disciples and their successors.[3] From Spain, the influence of Francisco de Vitoria's teaching spread to Portugal (to the University of Coïmbra), to Italy (through the Roman college of the Jesuits), and to the Low Countries where Leonardus Lessius (1551–1623), Franciscus Sylvius or du Bois (1581–1649), and Johannes Malderus (1563–1633) wrote commentaries on Thomas Aquinas inspired by the Spanish doctrines.

The school of Salamanca distinguished itself in philosophy and in natural and international law. The treatises of Francisco de Vitoria on the Indies and on the laws of war have even been republished by the Carnegie Endowment for International Peace.[4] Some of Vitoria's pupils occupied prominent positions: Domingo de Soto (1494–1560) represented Charles V at the Council of Trent and in 1548 became the Emperor's confessor; Diego de Covarrubias y Leyva (1512–1577), who wrote a treatise on money, was appointed Bishop of Ciudad Rodrigo and later President of the Council of Castile;[5] Martín de Azpilcueta, better known as Navarrus (1493–1586), was rector of the University of Coïmbra before being called to Rome in 1567, where he enjoyed the confidence of three successive popes and died a nonagenarian.[6] Among those influenced indirectly by Francisco

2. On usury, by far the best study available in English is the article of T. P. McLaughlin, "The Teachings of the Canonists on Usury (XII, XIII and XIV Centuries)," *Mediaeval Studies*, I (1939), 81–147, and II (1940), 1–22. Cf. Benjamin N. Nelson, *The Idea of Usury* (Princeton: Princeton University Press, 1949).

3. Marjorie Grice-Hutchinson, *The School of Salamanca, Readings in Spanish Monetary History, 1544–1605* (Oxford: The Clarendon Press, 1952). Although not written by a professional economist, this is an excellent little book.

4. *De Indis et de jure belli: Relectiones* (Washington, D. C., 1917). No. 7 of the series: The Classics of International Law.

5. *Veterum numismatum collatio* (Salamanca, 1550).

6. On Azpilcueta there is a study by Alberto Ullastres Calvo, "Martín de Azpilcueta y su comentario resolutorio de cambios; las ideas ecónomicas de un moralista español del siglo XVI," *Anales de Economía*, I (1941), 375–407, and II (1942), 52–95.

de Vitoria, mention should be made also of Luis de Molina (1535–1601), who occupied for more than twenty years the chair of theology at the University of Evora in Portugal. His analysis of value and price is especially valuable for its comprehensiveness.[7] Since economics was not recognized as an independent discipline, it is not surprising that the members of the school of Salamanca achieved greater distinction in other fields, but this is no reason why they should be ignored by economists or denied their due.

In form and content, the treatises published by the Spanish school continue the scholastic tradition with its constant appeal to authority, its display of references to support even the most trivial statements, and its love of subtle distinctions and definitions.[8] As in the past, attention remained focused on the observance of the rules of justice and on the lawfulness of various types of contracts. The moralists of the new school, however, attempted to provide fresh interpretations, to refine their concepts, to elaborate their analysis, to observe market conditions, and to bring their principles somehow into harmony with the requirements of expanding business and finance. Without changing completely the scholastic methods of analysis, the task was by no means an easy one. No wonder that the casuists of the Spanish school were only half successful; they revitalized scholasticism, it is true, but only for a time, without saving it from ultimate doom.[9]

Even more than the medieval Schoolmen, the later Doctors adhered to the theory that utility was the main source of value and that the just price, in the absence of public regulation, was deter-

7. Bernard W. Dempsey, *Interest and Usury*, with an Introduction by Joseph A. Schumpeter. This work discusses the theories of three Schoolmen, all belonging to, or influenced by, the school of Salamanca: Molina, Lessius and Lugo. On Molina, there is an unpublished doctoral dissertation by W. Seavey Joyce, *The Economics of Luis de Molina* (Harvard University, 1948).

8. Grice-Hutchinson, *op. cit.*, p. 40. Nevertheless, Earl J. Hamilton (*American Treasure and the Price Revolution in Spain, 1501–1650*, p. 295) labels Tomás de Mercado and others as "Spanish mercantilists." This label is certainly wrong: even the title of Mercado's treatise, *Summa de tratos y contratos de mercaderes* (1st ed.; Salamanca, 1569), indicates clearly that the approach is scholastic. Moreover, Spanish writers do not consider Mercado and other authors belonging to the school of Salamanca as mercantilists, but call them *jusnaturalistas* and *moralistas*, which is correct, in my opinion: José Larraz, *La época del mercantilismo en Castilla, 1500–1700* (2d ed.; Madrid, 1943), pp. 119, 122, and 131. Cf Andrés V. Castillo, *Spanish Mercantilism: Gerónimo de Uztáriz, Economist* (Columbia University Press, 1930), p. 45.

9. With reference to the philosophical restoration initiated by the school of Salamanca, the same views are expressed by Maurice De Wulf, *History of Mediaeval Philosophy*, II, 301–7.

SCHOLASTIC ECONOMICS 169

mined by common estimation, that is, by the interplay of the forces of supply and demand without any frauds, restraints, or conspiracies.[1] Domingo de Soto and Luis de Molina both denounce as "fallacious" the rule formulated by John Duns Scotus (1274–1308), according to which the just price should equal the cost of production plus a reasonable profit.[2]

Tomás de Mercado makes the pertinent remark that prices are as changeable as the wind.[3] Molina even introduces the concept of competition by stating that "concurrence" or rivalry among buyers will enhance prices, but that a flagging demand will bring them down.[4] Since similar statements are found in other authors, we may conclude that the Doctors of the new school generally accepted the idea that the just price, if not fixed by public authority, corresponded to the current or market price.[5]

Conditions of supply and demand are not the only factors that affect prices. There is also the influence of the volume of circulating media on the price level. The Spanish authors take the quantity theory for granted, since their treatises, almost without exception, mention that prices go up or down according to the abundance or scarcity of money.[6] Twelve years before Jean Bodin, or in 1556, Azpilcueta or Navarrus, attributes the rise of Spanish prices to the

1. Luis de Alcalá, *Tractado de los prestamos que passan entre mercaderes y tractantes* (Toledo, 1546), Part I, § 5, fol. 5ᵛ; Part II, § 11, fol. 22–23; Luis Saravía de la Calle, *Instrución de los tratos del comprar y vender* (Medina del Campo, 1544), cap. 2; Tomás de Mercado, *op. cit.*, lib. 2, cap. 8; Domingo de Soto, *De justitia et jure* (1st ed.; Salamanca, 1553), lib. VI, quest. 2, art. 3; Luis de Molina, *De justitia et jure* (Cuença, 1592), tract. II, disp. 348, § 8. Cf. Grice-Hutchinson, *op. cit.*, pp. 49, 72, 79, 82, 88. Soto expresses the rule as follows: *Sensus ergo est quod tantum valet res quanti vendi potest, seclusa vi, fraude et dolo.*

2. Soto, *op. cit.*, lib. VI, qu. 2, art. 3; Molina, *op. cit.*, tract. II, disp. 348, §8; and Mercado, *op. cit.*, lib. 2, cap. 11. Cf. Bernard W. Dempsey, "Just Price in a Functional Economy," *American Economic Review*, XXV (1935), 471–86.

3. *Op. cit.*, lib. 2, cap. 8: . . . *Aunque es mas variable (según la experiencia enseña) que el viento.*

4. *Op. cit.*, Tract. II (*de contractibus*), disp. 348, §4: *Multitudo emptorum concurrentium, plus uno tempore quam alio, et maiore aviditate facit pretium accrescere; emptorum vero raritas facit illud decrescere.*

5. Grice-Hutchinson, *op. cit.*, pp. 48, 80, 86–87, 105.

6. Molina, for example, states that prices and wages will be higher in a country where money is abundant than in another where it is scarce (*op. cit.*, tract. II, disp. 348, §4). Cf. Grice-Hutchinson, *op. cit.*, pp. 80, 105; Mercado, *op. cit.*, lib. 2, cap. 11; Cardinal de Lugo quoted by J. Brodrick, *The Economic Morals of the Jesuits*, p. 10. Cf. Bernard W. Dempsey, "The Historical Emergence of Quantity Theory," this *Journal*, L (1936), 174–84, and the "Comments" thereto by E. J. Hamilton, *ibid.*, 185–92. These comments only illustrate the fact that economists look in the wrong places for bibliographical guidance on scholastic economics.

influx of gold and silver from the New World.[7] He also observes that, because the flow reaches Spain first, the level of prices and of wages is higher there than in France.

The Spanish moralists devoted much more attention to foreign exchange than did the medieval Schoolmen. They noticed that in the trade with Flanders and Italy, the exchange rate was generally unfavorable to Spain, but they could not explain this phenomenon, since they ignored the balance-of-payments theory.[8] Instead, they sought to justify exchange transactions by arguing that the money had a greater purchasing power abroad than in Spain and that the rate had to be unfavorable in order to restore the purchasing power parity, a partial and ambiguous explanation, but typical of scholastic dialectics.[9] Among the Spanish moralists, a lively discussion was raised concerning the lawfulness of exchange between two places within the same realm. This practice, it was charged, served merely as a subterfuge to circumvent the usury prohibition.[1] In the debate the rigorist friars, headed by Domingo de Soto, eventually won out, and, through their influence at Court, secured in 1552 a royal decree forbidding internal exchange at any rate other than par. It is needless to say that the merchants soon discovered new ways of evasion. In trying to constrain the market, the moralists were fighting a losing battle.

One of the major developments of the sixteenth century was the rise of the fairs of Castile, Lyons, Frankfort-on-the-Main, and, above all, Besançon, as international clearing centers. From 1579 on, the Besançon fairs, while keeping their name, were actually held in

7. *Comentario resolutorio de cambios* (Salamanca, 1556), cap. 20, no. 51. For an English version of this passage, see Grice-Hutchinson, *op. cit.*, p. 95. Molina, whose text is, however, posterior to the book of Bodin, also refers to the price-raising effects of the influx of gold and silver from New Spain (*op. cit.*, tract. II, disp. 83, §13). Azpilcueta, or Navarrus, is not mentioned in the works of Hamilton.

8. Mercado, *op. cit.*, lib. IV, cap. 4; Soto, *op. cit.*, lib. VI, qu. 12, art. 2. Cf. de Roover, *L'évolution*, p. 81; Grice-Hutchinson, *op. cit.*, pp. 13–14.

9. *Ibid.*, pp. 57–58. Of course, this is not the purchasing-power-parity doctrine as understood today.

1. Those opposed to internal exchange were Francisco de Vitoria and Domingo de Soto (*op. cit.*, lib. VI, qu. 13, art. 1). On the other hand, Miguel de Palacios and Tomás de Mercado (*op. cit.*, tract. 4, cap. 8) considered it lawful. Francisco Garcia (*Trattato de tutti i contratti che nei negotii et commertii humani sogliono occorrere*, Brescia, 1596, cap. 36, §7), without being pro or con, simply states that, in Spain, internal exchange is prohibited by law. The same position is taken by Azpilcueta, or Navarrus (*op. cit.*, cap. 15, nos. 28–30), who is, however, very sceptical about the practical results of the prohibition. Cf. de Roover, *L'évolution*, pp. 108, 184, 195, 200, 202, 205.

Piacenza, on the initiative of the Genoese bankers who monopolized the financial business of the Spanish crown. To a certain extent, these fairs were institutions called forth by the scholastic doctrine, since it condemned the discounting of credit instruments but did not frown upon dealings in foreign exchange, unless they were overtly misused to evade the ban against usury. Thus the exchange business at the fairs became one of the main preoccupations of the moralists. The copious works of two Italians, Sigismondo Scaccia (c. 1568–1618) and Raphael de Turri (c. 1578–1666), not to speak of minor treatises, deal exclusively with this topic. The principal bone of contention was the lawfulness of the *cambio con la ricorsa*, a device which involved drafts and redrafts going back and forth between Genoa or another banking place and the fairs of Besançon.[2] To befuddle the theologians, the bankers had shrouded the *cambio con la ricorsa* in a veil of technical jargon and complicated bookkeeping. Stripped of its trappings, the *cambio con la ricorsa* loses all its mystery: in its naked form it is simply discount cleverly concealed under the form of fictitious exchange transactions. Nevertheless, the theologians and the jurists, approaching the problem from a legal point of view, found themselves caught in a web of technicalities and contradictions which contributed not a little to the discredit of scholastic economics.

In economics, the scholastic doctrine reaches its full maturity in the monumental works of Cardinals Juan de Lugo (1583–1660) and Giambattista de Luca (1613–1683), who should not be mistaken one for the other, although the similarity in name leads to confusion.[3] Despite an impressive display of scholarship, their works ill conceal the fact that the Doctors had exhausted the possibilities of their method and that further progress no longer depended upon more elaboration and refinement, but upon a complete renewal of the analytical apparatus.

III. THE DEMISE OF SCHOLASTIC ECONOMICS

The demise of scholasticism is not limited to economics, of course, but involves the entire scientific and philosophical system born in the medieval universities and still far from moribund on the eve of the seventeenth century. The scepticism of the Renaissance, it is true, had sapped the strength of the scholastic system but without being

2. *Ibid.*, pp. 80–81, for an example of *cambio con la ricorsa*. Further information is found in the recent book of Giulio Mandich, *Le pacte de Ricorsa et le marché italien des changes au XVIIe siècle* (Collection "Affaires et Gens d'affaires," No. 7, Paris: Armand Colin, 1953).

3. The work of Cardinal de Lugo, *Disputationes scholasticae et morales* (Lyons, 1642), was republished in 1869. Volume VII (*in quo de contractibus in*

able to destroy the still vigorous organism. Although derided and ridiculed by its opponents, scholasticism continued to exert far-reaching influence. It was confronted, however, with an increasingly hostile spirit, which provided a favorable climate for the reception of Cartesian philosophy. The real crisis did not come until the seventeenth century. In the face of the attack, the Aristotelians failed to realize that, in order to survive, they had to renew their methods. Instead, they stubbornly refused to accept the new discoveries in experimental science, with the inevitable result that their philosophy shared the fate of their antiquated astronomy, physics, and medicine, and along with them, fell into complete discredit.[4]

On the continent of Europe, and to a lesser extent in England, the dying Aristotelian system kept its hold on the universities, which thus became asylums for old fogies and citadels of bigoted pedantry. Learning deserted this musty environment and found a haven in the academies and in the salons of the eighteenth century.

It would be a grievous mistake to view the evolution of economics as divorced from that of the other sciences. The main reason why scholastic economics decayed was that its adherents were unable or unwilling to revamp their system and to discard the dead wood in order to preserve what was worth preserving. Nothing illustrates this failure better than the work of the late casuists of the seventeenth century, such as the treatise of Raphael de Turri. In it, the scholastic doctrine on the *cambium* contract reached maturity, but the subtle distinctions between licit and illicit exchange fail to cover up the fallacies and the inconsistencies which underlie the whole argument. Why should one form of exchange be lawful and not another? One can only agree with the mercantilist Malachy Postlethwayt, who in 1751 declared that the lawyers and divines with "their useless niceties" and "their fanciful divisions and subdivisions," instead of clearing up the matter, had "only perplexed and confounded it."[5] Already in the sixteenth century, the Dominican friar, Domingo de Soto, had sounded the alarm by stating that "the matter of exchange, although

genere et in specie agitur) contains the part dealing principally with economics. Cardinal de Luca wrote a popular work in the vernacular, *Il dottor volgare* (Rome, 1673, 9 vols.), which, as the title indicates, was designed to explain the doctrine of the Doctors to the public. He is also the author of a Latin treatise, *Theatrum veritatis et justitiae* (Rome, 1669–1681, 21 vols.) written only for scholars.

4. Maurice De Wulf, *op. cit.*, II, 309 ff. The late author, a pupil of Cardinal Mercier, was professor at the Catholic University of Louvain and at Harvard University.

5. "Bill of Exchange," *The Universal Dictionary of Trade and Commerce* (2d ed.; London, 1757), p. 277.

SCHOLASTIC ECONOMICS 173

sufficiently abstruse in itself, is being more and more obscured by the clever subterfuges of the merchants and the contradictory opinions of the Doctors."⁶ But he himself was a prisoner of his method and could not escape from the impasse.

There was nothing basically wrong with the scholastic theory on value and price. It rested on utility and scarcity, and Adam Smith did not improve upon it.⁷

The great weakness of scholastic economics was the usury doctrine. Canon law, dating as it does back to the early Middle Ages when most loans were made for consumption purposes, defined usury as any increment demanded beyond the principal of a loan. Since this definition was a part of Catholic dogma, the Schoolmen were unable to change it. As time went by, it became a source of increasing embarrassment. Tied to their definition, the Doctors were sucked deeper and deeper into a quagmire of contradictions. It is not that the Church ever seriously hampered business investments, but practical necessity placed before the moralists the well-nigh impossible task of legitimizing means for taking interest while safeguarding the principle that loans were gratuitous contracts. This difficulty was solved in two ways: (1) by the doctrine of extrinsic titles, and (2) by the rather artificial distinction between licit and illicit contracts. In the sixteenth century, the more lenient among the casuists undermined their own position still further by permitting the triple contract, according to which the borrower guaranteed to the lender a fixed return of, let us say, 5 per cent a year.⁸ In the end, the lawfulness of interest became a question of formality, that is, of drafting contracts in the proper form. Is it then surprising that casuistry acquired such a bad connotation and is today synonymous with sophistry and mental reservation?

6. *Op. cit.*, lib. 6, qu. 8, art. 1. This text was copied by other Doctors, see de Roover, *L'évolution*, p. 72.

7. Emil Kauder, "Genesis of the Marginal Utility Theory: From Aristotle to the End of the Eighteenth Century," *Economic Journal*. LXIII (1953), 638–50; *idem*, "The Retarded Acceptance of the Marginal Utility Theory," this *Journal*, LXVII (1953), 564–75.

8. The triple contract, as the name indicates, involves a combination of three contracts in one: (1) a partnership contract between the lender and the borrower sharing in profit and loss of the borrower's business, (2) an insurance contract by which the borrower guarantees restitution of the capital, and (3) another insurance contract by which the borrower guarantees the lender against any loss, if the latter foregoes his share in eventual profits, in exchange for a fixed but reduced return on his investment. Although the triple contract had been condemned, in 1586, by Sixtus V (1585–1590), the casuists continued to debate its lawfulness throughout the seventeenth century. "Usure," *Dictionnaire de Théologie Catholique*, XV (1948), cols. 2373–74.

174   *QUARTERLY JOURNAL OF ECONOMICS*

From the start, the usury doctrine became an easy target for the opponents of scholasticism. In a certain way, the Doctors had only themselves to blame: by their inconsistencies, they had exposed themselves to criticism and even ridicule.

The firing was opened in the sixteenth century with the fierce attack of Charles du Moulin (1500–1566), who advocated the toleration of a moderate rate of interest. He pointed out that the usury prohibition, meant to protect the debtor, had the opposite effect by increasing the cost of lending. Not content with marshaling serious arguments, he poked fun at the "jargon" of the Doctors and at their classification of *cambium* into real, dry, and fictitious exchange, rechange and "counter-change."[9] Du Moulin's book was premature and exposed its author to persecution for heresy.

In the seventeenth century, the blast came from another quarter; this time the casuists were criticized, not for their rigor but for their leniency, by the Jansenist, Blaise Pascal (1623–1662), illustrious philosopher, mathematician, and physicist, who, by the excellency of his style, won a name for himself in French literature. His *Lettres Provinciales* were scurrilous pamphlets, that created an enormous sensation. In the eighth letter, he attempts to confute the casuists for their opinion on usury and contracts. Of course, Pascal was an amateur in economics, as well as in theology. Nevertheless, there is no denying that his castigation was not entirely undeserved and that his victims had made concessions inconsistent with their basic principles.[1]

During the eighteenth century, the attack continues unabated. Whenever the *Philosophes* refer to the Doctors, they call them "casuists" with an undertone of scorn and contempt. They refer to them only to criticize; and when they borrow from them, they do not give them any credit. This attitude is typical of the Age of Enlightenment, which showed no appreciation of Gothic cathedrals or of things medieval, in general.

More than ever, the usury doctrine is the center of attack. According to Turgot (1727–1781), the prejudice against interest had been introduced "in centuries of ignorance" by theologians who did

9. Charles du Moulin, *Sommaire du livre analytique des contracts, usures rentes constituées, intérests et monnoyes*, in *Omnia quae extant opera* (Paris, 1681), Vol. II, No. 73: "Je laisse aussi leurs jargons et distinctions de change réal, fict et sec, rechange et contre-change." Cf. de Roover, *L'évolution*, p. 195.

1. To be specific, I refer to the comments of Pascal on the Mohatra contract, one of the subterfuges used in Spain. Pascal's main victim was the casuist, Antonio Escobar y Mendoza, whose major work is *Universae theologiae moralis receptores* (1st ed.; Lyons, 1652, 7 vols.).

SCHOLASTIC ECONOMICS 175

not "understand the meaning of the Scriptures any better than the principles of natural law."[2] Richard Cantillon (d. 1734) remarked sarcastically that *lucrum cessans* would entitle a man making "five hundred per cent" in his business to demand the same from his borrowers.[3] Abbé de Condillac frankly comes out with the assertion that the loan at interest is just and should be permitted. He goes on to state that legislators and "casuists" are confused on the subject and asks them pointedly why they disapprove of interest and not of exchange.[4] Is there really so much difference between distance in time (*distance de temps*) and distance of place (*distance de lieu*)? In France, during the eighteenth century, the law still proscribed the taking of interest, although this practice was generally tolerated with the connivance of the courts. The physiocrats waged an unsuccessful campaign for the enactment of a statute which would legalize contractual clauses stipulating the payment of interest. Such a law was not passed until October 12, 1789, after the outbreak of the French Revolution.

In Italy, the attack on the usury doctrine was even more insidious than in France, since it was carried on under the cover of orthodoxy. In 1744, there appeared a book in which the author, Marquess Scipione Maffei (1675–1755), pretended, on the surface, to defend the traditional doctrines, but, in the last chapters, ruined the entire edifice by advocating a new extrinsic title, never admitted by the theologians: the *lex principis*, that is, the law or custom of the land.[5] As a matter of fact, the purpose of the book was to justify the issue by the city of Verona of a municipal loan yielding interest at 4 per cent. Maffei's publication created such a stir that in order to appease the tempest, Pope Benedict XIV (1740–1758) was impelled to promulgate the encyclical *Vix Pervenit* (1745), which reasserted for the last time the old dogma with respect to usury.[6] Within a few months (1746), there appeared the second edition of Maffei's book without

2. "Réflexions sur la formation et la distribution des richesses," *Oeuvres de Turgot*, ed. Gustave Schelle, II (Paris, 1914), 577–78, §LXXIII:" Erreurs des scolastiques réfutées"; and "Mémoire sur les prêts d'argent" (1770); *ibid.*, III (Paris, 1919), 163. Cf. Jean François Melon, *Essai politique sur le commerce* (Paris, 1761), pp. 259 and 272.

3. *Essai sur la nature du commerce en général*, ed. Henry Higgs (London, 1931), pp. 208–10.

4. *Le commerce et le gouvernement considérés relativement l'un à l'autre*, in *Mélanges d'économie politique*, ed. Eugène Daire (Paris, 1847), I, 311–12.

5. *Dell'impiego del danaro, libri tre* (1st. ed.; Rome, 1744; 2d ed.; Rome, 1746).

6. de Roover (*L'évolution*, pp. 123–24 n.) gives a summary in French of the five points discussed in *Vix Pervenit*.

any substantial modification of the author's stand on the usury question. Yet this second edition published in full the text of the Encyclical, bore the imprimatur of the ecclesiastical authorities, and contained a dedicatory letter to Benedict XIV, a personal friend of the author. On scholasticism, the book of Maffei had a deleterious effect, since it implicitly redefined usury as any increment — not beyond the principal — but beyond *the moderate rate allowed by law or custom.*[7]

The new definition represented a radical departure from the basic norms of scholastic economics.[8] Books challenging the thesis of Maffei and restating the scholastic tradition were still being written in the beginning of the nineteenth century, but their authors were not men of any talent and they repeated the old, worn-out arguments without contributing anything new.[9] Scholasticism had ceased to attract the best minds: its discredit, except in ultra-conservative circles, was too profound.

After the *Code Napoléon*, adopted all over western Europe, had allowed the taking of interest, the Church, too, decided to abandon the old usury doctrine. It was quietly buried in 1830, when the Sacred Penitentiary issued instructions to confessors not to disturb penitents who lent money at the legal rate of interest without any title other than the sanction of Civil Law.[1] With this decision,

7. The same thesis was defended by the Jansenist, Nicolas Broedersen, in his book, *De usuris licitis et illicitis* (1st ed.; 1743). Abbé Ferdinando Galiani in his book, *Della moneta*, devotes to usury an equivocal chapter, in which he pays at least lip service to the traditional doctrine. See Arthur Eli Monroe, *Early Economic Thought, Selections from Economic Literature prior to Adam Smith*, pp. 300–7. Antonio Genovesi (1713–1769) in his book, *Lezioni di economia civile*, adopts the same point of view as Maffei and Broedersen.

8. According to the old canon law, any statutes allowing interest were anti-canonical. The Council of Vienne (1311–1312) explicitly declares them to be in contravention of divine and human law and orders the repeal of those in operation: *Decretales*, c. *Ex gravi*, in Clement., lib. 5, title 5, can. l, §1.

9. Count Monaldo Leopardi (1776–1847), *La giustizia nei contratti e l'usura* (Modena, 1834); Anonymous, *Analisi ragionata e critica dei libri tre su le usure dell'abbate Marco Mastrofini data in luce da un amico della verità* (Naples, 1835). Count Leopardi was the father of the famous poet, Giacomo Leopardi: his reactionary ideas were not limited to the usury question.

1. "Usure," *Dictionnaire de Théologie Catholique*, XV, cols. 2379 f. The new canon law, promulgated by Benedict XV in 1917, art. 1543, admits the validity of the legal title (*non est per se illicitum de lucro legali pacisci, nisi constet ipsum esse immoderatum*), although it still upholds the principle that a loan is *per se* a gratuitous contract. Further details about the decisions of the Roman congregations in 1830 and later may be found in Henry C. Lea, "The Ecclesiastical Treatment of Usury," *Yale Review*, II (1893–94), 379–85 (republished in *Minor Historical Writings and Other Essays*, Philadelphia, 1942, pp. 129–51). The interpretations of this author are generally unfavorable to the Church, but his factual information agrees with the *Dictionnaire de Théologie Catholique*.

SCHOLASTIC ECONOMICS 177

scholastic economics, which had emphasized usury so much, received its death blow.

IV. SCHOLASTICISM AND MERCANTILISM: A CONTRAST

The differences between mercantilism and scholastic economics are striking and profound. Yet, I do not know that a comparison has ever been attempted, although a clear perception of the contrasts has its importance for an understanding of the development of economic thought. There are even historians who profess to find the "prehistory" of economics among the vagaries of the mercantilistic pamphleteers, thus completely ignoring the contributions of the Doctors.[2]

Unlike mercantilism, scholastic economics enjoyed the unquestioned superiority of being an integral part of a coherent philosophical system. Although economics was not yet acknowledged as an independent discipline, it formed a consistent body of doctrine according to which economic relations ought to be ruled by the laws of distributive and commutative justice. In contrast, mercantilism was never more than a conglomerate of unco-ordinated prescriptions by which the authors of the mercantilistic tracts sought to influence economic policy, usually in a sense favorable to their private interests.[3]

The Doctors, as this name indicates, were all university graduates, trained in theology or in canon and civil law (*doctor utriusque juris*). Most of them were clerics, though there are some notable exceptions among the jurists, especially among the civilians, for instance, Messer Lorenzo di Antonio Ridolfi, who was a layman, a diplomat and a lecturer at the Florentine athenaeum.[4] The mercantilists, on the contrary, were with few exceptions self-trained merchants, with some literary talents, but without university degrees. Essentially, they were empiricists who, for better or for worse, were not encumbered by scholastic traditions. In this way they made their major contribution by developing the balance-of-trade theory, whereas the Doctors were unable to cut themselves loose from their traditional approach to the foreign exchange problem.

As a rule, the mercantilist writings were brief tracts on specific and controversial issues, which contrast markedly with the weighty and often pedantic treatises of the Doctors. Whereas the mercan-

2. For instance, Edward Heimann, *History of Economic Doctrines*, pp. 22–47.
3. A. V. Judges, "The Idea of a Mercantile State," *Transactions of the Royal Historical Society*, 4th Series, XXI (1939), 50.
4. For his biography, see Vespasiano da Bisticci, *Vite di uomini illustri del secolo XV* (Florence, 1938), pp. 401–5.

tilist pamphlets rarely refer to sources or provide marginal notes, the scholastic treatises literally bristle with references in support of nearly every statement, even the most commonplace. This sometimes annoying display of erudition, first introduced by the postglossators, received further encouragement from the humanists, who developed the habit of invoking the authority of the Ancients for everything.

By the very fact that the Doctors were moralists, their main preoccupation was with social justice and general welfare, but naturally with these ideals as they were conceived in the Middle Ages and the sixteenth and seventeenth centuries. The mercantilists, too, professed to further the cause of the commonweal; however, their declarations in this respect should not always be taken at their face value. All too often they serve as a screen for private interests. Most of the authors of mercantilist tracts had an ax to grind. This is especially true of the early mercantilists. Gérard de Malynes (fl. 1586–1641) was a perennial office-seeker who advocated exchange control in the hope that he himself would be appointed the controller. Misselden (fl. 1608–1654) and John Wheeler (fl. 1601–1608) were spokesmen for the Merchant Adventurers; and Thomas Mun (1571–1641) wrote his tracts in defense of the East India Company. As for Gresham (1519–1579), he was a shrewd and none too scrupulous manipulator of the money market, whose recommendations, although advantageous to the Queen, were apt to have unfavorable repercussions on English trade and on the volume of employment. The later mercantilists were less prejudiced, but their views were still warped by their narrow nationalism. Most of them rallied to the defense of the colonial system and sponsored aggressive measures to combat or to exclude foreign competition, an attitude which is alien to the spirit of scholasticism. Did not St. Thomas justify international trade by pointing out the fact that no nation is self-sufficient?[5]

As we have seen, the casuists of the seventeenth century were either unwilling or unable to rejuvenate their methods. They continued in the old ruts and made no effort to incorporate new discoveries, such as the balance-of-trade theory, into their traditional doctrines. The conservatism of the late scholastic writers thus became an impediment to further progress, and it is fortunate that the mercantilists displayed more initiative and did not hesitate to blaze new trails. True, their methods were not always sound, nor

5. Amintore Fanfani, *Storia delle dottrine economiche: il volontarismo* (3d ed.; Milan, 1942), p. 112. The reference is to *De regimine principum*, Book 2, chap. 3.

always successful, but they opened up new avenues for further research. The controversy of the early mercantilists about exchange control led to a premature proposal for the creation of a stabilization fund and eventually culminated in the formulation by Thomas Mun of the balance-of-trade theory.[6] The mercantilists also made the first clumsy attempts to use statistical data, and Sir William Petty (1623–1687) even made statistics the basis of his *Political Arithmetick*. Others pondered over banking schemes; and the studies of Charles Davenant (1656–1714) and Gregory King (1648–1712) on the behavior of grain prices put them on the track of the elasticity of demand.[7] The seventeenth century was the age of projectors. Nearly always, the aim was to influence public policy, whereas the scholastic writers were content to set up ethical standards, but left their practical realization to the often inefficient government authorities.

The scholastic writers regarded trade as an occupation which, although not evil in itself, endangered the salvation of the soul, as the merchants almost unavoidably succumbed to the temptations of usury, cheating, and unlawful gain: *et de hoc rarissime evadunt mercatores*, as St. Bonaventure (1221–1275), the Seraphic Doctor, testifies.[8] In this opinion, the other Doctors concur: without exception, they much prefer agriculture to trade. The mercantilist writers, of course, take exactly the opposite point of view.[9] In their eyes trade is the noblest of all professions.[1] Both agriculture and industry depend on trade to provide a market for their products and to give employment to the "poor."[2] The merchant, far from being regarded

6. de Roover, *Gresham on Foreign Exchange*, pp. 226–31, 250–65.

7. I take advantage of this opportunity to call the attention of the economists to an article by Luigi Einaudi, "La paternità della legge detta di King," *Rivista di storia economica*, VIII (1943), 33–38. The author attributes to both Davenant and King the discovery of the law stating that grain prices vary more than proportionately to the deviations of the harvest from the normal.

8. *Decretum Gratiani*: canon *Quoniam non cognovi*, Dist. LXXXVIII, canon 12; and canon *Qualitas lucri*, Dist. V, "de paenitentia," canon 2; *quia difficile est inter ementis vendentisque commercium non intervenire peccatum*. Cf. Schreiber, *op. cit.*, p. 129.

9. Jelle C. Riemersma, "Usury Restrictions in a Mercantile Economy," *Canadian Journal of Economics and Political Science*, XVIII (1952), 22.

1. See the encomium of trade by Thomas Mun, *England's Treasure by Forraign Trade* (London, 1664), chap. 21. Cf. Eli F. Heckscher, *Mercantilism* II, 281.

2. William D. Grampp, "The Liberal Elements in English Mercantilism," this *Journal*, LXVI (1952), 469. These ideas must have been current among the merchants on the continent as well as in England, since we find them also in Lodovico Guicciardini's famous description of Antwerp, first published in 1567: *Description de tous les Pays-Bas*, trans. François de Belleforest (Antwerp, 1582), p. 182; republished in *Tudor Economic Documents*, eds. R. H. Tawney and Eileen Power, III, 161.

with distrust, is extolled as the benefactor of humanity and the principal pillar of the State. This is what one might expect, since mercantilism was the economic system developed by, and for, the merchants.

In contrast to scholastic economics, mercantilism was amoral. The later mercantilists were interested in a large population and full employment only because they thought such conditions would stimulate trade and increase the economic power of the state.[3] Usury was no longer considered a voracious monster: Sir Josiah Child (1630–1699), Sir Thomas Culpeper the Elder, and others complained only that the interest rate, being higher in England than in Holland, favored the competition of the Dutch.[4] Trade has no soul and the individual did not count: why should the mercantilists be disturbed by moral issues?

One of the most striking characteristics of scholastic economics was universalism: regardless of origin and nationality, the Doctors are in fundamental agreement on method and principles. Although there may be, sometimes, sharp differences on points of detail or of practical application, all their treatises follow more or less the same pattern easily recognizable by anyone acquainted with scholastic literature. In the mercantilist camp, on the contrary, such uniformity in doctrine or method does not exist: neither between national schools nor between individual writers.

Among the mercantilists, "everyone is his own economist," according to the phrase so aptly coined by Professor E. A. J. Johnson. No one considers himself bound by precedent, and each author follows his own inspiration in selecting the appropriate method for dealing with his chosen topic.

Notwithstanding the great prestige of Eli F. Heckscher, I disagree with his statement that mercantilism strove toward unity.[5] As a matter of fact, non-scholastic economics in the seventeenth and eighteenth centuries varied greatly from country to country. In my opinion, the name "mercantilism" is appropriate only for British economics during that period. In Germany, one should speak of cameralism. One of its leading exponents, Johann Joachim Becher (1635–

3. E. A. J. Johnson, *Predecessors of Adam Smith*, pp. 247–52; Heckscher, *Mercantilism*, II, 159; Philip W. Buck, *The Politics of Mercantilism*, pp. 44–48. 65–66, 89–90.

4. Heckscher, *Mercantilism*, II, 286–89.

5. Heckscher, himself, in response to criticism of his book, was forced to concede that mercantilism failed as a unifying system: "Mercantilism," *Economic History Review*, VII (1936), 48. Cf. Herbert Heaton, "Heckscher on Mercantilism," *Journal of Political Economy*, XLV (1937), 374; J. F. Rees, "Mercantilism," *History*, New Series, XXIV (1939–1940), 130.

SCHOLASTIC ECONOMICS 181

1682), "was still strongly influenced by the venerable Aristotelian tradition," albeit that he considerably modified the scholastic views.[6] In France, the expression "Colbertism," rather than "mercantilism," should be used to designate the economic policy of Colbert. Moreover, this policy aroused much criticism from writers such as Vauban (1633–1707) and his cousin Boisguilbert (1646–1714), whose comments on the iniquities of the French tax system anticipated the physiocrats instead of owing something to mercantilist ideas.[7]

Although the United Provinces were the leading economic power in the seventeenth century, there exists as yet no adequate study on Dutch economic thought during this period.[8] At any rate, Hugo Grotius or de Groot deserves a niche in the gallery of famous economists. One can hardly classify him as a mercantilist; he was rather an Aristotelian who used scholastic methods to defeat scholasticism.[9] Even Pieter de la Court (1618–1685), although not an Aristotelian, is far too liberal to pass for a mercantilist.[1]

In Spain, after 1600, economic writers, without breaking with scholasticism, were mainly concerned with the country's ailments: vellon inflation, vagrancy, depopulation, and economic decline. Whether this concern with pressing social and economic problems labels them as mercantilists remains a debatable point.[2] As in Spain,

6. de Roover, "Monopoly Theory prior to Adam Smith," *op. cit.*, p. 519. There is a new book on Becher by H. Hassinger, *Johann Joachim Becher (1635–1682): ein Beitrag zur Geschichte des Mercantilismus* (Vienna, 1951). The author apparently regards Becher as a mercantilist. Heckscher, however, states that the German cameralists "were imbued with a spirit of their own" (*Mercantilism*, II, 263).

7. *Ibid.*, II, 264. Cf. Hazel van Dyke Roberts, *Boisguilbert, Economist of the Reign of Louis XIV*, p. 255: "Boisguilbert had completely shaken off mercantilist thought."

8. The best study is still that of Etienne Laspeyres, but it is almost a century old: *Geschichte der wirtschaftlichen Anschauungen der Niederländer und ihrer Litteratur zur Zeit der Republik* (Preisschriften gekrönt und herausgegeben von der Fürstlich Jablonowski'schen Gesellschaft, Vol. XI, Leipzig, 1863).

9. de Roover, "Monopoly Theory prior to Adam Smith," *op. cit.*, pp. 521–22.

1. Heckscher (*Mercantilism*, I, 351) admits that the Dutch were "less affected by mercantilist tendencies than most other countries." His treatment of Dutch writers is based entirely on the study of Laspeyres (*op. cit.*, II, 263) and, moreover, is very superficial. See the pertinent remarks of Heaton (*op. cit.*, pp. 371 f.) about Heckscher's neglect of Dutch economic thought and policy in the seventeenth century.

2. They are mercantilists according to Earl J. Hamilton, "Spanish Mercantilism before 1700," *Facts and Factors in Economic History: Articles by former Students of Edwin Francis Gay*, pp. 214–39. This is an introductory survey which lists a few tracts and makes some general comments on the contents of the economic literature in Spain from about 1600 to 1700. The Latin treatises, including the important work of Luis de Molina, are not discussed. After stating that

182   *QUARTERLY JOURNAL OF ECONOMICS*

so also in Italy the scholastic traditions were particularly strong, and persisted well into the eighteenth century along with other currents of thought originating in the merchant manuals of the Middle Ages.[3] In 1613, a Neapolitan writer, Dr. Antonio Serra, in fighting a scheme to regulate foreign exchange, formulated independently the balance-of-trade theory developed contemporaneously by the English mercantilists.[4] His proposals were dismissed, and his book was ignored for more than a century until abbé Ferdinando Galiani praised it as an outstanding performance. The witty abbé expresses his surprise that a book like Serra's was conceived "in an age of ignorance about economic matters," but he complains that the work is "tedious" reading because of its obscure style, its poor organization, and its "divisions and subdivisions" reminiscent of scholastic literature.[5] In other words, the abbé is a typical example of the eighteenth-century point of view. Another interesting fact is that Galiani considers the work of Serra to be scholastic, whereas most modern authors have classed it as a mercantilist pamphlet.[6]

The trouble is that the word "mercantilism" does not stand for a clear concept, but lends itself to confusion. The great specialist Heckscher, himself, has to admit that "mercantilism is simply a convenient term for summarizing a phase of economic policy and

most of the Spanish economic writers were ecclesiastics with no intimate knowledge of business or finance (pp. 229–30), Professor Hamilton calls them "mercantilists." Sancho de Moncada, one of the so-called Spanish mercantilists, was professor of theology in the University of Toledo, as Hamilton himself points out (*American Treasure*, p. 294). Other authors, including Andrés Villegas Castillo, Ramón Carande, Bernard W. Dempsey, Marjorie Grice-Hutchinson, and José Larraz, do not agree with Hamilton's classification. Only Gerónimo de Uztáriz (1670–1732), a late writer and statesman, seems to have come strongly under the influence of mercantilist thought. Cf. Ramón Carande, *Carlos V y sus Banqueros, la vida económica de España en una fase de su hegemonía, 1516–1556* (Madrid, 1943), p. 89.

3. Heckscher (*Mercantilism*, II, 263) implicitly admits that he is unacquainted with Italian economic literature. The famous tract of Bernardo Davanzati (1529–1606), *Notizia dei cambi*, written in 1581, was certainly based on merchant manuals, as appears clear from two manuscripts in the State Archives of Pisa: Fondo Alleati, Nos. 17 and 69. I owe this information to the kindness of Professor Federigo Melis of the University of Pisa.

4. *Breve trattato delle cause che possono far abbondare li regni d'oro e argento dove non sono miniere con applicazione al Regno di Napoli* in *Economisti del cinque e seicento*, ed. Augusto Graziani (Bari, 1913), 141–233. Selections from Serra's treatise, in English translation, are found in Monroe, *op. cit.*, pp. 143–67.

5. Ferdinando Galiani, *Della moneta* (Bari, 1915), p. 344.

6. Monroe, *op. cit.*, p. 144; Cossa, *op. cit.*, p. 178; Fanfani, *Storia, il volontarismo*, p. 171; Lewis H. Haney, *History of Economic Thought* (3d ed.), pp. 112–13; John M. Ferguson, *Landmarks of Economic Thought*, pp. 36–37.

SCHOLASTIC ECONOMICS 183

economic ideas."[7] It should be added that the term covers only those heterogeneous ideas that are non-scholastic in inspiration.

There are remnants of scholastic influence in many mercantilist writings, but surprisingly those traces have not been recognized, though they are not so difficult to spot. The mercantilists, of course, were unable to escape from the impact of several centuries of culture. Whether or not they knew it, they absorbed some of the ideas bequeathed by former generations.[8]

Gerard de Malynes is the writer in whose works the traditional views are the most perceptible. Whether he should be considered as a mercantilist or as a scholastic writer, is to my mind a moot question.[9] In any case, there can be no doubt that he forms the link between the two schools of thought. His insistence on the par as the only fair rate of exchange is simply a variant of the just price theory taken over from Dr. Thomas Wilson, himself a Doctor still imbued with scholastic traditions. According to Professor Jacob Viner, Malynes was poor in market analysis,[1] but there can be no question about his being well read and well acquainted with ancient and scholastic literature.[2] In his *Saint George for England*, a tract against usury, he describes the dragon called *Foenus politicum* as having two wings, *usura palliata* and *usura explicata*, and a tail, "inconstant *Cambium*."[3] This allegory is obviously sheer and unadulterated scholasticism. Malynes has also received credit for distinguishing between changes in the price level due to monetary factors and changes in the price of particular commodities due to the operation of the law of supply and demand. I strongly suspect that this idea did not originate with him but that he took it from a continental treatise, for he was by no means an original thinker and was addicted to plagiarism.[4]

7. "Mercantilism," *Economic History Review*, VII (1936–37), 54.

8. Heckscher (*Mercantilism*, II, 277) states: "Here one may perceive a tendency towards economic liberty that was never entirely broken off and therefore connected medieval and laizzez-faire ideals."

9. de Roover, *Gresham on Foreign Exchange*, pp. 285 f.

1. *Studies in the Theory of International Trade* (New York, 1937), p. 76.

2. Helen E. Sandison, "An Elizabethan Economist's Method of Literary Composition," *Huntington Library Quarterly*, VI (1942–43), 205–11. Professor Sandison shows that Malynes certainly "borrowed" from Sir Thomas More's *Utopia*. I may add that he also was acquainted with the works of Jean Bodin, Lodovico Guicciardini, Dr. Thomas Wilson, Aristotle, and most probably, Leonardus Lessius.

3. *Saint George for England allegorically described* (London, 1601); "Foreword to the Reader." On p. 61, Malynes mentions the extrinsic titles, *damnum emergens* and *lucrum cessans*.

4. In the sixteenth century, most of the scholastic writers accepted the quantity theory of money and stated that prices "generally" go up or down

184   *QUARTERLY JOURNAL OF ECONOMICS*

In a recent article, the mercantilists have been praised for the "liberalism" of their concepts.[5] Contrary to the conclusions of the author, it appears, however, that those so-called "liberal elements" are rooted in the doctrines of the medieval Schoolmen.[6] For one thing, the Doctors were uncompromising in their condemnation of monopoly for the reason that the monopolist exploits the public and makes an illicit gain by raising the price of his articles above the competitive level. For example, Cardinal Cajetan, commenting on the *Summa* of Thomas Aquinas states that monopoly offends freedom by compelling the public to pay a price higher than the one that would prevail in the market, if there were no such monopoly (*si huiusmodi monopolium non esset*).[7] The traditional feeling against monopoly was so strong that no mercantilist writer dared openly defy public opinion, even when his purpose was to justify the monopolistic practices of this or that trading company.[8] In the parlance of the mercantilists, "free trade," as I have pointed out in this *Journal*, meant freedom from restraints of any sort in internal as well as in foreign trade. Consequently, it corresponded to the French expression *liberté du commerce* and not to *libre échange*.[9] In the seventeenth century, protection in the modern sense was not yet born; the struggle was still a medieval struggle for the control of the carrying trade.[1] In dealing with the history of economic thought, it is not enough to know the writings of the economists; one must also know something

with the abundance or scarcity of money. Such a statement had even become commonplace.

5. Grampp, *op. cit.*, pp. 465–501.

6. *Ibid.*, pp. 500 f. So far as I know, the Schoolmen have never stated "that free individual behavior was inimical to the welfare of society." Heckscher (*Mercantilism*, II, 277) asserts the contrary and rightly states: "that even the medieval tradition was sympathetic to a certain sort of freedom. The medieval influence was thus not without importance to the notion of economic liberty under mercantilism." As late as the seventeenth century, the Anglican and Puritan divines continued to propound scholastic doctrine on just price, monopoly, and price discrimination. See the characteristic passages of Richard Baxter (1615–1691), a popular preacher, which are quoted by H. M. Robertson, *Aspects of the Rise of Economic Individualism: A Criticism of Max Weber and his School* (Cambridge, 1935), p. 17.

7. Text quoted by Fanfani, *Origini dello spirito capitalistico*, p. 123. Cf. Joseph Höffner, *Wirtschaftsethik und Monopole im fünfzehnten und sechzehnten Jahrhundert* (Jena, 1941), p. 107.

8. de Roover, *Gresham on Foreign Exchange*, p. 284. Such was certainly the purpose of John Wheeler, Edward Misselden, Thomas Mun, Sir Josiah Child, and Charles Davenant.

9. When French authors of the period mean *libre échange*, they use the expression: *liberté du commerce entre les nations*.

1. de Roover, *Gresham on Foreign Exchange*, pp. 282 f.

about the institutional framework and the social environment of the period.

Certainly, the English "mercantilists did not believe in an economy wholly or mainly directed by the State,"[2] but they wanted the state to pursue a policy favorable to the trading interests and they tended to defend the exclusive privileges of chartered companies and corporations.[3] Owing to the persistent influence of scholastic ideals, the mercantilists paid lip service to the goddess of "free trade," though the sincerity of their devotion is very much open to question, inasmuch as their pretenses conflict with their other aims. But then, mercantilism was not a logical system. It may even plausibly be argued that, unlike scholasticism, the much vaunted mercantile system was not a system at all.

V. Conclusions

The shortcomings of scholastic economics — and no effort has been made to conceal them — should not blind us to the greatness of the achievement. The Doctors correctly diagnosed the economic problem as one of scarcity. In their opinion, economics was a branch of ethics which determined the rules of justice that ought to preside over the distribution and the exchange of scarce goods. It is obvious that there would be no need for distribution or exchange, if goods could be obtained without effort in unlimited quantities.

The great difference between scholastic and contemporary economics is one of scope and methodology: the Doctors approached economics from a legal point of view. They attached an excessive importance to formalism, so that the study of economics nearly reduced itself to an investigation into the form and nature of contracts. Because of their preoccupation with ethics, the Doctors were also more interested in what ought to be than in what actually was. In the matter of usury, they made the fatal mistake of allowing this subordinate question to overshadow all other problems. Besides, the sophistication of the later casuists involved them more and more in a maze of contradictions, which, ever since the eighteenth century, have prejudiced economists against scholastic doctrines. The more concessions the casuists made, the more they undermined their own position. They were unwilling to face the fact that their distinction

2. Grampp, *op. cit.*, p. 495.

3. In order to enlist the support of the government, mercantilist writers and projectors never failed to stress the benefits which would accrue to the Royal Treasury, if their schemes were carried out (Heaton, "Heckscher on Mercantilism," *op. cit.*, p. 376).

between usurious and nonusurious contracts was based on mere legal technicalities.[4] After all, was it logical to allow a charge for the use of money in one case and to prohibit it in another?[5]

The Doctors, especially the members of the school of Salamanca, made one of their main contributions in developing a theory of value, based on utility and scarcity, which is more in line with modern thinking than that of Adam Smith. Because of his influence and prestige, he created a century of confusion on this topic by throwing out utility and by becoming entangled in the antithesis of value in use and value in exchange. The Doctors were also right in stressing from the beginning the principle of mutual advantage in any bargain or voluntary exchange.[6]

In the absence of fraud or collusion, the market price was supposed to be just, but the Doctors never questioned the right of public authorities to interfere, whenever, because of famine or other circumstances, either buyers or sellers would be seriously harmed by the free operation of the law of supply and demand. Perhaps in the nineteenth century, economists might have regarded the scholastic position as erroneous, but today we operate, in fact, on a just-price basis, since the government does not hesitate to regulate prices in times of national emergency. While the Doctors may have been correct in their analysis, they had the fault of many idealists of overlooking entirely practical difficulties: they assumed that it sufficed to set a price by decree in order to make it effective.

In accordance with the teachings of the Doctors, monopoly was almost everywhere considered a criminal offense. Incidentally, the Doctors rarely mention the guilds and then only to reprove them for their monopolistic practices.[7] I do not find evidence in their treatises that they favored the guild system, which is so often pictured as an ideal organization for Christian society or is recommended as a panacea against the evils of modern industrialism.[8]

4. Robertson, *op. cit.*, p. 118: "In practice, Calvin's position (that all usuries were not necessarily to be condemned) had been reached by Catholic teachers. The difference was mainly one of expression. Amongst the Catholics more depended upon the formalities of contracts."

5. See R. H. Harrod's remarks in a review of John P. Kelly, "Aquinas and Modern Practices of Interest Taking," *Economic Journal*, LVI (1946), 314.

6. Grampp (*op. cit.*, p. 466) credits the mercantilists with the formulation of this principle, although it is clearly stated by Thomas Aquinas, in his *Summa theologica*, II, ii, qu. 77, art. 1, corpus. Cf. Monroe, *op. cit.*, p. 54. John Buridan gives an even better analysis than Aquinas (Schreiber, *op. cit.*, p. 183).

7. Höffner, *Wirtschaftsethik und Monopole*, pp. 82, 92–94.

8. This is the point of view, for example, of the advocates of guild socialism, especially the earlier adherents of this school.   Cf. Arthur J. Penty, *Old Worlds*

SCHOLASTIC ECONOMICS   187

Among other contributions of the Doctors, one should not forget to mention their acceptance, by the sixteenth century, of the quantity theory of money and their speculations on the lawfulness of banking and dealings in foreign exchange. The latter discussion, starting as far back as the thirteenth century, paved the way to the balance-of-trade theory, developed by the English mercantilists in the Tudor and Stuart period. Unfortunately, the late casuists never paid any attention to this discovery and even allowed it to be used against them by their opponents.

One should not mistakenly assume that scholastic economics exerted no influence on business morality. The Church sought to enforce its code of social ethics in two ways: *in foro externo*, that is, through the courts, ecclesiastical and secular, and *in foro interno*, that is, through the confessional. In the Middle Ages, all over western Europe, usurers were constantly brought to court. It is true that the historian stops at the threshold of the confessional, but the numerous medieval wills providing for restitution of usury suggest that confession was far from being an ineffective means of enforcement.[9]

This is not the place to enter into a discussion of the Max Weber theory about the rôle of religion in the rise of capitalism. I question it, because the writings of the Doctors seem to show that the medieval Church neither favored nor hindered the development of capitalism. Like technological and scientific progress, capitalism grew outside the Church. It does not follow, however, that scholastic doctrines had no influence on the course of economic development. Quite the contrary. Recent research in economic history has established the fact that the usury prohibition profoundly affected the development of banking. Since the taking of interest was forbidden, the discounting of commercial paper was also ruled out, but the bankers cleverly shifted to exchange dealings as the basis of their operations. This shift changed the entire structure of the continental European banking system up to the time of the French Revolution.[1]

To consider scholastic economics as medieval doctrine is simply an error, and economists have bypassed a current of thought which

for New, a Study of the Post-Industrial State, pp. 44–49; Ralph Adams Cram, *Walled Towns* pp. 46, 80–82; G. D. H. Cole, "Guild Socialism," *The Encyclopaedia of the Social Sciences*, VII, 202–4.

9. Benjamin N. Nelson, "The Usurer and the Merchant Prince: Italian Businessmen and the Ecclesiastical Law of Restitution, 1100–1550," Supplement to *The Journal of Economic History*, VII (1947), 104–22.

1. de Roover, *L'évolution*, pp. 144–45.

runs parallel with mercantilism and reached out into the eighteenth century, connecting the *économistes* and even Adam Smith with Thomas Aquinas and the medieval Schoolmen.[2] Traces of scholastic influence still permeate eighteenth century economic thinking and sometimes appear in unexpected places, such as the *Encyclopédie* of Diderot and d'Alembert. The *Encyclopédie's* definition of price differs in no way from that given in scholastic treatises, and the same applies to the treatment of monopoly and dry exchange.[3]

In the case of Adam Smith, the ascendance which links him to scholasticism passes through his teacher, Francis Hutcheson, Samuel Pufendorf, and Hugo Grotius.[4] Smith's library contained copies of both Grotius and Pufendorf.[5] Moreover, there is evidence that Adam Smith read Grotius at the age of fifteen when he was a student at Glasgow College. At that time, his teacher was using as textbook a translation of Pufendorf's *De officio Hominis et Civis* by Gershom Carmichael (d. 1729), Hutcheson's predecessor in the chair of Moral Philosophy.[6] In his lectures on political economy, as already stated, Hutcheson dealt with the subject in scholastic fashion as a branch of natural jurisprudence, particularly as "a discussion of contracts."[7] When Adam Smith, himself, succeeded to the chair of Moral Philosophy, he modified this outline by transferring economics to the fourth part of "his course of lectures" devoted to matters not pertaining to justice, but to expediency.[8] This decision definitely constituted a break with the scholastic tradition. The outline of the course in Moral Philosophy, as taught by Francis Hutcheson and later by Adam Smith himself, clearly shows that the curriculum of Glasgow College, in the eighteenth century, never paid any attention to mer-

2. Professor Mabel Magee, my former colleague at Wells College, tells me that Seligman was an exception. According to her detailed notes on his course at Columbia University on the history of economic thought, he dealt with most of the writers mentioned in this article and did not consider scholastic economics as a medieval economic doctrine. I avail myself of this opportunity to thank Dr. Magee and another former colleague, Professor Jean S. Davis, for reading a draft of this article and making helpful suggestions.

3. According to the *Encyclopédie*, the price of commodities is set either by ordinance or by common estimation: the first is called the legal price (*prix légitime*) and the second, the current price (*prix courant*). The scholastic origin of this distinction is beyond question.

4. Grice-Hutchinson, *The School of Salamanca*, pp. 64–69, 76. Cf. William Robert Scott, *Adam Smith as Student and Professor* (Glasgow, 1937).

5. James Bonar, *A Catalogue of the Library of Adam Smith* (2d ed.), pp. 78, 151.

6. Scott, *op. cit.*, pp. 34, 112.

7. John Rae, *Life of Adam Smith*, p. 14.

8. *Ibid.*, pp. 54 f.

SCHOLASTIC ECONOMICS 189

cantilist thought, but always provided for some teaching of economic principles based on ethics and law, inherited from the medieval university. In the *Wealth of Nations*, Adam Smith, it is true, devotes several chapters to mercantilism but only to denounce it as a pernicious and "sophistical" system.

Two eighteenth century economists, abbé Ferdinando Galiani (1728–87) and abbé Etienne Bonnot de Condillac (1715–80), have been hailed by some historians as the first to anticipate the modern marginal utility theory of value by stating that value rests on the combination of two elements: utility and scarcity.[9] The question arises whether this idea originates with the two abbés or whether — what is more likely — they took it from the Doctors, possibly by way of the late casuists and the school of Salamanca, as Marjorie Grice-Hutchinson seems to think.[1] In my opinion, she is undoubtedly right, since it is highly improbable that cultured men in holy orders would be unacquainted with the extensive literature on moral theology. As far as Galiani is concerned, scholastic influence is noticeable in many passages of his essay on money, especially in his treatment of usury and *cambio*.[2] Furthermore, the chapter on value contains a quotation from Diego Covarrubias y Leyva, one of the leading representatives of the school of Salamanca.[3] Consequently, Galiani certainly knew his work, and hence there was no breach of continuity.

As this study shows, modern economics owes the Schoolmen and their successors a greater debt than is commonly acknowledged. It also illustrates the merits and the defects of the legal approach to economics. What really caused the downfall of scholastic economics was the refusal of the late casuists to revise and to modernize their methods. Perhaps their whole system was in need of a complete overhauling. Nevertheless, it contained much that was worth pre-

9. Galiani, *op. cit.*, Book I, chap. 2, pp. 25–45; and Condillac, *op. cit.*, Vol. I, chaps. 1 and 2, pp. 248–57. In a footnote, the editor, Eugène Daire, blames Condillac for not following in the footsteps of Quesnay and Adam Smith and not adopting their distinction between *value in use* and *value in exchange!*

1. *Op. cit.*, pp. 63–64, 76.

2. *Op. cit.*, Book 5, chaps. 1 and 4, pp. 289–96, 303–7. Galiani's definition of usury, as any gain above the principal accruing from a *mutuum*, is still purely scholastic.

3. *Op. cit.*, Book I, chap. 2, p. 26. The most recent and much the best biographical study on abbé Galiani is that of President Luigi Einaudi, "Galiani economista," *Saggi bibliografici e storici intorno alle dottrine economiche* (Rome, 1953), 269–305. This study was first published in German under the title "Galiani als Nationalökonom," *Schweizerische Zeitschrift für Volkswirtschaft und Statistik*, LXXXI (1945), No. 1. An English version of the first part of Einaudi's study is available in Henry William Spiegel (ed.), *The Development of Economic Thought* (New York, 1952), pp. 62–82.

serving and which was preserved in actual fact. Valuable ideas may lie buried for a time but they eventually spring up. Like other sciences, economics grows slowly by accretion. Despite many currents and cross currents, continuity is perhaps the most impressive phenomenon in the history of economic doctrines.

RAYMOND DE ROOVER.

THE GRADUATE SCHOOL
BOSTON COLLEGE

[5]

The Concept of the Just Price:
Theory and Economic Policy

IN THE view of many economists the just price is a nebulous concept invented by pious monks who knew nothing of business or economics and were blissfully unaware of market mechanisms. It is true that certain writers, Catholics and non-Catholics alike, have done their best to accredit this fairy tale and to propagate the notion that the just price, instead of being set by the allegedly blind and unconscionable forces of the market, was determined by criteria of fairness without regard to the elements of supply and demand or at least with the purpose of eliminating the evils of unrestrained competition.

According to a widespread belief—found in nearly all books dealing with the subject—the just price was linked to the medieval concept of a social hierarchy and corresponded to a reasonable charge which would enable the producer to live and to support his family on a scale suitable to his station in life.[1] This doctrine is generally thought to have found its practical application in the guild system. For this purpose the guilds are presented as welfare agencies which prevented unfair competition, protected consumers against deceit and exploitation, created equal opportunities for their members, and secured for them a modest but decent living in keeping with traditional standards.[2] One of the main champions of this idyllic view is Max Weber (1864-1920), who describes the guilds as at least originally founded on the subsistence principle (*Nahrungsprinzip*) and as following a livelihood policy by

[1] William Ashley, *An Introduction to English Economic History and Theory* (4th ed.; 2 vols.; London: Longmans, Green, 1920), I, Part II, 391; John M. Clark, *The Social Control of Business* (2d ed.; New York: McGraw-Hill Book Co., 1939), pp. 23-24; Shepard B. Clough and Charles W. Cole, *Economic History of Europe* (rev. ed.; Boston: D. C. Heath, 1946), pp. 31, 68; George Clune, *The Medieval Gild System* (Dublin: Browne and Nolan, 1943), p. 55; Alfred de Tarde, *L'idée du juste prix* (Paris: Félix Alcan, 1907), pp. 42-43; Joseph Dorfman, *The Economic Mind in American Civilization* (3 vols.; New York: Viking Press, 1946-49), I, 5; N. S. B. Gras, *Business and Capitalism* (New York: Crofts, 1939), pp. 122-23; Herbert Heaton, *Economic History of Europe* (1st ed.; New York: Harper, 1936), p. 204; George O'Brien, *An Essay on Medieval Economic Teaching* (London: Longmans, Green, 1920), pp. 111-12; Leo S. Schumacher, *The Philosophy of the Equitable Distribution of Wealth* (Washington, D.C.: The Catholic University of America, 1949), p. 47; James Westfall Thompson, *An Economic and Social History of the Middle Ages, 300–1300* (New York: Century Co., 1928), p. 697. This list is by no means exhaustive.

[2] For example, Arthur J. Penty, *A Guildman's Interpretation of History* (New York: Sunrise Turn, n.d.), pp. 38-46.

New Viewpoints on Familiar Subjects 419

regulating output, technique, quality, and prices.[3] Another German economist, Werner Sombart (1863–1941), goes even further: according to him, not only the medieval craftsmen but even the merchants strove only to gain a livelihood befitting their rank in society and did not seek to accumulate wealth or to climb the social ladder. This attitude, he claims, was rooted in the concept of the just price "which dominated the entire period of the Middle Ages." In support of this statement Sombart refers to the writings of Henry of Langenstein, the Elder (1325–1397).[4]

This is a clue. Indeed, Heinrich von Langenstein states that if the public authorities fail to fix a price, the producer may set it himself, but he should not charge more for his labor and expenses than would enable him to maintain his status (. . . *per quanto res suas vendendo statum suum continuare possit*).[5] And if he does charge more in order to enrich himself or to improve his station, he commits the sin of avarice. Sombart is by no means the first to cite this text. In so far as I have been able to discover, it was first mentioned by Wilhelm Roscher (1817–1894) in 1874.[6] Since it fitted in so well with prevailing preconceptions, it was regarded as a characteristic formulation of the scholastic doctrine of the just price and copied by one author after another, including Rudolf Kaulla,[7] Sir William Ashley,[8] R. H. Tawney,[9] and Amintore Fanfani,[10] to mention only a few among the most prominent. Thus Langenstein's text exerted enormous influence.

---

[3] Max Weber, *General Economic History,* translated by Frank H. Knight (London: Allen & Unwin, n.d.), pp. 138–43. The author recognizes that the guilds, in the course of time, tended to become monopolistic organizations.

[4] Werner Sombart, *Der moderne Kapitalismus,* (2d rev. ed.; Munich: Duncker & Humblot, 1916), I, 292–93.

[5] Heinrich von Langenstein, also called Henricus de Hassia (Hesse), *Tractatus bipartitus de contractibus emptionis et venditionis,* Part I, cap. 12, published in Johannes Gerson, *Opera omnia,* IV (Cologne, 1484), fol. 191. No more recent edition is available. Langenstein's treatise was omitted from later editions of Gerson. The most detailed study of Langenstein's economic ideas is in Manuel Rocha, *Travail et salaire à travers la scolastique* (2d ed.; Paris: Desclée de Brouwer, 1933), pp. 21–48, esp. p. 44. Cf. Edmund Schreiber, *Die volkswirtschaftlichen Anschauungen der Scholastik seit Thomas v. Aquin* (Jena: Gustav Fischer, 1913), pp. 196–202.

[6] *Geschichte der National-Oekonomik in Deutschland* (Munich, 1874), pp. 19–20.

[7] "Die Lehre vom gerechten Preis in der Scholastik," *Zeitschrift für die gesamte Staatswissenschaft,* LX (1904), 598 ff., and *Theory of the Just Price* (London: Allen and Unwin, 1940), p. 44.

[8] *English Economic History,* I, Part II, 391 and 474, n. 45. The reference is to Roscher.

[9] *Religion and the Rise of Capitalism* (rev. ed.; New York: Harcourt, Brace, and Co., 1937), pp. 41–42 and 295, n. 56.

[10] *Le origini dello spirito capitalistico in Italia* (Milan: Vita e Pensiero, 1933), p. 7. He also refers to Sombart.

420   *Raymond de Roover*

It was used as historical justification for the theory of the living wage and was given wide currency by the supporters of guild socialism, who expected to cure the ills of modern industrialism by resurrecting the medieval guilds. In a subtle way Langenstein was even drafted in defense of the corporate state.

As a matter of fact, Langenstein enjoys such popularity that economic historians usually take his statement as typical of the scholastic doctrine on the just price.[11] I question very much whether there is the slightest justification for according him so much credit and for considering his statement as authoritative and representative. Langenstein was not one of the giants in medieval philosophy but a relatively minor figure. Like his master, Buridan (d. after 1358), he was a nominalist and a follower of William of Ockham (ca. 1300–1349), whose doctrines were tainted with heresy and were opposed both by the Scotists and the Thomists. As a disciple of Ockham, Langenstein stood more or less outside the main current of scholastic thought.[12] What applies to philosophy applies also to economics. Langenstein's value and price theory was strongly influenced by Buridan's and also emphasized psychological and individual factors as price determinants. I have found that Langenstein is rarely cited by later scholastic authors, a sure indication that his writings did not carry much weight. His influence may have been greater, however, in central and eastern Europe, where the leading universities (Vienna, Prague, and Cracow) around 1400 were strongholds of nominalism. It is quite possible that Langenstein inspired such men as Matthew of Cracow (d. 1397) who, I have been told by Paul Czartoryski, also wrote on economic questions. In any case, the prestige which Langenstein enjoys today among economic historians is due to the mere chance that his pronouncements on the just price were put into circulation and hailed as oracles by the German economists of the historical school and their English followers.

The purpose of this paper is to demonstrate that the generally accepted definition of the just price is wrong and rests on misinterpretation of the scholastic position on the matter. According to the majority of the doctors, the just price did not correspond to cost of production

[11] This observation is made by Bernard W. Dempsey, S.J., "The Economic Philosophy of St. Thomas," in Robert E. Brennan, ed., *Essays in Thomism* (New York: Sheed and Ward, 1942), p. 250.

[12] Maurice De Wulf, *Histoire de la philosophie médiévale* (5th ed.; 2 vols.; Paris: Félix Alcan, 1924–25), II, 191. Cf. Joseph Höffner, *Statik und Dynamik in der scholastischen Wirtschaftsethik* (Cologne: Westdeutscherverlag, 1955), pp. 19–22. This author points out that the idea of social status and the subsistence principle was stressed by the nominalists and not by their opponents, the Thomists.

New Viewpoints on Familiar Subjects   421

as determined by the producer's social status, but was simply the current market price, with this important reservation: in cases of collusion or emergency, the public authorities retained the right to interfere and to impose a fair price.[13] In order to straighten out the existing confusion, it will also be shown how this doctrine was translated into policy, particularly in connection with the guilds.

For the inception of the scholastic doctrine of the just price, one of the fundamental texts is the canon *Placuit,* which is really a capitulary issued in 884 by Karloman, King of France,[14] but incorporated by Raymond of Pennaforte (1180–1278) in the canon law.[15] This canon states that parish priests should admonish their flocks not to charge wayfarers more than the price obtainable in the local market (*quam in mercato vendere possint*). Otherwise, the wayfarers can complain to the priest, who is then required to set a price with "humanity." This text, it seems to me, clearly equates just price with market price and does not lend itself to a different interpretation.

In the works of Albertus Magnus (1193–1280) and especially in those of Thomas Aquinas (1226–1274), the passages relating to price are so scattered and seemingly so conflicting that they have given rise to varying interpretations. By selecting only those passages favorable to their thesis, certain writers even reached the conclusion that Albertus Magnus and Thomas Aquinas had a labor theory of value and adumbrated Karl Marx (1818–1883).[16] To prove their point these writers used chiefly the comments of the two theologians on Aristotle's *Nicomachean Ethics,* where it is stated that commutative or contractual justice requires strict equivalence between what is received and what is given and that any exchange violating this rule is unfair. This is then construed in a Marxian sense as meaning that price, to be just, should always correspond to cost, which in the Middle Ages was chiefly labor cost.[17] The trouble is that such an explanation contradicts

---

13 The same point of view is represented by Joseph Höffner (note 12) and by John T. Noonan, Jr., *The Scholastic Analysis of Usury* (Cambridge: Harvard University Press, 1957), p. 86.

14 Alfredus Boretius and Victor Krause, eds., *Capitularia Regum Francorum* (Monumenta Germaniae Historica, Legum, Sec. II, Hanover, 1892), 375. This capitulary found its way into the canon law through the collections of Burchard of Worms and Yvo of Chartres.

15 *Corpus juris canonici, Decretales: in X,* III, 17, 1.

16 The main exponent of this thesis is Selma Hagenauer, *Das "justum pretium" bei Thomas von Aquino* (Stuttgart: W. Kohlhammer, 1931). Cf. Tawney, *Religion,* p. 36.

17 As a matter of fact, Aquinas comes close to saying that any exchange of two commodities should be based on the ratio between the amounts of labor expended on each. Thomas Aquinas, *Commentaria in X libros ethicorum ad Nicomachum,* lib. V, lect. 7, 8, 9 (Parma edition of *Opera omnia,* XXI, 168, 171, 172).

Raymond de Roover

statements made elsewhere by Albertus Magnus and Thomas Aquinas. Moreover, the texts in question are open to another interpretation which would do away with any inconsistency. In their comments on Aristotle both Albertus and Aquinas insist that arts and crafts would be doomed to destruction if the producer did not recover his outlays in the sale of his product.[18] In other words, the market price could not fall permanently below cost. If so, there is no contradiction, since the market price would then tend to coincide with cost or to oscillate around this point like the swing of a pendulum. Besides, Thomas Aquinas himself recognizes that the just price cannot be determined with precision, but can vary within a certain range, so that minor deviations do not involve any injustice.[19] This second interpretation, of course, is not in accord with Marxian dialectics; but it agrees with classical and neoclassical economic analysis. It is also consonant with the later development of scholastic thought.

Whatever the meaning of these obscure passages, Albertus Magnus and Thomas Aquinas are more explicit, if less analytical, in other works where they give their own opinions and do not try to elucidate Aristotle's. The first, in his comments on the *Sentences* of Peter Lombard, defines the just price as follows: What goods are worth according to the estimation of the market (*secundum aestimationem fori*) at the time of the sale.[20] Thomas Aquinas nowhere puts the matter so clearly, but he tells the story of a merchant who brings wheat to a country where there is dearth and knows that others are following with more. May this merchant, Aquinas asks, sell his wheat at the prevailing price (*pretium quod invenit*) or should he announce the arrival of fresh supplies and thus cause the price to fall? The answer is that he may sell his wheat at the current price without infringing the rules of justice, although, Aquinas adds almost as an afterthought, he would act more virtuously by notifying the buyers. In my opinion this passage destroys with a single blow the thesis of those who try to make Aquinas into a Marxist, and proves beyond doubt that he considered the market price as just.[21]

---

[18] Albertus Magnus, *Liber V ethicorum*, tract. 2, cap. 7, No. 28, in his *Opera omnia* (Paris, 1891), VII, 353; Aquinas, *Comment. in X libros ethicorum*, lib. V, lect. 7, 8.

[19] *Summa theologica*, II, ii, qu. 77, art. 1, ad. 1. Cf. Arthur E. Monroe, *Early Economic Thought* (Cambridge: Harvard University Press, 1948), p. 56.

[20] Albertus Magnus, *Commentarii in IV sententiarum Petri Lombardi*, Dist. 16, art. 46, in *Opera omnia*, XXIX (Paris, 1894), 638. Cf. J. B. Kraus, S.J., *Scholastik, Puritanismus, und Kapitalismus* (Leipzig: Duncker & Humblot, 1930), p. 53.

[21] *Summa theologica*, II, ii, qu. 77, art. 3, ad. 4. The story is taken from Cicero, *De officiis*, iii. 12. My conclusion agrees with that of Armando Sapori, "Il giusto prezzo nella dottrina di san Tommaso e nella pratica del suo tempo," *Studi di storia economica (secoli XIII–XIV–XV)* (3d rev. ed.; 2 vols.; Florence: Sansoni, 1955), I, 279.

New Viewpoints on Familiar Subjects 423

This interpretation, moreover, agrees with that of Cardinal Cajetan
(1468–1534), the authoritative commentator on the *Summa*. In connection with question 77 *secunda secundae,* which deals with the sales
contract, he concludes that according to Aquinas the just price is "the
one, which at a given time, can be gotten from the buyers, assuming
common knowledge and in the absence of all fraud and coercion."[22]
He then goes on to describe the market mechanism and to show how
prices rise or fall in response to changes in demand or supply.

Those who say Thomas Aquinas favored cost of production rather
than market valuation as the criterion of justice claim that the later
scholastic doctors, yielding to the pressure of rising capitalism, modified
his doctrine in this respect.[23] Since Aquinas upheld market valuation
instead of cost, however, there was no change, but a continuous tradition involving, it is true, elaboration and refinement as economic
development raised new problems and as discussion revealed flaws
in previous analysis.

Some of the most valuable contributions were made by Bernardino
of Siena (1380–1444), perhaps the ablest economist of the Middle Ages.
Although usually a follower of John Duns Scotus, he espouses the
Thomist position on price. According to San Bernardino, price is a
social phenomenon and is set not by the arbitrary decision of individuals, but *communiter,* that is, by the community.[24] How? There are
two possibilities: The price of a commodity can be fixed either by the
public authorities for the common good, or by the estimation currently
arrived at in the market (*secundum aestimationem fori occurrentis*).[25]
The first is the legal price; the second is called later the natural price.
Citing Henricus Hostiensis (d. 1271), San Bernardino stresses the fact
that the market price has to be accepted by the producer and is fair
whether he gains or loses, whether it is above or below cost.[26] This
point was further elaborated by the Dominican friar, Tommaso
Buoninsegni (d. 1609). In his treatise on licit traffics he points out that

[22] Comments on *Summa theologica,* II, ii, qu. 77, art. 1 (Leonine edition, VI, 149). Cf. Lewis
Watt, "The Theory Lying Behind the Historical Conception of the Just Price," in V. A. Demant,
ed., *The Just Price* (London: Student Christian Movement Press, 1930), p. 69.

[23] Tawney, *Religion,* p. 40; Tarde, *Juste prix,* pp. 51–52.

[24] This was the traditional doctrine derived from the Roman law. Accursius (1182–1260),
Glossa ordinaria to *Digest,* XXXV, 2, 63: "Res tantum valet quantum vendi potest, sed communiter" ("Goods are worth as much as they can be sold for, commonly").

[25] San Bernardino of Siena, *De evangelio aeterno,* sermon 35, art. 2, cap. 2, and sermon 33,
art. 2, cap. 7, part 2, §5, in his *Opera omnia,* IV (Florence–Quaracchi: St. Bonaventure Press,
1956), 157–58, 197. Cf. Franz Josef Hünermann, *Die wirtschaftsethischen Predigten des hl.
Bernardin von Siena* (doct. diss., Münster; Kempen–Niederrhein: Thomas Druckerei, 1939),
pp. 80 ff.

[26] Bernardino, *De evangelio,* sermon 33, art. 2, cap. 7, part 2, §5. Cf. Fanfani, *Origini,* p. 13.

the just price does not have gradations, because buyers, if they are well informed, as they usually are in a wholesale market, will not pay more than the current price.[27] In other words, for the same commodity there can be only one price in the same market.

By the sixteenth century the majority of the scholastic doctors agreed that the just price was either fixed by law or determined by common estimation (*communis aestimatio*). There has been some discussion about the meaning of this phrase, but it appears to be identical with *aestimatio fori,* or market valuation, since the two expressions were used interchangeably by the scholastics.[28] Moreover, it is not clear how a community acting collectively could arrive at a price except by the chaffering of the market, certainly not by taking a vote, for example.

The dissenters were only a few followers of John Duns Scotus (1265–1308), such as John Mayor (1469–1550), another Scot, and Johannes Consobrinus, or João Sobrinho (d. 1486), a Portuguese who taught for some time in England.[29] Like their leader, they maintained that the just price corresponded to cost including normal profit and compensation for risk.[30] Unlike Langenstein, they did not worry about social status.

The theory of Duns Scotus was denounced most vehemently as fallacious by the School of Salamanca, founded by the great jurist, Francisco de Vitoria (*ca.* 1480–1546). More than ever emphasis was put on the fairness of the current market price. Without exception, Vitoria and his disciples insist that attention be paid only to supply and demand, without regard for labor costs, expenses, or incurred risks; inefficient producers or unfortunate speculators should simply bear the consequences of their incompetence, bad luck, or wrong forecasting.[31]

---

[27] Tommaso Buoninsegni, O.P., *Trattato de' traffichi giusti et ordinarii* (Venice, 1588), cap. 11, Nos. 1 and 2.

[28] Raymond de Roover, "Joseph A. Schumpeter and Scholastic Economics," *Kyklos,* IX (1957), 133–34. A different interpretation is given by Abram L. Harris, *Economics and Social Reform* (New York: Harper & Brothers, 1958), pp. 318–22. In support of his views he quotes a definition given by Heinrich Pesch (1854–1926), but it is clear that the latter's value theory stems directly or indirectly from Langenstein, whose doctrine is not representative of scholasticism.

[29] John Duns Scotus, O.F.M., *Quaestiones in librum quartum sententiarum,* dist. 15, qu. 2, No. 23, in his *Opera omnia,* XVIII (Paris, 1894), 318; Moses Bensabat Amzalak, *Frei João Sobrinho e as Doutrinas Económicas da Idade Média* (Lisbon: Gráfica Lisbonense, 1945), pp. 257 ff.

[30] Risk is specifically mentioned, since Scotus states that a merchant who suffers damage through shipwreck or fire can recoup this loss on the sale of other goods.

[31] Marjorie Grice-Hutchinson, *The School of Salamanca: Readings in Spanish Monetary Theory, 1544–1605* (Oxford: Clarendon Press, 1952), pp. 48, 72, 81–82, 86; Demetrio Iparraguirre, *Francisco de Vitoria, una teoria social del valor económico* (Publicaciones de la

New Viewpoints on Familiar Subjects   425

Although the whole discussion on the just price assumed the existence of competitive conditions, it is strange that the word "competition" never occurs in scholastic treatises until the end of the sixteenth century, when it is used by Luis de Molina (1535-1601). Discussing price formation in an open market, he states that "competition (*concurrentium*) among buyers—brisker at one time than at another—and their greater avidity will cause prices to go up, whereas paucity of purchasers will bring them down."[32] The Spanish school accepted as a matter of course the quantity theory of money and the proposition that prices "generally" will rise or fall in response to expansion or contraction of the monetary circulation.[33]

Whenever the free market failed to function properly, the public authorities, according to the scholastic doctrine, had not only the right but the duty to step in by means of price regulation. When there was a legal price, it superseded the market price and was binding, unless the regulations were manifestly out of date or openly disobeyed, with the authorities making no attempt at enforcement.[34] In other words, the moralists realized perfectly well that it was useless to fix prices by decree if nothing was done to make them effective.

Discussion of this issue does not start until the fourteenth century, and one of the first advocates of price fixing was the Frenchman Jean Gerson (1362-1428), *doctor christianissimus* and at one time chancellor of the University of Paris. He suggested that price fixing be extended to all commodities, on the ground that no one should presume to be wiser than the lawmaker.[35] This suggestion, however, found few supporters, as the impracticality of the whole scheme became apparent. In fact, medieval price regulation usually embraced only a few basic necessities, such as wheat, bread, meat, wine, and beer. Legal prices were usually ceiling prices. But they could be minima, below which a buyer could not go, if the rate was set in favor of the seller.[36]

Universidad de Deusto, 1st series, Vol. VIII; Bilbao: Mensajero del Corazón de Jesús, 1957), pp. 55–56, 74–81; Joseph A. Schumpeter, *History of Economic Analysis* (New York: Oxford University Press, 1954), pp. 98–99; Raymond de Roover, "Scholastic Economics: Survival and Lasting Influence from the Sixteenth Century to Adam Smith," *Quarterly Journal of Economics,* LXIX (1955), 169.

[32] Luis de Molina, *De justitia et jure* (Cuença, 1592), Tract. 2 *(De contractibus),* disp. 348, §4.

[33] Grice-Hutchinson, *School of Salamanca,* pp. 51–52, 95, 113.

[34] Alphonsus Liguori (1696–1787), *Theologia moralis,* Book III, Tract. 5, cap. 3, dub. 8, art. 1, No. 803, in his *Opere,* V (Turin, 1888), 645.

[35] Johannes Gerson, *De contractibus,* consid. 19 in his *Opera omnia,* III (Antwerp, 1706), col. 175.

[36] This point is emphasized by Leonardus Lessius, S.J., *De justitia et jure* (Paris, 1606), lib. 2, cap. 21, dub. 2, §13.

426 *Raymond de Roover*

One weakness of the scholastic doctors was that they were interested only in laying down principles and tended to overlook practical difficulties, which, they claimed, did not concern the theologians but were the province of the "politicians." An extreme position was taken by Martin Azpilcueta (1493–1587), better known as Navarrus, who opposed all price regulation because it was unnecessary in times of plenty and ineffective or harmful in times of dearth.[37] Several others, among them Molina, looked upon price regulation with the same disfavor.

Since scholastic doctrine favored competition, it is logical that all forms of price discrimination were condemned. Already in the thirteenth century both Thomas Aquinas and John Duns Scotus formulated the rule that a seller was not allowed to sell dearer because his wares were greatly wanted by a prospective buyer.[38] An even better statement is found in San Bernardino of Siena who, citing the canon *Placuit* mentioned above, underscores the point that price should be the same to all and that no one is allowed to charge strangers more than local customers or to take advantage of a buyer's ignorance, rusticity, or special need.[39] Instead of *Placuit*, certain writers quote a text from the *Digest*, which says that the seller may not exploit a buyer's affection or desire for a particular article, whence the expression *pretium affectionis*, which in scholastic literature designates a discriminatory price.[40] In any case there was no disagreement about the unethical character of price discrimination.

The scholastics, theologians as well as jurists, were also unanimous in regarding monopoly as a deleterious practice, inimical to the commonweal. Monopoly was defined broadly so as to include any pacts or rings formed to keep up or to depress prices above or below the competitive level. Consequently, this concept included what is today called monopsony, oligopoly, and any other monopolistic practices. In the opinion of the scholastics monopoly was an offense against liberty; it assumed a criminal character because it rested usually on

[37] Cardinal Juan de Lugo, S.J. (1583–1660), *De justitia et jure, disputationes*, disp. 26, sec. 4, No. 50, in his *Opera omnia*, VII (Paris, 1893), 337.

[38] Aquinas, *Summa theologica*, II, ii, qu. 77, art. 1, *corpus;* Duns Scotus, *Quaestiones*, lib. IV, dist. 15, qu. 2, No. 16, in *Opera omnia*, XVIII, 289; Monroe, *Economic Thought*, p. 55.

[39] *De evangelio*, sermon 33, art. 2, cap. 5, in *Opera omnia*, IV, 148–49, and Luciano Banchi, ed., *Le prediche volgari di san Bernardino*, III (Siena, 1888), predica 38, 246. Cf. Fanfani, *Origini*, p. 110.

[40] *Corpus juris civilis, Digest*, XXXV, 2, 63. The text really refers to a slave whose father is a freeman; it states that the slave's owner cannot charge more than the market price if the father wants to buy and adopt his offspring. In the Middle Ages this text was stretched to cover all cases of price discrimination.

New Viewpoints on Familiar Subjects 427

collusion or "conspiracy"—this phrase actually occurs again and again in scholastic treatises.[41] Perhaps the best treatment on the subject is found in the writings of the Belgian Jesuit Leonardus Lessius (1554–1623). He admits that not all monopolies are iniquitous and that a prince, if he has good reasons, may grant exclusive privileges. He must then, however, fix a fair price giving due consideration to all attending circumstances (*spectatio circumstanciis omnibus*), such as cost, risk, and market conditions, presumably by striking a compromise between conflicting criteria, as public utility commissions do today.[42] To my mind there is no doubt that the conspiracy idea of the antitrust laws goes back to scholastic precedents and is rooted in the medieval concept of the just price.[43]

The doctrine of the market price of course applied only to staple products, on which competition, to use David Ricardo's phrase, operated without restraint. The scholastics also discussed the case of luxuries, such as thoroughbred dogs, birds of paradise, rare pictures, rich tapestries, and the like, for which there was no regular market. On this subject the doctors were unable to reach an agreement. Some, as for example Francisco de Vitoria, proclaimed that the seller of such superfluities and frivolities could accept what an informed buyer offered to pay, provided of course that there was no fraud, deceit, or coercion.[44] Others, such as Lessius, contended that the price of such articles should be set by experts (*ex judicio intelligentis mercatoris*).[45] The Blessed Angelo Carletti da Chivasso (d. 1495) found it difficult to make a rule but thought that the seller should determine the price honestly after considering such pertinent facts as scarcity, trouble, and risk.[46]

For completeness it should perhaps be added that the Reformation wrought little change and that the Protestant divines, Max Weber notwithstanding, continued to expound the scholastic doctrine on the just price without altering it in the least. I do not see, for example, why the Puritan preacher Richard Baxter (1615-1691) should be denounced as an abbeter of capitalism because he mentions that the just price is the

---

[41] Bernardino, *De evangelio*, sermon 33, art. 2, cap. 7, part 1, §5, in *Opera omnia*, IV, 153. Cf. Joseph Höffner, *Wirtschaftsethik und Monopole im fünfzehnten und sechzehnten Jahrhundert* (Jena: Gustav Fischer, 1941), pp. 53, 135–56.

[42] *De justitia et jure*, lib. 2, cap. 21, dub. 20, §148.

[43] Schumpeter, *History of Economic Analysis*, pp. 154–55; William L. Letwin, "The English Common Law Concerning Monopolies," *The University of Chicago Law Review*, XXI (1953–54), 355–61; Raymond de Roover, "Monopoly Theory Prior to Adam Smith: A Revision," *Quarterly Journal of Economics*, LXV (1951), 501–2, 507.

[44] Iparraguirre, *Francisco de Vitoria*, pp. 59–65.

[45] Lessius, *De justitia*, lib. 2, cap. 21, dub. 3, Nos. 15, 16.

[46] Angelo da Chivasso, O.F.M., *Somma angelica* (Venice, 1593), Part II, rubr. *Venditione*, §5.

428   *Raymond de Roover*

market price in the absence of a rate set by law.[47] The doctrine of the just price was brought to the shores of America by the Puritan ministers. As a sample of their doctrines I shall merely mention the five rules for trading proposed by the Reverend John Cotton (1584–1642).[48] They differ from scholastic doctrine only in one respect: the medieval doctors did not approve of price increases on credit sales, because such a practice involved concealed usury.

A few words need to be said about the practical application of the doctrine of the just price. How was it translated into policy? And was this policy consistent with its theoretical postulates? Perhaps the authorities followed a vacillating course and wavered between the enforcement of competition on the one hand and the protection of monopoly on the other hand. In the Middle Ages the implementation of economic policy rested to a large extent, if not exclusively, with the municipal authorities of cities, towns, and boroughs. This is especially true of the Italian city states and the quasi-independent *Reichsstädte* in Germany. In England and France, however, royal government had not entirely renounced its sovereign rights and often took advantage of economic and social conflicts to assert its authority. Nevertheless, even in these two monarchies the towns were the main policy-making agencies. They followed one policy with respect to foodstuffs that they drew from the countryside and another with regard to the manu-factured products that were made within the walls. "Thus," in the words of John M. Clark, "there were laws, of town origin, aiming to enforce competition in the things the townsmen bought, while the guild regulations limited and controlled competition in the things they sold." [49] Although this may be an oversimplification, it contains a great deal of truth. One has to remember, however, that realities involve complications too readily overlooked in making general statements.

With regard to victuals the aim of town policy was very simply to secure abundant supplies as cheaply as possible.[50] For this purpose reliance was placed on the enforcement of competition, and the peasants

---

[47] H. M. Robertson, *Aspects of the Rise of Economic Individualism: A Criticism of Max Weber and His School* (Cambridge, Eng.: The University Press, 1933), p. 17.

[48] N. S. B. Gras and Henrietta M. Larson, *Casebook in American Business History* (New York: Crofts, 1939), p. 59; Tawney, *Religion*, pp. 128–30; E. A. J. Johnson, *American Economic Thought in the Seventeenth Century* (London: P. S. King & Son, 1932), pp. 123–30. The latter is surprised to find that supply-and-demand was understood when the doctrine of "just price" was still the dominant note!

[49] *Social Control of Business*, p. 23.

[50] "Ad hoc ut maior copia victualium in civitate habeatur,": quoted from a Florentine statute by Sapori, *Studi*, I, 294.

New Viewpoints on Familiar Subjects   429

of the surrounding district were encouraged and, if necessary, compelled to bring their products to the market and to sell them directly
to the consumer, thereby eliminating all middlemen, hawkers, or
brokers.[51] As Hans van Werveke correctly points out, this provisioning
policy (*politique de ravitaillement*) was practiced throughout western
Europe from Sicily to England.[52] Everywhere measures were taken
against engrossers (*accapareurs*), forestallers (*recoupeurs*), and regraters (*regrattiers*) who tried to accumulate stocks, to prevent supplies
from reaching the market, or to form corners in order to drive prices
up.[53] Medieval records are full of references to engrossers or forestallers
who were caught, dragged into court, and fined or punished with
exposure on the pillory.[54] This applies not only to England but to the
Continent as well. Those who escaped conviction in the secular courts
were still punishable *in foro conscientiae*; according to canon law,
monopoly profits were *turpe lucrum,* which, like usury, was subject
to restitution.[55] In dealing with the Middle Ages it would be a grievous
error to ignore the confessional as a means of enforcement.

Unfortunately, crop failures created a recurrent problem, especially
in the case of grain, because bread was the staple food and there were
no suitable substitutes. Since the demand for cereals was highly
inelastic, prices went up to fantastic heights in case of dearth.[56] Under
those circumstances it would have been folly to rely on the automatic
operation of competition. In order to avoid bread riots and mass
starvation the authorities were forced to resort to regulation, and it is
here that difficulties began. The scholastic authors were full of illusions
about the omniscience, honesty, and efficiency of public authorities.

The history of price regulation remains to be written, but we know

[51] Henri Pirenne, "Les anciennes démocraties des Pays-Bas," in *Les villes et les institutions
urbaines* (6th ed.; 2 vols.; Paris; Félix Alcan, 1939), I, 196–99; *idem,* "Le consommateur au
moyen âge," *Histoire économique de l'Occident médiéval* (Bruges: Desclée de Brouwer, 1951),
pp. 532–34.

[52] "Les villes belges: histoire des institutions économiques et sociales," in *La ville,* Vol. II:
Institutions économiques et sociales (Recueils de la Société Jean Bodin, No. 7; Brussels: Editions
de la Librairie Encyclopédique, 1955), p. 564. For Sicily: Antonio Petino, *Aspetti e momenti di
politica granaria a Catania ed in Sicilia nel Quattrocento* (Catania: Università di Catania, 1952),
p. 31.

[53] In German the terms are *Aufkauf, Vorkauf,* and *Wiederkauf.* Jean Schneider, "Les villes
allemandes," *La ville,* II, 432–33. It was not always possible to eliminate middlemen entirely.

[54] L. F. Salzman, *English Industries of the Middle Ages* (Oxford: Clarendon Press, 1923),
p. 314.

[55] *Corpus juris canonici, Decretum Gratiani:* c. *Quicumque tempore,* Causa xiv, qu. 4, c.
9. This is article 17 of a capitulary issued by Charlemagne in 806.

[56] This statement is fully supported by statistical data. See, for example, Charles Verlinden,
J. Craeybeckx, and E. Scholliers, "Mouvements des prix et des salaires en Belgique au XVIe
siècle," *Annales (Economies, Sociétés, Civilisations),* X (1955), 173–98.

430 *Raymond de Roover*

it to be a tale of woe.[57] In the absence of a well-organized system of allocation and rationing, price controls were bound to break down, and it is not surprising that previous to 1800 their administration was often haphazard, vexatious, inefficient, and arbitrary. A crude form of rationing, common all over Europe, was to freeze the price of bread but to vary the size of the loaf with the price of breadstuffs.[58] As the latter increased, the penny or twopenny loaf became smaller and smaller. Price fixing usually made matters worse instead of better and inevitably led to the emergence of a black market and widespread concealment of available stocks. A more successful device was to store supplies in public granaries and to sell them to the poor below market price in time of dearth.[59] The creation of such granaries, unfortunately, did not become a regular policy until the eighteenth century, when it was adopted by the Prussian state.[60] Another expedient was to appropriate public funds for purchases abroad and to sell the imported grain at a loss in the local market. The result was usually to relieve the situation, to lower prevailing prices, and to bring stocks out of hiding. In many instances panicky authorities were only goaded into action by the fear of mob violence and then proceeded to seize stocks and to find scapegoats among minor offenders.[61]

The public authorities, for all their inefficiency, probably achieved some measure of success in avoiding worse troubles. I am convinced that the problem was not one that could have been solved by reliance on the

[57] An excellent monograph provided with a valuable bibliography is the following: Hans Conrad Peyer, *Zur Getreidepolitik oberitalienischer Städte im 13. Jahrhundert* (Vienna: Universum, 1950). Other studies of the same kind are: H. G. von Rundstedt, *Die Regelung des Getreidehandels in den Städten Südwestdeutschlands und der deutschen Schweiz im späteren Mittelalter und im Beginn der Neuzeit* (Stuttgart: W. Kohlhammer, 1930) and L. Klaiber, *Beiträge zur Wirtschaftspolitik oberschwäbischer Reichsstädte im ausgehenden Mittelalter* (Stuttgart: Kohlhammer, 1927).

[58] Examples abound. For Belgium, see Verlinden *et al.*, art. cited in n. 56, above, p. 185; for Germany, see Klaiber, *Beiträge*, p. 62; for France, see Gustave Fagniez, *Documents relatifs à l'histoire de l'industrie et du commerce en France*, (2 vols.; Paris: Alphonse Picard, 1898–1900), II, 291, No. 164; for England, Ashley, *English Economic History*, I, Part I, 188–89; for Italy, Peyer, *Zur Getreidepolitik*, p. 145.

[59] Example in Basel during the fifteenth century: Hermann Bruder, *Die Lebensmittelpolitik der Stadt Basel im Mittelalter* (Achern im Breisgau, 1909), p. 3.

[60] This is a reference to the *Magazinpolitik*, or ever-normal granary, initiated by Frederick William I, King in Prussia (1713–40) and continued by his son and successor, Frederick the Great (1740–86): R. de Roover, "Monopoly Theory," p. 520. In France beginnings were made with the same policy but did not produce tangible results: Earl J. Hamilton, "Origin and Growth of the National Debt in France and England," *Studi in onore di Gino Luzzatto* (4 vols.; Milan: A. Giuffré, 1950), II, 249.

[61] Enrico Fiumi, "Sui rapporti economici tra città e contado nell'età comunale," *Archivio storico italiano*, CXIV (1956), 58.

New Viewpoints on Familiar Subjects   431

free operation of competition. The theologians of the Spanish school were doubtless overoptimistic in assuming that removal of controls was the best solution in times of critical shortage of essential commodities. As the experience of two world wars has shown, the institution of controls is an unavoidable measure when demand greatly exceeds the available supply at reasonable prices.

The scholastic writers, in their weighty treatises, rarely mention the guilds, but when they do, it is not to praise them for their humanitarian livelihood policy but to blame them for their monopolistic practices. Thus, San Antonino (1389–1459) accuses the clothiers, or *lanaiuoli,* of Florence of paying their workers in truck or in debased coins.[62] In England John Wycliffe (*ca.* 1324–1384) curses the free masons and other craftsmen because they "conspire" together to ask more than a rightful wage and to oppress other men.[63] An equally virulent attack is found in the so-called *Reformation of Emperor Sigismond* (1437); the author of this proposal would abolish all guilds because they abuse their control of town governments to exploit the public.[64]

Monopoly was the essence of the guild system.[65] This statement applies chiefly to the craft guilds, which were associations of small independent masters. They often entered into secret compacts to fix prices at the expense of the consumer. There was, however, another kind of guild—much less common—which was mainly found in the textile industry. Instead of being composed of independent masters it was made up of artificers, such as weavers, dyers, fullers, or finishers, who worked for wages and combined to protect themselves against exploitation by their employers and to obtain better pay. They even went so far as to organize strikes. This second type resembled more closely the modern labor union. It is important to distinguish between these two kinds of guilds.[66] No such distinction was made by the

---

[62] *Summa theologica* (Verona, 1740), Part II, tit. 1 *(De avaritia)*, cap. 17, §§7, 8. The truck system existed also in Lucca (1419): Giovanni Sercambi, *Croniche,* ed. Salvatore Bongi, III (Lucca, 1892), 252. It was found even in Flanders: Henri Pirenne, *Histoire de Belgique,* I (5th rev. ed.; Brussels: M. Lamertin, 1929), 282.

[63] John Wycliffe, *The Grete Sentence of Curs Expounded,* in Thomas Arnold, ed., *Select English Works of Wyclif,* III (Oxford, 1871), 333. Cf. Tawney, *Religion and Capitalism,* pp. 27, 293.

[64] J. B. Ross and Mary M. McLaughlin, eds., *The Portable Medieval Reader* (New York: Viking Press, 1949), pp. 314–15.

[65] Tawney (*Religion,* p. 27) fully admits this point. Cf. Emile Coornaert, *Les corporations en France avant 1789* (3d ed.; Paris: Gallimard, 1941), p. 265.

[66] Niccolò Rodolico, *La democrazia fiorentina nel suo tramonto, 1378–1382* (Bologna: Nicola Zanichelli, 1905), pp. 95 ff.

Raymond de Roover

scholastics, who were not favorably disposed toward any alliances, whether of masters or of workers. Molina, for example, condemns them both indiscriminately as detrimental to the commonweal.[67]

In order to avoid confusion it may be desirable to deal first with the ordinary craft guild of independent artisans, such as bakers, butchers, shoemakers, and so forth. It is often asserted that such guilds set prices supposedly enabling their members to earn a decent living.[68] It cannot be denied that they did so in many cases, but it must be stressed that such action was an abuse, unless the rates established by the guilds had received official sanction.[69]

According to scholastic doctrine the fixing of prices was entrusted to the public authorities, but I have not found that this function was delegated to private interests, such as guilds. In this matter practice corresponded to theory. In England at least the law forbade the guilds to set prices "for their singular profit and to the common hurt and damage of the people"; victualers especially were not permitted to form "confederacies" for this purpose.[70] The same rule prevailed in Germany as long as the territorial princes retained some control over the towns.[71] Thus, in Cologne, according to a decision of 1258, the archbishop retained the right to police the market because the guilds depresssed prices when they bought and raised prices when they sold.[72]

---

[67] *De justitia et jure,* tract. II, disp. 345, §2. I wish to stress the point that accusations of conspiracy were made against both types of guilds, because there has been a confused controversy on this issue: Ernst Kelter, "Die Wirtschaftsgesinnung des mittelalterlichen Zünftlers," *Schmollers Jahrbuch für Gesetzgebung, Verwaltung und Volkswirtschaft im Deutschen Reiche,* LV² (1932), 749–75; Adriaan van Vollenhoven, "Die Wirtschaftsgesinnung des mittelalterlichen Zünftlers: eine Kritik," with rejoinder by Kelter, *ibid.,* LIX (1935), 298–316. Van Vollenhoven errs in assuming that indictments of conspiracy were aimed at only the labor-union type of guild: abundant evidence to the contrary is found in the Italian statutes. Kelter rightly emphasizes that guild policy clashed with municipal policy of abundance and cheapness. Cf. Ugo Froese, *Der Wirtschaftswille im deutschen Hochmittelalter* (Giessen, Konrad Triltsch 1936), pp. 47 ff.

[68] Clune, *Gild System,* p. 56. On the antinomy between subsistence and profit motive as the ruling principle of guild policy see Friedrich Lütge, "Die Preispolitik in München im hohen Mittelater; ein Beitrag zum Streit über das Problem 'Nahrungsprinzip' oder 'Erwerbsstreben,'" *Jahrbuch für Nationalökonomie und Statistik,* CLIII (1941), 162–202.

[69] George Unwin, *The Gilds and Companies of London* (New York: Charles Scribner's Sons, 1909), p. 92; John Clapham, *A Concise History of Britain from the Earliest Times to 1750* (Cambridge, Eng.: University Press, 1951), p. 132.

[70] Statutes of the Realm: 15 Henry VI, c. 6 (1437); 19 Henry VII, c. 7 (1504); and 22 Henry VIII, c. 4 (1531). Cf. Lujo Brentano, "On the History and Development of Gilds," in Toulmin Smith, ed., *English Gilds* (London: Early English Text Society, 1870), pp. cxxxi, cxl, cxlix, clvii.

[71] Kelter, "Wirtschaftsgesinnung," p. 762.

[72] Ernst Kelter, *Geschichte der obrigkeitlichen Preisregelung,* I: *Die obrigkeitliche Preisregelung in der Zeit der mittelalterlichen Stadtwirtschaft* (Jena: Gustav Fischer, 1935), 34. The title of this book is deceptive; it deals chiefly with Cologne.

New Viewpoints on Familiar Subjects 433

Even in Italy municipal statutes usually restrained the guilds from making any secret agreements to keep prices up or down.[73] The best example is perhaps Florence; although it was a stronghold of the guild system, the ordinances of justice of 1293 and later statutes contained provisions outlawing all "conspiracies," monopolies, leagues, or pacts for the purpose of manipulating prices. Delinquents incurred a heavy fine of £1,000 *di piccioli,* although I know of no instance in which this penalty was ever imposed.[74]

This leniency contrasts sharply with the drastic measures taken in Florence to thwart any attempt by the workers in the woolen and silk industries to form brotherhoods. In both these industries the guild was controlled by the master manufacturers or industrial entrepreneurs. The statutes of these industrial guilds most severely proscribed any conjurations, machinations, or conventicles among the artificers and journeymen subject to the guilds' jurisdiction.[75] In 1345 a wool carder, Ciuto Brandini, actually suffered capital punishment, although his only crime was that he had tried to organize a confraternity among his fellow workers.[76] In the indictment he is described as a man of ill fame and foul language and is accused of forming an illegal "congregation," threatening peace and order, and imperiling the life and property of the citizens.[77] Similar conditions existed in other textile centers, not only in Italy, but also beyond the Alps, even in Toulouse, a minor center.[78] In Flanders, around 1300 still the major cloth-producing

[73] Gunnar Mickwitz, *Die Kartelfunktionen der Zünfte und ihre Bedeutung bei der Entstehung des Zunftwesens* (Helsingfors: Centraltryckeriet, 1936), pp. 20 ff. Mickwitz also presents evidence relating to England, France, and Germany.

[74] *Statuti populi et communis Florentiae,* I (Florence, 1778), 302–3, 426–27: ordinamenta justitiae (1293), rubr. 21 and statuta (1415), lib. 3, rubr. 87.

[75] Anna Maria E. Agnoletti, ed., *Statuto dell'Arte della Lana di Firenze, 1317–1319* (Florence: Felice Le Monnier, 1940), pp. 114–15: statute of 1317, lib. 2, art. 19; Umberto Dorini, ed., *Statuti dell'Arte di Por Santa Maria* (Florence: Leo S. Olschki, 1934), pp. 153–54: statute of 1335, rubr. 134. To forbid labor unions this statute invokes the brotherhood of men (!) and the right to work; all artificers are free to exercise their craft without any impediment (*attribuendo libertatem cuilibet artifici de suo misterio exercendo absque impedimento*). This statute was ratified by the Commune to the extent that it contained nothing against (1) the Catholic faith, (2) the usury doctrine, and (3) the antimonopoly legislation (p. 207). The Arte di Calimala or merchants' guild enacted similar provisions against associations of dyers, menders, and finishers. Giovanni Filippi, *L'arte dei mercanti di Calimala in Firenze ed il suo più antico statuto* (Turin, 1889), p. 160: statute of 1301. lib. 5, art. 4.

[76] Rodolico, *Democrazia fiorentina,* pp. 119–20.

[77] The text of the indictment is published by Niccolò Rodolico, *Il popolo minuto* (Bologna: Zanichelli, 1899), pp. 157–60, No. 14.

[78] Rodolico, *Democrazia,* pp. 96–104; Sister Mary Ambrose Mulholland, "Statutes on Cloth-making, Toulouse, 1227," in J. H. Mundy *et al.,* eds., *Essays in Medieval Life and Thought: presented in Honor of Austin P. Evans* (New York: Columbia University Press, 1955), p. 178 (art. 24).

Raymond de Roover

region in Europe, the patricians and clothiers who ran the town governments passed the most cruel legislation to cow the workers, to ban
suspicious assemblies, and to put down strikes.[79] In Ypres the penalty
was blinding and perpetual banishment. In 1280 or 1281 ten strikers
were thus disfigured.[80] This inhuman punishment did not prevent an
outburst which swept the patricians out of power and caused a long
period of unrest. In any case, the evidence is clear. The theory of the
just price was applied also to wages and was used or misused to brand
workers' associations as intolerable conspiracies, even when they were
concealed under the form of religious fraternities.[81]

The general conclusion of this study can be briefly stated. The
scholastics were more favorable to freedom or competition than is
generally assumed. Their hostility toward monopoly was especially
marked. Contrary to a widespread belief they certainly did not rely on
the price system to maintain the social hierarchy. As a matter of fact,
small masters operating under conditions of competition were not
likely to accumulate great wealth. Social status in the Middle Ages
depended chiefly on inequality in the distribution of property, mainly
land, and the levying of dues (feudal payments or tithes) for the
benefit of the ruling classes. There was one exception: in Italy the
merchants and bankers outrivaled the feudal nobility.[82]

RAYMOND DE ROOVER, *Boston College*

[79] The jurist Phillippe de Beaumanoir (1246–96) declares all leagues among artificers to
be illegal: *Coutumes de Beauvaisis*, I, ch. xxx, art. 884 (Paris: Picard, 1899), 446. This passage
is also published in Fagniez, *Documents*, I, 290.

[80] G. Des Marez, "Les luttes sociales à Bruxelles au Moyen Age," *Revue de l'Université de
Bruxelles*, XI (1905–6), 298.

[81] Rodolico, *Democrazia*, p. 116.

[82] After this paper had been read, Fritz Redlich kindly called my attention to a little-known
enactment of Emperor Frederic I (1158) according to which sutlers who sold their wares to
the soldiery at a price higher than the one prevailing in the neighboring markets exposed
themselves to severe punishment, including confiscation of their merchandise, whipping, and
branding with a hot iron on both cheeks. This is a rather drastic way of enforcing competition
and preventing price discrimination! *MGH*, Legum, Sectio IV, I, 241, No. 173, art. 17.

[6]

ECONOMIC THOUGHT OF ISLAM: IBN KHALDUN

> "... who brings forth the green
> pasture and then turns it to
> withered grass."
>
> *The Koran, Sura 87.*

This essay has to do mainly with the economics of Ibn Khaldūn (1332–1406), historian and statesman of prominent Arab descent and medieval Islam's greatest economist, who spent most of his stormy life in northwest Africa and Egypt, engaged either in scholarly undertakings or in judicial and other governmental activities. His economic opinions, apparently the most advanced of those expressed in medieval Islam,[1] are to be found principally in *The Muqaddimah*, originally intended as an introduction to his history (*Kitāb al-ʿIbar*) of the Arab and Muslim world and its pre-Islamic antecedents, though finally transformed into an exposition of the sources of historical change at work in that world.[2] *The Muqaddimah*, initially completed in 1377, continued to be corrected or added to until shortly before the author's death; though manuscript copies were numerous, it was not issued in printed form until in the 1850's.[3]

[1] When medieval Islam terminated does not coincide with when medieval Christendom terminated, for the Arabic world did not experience a Renaissance as did the West. "Until comparatively recent times ... the Arab retained his medieval outlook and habit of mind, and was in no respect more enlightened than his forefathers who lived under the 'Abbasid Caliphate." So concludes Reynold A. Nicholson, in *A Literary History of the Arabs* (Cambridge), 1930, p. 443. Indeed, until the early twentieth century it was commonly believed that the world of Islam was incapable of economic development. See under "tidjāra" (i.e., commerce), *Encyclopedia of Islam*, IV, Leiden, 1934, pp. 750–51. An impression of the religious attitude of Islamic authors toward economic activity may be had from Helmut Ritter, *Das Meer der Seele*, Leiden, 1955.

[2] I have used Franz Rosenthal's splendid, annotated translation of *The Muqaddimah* (3 vols.), London, 1958; it includes the introduction and Book One of Ibn Khaldūn's World History, entitled *Katāb al-ʿIbar*. Selections from *The Muqaddimah* were translated and arranged by Charles Issawi and published as *An Arab Philosophy of History*, London, 1950. The literature relating to Ibn Khaldūn is very extensive. A good account of his "new science of culture" is that of Muhsin Mahdi in *Ibn Khaldūn's Philosophy of History*, London, 1957. Walter J. Fischel's selected bibliography of works by and about Ibn Khaldūn are included in Rosenthal, *op. cit.*, III, pp. 485–512; other items are noted in Rosenthal's "Introduction", *ibid.*, I, pp. xliii–xlv, lxiv–lxv. Hereinafter I shall refer to this work merely by citing the volume number in large Roman numerals; pagination in small Roman numerals in Vol. I refers to Rosenthal's introduction, etc.

[3] On the evolution of the text, together with comments on the manuscripts extant and on the printed editions, see Rosenthal (I, pp. lxxxviii–cix).

What Ibn Khaldūn has to say about economic matters is important not so much because his is esteemed a great mind,[4] or because he was a highly original thinker, or even because he came in time to be looked upon as one who had anticipated a variety of "modern" notions. It is important rather because he had "a deep insight into the essentials of the accumulated knowledge of his time", could evaluate the manifestations of the culture of his day, could reflect faithfully the understanding which contemporary lawyers and jurists had of practical economic and financial matters that normally were not treated in books (I, pp. xliii, lxxxii ff., lxxxvi), and could break with the approaches of earlier writers on economic issues. His economic observations flowed principally from his concern with the rise and fall of ruling dynasties (or the "states" they constituted) and with the role of crafts, together with their acquisition and their correlation with the level of "civilization" or culture. These observations, however, coming at a time when the medieval Muslim world had lost its elan, had little immediate influence; not until much later did their significance begin to be fully appreciated.[5]

I. *Economics in the Islamic Scheme of Science*

Economics, such as it was, did not occupy an important position in the medieval Islamic scheme of science, and the traditional character of Islamic

[4] Rosenthal writes: "Here was a man with a great mind, who combined action with thought, the heir to a great civilization that had run its course, and the inhabitant of a country with a living historical tradition" (I, pp. lxxxvii); and he approves (I, p. cxv) A. J. Toynbee's assessment of Ibn Khaldūn's contribution as "undoubtedly the greatest work of its kind that has ever yet been created by any mind in any time or place". See Toynbee, *A Study of History*, 2d. ed., III (London, 1935), p. 322; also P. A. Sorokin, *Social and Cultural Dynamics*, IV (New York, 1941) on the place of Ibn Khaldūn's cycle theory in the history of such theories. Rosenthal notes also that, while Ibn Khaldūn lacked the equipment to make "original contributions of note to any of the established disciplines" (I, p. xliii), his experience in government and tribal politics was extensive, and he possessed "remarkable detachment" respecting what he observed, together with a markedly realistic outlook and a capacity for ruthless and opportunistic action when essential to his purposes (I, pp. xxxv–lxvi, esp. xxxvi–lii, lxi–lxvi). His experience contributed much more to his thought than did his reading, W. I. Fischel points out in "Ibn Khaldūn's Activities in Mamlūke Egypte (1382–1406)", in Fischel, ed., *Semitic and Oriental Studies* (Berkeley, 1951), p. 104.

[5] While he coupled with his account of the decline of the intellectual sciences in Western Islam a statement that they were flourishing in Christian Europe, he did not comment on this renaissance or attempt to explain it (III, pp. 117–18). A. L. Tibāwī concludes that "the philosophy of (Muslim) education" remained "as al-Ghazālī left it" and that, while Ibn Khaldūn managed to be original about it within the traditional framework, "the philosophy of Muslim education remained on the whole static" after his time. See "The Philosophy of Muslim Education", *Islamic Quarterly*, IV, 1957, pp. 86–89. Inasmuch as education, being the concern of the individual rather than of the state, fell into the hands of the theologians, it could not become dynamic or widespread. See Reuben Levy, *The Social Structure of Islam* (Cambridge, 1957), pp. 298–99; H. A. R. Gibb, *Mohammedanism: An Historical Survey* (2d. ed., New York, 1955), pp. 111–12, also chap. 10. On the organization, etc., of Muslim education, especially in Egypt up to 1250 A.D., see Ahmad Shalaby, *History of Muslim Education*, Beirut, 1954.

society did not make for the improvement of this position. Such attention as was given to "theoretical" economics seems to have been prompted less by an early and persisting interest in taxation[6] than by contact with Greek philosophical and scientific writings, especially those of later Platonic and neo-Platonic orientation,[7] which became known to Arabic scholars and which, though primarily philosophical or natural-scientific in orientation,[8]

---

[8]   E.g., see Abu Yūsuf (Yaʿqūb b. Ibrāhīm), *Le livre de l'impôt foncier (Kitāb al-Kharāj)*, translated and annotated by E. Fagnan, Paris, 1921; Yahyā Ben Ādam, *Taxation in Islam (Kitāb al-Kharāj)*, translated and annotated by A. Ben Shemesh, Leiden, 1958. These works, two of the three that survive of some 21 such compositions, reflect Islamic thought about 800 A.D. at which time the influence of Greek thought had not yet made itself felt; for Yahyā b. Ādam died in 818 A.D., 20 years after Abu Yūsuf (*ibid.*, p. ix). Abu Yūsuf's work, done at the request of the caliph Hārūn al-Rashīd, was judicial (though somewhat casuistical) and hence concerned with the determination of legal rules, he having been an organizer of one of the several Islamic legal schools which emerged in the eighth century. Yahyā b. Ādam's work is a book of Hadīth, or traditions going back to Mohammed, which constitute, along with the Koran, the two main sources of Islamic legal speculation. See *ibid.*, pp. 1–7; also M. J. Kister's comments on the implications of some of these traditions, in *Journal of Economic and Social History of the Orient*, III (1960), pp. 326–34. See also Levy, *op. cit.*, pp. 167–68, 296; references in note 8 below. On the kharāj (i.e., land tax) as well as other taxes and sources of public revenue see Levy, *op. cit.*, pp. 23–24, 58, 303–24; N. P. Aghnides, *An Introduction to Mohammedan Law and Bibliography* (New York, 1916), especially Part II, on "financial theories". On the inter-country diversity of early Islamic taxation see Levy, *op cit.*, chap. 8, and D. C. Dennett, *Conversion and the Poll Tax in Early Islam*, Cambridge, 1950; also Fredde Løkkegaard's monograph relating principally to Iraq, *Islamic Taxation in the Classic Period*, Copenhagen, 1950. On the replacement of tribal by individual ownership under Islam, and its relation to taxation as well as the encouragement of cultivation see Ali Abd Al-Kader, "Land Property and Land Tenure in Islam", *Islamic Quarterly*, V, 1959, pp. 4–11.

[7]   Most of the translations were done between A.D. 800 and A.D. 1000. The translators, usually Christians, translated "from Syriac versions or, less frequently, from the Greek original". Almost all of Aristotle's treatises (with the exception of the *Politics*, which apparently was not much studied in the Imperial Age) as well as the leading dialogues of Plato and the works of later authors and commentators, only some of whose works were known to the West, were translated. See Richard Walzer, *Greek into Arabic: Essays on Islamic Philosophy* (Cambridge, 1962), pp. 5–8, 29–35, 60–128, 142 ff., 220 ff., 236–39; also *idem*, "The Rise of Islamic Philosophy", *Oriens*, III (1950), pp. 1–19. See also De Lacy O'Leary, *Arabic Thought and Its Place in History* (London, 1954), chaps. 1, 4, 6 and *How Greek Science Passed to the Arabs*, London, 1948; Levy, *op cit.*, chap. 10; T. J. de Boer, *The History of Philosophy in Islam*, London, 1933, chaps, 1–3; R. Arnaldez, "Sciences et philosophie dans la civilisation de Bagdad sous les premiers 'Abbāsides", *Arabica*, IX (1962), pp. 357–73.

[8]   While Ethics commanded little attention in late Greek philosophical schools, it did receive considerable attention at the hands of Muslim authors under Greek influence. E.g., see Levy, *op. cit.*, pp. 215–28; Walzer, *Greek into Arabic*, pp. 17, 32, 221–27, 232, 239–45. Islamic philosophical ethics were based essentially on Plato as was Islamic political theory; stress was placed upon the four Platonic virtues (wisdom, temperance, valor, justice), though generosity and a variety of minor virtues associated with major virtues were included in the scheme of virtues (in keeping with Neoplatonic moral philosophy). *Ibid.*, pp. 222–23, 240–41. See also Dwight M. Donaldson, *Studies in Muslim Ethics* (London, 1953), pp. 119, 126–27, 274–75. This stress, as manifested, was not particularly favorable to material progress.

ECONOMIC THOUGHT OF ISLAM   271

eventuated in "a renaissance of Plato's political philosophy in Islam."[9] The rationalistic spirit underlying Greek philosophical inquiry was not entirely absorbed into Islamic science and philosophy, however, and this may have accentuated static elements in Islam. Not only was erudition unduly stressed; Islamic philosophy also was looked upon as a source of support for a Muslim natural theology, and inquiry was constrained in so far as it was believed that Muslim law, based largely upon the divinely inspired Koran and Prophetic Tradition, was essentially immutable.[10] Moreover, the "Mohammedan legal system" itself lacked an "evolutionary outlook on life"; its rules, though not hard and fast enough to prevent all change, especially in the sphere of commerce and extra-canonical administrative law,[11] were rigid enough, at

[9] E. I. J. Rosenthal, *Political Thought in Medieval Islam* (Cambridge, 1958), p. 6. Haroon Khan Sherwani implies that the incentive given to Muslim thought by the translation of Greek authors has been exaggerated. See his *Studies in Muslim Political Thought and Administration* (2d. ed., Lahore 1945), pp. 38–47. See also S. Mahmassani's argument that Muslim jurists, believing the *shari'a* to be of divine origin, were little influenced by Roman law. See his *Falsafat Al-Tashrī Fi Al-Islam* (translated by F. J. Ziadeh, Leiden, 1961), pp. 136–45. Scholarship reveals, however, the presence in Muslim law of a variety of elements of Roman or occidental provenance. E.g., see E. Gräf, *Jagdbeute und Schlachttier im islamischen Recht* (Mainz, 1959), pp. 194 ff., 202, 210 ff., 340 ff.; J. Schacht, *The Origins of Muhammadan Jurisprudence*, Oxford, 1950; E. Tyan, *Histoire de l'organisation judiciaire en pays d'Islam*, 2d. ed., Leiden, 1960.
[10] See Walzer, *Greek into Arabic*, chaps. 1–2, on role of Islamic philosophy. According to E. I. J. Rosenthal (*op. cit.*, p. 6), "the *Falasifa*", Arabic writers who based their study directly on the Greek text, "are strongly under the influence of the Shari'a" (i.e., that which is known as a result of divine revelation) in addition to that of Plato and Aristotle. See also Gibb, *Mohammedanism*, chap. 6; Levy, *op. cit.*, chaps. 4, 6; Aghnides, *op. cit.*, I, Part I; O'Leary, *Arabic Thought*, p. 135. According to G. E. von Grunebaum, *Medieval Islam* (2d. ed., Chicago, 1953), p. 110, "the very urge to have every detail covered by prophetic precedent forced a certain amount of forgery. Modern practices had to be justified or combated, and a *hadīt* was the only weapon to achieve either". On circumstances affecting change in Islamic thought see also *ibid.*, pp. 39–42, 231–32, 253–57, 283, 344; Aghnides, *op. cit.*, pp. 26–29; pp. 12–13 of translation by A. Ben Shemesh, cited in note 6 above; Alfred Guillaume, *Islam* (Harmondsworth, 1954), chap. 5, esp. pp. 91–101. On the extent to which the Muslim legal system was evolutionary see Mahmassani, *op. cit.*, Parts 3–4. See also Majid Khadduri and Herbert J. Liebesny, *Law in the Middle East*, Vol. I, *Origin and Development of Islamic Law*, Washington, D.C., 1955. In reality, of course, Muslim law has proved less immutable in the face of changing conditions than some accounts suggest; see J. N. D. Anderson, *Islamic Law in the Modern World*, New York, 1959.
[11] See Aghnides, *op. cit.*, Part I, chap. 11; Levy, *op. cit.*, chap. 6. Religious or ideological attitudes affected taxation, finance, and other dimensions of Muslim economic life. For example, payment of zakat, the tax intended principally for welfare purposes, has been described as an act of worship; Islamic finance as well as the economic system of Islam has been described as resting, at least in part, upon the sayings and practices of the Prophet. See Sh. Ata Ullah, *Revival of Zakat* (Lahore, n.d.), p. 17; Levy, *op. cit.*, p. 341; S. A. Siddiqi, *Public Finance in Islam* (Lahore, 1952), p. xii; Mazherrudin Siddiqi, *Marxism or Islam* (Lahore, 1954), chaps. 10–11. Actual practices do not, of course, always conform to prescribed standards. See Levy, *op. cit.*, chaps. 6–7; E. Ashtor, on nonconformity of tax practice with theological theory, in "Le coût de la vie dans l'Égypte médiévale", *Journal of Economic and Social History of the Orient*, III (1960), pp. 72–73; also Claude Cahen, "Contribution à l'étude des impôts dans l'Égypte médiévale", *ibid.*, V (1962), pp. 244–78.

272   JOSEPH J. SPENGLER

least in societies dominated as were the Islamic by custom and tradition, to deaden the hope of collective material progress.[12] Furthermore, even though Greek political philosophy, with its emphasis upon rationalistic inquiry, became popular in and after the time of al-Fārābī (died in A.D. 950), its influence upon practice was quite limited at best and did not remain effective even as far east as Persia. Indeed, Muslim penetration into India, though it made Iranian culture, thought, language, and administrative practice dominant there, did not carry with it Greek philosophy, probably because its influence in Persia had diminished and conditions conducive to its spread were not present in Muslim India.[13]

Muslim writers classed "economics" as a practical science, along with politics and ethics, in keeping with a classificatory scheme supposedly originated by Eudemus (pupil of Aristotle) and utilized by Christian authors from Boethius to Thomas Aquinas.[14] Of the nine Muslim (or Koran-oriented)

[12] "The idea of social progress through increase in knowledge is foreign to the Muslim Middle Ages", observes Grunebaum, *op. cit.*, p. 248; cf. p. 257. He identifies but one Muslim author, al Mas'ūdī (d. 957), with a strong belief in scientific progress (*ibid.*, p. 347 n.) and points to the contempt in which the squalid masses were held by the leading castes as a factor contributing to the disinclination of Muslim ruling circles to support technical progress (*ibid.*, pp. 343–44). Koranic injunctions respecting human equality were never more than partially observed. See Levy, *op. cit.*, pp. 53–73.

[13] Grunebaum, *op. cit.*, pp. 202 ff.; Nicholson, *op. cit.*, p. 444. On the tenth century Persian Renaissance, see Soheil M. Afnan, *Avicenna His Life and Works* (London, 1958), chap. 1. The absorption of the caste system of India (exclusive of the kshatriya) into Indian Islam, despite Islam's being in theory an egalitarian theocracy, may be attributable to Iranian influence inasmuch as an explicitly four-class pyramid, together with very little interclass mobility, existed under the Sassanians. See Grunebaum, *op. cit.*, pp. 202–203; Levy, *op. cit.*, pp. 72–74; R. Ghirshman, *Iran* (Harmondsworth, 1954), pp. 309 ff. The caste system under Indian Islam is described in Sir Denzil Ibbetson's classic *Panjab Castes* (Lahore, 1916), based on the Census of 1881 and first published in 1883; see also Murray T. Titus, *Indian Islam* (London, 1930), pp. 168–72, 190–91; S. M. Jaffar, *Some Cultural Aspects of Muslim Rule in India*, Lahore, 1950. In his chapter on castes in India, al-Bērūnī, writing in the early eleventh century, describes the caste system (which he sketches) as the greatest obstacle to Hindu-Muslim "understanding" and remarks that "we Moslems ... stand entirely on the other side of the question, considering all men as equal, except in piety"; but he does not indicate whether those converted to Islam became free of caste ties. See his *India* (translated by Edward C. Sachau), I (London, 1914), pp. 99–104, esp. p. 100. Al-Bērūnī often compares Indian and Greek views, but does not discuss political theory. Such comparisons are not set down, however, by Abul Fazl-I'Allami, in his *Ain-I-Ākbari* (3 vols., translated by H. Blochmann and H. S. Jarrett and revised by D. C. Philpott and Jadu-Nath Sarkar), Calcutta, 1939–48. In this work, a manual of Akbar's empire and a summary of Hindu history, customs, and philosophy, the caste system is briefly described, but not assessed in light of Muslim belief, and comparison "with the systems of Greece and Persia" is declared outside the author's intention. *Ibid.*, III, pp. 126–32, 421–22. Writing as late as 1923, however, J. Stephenson reports that treatises on moral philosophy, by Nasiruddin Tūsī (1200–1274), Persian Muslim assimilator of Platonic and Aristotelian ideas, were still being read in India and Persia. See "The Classification of the Sciences according to Nasiruddin Tusi", *Isis*, V (1923), pp. 329, 331. The widespread use of Persian in Muslim India may have fostered the reading of Tūsī's work. On his views see below.

[14] See Stephenson, *op. cit.*, pp. 334–36; Rosenthal, *Political Thought*, pp. 143, 165, 269. On the classification of sciences by Aristotle (who distinguished theoretical, productive,

ECONOMIC THOUGHT OF ISLAM   273

sciences in vogue in the early Abbasid period (750+) when Baghdad came to outshine all but Constantinople, only jurisprudence (fiqh) and "sciences" concerned with the interpretation of the Koran and of "Apostolic Tradition" (hadīth) were at all likely to be confronted by economic questions (e.g., taxation), and then in an administrative or ethical guise.[15] Even so, the "Muslim sciences" could influence the way Muslim writers theorized about economic issues, for authority carried weight in the Islamic world, and in the ideal Muslim state (an egalitarian, lay theocracy, or as some prefer, "nomocracy") all spheres of life (including the economic) were interrelated and under the governance of Divine Law as expressed in Koran, Sunnah, and Hadīth.[16]

---

and practical sciences, with ethics and politics the main practical branches) and later writers, see George Sarton, *Introduction to the History of Science*, III (Baltimore, 1927), pp. 76–77; also John H. Randall, Jr., *Aristotle*, New York, 1960, chaps. 3, 12–13. Al-Fārābī's treatment of the sciences has recently been translated by A. G. Palencia as *Catálago de las Ciencias*, Madrid, 1953. On his and Avicenna's treatment see also Hilmi Ziya Ülken, *La Pensée de L'Islam* (translated by G. Dubois, Max Bilen, and the author, Istanbul, 1953), chaps. 22–23, esp. pp. 398–414, 430–35. Ülken touches on the sciences in his accounts of several other authors. Averroes, following Aristotle, described politics as a practical science of action. See E. I. J. Rosenthal (trans.), *Averroes' Commentary on Plato's Republic* (Cambridge, 1956), pp. 111–12, 150–51, 255, 264. Al-Ghazālī gave politics a partially religious orientation. See his *The Book of Knowledge* (translated by N. A. Faris) (Lahore, 1962), pp. 27–30. Much of Al-Ghazālī is in summary form in G. H. Bousquet, *Ihyā' 'Oloum ed-Dīn ou vivification des sciences de la foi*, Paris, 1955. *The Book of Knowledge* is the first book in the first part of the *Ihyā'*, the second part of which deals with economic and other ethics.

[15] On these sciences and changes in Muslim classifications, see Grunebaum, *Islam* (No. 4 of Comparative Studies of Cultures and Civilizations, edited by Robert Redfield and Milton Singer, Memoirs of the American Anthropological Association, April, 1955), chaps. 5, 9. See also Levy, *op. cit.*, pp. 150, 215–41, chap. 10; Franz Rosenthal, *A History of Muslim Historiography* (Leiden, 1952), pp. 28–48; Mahdi, *op. cit.*, pp. 82 ff., 139–46; Nicholson, *A Literary History of the Arabs*, pp. 282–84, also 362–64; E. G. Browne, *Literary History of Persia*, I (Cambridge, 1929), pp. 383–88; M. Plessner, *Die Geschichte der Wissenschaften im Islam* (Philosophie und Geschichte, No. 31), Tübingen, 1931; L. Gardet and M. M. Anawati, *Introduction à la théologie musulmane* (Paris, 1948), pp. 101–24 on "le Kalām et les sciences musulmanes".

[16] See Grunebaum's description of government in Islam as envisaged in classical, medieval Islamic political science, *Islam*, chap. 7; also Louis Gardet, *La cité musulmane; vie sociale et politique* (Paris, 1954), esp. Parts I–II, and E. I. J. Rosenthal's evaluation of this work in the *Islamic Quarterly*, II (1955), pp. 237–39. On the role of authority in and before Islamic times see A. L. Tibāwī, "The Idea of Guidance in Islam", *ibid.*, III (1956), pp. 139–56. Indicative of the economically regulatory role of Islam in urban centers are the manuals designed to guide the muhtasib (or censor) in the definition and performance of his religio-political duties. Among the few of these manuals known today is one influenced by Ghazālī (see Donaldson, *op. cit.*, pp. 160 ff.) and others, the *Ma'ālim al-Qurba*, by Ibn al Ukhuwwa, probably an Egyptian, who died in 1329 A.D. This work, translated and edited by Reuben Levy, in the E. J. W. Gibb Memorial Series, No. 12, n.s., was published in the original and translated in 1938 (Cambridge). On the role of the muhtasib see Levy, *Social Structure of Islam*, pp. 333–39; also under "sinf" (gild) in the *Encyclopedia of Islam* (Leiden, 1934), IV, pp. 436–37; also Grunebaum, *Islam*, pp. 137–38, where it is indicated that the muhtasib "is the successor of the agoranomos of the Greek and Hellenistic cities". See also *ibid.*, chap. 8, on Muslim town structure.

These sciences could thus govern what questions were asked and how they were asked, at least so long as the author was carrying on his inquiry in terms of the ideal rather than of the actual Muslim world; they could thus freeze inquiry except in so far as Muslim science and ideals underwent change.[17] In Ibn Khaldūn's case escape lay in his concern with the real rather than with the ideal Muslim world.

Economic matter did not go undiscussed. Economic activity being subject to such constraints as flowed from the Koran (e.g., against *riba*, signifying profit or interest) or from the *sunnah* (i.e., Mohammed's sayings, deeds, or tacit approvals), the implications of the supposed constraints were examined.[18] These examinations did not involve explicit economic analysis, of course; they had to do rather with the content of economically-oriented regulations based upon the Koran and the sunnah. The significance of these constraints seems to have been delineated principally in compilations of traditions, of which there were a great many,[19] and in manuals for the guidance of the muḥtasib, who enforced religious and moral precepts. In a leading such manual, the *Ma'ālim al-Qurba* (whose author died in A.D. 1329), concerned with preventing illegal acts and with enforcing "what is due" to God or man, conditions essential to the legal conduct of commerce and of some seventy

[17]   At least one major author, al-Ghazālī, classifies politics (in conjunction with which he treats economic matters) as one of the sciences connected with religion as were also metaphysics, ethics, and psychology. See Sherwani, *op. cit.*, pp. 155–56; al-Ghazālī, *The Book of Knowledge*, pp. 27–30, 36–41, 45–46, 53–54, and the third book, in the second part of the Ihyā', dealing with "The Ethics of Earnings and Livelihood". Muslim thought did not, of course, remain completely static any more than does any system of thought, though the changes probably were not of significance for economic science until modern times. On the susceptibility of Muslim thought to change see Gibb, *op. cit.*, passim; J. Hans, *Dynamik und Dogma in Islam*, Leiden, 1960; Ülken, *La Pensée de L'Islam*; W. C. Smith, *Islam in Modern History* (New York, 1961), chaps. 1–2; J. M. S. Baljon, *Modern Moslem Koran Interpretation* (Leiden, 1961), esp. pp. 116–18 on *riba* (interest); Jacques Austruy, *L'Islam face au développement économique*, Paris, 1961.

[18]   See, for example, A. J. Wensinck, *A Handbook of Early Muhammadan Tradition* (Leiden, 1927), esp. under alms, barter, coins, credit, debts, usury, wealth.

[19]   Illustrative are the sections "On Selling", in the *Al-Sahīh* (Cairo, 1334 A.H.), by Abu al-Husayn Muslim al-Nīsābūri (206–261 A.H.), one of two such authentic compilations. See S. Mahmassani, *op. cit.*, pp. 71–72. For example, Muslim insists on the importance of a buyer's examining an article prior to its sale and he lays down various conditions which must be present before higgling can eventuate in a valid sale. Cheating is described as unjust. The sale of unripened crops is forbidden since such a transaction might involve speculation or usury which is forbidden. While rent of land for money was permitted, rent for a share of the crops was prohibited inasmuch as such arrangement involved speculation and risk. It was permissible, however, to collect 0.2–0.5 of the crops on land owned by Jews and Christians in areas invaded by Muslims. Trade in wine and pork was prohibited as were transactions involving futurity *and* interest. Monopoly was prohibited since it involved excessive profits. Sale to a non-partner of a partner's share of property owned in partnership is permissible only in the event a partner does not want it at the going price. See Vol. I, pp. 600–42. North African ulema ranked Muslim's compilation most worthy after the Koran. Mahmassani, *op. cit.*, p. 72. On trading companies, profit distribution, etc., see *"Shirka"*, *Encyclopedia of Islam*, IV, pp. 380–81.

activities or occupations are set down. Many commercial transactions are forbidden, among them usury, invalid hire and partnership, transactions involving unsanctioned futurity and (hence) speculation or interest, and sales or purchases which violate ritual or fail to meet all determinants of legality. Various actions bearing upon exchange (e.g., debasement of coinage, fraudulent misrepresentation, use of false weights or measures, adulteration, forestalling, and hoarding) are also prohibited. *Ribā* (illicit gain) "is forbidden by God. Brokers who deal in money and traders in foodstuffs must beware of it, for only in money and foodstuffs is there *ribā*. The money-changer must not grant credit and receive increment". "To earn a livelihood by money-changing involves great risk to those who engage in it". "Any loan bringing benefit [to the lender] is unlawful". Regarding the fixation of prices by agents of the state opinion varied; the muḥtasib could not fix "the prices of commodities in opposition to the owners", but the imam could or might determine such prices.[20] Chapters relating to various trades, crafts, and professions have to do with hygiene, prevention of adulteration, assurance of craft or professional skill, and the honesty and integrity of practitioners, and so on.[21]

Economic matters were touched upon also in other works. In the tenth century, if not earlier, tracts were devoted to the conduct of commercially oriented crafts[22] of which, as Ibn Khaldūn's and other reports suggest, there

[20]   The above statements are based on Ukhuwwa's *Ma'ālim al-Qurba*, pp. 6–29, 40–43, 46–47. See also *Encyclopedia of Islam*, under "riba" (*ibid.*, III, pp. 1148–50), and "tidjara" (*ibid.*, IV, pp. 747–50), and "sarf" or money-changing (*ibid.*, IV, p. 169). According to W. J. Fischel, *Jews in the Economic and Political Life of Medieval Islam* (London, 1937), p. 13, tenth-century Arab sources "reveal a prodigious desire to accumulate money" and great fear of losing it.

[21]   *Ma'ālim al-Qurba*, pp. 30–40, 43–68, 89–98. See also Levy, *Social Structure of Islam*, pp. 220, 255–58, 336–38. "These various restrictions upon normal commerce have either been openly disregarded by many Muslims, so that trade has been carried on according to local custom, or have led to the adoption of subterfuges and legal fictions in order that the letter of the law might be observed while transactions went forward as necessity and custom demanded." *Ibid.*, p. 256, also pp. 257–58 on evasive expedients and dependence upon the protection of custom. See also "riba", *Encyclopedia of Islam*, IV, p. 1150; Mahmassani, *op. cit.*, pp. 119–26, 154–55, 203–04. Despite their evasion of religious restrictions on finance and speculation, Muslim merchants were handicapped thereby, R. S. Lopez concludes. See his account in M. Postan and E. E. Rich, eds., *The Cambridge Economic History of Europe*, II (Cambridge, 1952), pp. 283–88. On medieval Arab letters of credit, government borrowing, and insecurity of wealth, see Fischel, *Jews in . . . Islam*, pp. 13–29, 73, 87, also Claude Cahen, "Un traité financier inédit d'époque Fatimide-Agyubide", *Journal of the Economic and Social History of the Orient*, V (1962), pp. 139–59. See note 30 below.

[22]   See Browne, *Literary History*, I, pp. 378–83; Sarton, *op. cit.*, III, pp. 1771–72; Solomon Gandz's note on "The Rule of Three in Arabic and Hebrew Sources", *Isis*, XXII (1934), pp. 219–22. This rule is discussed in Arabic algebras (which usually contained a chapter on business transactions even as did European works), apparently having been introduced (along with loan words describing "general, fixed market" prices and individual prices arrived at through higgling) by Aramaic-speaking merchants trading directly or indirectly with Arabs, Persians, and Hindus centuries before Islamic times. Gandz refers particularly to an early ninth-century Arabic algebra. Ibn Khaldūn refers to a number of Spanish Muslim business arithmetics (III, pp. 126–27). See also H. Ber-

276   JOSEPH J. SPENGLER

were many.[23] The "Mirrors for Princes", introduced into Arabic literature
from Persia in the eighth century, sometimes included, besides general matter
on the art of government and pleas for "justice" and the subjects' "welfare",
discussions relating to taxation and other economic questions.[24] "Economics",
when introduced into the Muslim scheme, was little more than household
management, though as set out in the Neopythagorean *"Bryson"* rather than
as in Aristotle's *Politics* (in which household management is treated), which
apparently was not known to the *Falāsifa* though they drew on Aristotle's
Ethics[25] and on some of Plato's political writings.[26] While the analytical

---

nadelli, "The Origins of Modern Economic Theory", *Economic Record*, XXXVII, 1961,
pp. 320–38.
[23] How numerous, varied, and specialized were crafts in Muslim parts of the Mediterranean area is suggested by S. D. Goitein's "The Main Industries of the Mediterranean
Area as Reflected in the Records of the Cairo Geniza", *Journal of the Economic and
Social History of the Orient*, IV (2), 1961, pp. 168–99. Specialization in food supply
did not, of course, insure hygiene (*ibid.*, pp. 194–95), the absence of which, however,
seems to have exacted heaviest toll among the holy, Tomas of Margâ's account of the
death of Rabban Gabriel suggests. "And the holy man fell ill of a disease of the bowels
and suffered from diarrhoea for four months, like the majority of holy men who have
departed and will depart from the world." See *The Book of Governors: The Historia
Monastica of Thomas, Bishop of Margâ A.D. 840* (translated from the Syriac by E. A.
W. Budge), II (London, 1893), p. 680. The tenth-century Pure Brethren, while defining
those trades as essential, dignified the work of all tradesmen by noting that each imitated
the Creator. See Y. Marquet, "La place du travail dans la hiérarchie ismâ'ilrenne
d'après l'Encyclopédie des Frères de la Pureté", *Arabica*, VIII (1961), pp. 232–36.
[24] E. I. J. Rosenthal, *Political Thought*, pp. 3, 41, 50, 63–83, 221–22, 249, 251–56;
G. Richter, *Studien zur Geschichte der Alteren Arabischen Fürstenspiegel*, Leipzig, 1932.
Two late eleventh-century "mirrors" have been translated into English: Kai Kā'ūs ibn
Iskander, *A Mirror for Princes* (The Qābūs-nāma), translated by Reuben Levy, London,
1951; Nizam al-Mulk, *The Book of Government or Rules for Kings* (The Siyāsat-nāma),
translated by Hubert Darke, London, 1960. Moderateness in taxation and rent collection
is counseled in the latter (chaps. 4–7, 37) while in the former advice is given respecting
buying and selling, the use of wealth, and the conduct of agriculture, merchandising, and
other crafts (pp. 90–95, 109–11, 211–12, 156–65, 237–39). The counsel is expressed
quite simply, and without analysis. Economic matter was not included in *Le Livre de
L'Agriculture* (Kitab al-Felahah), by Ibn al-ʿAwāmm, translated from the Arabic by
J. J. Clement-Mullet and published in Paris in 1864. This work was composed in Seville
in the twelfth century A.D. (*ibid.*, I, preface, pp. 17–18) and was known to Ibn Khaldūn
(see III, pp. 151–52).
[25] Some knew the *Topica* or the *Rhetoric* but did not find therein a basis for developing a theory of the margin. E.g., see my "Aristotle on Imputation and Related Matters",
Southern Economic Journal, XXI (1955), pp. 371–89. There were Arabic translations of
the first book of *Economics*, wrongly attributed to Aristotle, and of "the book of Rufus"
possible the work of a Philodemus. See under "tadbīr", *Encyclopedia of Islam*, IV,
p. 595.
[26] E. I. J. Rosenthal, *Political Thought*, pp. 143, 165, 187, 269, 285, 295, 300; Afnan,
op. cit., pp. 231–32. The role of the unidentified Greek, "Bryson", or "Brason", or
Brasson (Brússon), whose work was unknown to the West, is treated by Martin Plessner
in *Der OIKONOMIKOC des Neupythogoreers 'Bryson' and sein Einflusz auf die Isla-
mische Wissenschaft*, Heidelberg, 1928; see pp. 1–8 on "Bryson" and pp. 9–143 on the
translations and their influence; texts and translations are given, pp. 144–274. An annotated English translation setting the work in its late Hellenistic context is needed. On

ECONOMIC THOUGHT OF ISLAM   277

aspects of commerce were largely neglected, its conduct was described, trading having been approved in the Koran (which probably reflected commercial Mecca), with Arab traders ranging eastward from the homeland through South Asia to China and southward to Mombasa.[27] Moreover, ethical implications of trade came to command increasing attention, and trade itself was declared subject to restraint, even in Muhammad's day, on the ground it might entail behavior inimical to man's eternal salvation.[28] There was also much interest in geography, in part because of interest in trade and because the vast extent of the Muslim world permitted wide and varied travel which yielded geographic as well as economic information.[29] Arab historical works contributed little to economic analysis, in part because history was not a science according to the canons which the Muslims took over from the Greeks.[30]

Platonism among the Arabs see Franz Rosenthal, "On the Knowledge of Plato's Philosophy in the Islamic World", *Islamic Culture*, XIV (1940), pp. 387–422.

[27] On the highly commercial character of pre-Islamic Mecca, see Henri Lammens, *La Mecqua à la Veille de L'Hégire* (Beirut, 1924), chaps. 8–13. P. Grierson notes, however, that in Arabia in Muhammad's time payments were made mostly in bullion. See "The Monetary Reforms of 'Abd Al-Malik", *Journal of the Economic and Social History of the Orient*, III (1960), p. 257. See also Grunebaum, *Medieval Islam*, pp. 215–17; also P. K. Hitti, *History of the Arabs* (2d. ed., London, 1940), pp. 58–59 on traders in Southern Arabia in pre-Islamic times. When Mohammad clothed his theology in the language of trade, he reflected the generations-old commercial background of his city and people who readily comprehended Koranic statements which described the mutual relations between Allah and man in marketing and accounting terminology. See Lammens, *op. cit.*, pp. 216–20; Charles C. Torrey, *The Commercial-Theological Terms in the Koran* (Leiden, 1892), esp. pp. 2–6, 35–36, 46–50; also E. Cohn, *Der Wucher in Qor'an, Chedith und Fiqh*, Berlin, 1903; F. Arin, *Recherches Historiques sur les Opérations Usuraires et Aléatoires en Droit Musulman*, Paris, 1929.

[28] See under "tidjāra" (commerce) in *Encyclopedia of Islam*, IV, p. 747.

[29] C. R. Beazley, *The Dawn of Modern Geography*, London, 1897, pp. 393–468; Nicholson, *op. cit.*, pp. 356–57; Charles Issawi, "Arab Geography and the Circumnavigation of Africa", *Osiris*, X (1952), pp. 117–28. Mahdi, *op. cit.*, pp. 142–43. New acquaintance with Greek geographical works also stimulated Muslim interest in geography. *Ibid.*, pp. 142–43.

[30] In his preface to his *Journal d'un bourgeois du Caire* (Paris, 1945), an annotated translation of Ibn Iyas's chronicle of events in 1501–1510, Gaston Wiet comments on the "disconcerting incuriosity" of Arab authors respecting economic events. On historiography see F. Rosenthal, *Muslim Historiography*, pp. 29–31–47. Rosenthal (*ibid.*, p. 46) refers to a certain wazir, Ibn Al-Tiqtaqa ("the rapid talker"), who disliked having "the ruler study historical works, since they might teach him to exploit his subjects on his own and to dispense with the services of the wazir". See his *Al Fakrhi* (translated by C. E. J. Whitting, London, 1947), p. 3. This wazir's political theory resembled both that of Ibn Khaldū (who was not affected thereby) and the Indian thesis that a ruler owes his subjects protection in exchange for their allegiance and support. See E. I. J. Rosenthal, *Political Thought*, pp. 62–67. Information on taxation, banking, etc., is to be found in some historical works. E.g., see *The Eclipse of the Abbasid Caliphate*, by Miskawaihi (d. 1030 A.D.) and translated by H. F. Amedraz and D. S. Margoliouth, Oxford, 1921; also Gaston Wiet's translation, "Le traité des famines de Maqrīzī", *Journal of the Economic and Social History of the Orient*, V (1962), pp. 1–90, on crop failure, famine, taxation, and depreciation of money.

278   JOSEPH J. SPENGLER

Turning now parenthetically to the so-called "Bryson", the source of Greek inspiration, we find him dealing with economic questions in terms of the household (which includes, besides the head, four additional elements, money, servants or slaves, wife, and children) and of division of labor on a craft basis, and with the acquisition, conservation, and use of property. The practitioner of each craft depends for most of his needs upon the practitioners of other crafts (or professions) and disposes of most of his services to these practitioners. The crafts are thus interrelated as links in a chain, with no one craft capable of overwhelming the others. Out of this reciprocal interdependence arises the city wherein the crafts are gathered so that each can more readily serve others and be served by them. This interdependence also gives rise to the requirement of money (gold, silver, copper) to serve (so moderns would say) as means of exchange, unit of account, and store of value; for the wants and supplies of individuals are not always so synchronized that each can obtain what he needs at once when he needs it and simultaneously have available for its purchase products of his own craft in immediately salable form. Money overcomes this lack of synchronization. Bryson counsels the householder or craftsman to avoid various undesirable forms of behavior (among them avarice, niggardliness, waste, snobbery, and mismanagement) and to guard his property by prudently spending his income and investing part of it. The householder should not spend more than he earns, lest he reduce his capital. He must save in order to be able to meet unfavorable events as well as to increase his capital; he must avoid ventures which he is incapable of carrying out and he must not allow his invested money to remain long out of his hands. He should confine his selling to his wares even though they yield little profit and he might turn a profit by selling his immobile property. The buying and management of different types of slaves is discussed, along with the role of the wife, her duties and her contribution to the administration of the household, and various aspects of the business of rearing and educating children and launching them on careers.[31]

The views of Bryson are sometimes reflected as may be those of Plato (on whom Bryson drew in part) in Muslim accounts of the genesis of state and economy. Indeed, it has been said that "the whole economic literature of Islam can be traced to the *Economics* of Bryson".[32] Allegedly among the earliest of the Muslim authors so influenced was Ibn Abi'r-Rabiʿ, supposedly

---

[31] See Plessner's translation, in *op. cit.*, pp. 214 ff. The lot of the slave seems to have been easier under Islam than in late Greek times. E.g., see on slavery in Islam, Levy, *Social Structure of Islam*, pp. 73–89; S. D. Goitein, "Slaves and Slavegirls in the Cairo Geniza Records", *Arabica*, IX (1962), pp. 1–20.

[32] See "Tadbīr", *Encyclopedia of Islam*, IV (Leiden, 1934), pp. 595. Plessner identifies a number of the authors influenced by Bryson in *op. cit.*, pp. 29–49, 104–43. Miskawaih (died A.D. 1030) includes a reference to Bryson's discussion of child-rearing in his moral philosophy based largely on Galen and commentators on Plato and Aristotle. See Walzer, *Greek into Arabic*, pp. 220–22.

ECONOMIC THOUGHT OF ISLAM   279

a ninth-century philosopher.[33] He traces "wages, prices, profit and loss and all other economic phenomena", together with rural-urban population distribution, to man's inclination to co-operative action and to his inability to satisfy his wants other than through "mutual help and co-operation"; and (with Plato) he observes that justice "consists in placing everything in its proper place and giving everyone his due."[34] Al-Fārābī, tenth-century founder of Arabic political philosophy, has little to say of economic issues as such, though his discussion of household and city (in organic terms) may reflect Bryson and the view that the state has its origin in mutual need.[35] His account of division of labor in the "ideal city" emphasizes that each citizen must limit himself to "a single art", since men differ in aptitude, improve skills with practice, and are capable of supplying all needs only if each is responsible for a specific assignment.[36] Al-Fārābī does not examine the relationship of specialization to prices, distribution, and the use of money, though he indicates that each individual is entitled to his deserts or portion and that support should be provided for priests, secretaries, etc., and possibly for certain needy.[37] His neglect of economics and economic issues may reflect his view that the household and various other groupings are inferior to the state.[38]

---

[33] Sherwani, op. cit., p. 46. Plessner, however, assigns this author to the thirteenth century. Op. cit., pp. 32–34. D. M. Dunlop convincingly shows he came after al-Fārābī. See Dunlop's annotated translation of al-Fārābī's Fusūl Al-Madani, Cambridge, 1961, pp. 5–7.

[34] See Sherwani's summary, op. cit., pp. 49–50, 55. Ibn Abī'r-Rabī' advocates that agriculture, because of its importance, be taxed lightly, and that state expenditure fall short of state income. Ibid., pp. 50, 59. The role of slavery, together with public and private uses of "wealth", is discussed in ibid., pp. 58–60. Giving each "his due" is enjoined, within limits, in The Koran, 17, 24 ff., also 30. See translation by N. J. Dawood of The Koran (Penguin Classics, Harmondsworth), pp. 229, 189. For a somewhat different translation see A. J. Arberry, The Koran Interpreted (London, 1955), II, pp. 108–09; I, p. 305.

[35] See Fusūl Al-Madanī, (cited in note 33 above), pp. 36–37, 82. See also E. I. J. Rosenthal, Political Thought, pp. 125–29, 273–74; Sherwani, op. cit., pp. 86–91, also 76–78 on al-Fārābī's anticipation of Hobbes's compact theory.

[36] Fusūl, pp. 55–56. The function of habit is not discussed at this point though the role of habit in fixing virtue in the individual is treated earlier. Ibid., pp. 31–33. Love as well as mutual need bind the components of a city together. Ibid., pp. 36–37, 53–54.

[37] Ibid., pp. 54–55, 56–57. Al Fārābī distinguished between the ideal city or state to which the comments above apply and alternative theoretical and actual forms. Ibid., pp. 39, 55, 82; also F. Dieterici, Die Staatsleitung von Alfarabi (Leiden, 1904), pp. 50–89, and his translation, Der Musterstaat (Leiden, 1904), of al-Fārābī's account of the model state, esp. pp. 84–128. See also E. I. J. Rosenthal, Political Thought, pp. 126–28, 133, 135–37. Plato had mentioned support of priests and secretaries in his Politicus, 290 A–E.

[38] Sherwani, op. cit., pp. 75–76; E. I. J. Rosenthal, Political Thought, pp. 118, 165, 269. Avempace (d. 1138) played down economics as a science even as did al-Fārābī. Ibid., pp. 118, 165, 269. Averroes (1126–98) also subordinated economics to politics. See E. I. J. Rosenthal, "The Place of politics in the Philosophy of Ibn Bājja (Avempace)", Islamic Culture, XXV (1951), pp. 199 ff., and Averroes' Commentary, pp. 150–51, 264–65. Averroes, perhaps reflecting Bryson's influence, came close to expressing a nominalist view of money. Ibid., pp. 148–49, 211–12, 286–87.

Avicenna (980–1037), Al-Ghazālī (1058–1111), Nasīr al-Dīn Tūsī (1201–74), and Tūsī's vulgarizer, Al-Dawwānī (1427–1501), in their treatment of household economics as a separate science, reflect Bryson's influence as well as that of Aristotle and Plato (in respect to ethics and politics). Society as envisaged in Avicenna's work is a controlled hierarchy, with government flowing out of the co-operatively satisfiable needs of men, with commercial and other interpersonal transactions highly regulated, with provision for the support of both the disabled and the general welfare, and with households conducted in conformity with Bryson's counsel.[39] Ghazālī, noting that cities and the state arose out of the advantages men derived from division of labor and co-operation and that each should engage in a useful activity, points to the importance of unencumbered trade and exchange and the need for money to facilitate it.[40] Tūsī (of Asian origin as were Ghazālī, al-Fārābī, Avicenna, and Al-Dawwānī), allegedly treacherous adviser to Hulagu (destroyer of Baghdad),[41] followed Bryson quite closely;[42] his exposition was subsequently epitomized and popularized by Al-Dawwānī.[43]

Book II of Al-Dawwānī's work, on "the domestic state", has to do primarily with constituents of the household and their management, with the wives, children, slaves and servants, and income and property. Income was to be had from the professions and crafts, from agriculture, and from trade, though some held that the dependence of trade upon capital made it a more precarious source of income. "Mean" occupations and iniquitous and infamous sources of income were to be avoided, and "affluence" (than which "no" worldly "station . . . is better") was to be sought, if possible, in a profession comprehending "equity" and "not far removed from temperance and refinement." Moderateness in expenditure was counseled, together with saving

---

[39] Plessner, *op. cit.*, pp. 42–47; E. I. J. Rosenthal, *Political Thought*, pp. 143, 151–54, 239, 269, 285; Afnan, *Avicenna*, pp. 230–32.

[40] *The Book of Knowledge*, pp. 27–30, 146; Sherwani, *op. cit.*, pp. 154–55, 157–62, also p. 171 on the necessity that taxation be conducted in full compliance with the law. See also Plessner, *op. cit.*, pp. 131–36; E. I. J. Rosenthal, *Political Thought*, pp. 39, 239. In keeping with the widely accepted Muslim view that trade and craftsmanship are honorable sources of livelihood, and with his own view that their pursuit provided support in this world and access to the next world, Ghazālī believed, Grunebaum states, that only "the ascete, the mystic, the scholar, and the public official are exempt from the duty of earning bread by the work of their hands or by commerce". See Grunebaum, *Medieval Islam*, p. 215. "The markets", wrote Ghazālī, "are God's tables and whoever visits them will receive from them". Cited in *ibid.*, p. 215. For other favorable views of trade and crafts, see *ibid.*, pp. 215–18. His nominalist view of money clearly reflects Bryson's influence. See G.-H. Bousquet, "La monnaie selon un mystique musulman du XIᵉ siècle", *Revue d'économie politique*, LXIII (1935), pp. 238–40.

[41] Browne, *op. cit.*, II, pp. 12–13, 456–57, 484–86.

[42] Plessner, *op. cit.*, pp. 62–104. "Tūsī's *Economics* was regarded for all-time in Islam as the final model". See "Tadbīr", *Encyclopedia of Islam*, IV (Leiden, 1934), p. 595. Some of Tūsī's work was known to Ibn Khaldūn (I, xlv; III, 148, 315).

[43] *Ibid.*, pp. 104 ff.; E. I. J. Rosenthal, *Political Thought*, pp. 211–13, 246–47, 299–301. Al-Dawwānī's work was translated into English by W. F. Thompson, under the title, *Practical Philosophy of the Mohammedan People*, London, 1839.

and diversification of the investment of savings. Among the expenditures approved, besides those upon household needs, were alms, presents designed to win favors, and what amounts to "protection" and blackmail.[44] Efficient conduct of household affairs entailed the use in transactions of money, "the guardian of equity and the minor arbitrator of life", in part because its use in place of barterable commodities saved considerable transport cost.[45]

Al-Dawwānī, following Tūsī closely, developed the equity-maintaining role of money in Book I, concerned primarily with "the individual state" and ethics. Money, in its capacity as unit of account, intermediated as a common denominator between producers of unlike goods and thereby facilitated their interchange. Money could perform this role, however, only if "rectitude" and "discipline" (order) were maintained by the Prince and under "the holy institute of God".[46] Equity required also that each member of an economic class (principally bureaucratic personnel, rhetoricians, computing experts, soldiers, and suppliers of food, clothing, etc.) "be kept in his appropriate position" and so be enabled to become expert therein.[47]

The role of "reciprocal co-operation and interchange", so essential to man's security and support and perfection, is treated in Book III, on "the political state". Men differ in "aim and character" and nature and hence in skill and occupation, with the result that everyone is somewhat dependent upon others and obliged in turn to apply himself for others. In consequence of this need for "reciprocal co-operation", men must congregate in cities and other communities and make provision for government, law, an executive, and currency in order that the maintenance of all may be assured, each may be rendered "content with his rightful portion", and violence and reciprocal injury may be averted.[48]

Greek influence as represented in Bryson's work is present even in a hand-

[44] *Ibid.*, pp. 245–311. "Abrússan" (i.e., Bryson) is referred to in the discussion (pp. 245–50) of the household economy. On the "mean" occupations see R. Brunschvig, "Métiers vils en Islam", *Studia Islamica*, XVI (1962), pp. 41–60.

[45] *Ibid.*, p. 251.

[46] *Ibid.*, pp. 123–29, also pp. 399, 406, on the Prince's equity-preserving role. Equity is described as the paramount virtue, superior even to wisdom, courage, and temperance. *Ibid.*, pp. 52–64, 112 ff., which follow Tūsī closely. Aristotle's geometrical proportion arrangement is employed. *Ibid.*, pp. 124–25.

[47] *Ibid.*, pp. 320, 373–75. Elsewhere he identifies four main occupational classes: men of pen (lawyers, divines, "statisticians" [record-keepers?], etc.); men of business (merchants, artisans, craftsmen); men of sword (soldiers, guardians); and husbandmen, who alone produce what had no previous existence in contrast to the others who add "nothing", merely changing the form, place, or ownership of a thing. *Ibid.*, p. 389. See also *ibid.*, pp. 391–94, for five-fold classification of men based on their ethical qualities. Compare the various class systems mentioned in Levy, *Social Structure of Islam*, chap. 1, esp. pp. 59–71. In a forthcoming study Grunebaum will present evidence that divisions of society into four occupational classes are of Persian ancestry whereas divisions into three are of Greek ancestry. See also note 13 above. Maqrīzī divided the medieval Egyptian population into seven economic classes. See Wiet, "Le Traité...", *loc. cit.*, pp. 71–75.

[48] Al-Dawwānī, *op. cit.*, 318–22, 326–27.

282   JOSEPH J. SPENGLER

book for merchants, *Kitâb al-ishâra ilâ mahâsin al-tijâra*, written in or around
the 12th century[49] by Ja'far al-Dimashqî who treated trade and the accumulation of wealth more favorably than did Ibn Khaldūn.[50] He explains how
man's dependence upon division of labor and co-operation makes necessary
use of a suitable means of exchange (e.g., gold and silver)[51] and he indicates
measures essential to the accumulation and protection of wealth.[52] His main
concern, however, is to provide guidance for three categories of traders (the
wholesaler, the traveling merchant, and the exporter) who live by buying and
selling. Merchants must be able to judge the qualities of the commodities
they handle, to select dependable assistants or associates, to size up price
and market situations, and to protect themselves against spoilage, market
shifts, robbers, rulers, swindlers, etc.[53] They must be familiar with various
kinds of sales (e.g., for cash at specified prices, on instalment plan, etc.);
with the usual supply or "average" prices of the goods they handle, together
with the manner in which these prices fluctuate above and below the usual
level;[54] with changing conditions of supply and demand;[55] and with the arts
of measuring, weighing, counting, and calculating.[56] One profits, in general,
by buying a commodity from one who is not reluctant to sell a good at a
relatively low price and subsequently selling it to one who must have this
commodity.[57] The wholesale merchant must be alert to producer costs,

---

[49]   This influence is present also in Ibn Abī al-Rabī's *Kitâb sulūk al-malik fī tadbīr
al mamâlik*, written in the 13th century. See Helmut Ritter, "Ein arabisches Handbuch
der Handelswissenschaft", *Der Islam*, VII (1917), pp. 9–10.
[50]   For Ritter's translation of this booklet see *ibid.*, 45–91, and for his introduction,
including comments on Bryson's influence, Arabic treatment of commodities, and
Islam's economic ethic, see *ibid.*, pp. 1–45. Dimashqī's title indicates that his booklet
has to do with the virtues and good points of trade, the judging of commodities, and the
tricks of swindlers.
[51]   *Ibid.*, pp. 47–53.
[52]   He who would conserve his wealth spends no more than he takes in, provides against
unforeseen contingencies, refuses to engage in activities for which he is not equipped,
avoids investment in that for which demand is small and irregular (e.g., a scholarly
book), and sells fixed capital instead of commodⱪies only when the profit realizable
from the former sale is very much higher than that on the latter (*ibid.*, pp. 75–77). One
must also avoid waste and guard one's property against confiscation, etc. (*ibid.*, pp. 79–
91) as well as administer it well and be free of the prompting of avarice, niggardliness,
etc. (*ibid.*, pp. 77–79).
[53]   *Ibid.*, pp. 53–54, 56–58, 62–63, 71–75. On the classification of possessions into gold
and silver, commodities, fixed capital, and living creatures (slaves, draft and other
animals) see *ibid.*, pp. 45–46, also Ritter's comments, pp. 16–26. On professional, practical, and mixed occupations other than trade and on earnings based on power see
ibid., pp. 55–61.
[54]   *Ibid.*, pp. 54–56, 59.
[55]   *Ibid.*, pp. 55–56.
[56]   *Ibid.*, p. 62.
[57]   *Ibid.*, pp. 63–65. In his comments on household economy he indicates that foodstuffs
should be bought when plentiful and then stored; that winter clothing should be bought
in summer and summer clothing in winter when prices are low; that slaves, cattle, and
houses should be bought when subsistence is expensive, and land, mills, etc., when

relevant possible changes in supply or demand, and circumstances affecting transport, quality of government, etc.; and he should accumulate his stock over time and thereby avert or minimize losses through sudden price changes. The traveling merchant must know about relevant prices in his own and other countries, about the use of agents, and about the effect of excises on his profits. Exporters must know how to use agents and share profits with them.[58]

In what measure Ibn Khaldūn was influenced by the writings of the authors just passed in review, or by others, is hard to determine. The belief that the state and other human associations emerged because of man's insufficiency as an individual and his consequent need to co-operate apparently was widely held (having been effectively treated in Plato's political works) and must have been known to Ibn Khaldūn. He developed it, together with a solution of the Hobbesian problem,[59] somewhat uniquely and differently than did Avicenna (I, pp. lxxiii–lxxvi), however. Ibn Khaldūn's cycle theory, while it somewhat resembled earlier cycle theories (I, pp. lxxi–lxxxii), was much more effectively developed, and his treatment of imitation and habit were more pertinent than that of writers mentioned earlier. His superior handling of economic matter certainly warrants Plessner's observation that Islamic economics began with Ibn Khaldūn.[60] It remains true, however, that he knew or drew on many sources, among them Fürstenspiegel and administrative writings, so much so that, his translator infers, practically "every matter of detail" in his work "had been previously expressed elsewhere" (I, p. lxxxv). Yet his contribution was momentous, consisting as it does in the structure he erected out of these bits and details.

II. Economics and Other Sciences in the "Muqaddimah"

What Ibn Khaldūn has to say of crafts and science is essentially in keeping with Muslim tradition, though he failed to identify economics, geography, and politics as specific or practical sciences. When discussing (chap. 5) crafts, together with their roles and fortunes, he describes five as "necessary" (agriculture, architecture, tailoring, carpentry, and weaving) and five as "noble" (midwifery, calligraphy, book production, singing, and medicine), so-called

---

subsistence is cheap; and that weapons should be bought in times of quiet when they are not in demand. *Ibid.*, p. 79.

[58] *Ibid.*, pp. 66–70.

[59] On this problem see Talcott Parsons, *Structure of Social Action*, New York, 1937, *passim*. The Hobbesian assumption of persisting conflict in the absence of absolute rule had wide acceptance in the world of Islam where (as in other parts of Asia) great weight was attached to the regulative sanction of *fear*. E.g., see Baron Carra de Vaux's account of al-Fārābī's ignorant and error-ridden state, in his *Les penseurs de l'Islam*, IV (Paris, 1923), pp. 12–18.

[60] Plessner, *op. cit.*, p. 142. Ibn Khaldūn's direct knowledge of Greek authors was very limited. See W. J. Fischel, *Ibn Khaldūn and Tamerlane* (Berkeley, 1952), p. 84.

because their practitioners have contact "with great rulers" (II, pp. 355-56). Skill in a craft (as in a science, or in the craft of instructing in a science) is the result of appropriate habits (i.e. "firmly rooted" qualities) acquired through repetition (II, pp. 346–47, 426). Here, therefore, as in his discussion of the cumulation and diffusion of civilization and its capacity to survive vicissitudes, Ibn Khaldūn counts upon socio-psychological processes, upon habituation and diffusion through the imitation of the habits of others, which play a strategic part in his analysis of socio-economic fluctuations as well as in that of education (I, pp. lxxxiii–lxxxv; II, pp. 424–33).

Man's capacity for science flowed from his "ability to think" whilst his "soul" served as the "storehouse of human science" (III, p. 281). This capacity afforded him knowledge of both the "world of spirits" and the world of human beings (III, pp. 411–24) and could result in systematic treatment by anybody of subject matter (I, p. 79).[61] It had given rise, especially among the Greeks and the Persians,[62] to the philosophical or intellectual sciences based upon speculation and research (I, p. 78; III, pp. 111–117). Science tended to flourish, however, only where civilization was high (e.g., as in the East compared with the Maghrib) and where it had support (as in Egypt, with its many endowments) (II, pp. 427–37).[63]

Among the intellectual sciences he included: logic, which protects "the mind from error"; mathematics, which embraced music, algebra, geometry (which included surveying and optics), arithmetic and its branches associated with business and inheritance, and astronomy (including astrology); physics, which had to do with the behavior of "bodies" and which also included medicine and agriculture; and metaphysics, concerned with "existence as such" and in conjunction with which sorcery, talismans, magic, and alchemy are also discussed and evaluated, especially on religious grounds (III, pp. 111–246; also I, pp. 184–245). The traditional (or transmitted) Muslim sciences, unlike the philosophical, were based upon religious authority in the form of the Koran and the Sunnah and what is required for the understanding

[61] Systematic treatment apparently was an essential ingredient of science. E.g., see III, p. 80, where he implies that systematic treatment made a "science of sufism" as well as of Koranic interpretation, jurisprudence, "the science of tradition, and other disciplines".
[62] Ibn Khaldūn was under the influence of the tradition that Alexander had transmitted Persian sciences to the Greeks who improved them, with Islam reviving interest in them after Christianity had neglected them. In reality, various Greek works had been translated into Persian and in turn from Persian into Arabic. See F. Rosenthal's interesting *The Technique and Approach of Muslim Scholarship (Analecta Orientalia*, No. 24, Rome, 1947), p. 73.
[63] The Turkish amirs in Egypt "built a great many colleges, hermitages, and monasteries, and endowed them with mortmain endowments that yielded income" and "saw to it that their children would participate in the endowments, either as administrators" or otherwise. The amirs did this "because chicanery and confiscation are always to be feared from royal authority" and they were "slaves or clients" of the "Turkish dynasty". (II, p. 435). Ibn Khaldūn was generally alert, as in this instance, to the economic motive underlying some action.

of these sources. They included (among others) sometimes casuistic juris-prudence (which had to do with inheritance laws as well as with God's laws), "the sciences concerned with Prophetic traditions (hadīth)", dialectics, "specu-lative theology" (which sometimes bordered upon metaphysics and which was no longer needed inasmuch as "heretics and innovators" had been destroyed), and dream interpretation (II, pp. 436–63; III, pp. 1–110). There were also the Arabic-language sciences (lexicography, grammar, syntax and style, and literature) auxiliary to the religious sciences (III, pp. 298–99, 319–44). Ibn Khaldūn was highly critical of the orientation of the philo-sophical sciences, together with alchemy and astrology, because they had become at variance with the traditional sciences and religion and hence tended to be harmful to the state and good order (II, pp. 246–58; III, pp. 258–80).[64]

His failure to identify economics or politics explicitly as a science reflects his overriding concern with his new science of culture and his approach to the subject matter of economics and politics. So also does his neglect of the role which scientific progress might play in improving man's economic lot (given Ibn Khaldūn's belief that "civilization" tends to fluctuate, and with it the state of science, between a level typical of nomadic peoples and a level of the sort temporarily attained in prosperous parts of the Muslim world). His concern was the explanation of "civilization and social organization", and not prescrip-tion in keeping with ethical requirements.[65] He apparently assumed that Greek politico-economic and other abstract models had little applicability or explanatory power respecting social reality, and this assumption probably was strenghtened by his hostility to the scepticism manifested by philosophers (especially al-Fārābī and Avicenna) and to their conceptions of "happiness" (III, pp. 246–58). He apparently feared that a too abstract approach to political and economic questions might, by generating excessive speculation, blind the inquirer to relevant circumstances.[66] Presumably what was required

[64] He advises the student not to study "logic" until after he has become "saturated with the religious law and has studied the interpretation of the Qur'an and jurispru-dence". (III, pp. 250–58). He condemns astrology because it would disclose God's "secrets" (III, p. 264) and alchemy because it would undertake to accelerate natural processes and foil God's plans (III, pp. 275–79). The alchemist, were he successful in cheapening gold and silver, would undermine God's intention that "gold and silver, being rare, should be the standard of value by which the profits and capital accumula-tion of human beings are measured" (III, p. 277). Proponents of alchemy were likely to be philosophers (such as al-Fārābī) who could not make a living, or "students" bent on fleecing seekers after easy wealth (III, pp. 270, 280).
[65] I, pp. 77–78, 343 ff.; II, pp. 426–27. See also below; also Mahdi, *op cit.*, pp. 82–84, 156–59, 166–72, 228–32, 289–91. See note 68 on several earlier writers who manifested a socio-phychological approach in explaining human behavior, though not Ibn Khaldūn's great knowledge of nomadic life and culture. See also Rosenthal's Introduction to his translation, I, pp. lxxiii–vi, on the possible influence of Avicenna and others on his thought.
[66] Scholars abstract ideas "from the *sensibilia* and conceive (them) in their minds as general universals, so that they may be applicable to some matter in general but not to

286   JOSEPH J. SPENGLER

was an empirico-historical approach which yielded generalizations based upon past experience. Such at least was Ibn Khaldūn's approach, though he did not include history in his list of sciences.[67]

Ibn Khaldūn's main concern was to explain "social organization" or "civilization", together with its essential and its accidental characteristics and preconditions (I, pp. 77–79), a concern that was quite novel and that called for a science with an interdisciplinary approach which embraced knowledge of "politics"[68] and of various social activities, among them those economic in character. Only exhaustive inquiry could suffice; short presentations were misleading (I, pp. 10–14). History (in his opinion a "discipline" properly "accounted a branch of philosophy") was perhaps the instrument most essential to man's acquiring understanding of human civilization, given that the historian was suitably equipped and employed adequate methods. Such a historian needed to embody many qualities and aptitudes: capacity for speculation as well as for use of explanatory concepts (e.g. "group feeling"); extensive knowledge of man's past, of "the nature of things", and of sciences which enable the scholar to probe the information at his disposal, awareness of the significance of comparisons in space and time; and alertness to the falsity present in purported information and quantitative data (I, pp. 6–22, 55–58, 62–65, 71–73. Given Ibn Khaldūn's main concern and given his approach to its study, it was inevitable that economic matter, if not always economic analysis, would occupy a high place in his search for explanation and generalization, despite the importance he assigned otherworldly aims.[69]

any particular matter, individual, race, nation, or group of people . . . Scholars are accustomed to dealing with matters of the mind and with thoughts. They do not know anything else. Politicians, on the other hand, must pay attention to the facts of the outside world and the conditions . . . When they look at politics, (scholars) press (their observations) into the mold of their views and their way of making deductions. Thus, they commit many errors . . . The average person restricts himself to considering every matter as it is . . . His judgment is not infected with analogy and generalization . . . Such a man, therefore, can be trusted when he reflects upon his political activities . . ." III, pp. 308–10.
[67] However, see next paragraph. On the role of history see Franz Rosenthal, *Muslim Historiography*, pp. 14–15, 29–40; Mahdi, *op cit.*, chap. 3. Ibn Khaldūn believed that human affairs might be subject to supernatural influence, but only occasionally and in so restricted a sense that the processes of history remained unaffected (I, pp. lxxii ff.).
[68] Politics per se, being prescriptive and non-explanatory, did not suffice. "Politics is concerned with the administration of home or city in accordance with ethical and philosophical requirements, for the purpose of directing the mass toward a behavior that will result in the preservation and permanence of the (human) species" (I, p. 78). Elsewhere he indicates "the common people" to be a "stupid mass" (II, p. 196), and rhetoric a means toward their control (I, p. 78; III, p. 368). Ibn Khaldūn could have gotten a notion of ordered change and complex social interdependence from al-Masʿūdē, with some of whose work he was acquainted. See Grunebaum, *Medieval Islam*, pp. 284, 331, 339–40 n., 347 n. As-Sakkākī (d. 1229) also had noted the influence of milieu on thought. *Ibid.*, pp. 339–40 n., and "As-Sakkākī on Milieu and Thought", *Journal of the American Oriental Society*, LXV (1945), p. 62.
[69] "The purpose of human beings is not only their worldly welfare. The entire world is trifling and futile . . . The purpose (of human beings) is their religion, which leads them to happiness in the other world" (I, p. 386). "Political laws consider only worldly

ECONOMIC THOUGHT OF ISLAM   287

It was also inevitable that he would be much interested in causation and causality (II, pp. 414–16; III, pp. 34–39), a matter often disregarded by Muslim historians and chroniclers.[70]

The geographical and political factors taken into account by Ibn Khaldūn in his analysis of social organization were mainly those relevant to the Muslim West. In keeping with Greek geography (as taken over by the Muslims) and its emphasis upon the incidence of environment on man's behavior, he indicated that the middle (less extreme) regions of the earth (which included the Muslim world) were best suited to man's physique and to the development of civilization inasmuch as excessive heat or cold were unfavorable to the human body, temperament, and inclinations (I, pp. 167–76; also II, p. 235). He remarked, however, that the abundance of food characteristic of fertile areas might affect bodily and mental behavior adversely (I, pp. 177–83).

In his account of the role of government, in which he concentrated upon the Muslim apparatus of state and upon the social process underlying the rise and fall of dynasties and the resulting fluctuations in the functioning of the state (or dynasty and its agents), his empiricism led him to dismiss the utopian or model state (e.g., of al-Fārābī) as hypothetical and unreal (II, p. 138) and to recognize that the ideal egalitarian theocracy of Islam (represented supposedly in the first four caliphates) had tended to become a ruler-dominated state. Indeed, he treats the state and the dynasty ruling it (both denominated *dawlah*), as virtually co-terminous and hence subject to the same course of events (I, p. lxxx). At the same time, while he did not completely abstract the idea of "state", he seems to have inferred, as E. I. J. Rosenthal suggests, that the state "was an end in itself with a life of its own, governed by the law of causality, a natural and necessary institution" and the socio-political unit which "alone makes human civilization possible".[71] He apparently took it for

interests . . . it is necessary, as required by religious law, to cause the mass to act in accordance with the religious laws in all their affairs touching both this world and the other world" (I, p. 387). Hence the importance of the caliphate which embodied religious authority (I, pp. 387 ff., 415 ff.).

[70] E.g., see E. Blochet's comments on this disregard in his introduction (p. 7) to *Introduction à l'histoire des Mongols*, by Fadel Allāh Rashīd Ed-Dīn, London, 1910; Rosenthal, *Muslim Historiography*, pp. 100–04. See Mahdi, *op. cit.*, pp. 232–84 and passim on Ibn Khaldūn's concern with causation.

[71] E. I. J. Rosenthal, *Political Thought*, p. 84. "Islam knows no distinction between a spiritual and a temporal realm, between religious and secular activities. Both realms form a unity under the all-embracing authority of the *Sharī'a*", or prophetically revealed law of Islam based on the Koran, the Sunna (or exemplary life of Mohammed), and Hadith (or authentic traditions). See *ibid.*, pp. 2, 8; also, on egalitarian theocracy, Louis Gardet, *La cité musulmane*, pp. 31–68. In reality, however, as Ibn Khaldūn observed, the caliphate, or "earthly political form" of this theocracy, becomes transformed into "the mulk or power-state" when, as often happens, the "authority of the *Sharī'a* is impaired". See Rosenthal, *Political Thought*, pp. 117, 84–86, 92, 94–97. On types of authority in the *Muqaddimah* see I, pp. 380–82, also 414–28. On types of state see II, pp. 137–39, where after distinguishing between the rational state and the state based on divine law, together with the utopian state, Ibn Khaldūn further distinguishes be-

granted that, in the absence of ethical or religious norms to which both ruler and ruled voluntarily conformed, governmental decisions would be unjust and at variance with the worldly aspirations of the ruled (I, pp. 385–88; II, p. 285). In his discussion of caliphal functions and offices he noted that some were associated with authority in general, among these the mint and the ministries in charge of tax collection and expenditures, so important because money and the soldiers therewith hired (along with "the pen", or ministry of correspondence) constituted the three "pillars" of royal authority (I, pp. 80–82; II, pp. 4, 22–29, 46–48);[72] but he treated the "office of market supervisor", charged with prevention of fraud, as a "religious position", perhaps because of its disciplinary role (I, pp. 462–63, also p. 260–61). His counsel to rulers, while usually realistic, sometimes reflected the "Mirrors for Princes" literature (II, pp. 140–56).[73] Thus he urged rulers to appoint able officials (II, pp. 3 ff.) and to avoid "injustice, the ruin of civilization" (II, pp. 103–111); and he cautioned them against both excessive cleverness and excessive severity, remarking that tyranny destroys nations (I, pp. 382–85).

Ibn Khaldūn, while very conscious (as were many Muslim authors) of the propensity to change in human affairs, together with the uncertainty resulting, did not envisage this change as assuming the form of continually cumulating progress, nor did he anticipate a theory of organic evolution even though he several times expressed himself in terms of what appears to be the "chain of being" (I, pp. 194–95; II, p. 422–23), a conception conducive to evolutionary theory.[74] He looked upon man's intellectual powers as constant, though his

---

tween the welfare-orientated rational state of the Persian philosophers and the rational state in which the ruler is interested (as "all rulers" are) in maintaining his rule "through the forceful use of power".

[72] On the functions and behavior of the secretary or bureaucrat see II, pp. 29–35. Ghazālī, of whose theological works Ibn Khaldūn approved (III, pp. 28–29, also p. 229), had divided the population of countries "into (i) farmers, husbandmen, and handicraftsmen, (ii) men of the sword, and (iii) those who take money from the first grade in order to distribute among the second, whom he calls the Men of the Pen." See Sherwani, op. cit., p. 160. Ghazālī endorsed the opinion of the sages that "religion depends on kingship, kingship on the army, the army on wealth, wealth on material prosperity and material prosperity on justice." See A. K. S. Lambton, "The Theory of Kingship in the Nasīhat Ul-Mulūk of Ghazālī", Islamic Quarterly, I, 1954, p. 54.

[73] See F. Rosenthal's comments, I, p. lxxxv. Ibn Khaldūn also mentions the eleventh-century Al-Māwardī's Ordinances of Government, translated by E. Fagnan as Les statuts gouvernementaux, Algiers, 1915; but this author is concerned with political and religious issues in their ethical aspects rather than with economic issues other than taxation, public expenditure, and the prevention of fraud. See E. I. J. Rosenthal, op. cit., pp. 27–37, 235–38; Grunebaum, Islam, chap. 7, and Medieval Islam, pp. 156–66; Sherwani, op. cit., pp. 107–22.

[74] Ibn Khaldūn is not referred to in A.O. Lovejoy's classic The Great Chain of Being, Cambridge, 1936. It has been incorrectly inferred that both Ibn Khaldūn and Al-Bērūnī (whose work could have been known to Ibn Khaldūn) anticipated Darwin. Al-Bērūnī (973–1048) sometimes expressed himself in quasi-Darwinian terms. Thus he observed (see India, chap. 47) that since "increase" due to "sowing" is "unlimited, whilst the world is limited", there is selection either by "the agriculturalist" or by "Nature", and if "the

capacity for performance varied with the kinds of habits he acquired; there existed no ground for postulating man's continual retrogression just as there existed no warrant in man's experience for supposing that his cultural progress would not come to a halt and give way, at least for a time, to cultural retrogression. In sum, in the Muslim world he studied (mainly North Africa and Spain), civilization or culture had moved somewhat cyclically, fluctuating between nomadism and sedentary civilization.[75] This more or less cyclical movement reflected an essentially universal quality of culture, Ibn Khaldūn's exposition and analysis suggest, even though his concrete account is bound in time and space to a portion of the Muslim world. It is by no means clear, however, how nearly he succeeded in distilling the universal attributes of cultural fluctuation from the concrete attributes and manifestations he encountered in the history of Spain and North Africa and the adjacent world. One may infer a universal model or set of processes from his analysis, but one may not suppose that Ibn Khaldūn apprehended or intended so universal a model, given the concrete character of his account.[76]

III. *Politico-Economic Fluctuation*

Inasmuch as many of Ibn Khaldūn's economic findings seem to flow from his efforts to account for the politico-economic cycles he discovered in the history of Islam and the Middle East, I shall outline his cycle theory first and then inquire more specifically into these findings in Section IV. His theory, which is political and sociological as well as economic in nature, is rather loosely

---

earth is ruined, or is near to be ruined, by having too many inhabitants, its ruler ... sends it a messenger for the purpose of reducing the too great number"; or at least he so interpreted Indian thought. As J. C. Wilcynski shows, however, al-Bērūnī did not appreciate the significance of his observations or attempt to weld them into a coherent theory. See "On the Presumed Darwinism of Alberuni Eight Hundred Years before Darwin", *Isis*, L (1959), pp. 459–66. See also K. G. Bosch, "Ibn Khaldūn on Evolution", *Islamic Review*, XXXVIII (5, 1950), pp. 26 ff.

[75] I, pp. lxxxiii–lxxxv; II, pp. 424–33; section IV of this essay. Muslim historians probably attached as much importance to experimentation as did Muslim scientists who did not (as did medieval European scientists) assign increasing significance thereto; they occasionally stressed the importance of eyewitnesses. It was assumed that Muslim scholars, in or near their late teens, would have mastered as much knowledge as they would ever acquire; so there was "not much room for the concept of individual development in Muslim civilization". F. Rosenthal mentions several scholars who believed that knowledge would continue to cumulate, but he indicates that "change rather than development was supposed to govern the relationship of successive generations". Similarly, Muslim theories about the interdependence of civilizations merely implied the existence "of a certain element of change, which may mean improvement, or deterioration"; while those about the origins of science "also did not favor the assumption of progressive development". See F. Rosenthal, *The Technique and Approach of Muslim Scholarschip*, pp. 65–69, 74.

[76] See however Mahdi, *op. cit.*, chaps. 4–5.

stated, in part because it was inferred from what had supposedly taken place in the five or six centuries preceding his time.

Ibn Khaldūn's cycle theory runs in politico-economic terms. In skeletal form it proceeds as follows. A new dynasty comes into being and as it acquires strength, it extends the area within which order prevails and urban settlement and civilization can flourish. Crafts increase in number and there is greater division of labor, in part because aggregate income rises, swelled by increase in population and in output per worker, and provides an expanding market, a very important segment of which is that supported by governmental expenditure. Growth is not halted either by a dearth of effort or by a shortage of demand; for tastes change and demand rises as income grows, with the result that demand keeps pace with supply. Luxurious consumption and easy living serve, however, to soften both dynasty and population and to dissipate hardier qualities and virtues. Growth is halted by the inevitable weakening and collapse of the ruling dynasty, usually after three or four generations, a process that is accompanied by deterioration of economic conditions, decline of the economy in complexity, and the return of more primitive conditions.

It did not suffice for Ibn Khaldūn to postulate the emergence of a strong ruler; for a ruler always tended to emerge in virtue of the anarchic conditions which usually obtained when there was no ruler (I, pp. 284, 380–82; II, pp. 137, 300–01). It was necessary also to account for the emergence of a sufficiently strong dynasty, this being a necessary precondition (as the long essentially townless history of the Berbers suggested) to extensive urban settlement, the construction of large cities, and the evolution of civilization, or complex socio-economic organization and specialization (I, pp. 89, 280, 448–49; II, pp. 137–38, 235–44, 266–67). Such a dynasty could emerge only if those united by "group feeling" were sufficiently numerous and happened to pass under the leadership of a noble and very prestigious chieftain who could extend the sway of his group over other groups, convert his chieftainship into governmental or royal authority and the capability of ruling "by force" (I, pp. 137–38, 269–89), and seize control of territory under the rule of a now weakened dynasty (II, pp. 128–31, 298–99). Life under desert and other primitive conditions, though conducive to poverty, made for courage and strong group feeling and thus facilitated conquest and the extension of a group's sway (I, pp. 257–63, 282–89, 291–99), an extension that was also assisted at times by the liking of nomads, even though poor and equipped with salutary customs and simple tastes, for urban life and products (I, pp. 252–55; II, pp. 279–80, 291). Yet, when such royal authority came into being its period of ascendancy was limited; normally a royal family (incapable of retaining its virtues and prestige in a luxury-ridden, urban milieu) could last no more than three or four generations (i.e., 120 or more years; I, pp. 278–81, 343–46), though its authority might pass to some other potentially dynastic branch of the nation if group feeling remained sufficiently strong (I, pp. 296–99), or to

ECONOMIC THOUGHT OF ISLAM   291

a successor dynasty made up of former clients of its predecessor (I, pp. 285–86). Urban sedentary civilization (though initially subject to contraction of various sorts; I, pp. 328–32; II, pp. 124–26, 270–71, 297–301) was not necessarily doomed to replacement by a more primitive and even nomadic culture (as often accompanied Arab conquest of civilized lands; I, pp. 302–08). A declining culture was subject to revival; for "sedentary culture was always transferred from the preceding dynasty to the later one" (I, p. 351) which might re-invigorate it. The state of such a culture at the time of transfer depended, of course, on how powerful the retiring dynasty had been and on how long and how firmly sedentary a culture had been experienced and established (II, pp. 238–42, 279–80, 286–91).

The life-span of a dynasty, or state, is typically subdivisible into four or five stages. The first generation retains the simple tastes and tough desert qualities that elevated it, its members are animated by group feeling (sometimes re-enforced by religious belief; I, pp. 318–27), property and person are assured security, and taxes are not oppressive. The second generation, morally inferior to the first though superior to those that follow, experiences a weakening of the qualities associated with desert life as well as of its group feeling; power becomes concentrated in the hands of the royal family; the mode of living becomes much more luxurious and enervating, and there is some increase in royal expenditure; and the ruler becomes separated from both his relatives and the population at large, though in lesser measure than in the two following generations. With the advent of the third generation the qualities acquired through desert life disappear as does group feeling, and the ruler, his authority now complete, spends heavily upon construction and upon his retainers and soldiers, with the result that the burden of luxurious expenditure and taxation increases even though tranquility and contentment prevail. Under the fourth generation and in the fifth or final stage of the seemingly recurring cycle of socio-economic change, heavy expenditure, much of it in the form of "waste and squandering", continues, fed out of treasure cumulated in the past and out of such revenue or income as can be got out of an already over-taxed population, until finally shrinkage of revenue consequent upon shrinkage of the capacity of an overburdened economy to produce revenue results in shrinkage of the ruler's soldiery and hence in the dissipation of his ability to remain in power.[77]

With this sequence of generations, Ibn Khaldūn found associated a complex

[77] On the four generations see I, pp. 278–80, 285, 313–22, 342–46, 372–74; II, pp. 118–23, 284, 297–301; and on the five stages, I, pp. 353–55. See also I, pp. 356–81 on inter-dynasty differences in wealth, revenue, and expenditure, on how wealthy a few dynasties were, on the ruler's loss of support among his own people and his increasing resort to hirelings and clients who gradually win control over him and thus prepare the dynasty's demise. On the nature and the exploitative character of the Muslim revenue system at the time when the simpler Umayyads gave way to the luxurious Abbasids, see Levy, op. cit., pp. 299–328; also Donaldson, op. cit., chaps. 1–2, on the simpler tastes and values initially regnant in the Arab world.

of economic changes initially favorable but eventually more and more inimical to economic development and expansion. In his account he implies the operation of secondary or multiplier effects and of limitations to expansion imposed by dearth of manpower, but this implication is never made explicit or given even quasi-theoretical form. Order and urban settlement and the construction of urban overhead capital and public edifices came in the wake of ascending dynasties (particularly when these represented or had access to high civilization) and progressed until the ruling dynasty began to decline (II, pp. 235–71, 299–301). Civilization flourished under the aegis of a new dynasty, above all in the dynasty's capital city, especially when sedentary culture had already long been present in a country and enabled crafts to multiply and division of labor to extend (II, pp. 286–301, 349–52). Initially taxes would be low, in keeping with Islamic law, with the result that enterprises would increase in number and size and thus permit tax base, tax revenue, and governmental surplus to grow. In time, however, royal expenditure increased, with the result that private expenditure, especially upon non-necessities, also increased and intensified the money cost of manpower and other objects of royal expenditure. It then became necessary for the government, if it would continue expenditure at a high and rising rate, to increase assessments and tax rates and to levy more and higher customs duties. Presently taxation began to eat so heavily into business profit that business enterprise was discouraged, finally diminishing in amount with the result that tax revenue declined. This adverse effect was intensified when the now frustrated government, still bent upon continuing an insupportable rate of expenditure, not only increased taxes and tax rates (or permitted tax collectors to do so) but also engaged in commercial enterprise and undertook to buy monopsonistically and sell monopolistically, with the result that business activity was discouraged and tax revenue shrunk further. In these circumstances the dynasty was prompted to expropriate its remaining wealthy subjects as well as to have recourse to forced labor. Not enough money could or would be forthcoming, however, and the dynasty, its money foundation undermined, would presently find itself unable any longer to support its soldiery (i.e., its military foundation) to their satisfaction, and its disintegration, already under way, would be accelerated, especially if famine and pestilence occurred as a result of oppressive rule.[78] This disintegration process was intensified also as decline in governmental revenue entailed decline in government purchases and hence in the profitability of enterprises dependent upon governmental purchases (II, pp. 102–03). It was intensified also by the growing insecurity of private property and the resulting disinclination of cultivators and urban enterprisers (II, pp. 103–111) to extend their holdings and augment their productive

[78] The five sentences preceding are based upon II, pp. 89–102, 108–11, 117–28. On famine and pestilence, see II, pp. 135–37. It is after the second generation that decay sets in (II, pp. 97–98, 135; I, p. 346).

ECONOMIC THOUGHT OF ISLAM 293

activities. Interruption and reversal of the degenerative process described could now be realized only through the replacement of the regnant senile dynasty by a new one (II, pp. 117–18).

Ibn Khaldūn's cyclical interpretation of history thus allowed only limited economic progress. It was possible for populations to rise far above the primitive mode of economic life characteristic of nomadic peoples, and sedentary culture could become sufficiently imbedded in countries to prevent its complete destruction in periods of decline except under most unusual conditions. In such event, when periodic decline set in, particular centers would decay, only in time to give place to others which might flourish. There was thus a bottom below which retrogressive forces seldom carried a nation's economy. But there was also a ceiling. This was set by the eventual proclivity of dynasties to waste the substance of the underlying population and dissipate their economic strength, with the result that economic development was interrupted in the neighborhood of this ceiling if not earlier and made to give place to economic retrogression. Economic activity thus fluctuated within a fairly fixed range rather than about a rising trend.[79]

IV. *Economics Proper*

Ibn Khaldūn's essentially economic observations, though they relate largely to "various aspects of making a living", are not entirely separable from his discussion of such matters as rural-urban differences, the sociological basis of group power, and the process of detribalisation. As has been noted, he contrasts the "desert-life" (or Bedouin mode) and similar backwoods environments with "sedentary" urban environments where most craft and other economic activities are carried on and where social organization for co-operation (though it usually embraces considerable agricultural activity) is far more complex than among nomads and other non-urban peoples. Urban settlements are the products of dynasties who employ both reward and force to bring them into being, inasmuch as urban settlement is a most effective source of defence and a means to far greater tranquility, relaxation, and co-operation than human beings ordinarily seek or can achieve outside cities (II, pp. 235–38) The size of such settlements depends principally upon the strength and duration of a dynasty (and its continuation, if any) in power

[79] One might reduce Ibn Khaldūn's argument to terms of a model reminiscent of J. R. Hicks's, but without a rising floor and ceiling. See his *A Contribution to the Theory of the Trade Cycle* (Oxford, 1950), pp. 96–98. Studies of price movements suggest greater price stability than Ibn Khaldūn's cyclical theory might call for. See Ashtor, "Le coût de la vie", *loc. cit.*; "L'évolution des prix dans le proche-orient à la basse époque", *Journal of the Economic and Social History of the Orient*, IV (1961), pp. 15–46; "Matériaux pour l'histoire des prix dans l'Égypte médiévale", *ibid.*, VI, 1963, pp. 158–89.

and secondarily upon whether its work is carried on by a successor dynasty; for city construction entails great investment, the use of powerful machinery, and careful location and planning for purposes of defense, provisioning, health, etc. (II, pp. 238–49). A dynasty could not effectively undertake such urban construction until it was able to dispense with that "group feeling" ('*asabīyah*), or likemindedness and consciousness of kind and of belonging to a group (originally related by blood), which was essential to a tribe's survival in the desert (I, pp. 261–83), and which tended to give rise to powerful leaders and "royal authority" (I, pp. 284–89, 295–300) and eventually to dynastic power and sometimes even to dynasties so well established that their power rested largely or entirely on bases other than mere group feeling (I, pp. 313–19).[80] These bases were principally soldiers and money wherewith to support a military and power structure (I, pp. 80–81; II, pp. 23, 118–19); but he cited with approval a Persian ruler's observation that the availability of money depended upon the volume of economic activity which depended in turn on how justly a ruler governed (I, pp. 80–81). Elsewhere he noted that governmental injustice was common (II, pp. 285, 330).

Ibn Khaldūn may be said to be explaining how tribalism and tribal values (especially those encountered among the "Bedouins") could and did sometimes generate a non-tribal "state" in which co-operative mechanisms (including, as will be indicated, division of labor under the guidance of the market) based upon other than tribal ties might function. Such complicated mechanisms were not adapted to tribe-ridden peoples (I, pp. 332–36), or to life in the desert and the values to which it gave rise (I, pp. 261–65); this suggestion Ibn Khaldūn seems to substantiate in his remarks about the "Bedouins" (I, pp. 332–36) and in his many comments upon the destructive proclivities of the Arabs and upon their lack of interest in urban settlements and unfamiliarity with crafts, etc. (I, pp. 265–66, 302–10; II, pp. 226–70, 353–54). Yet, it was these mechanisms that made urban civilization superior to desert civilization and, as a rule, enabled urban populations to dominate desert tribes and groups (I, pp. 308–10). The process of detribalization and of the regalization of rulership would be hastened by the advent of effective spokesmen for a universal religion as had happened in the early years of Islam (I, pp. 305–06, 319–37, 414–28).

His discussion of economic behavior thus flows from his concern with "civilization" ('*umrān*), or culture, denoting human social organization (I, pp. 79 ff.), fluctuations in which gave rise to his cyclical theory based upon his observation of the variation of "civilization" with dynasty as dynasties neces-

---

[80] The nature of the concept of "group feeling" is discussed by Helmut Ritter, in "Irrational Solidarity Groups: A Socio-Psychological Study in Connection with Ibn Khaldūn", *Oriens*, I (1948), pp. 1–44. This finding may be compared with F. H. Giddings' "like-mindedness" and "consciousness of kind", in his *Elements of Sociology* (New York, 1898), chap. 12.

ECONOMIC THOUGHT OF ISLAM   295

sarily rose and fell.[81] Men, being political animals, formed organizations, not because they were driven thereto by instinct but because they recognized reciprocal need. Whether they lived in deserts or in cities they must, if they would effectively satisfy their needs (especially for food and defense), enter into social organizations; for man's capacity as a producer and performer was vastly greater when he functioned within a system of specialization and co-operation than when he carried on largely in isolation from his fellows (I, pp. 89 ff.; II, pp. 301, 417–19). Underlying man's social organization was his "ability to think" (an ability that varied with the individual) and consequently to take steps essential to the formation and the subsequent improvement of useful associations (II, pp. 411–19). The extent to which "civilization" developed varied in space and time (II, p. 369), being dependent in part upon how favorable or unfavorable the physical environment was (I, pp. 104–09, 119, 167–76; II, pp. 431–32), upon the size of the population (II, pp. 270–74, 351–52, 434; III, pp. 149), upon the phase in which a culturally fluctuating 'state' or dynasty found itself, upon the favorableness of economic conditions (e.g., whether or not taxation was excessive, whether government was interfering unduly with private enterprise or otherwise behaving unjustly),[82] and so on. Perhaps the most important of the forms of co-operation or organization into which men entered was division of labor (by craft or profession rather than by task) which greatly increased output per worker[83] (I, pp. 89–91; II, pp. 271–74), elevated a community's capacity

[81] "Dynasty and royal authority have the same relationship to civilization as form has to matter. (The form) is the shape that preserves the existence of (matter) through the (particular) kind (of phenomenon) it represents. One cannot imagine a dynasty without civilization, while a civilization without dynasty and royal authority is impossible, because human beings must by nature co-operate, and that calls for a restraining influence. Political leadership, based either on religious or royal authority, is obligatory as (such a restraining influence). This is what is meant by dynasty . . . The disintegration of one of them must influence the other" (II, pp. 300–01).

[82] II, pp. 89 ff., 95, 103, 135, 146. Ibn Khaldūn emphasized the depressive influence of the Black Death which carried away both his parents as well as many of his associates (I, xl), This "destructive plague" greatly decreased "civilization" by devastating nations and populations and laying waste to cities, buildings, roads, etc. (I, p. 64). He does not indicate when recovery set in or whether, as Karl F. Helleiner supposes, the resulting demoralization checked economic development for many decades (see "Population Movement and Agrarian Depression in the Later Middle Ages", *Canadian Journal of Economics and Political Science*, Vol. 15 (1949), pp. 368–77). Elsewhere (II, pp. 136–37), however, he indicates that in the later and declining years of dynasties pestilences are more frequent, being sequels to famines, unrest, and "corruption" of the air consequent upon excessive concentration of the population in cities. Presumably North Africa had not recovered from destruction brought by nomadic invasions after the mid-eleventh century.

[83] How specialization and co-operation increased output per worker is not analyzed as it was later, for example, by Adam Smith and his successors. Presumably specialization made for proficiency, co-operation made possible undertakings beyond the power of an individual, and skill and knowledge accumulated where men were congregating and co-operating. E.g., see I, pp. 89–91; II, pp. 271–74, 418–19; also II, pp. 238–39, 241 on the use of power-multiplying machines when the extent of co-operation and (pre-

296   JOSEPH J. SPENGLER

to produce above that required to supply elemental wants, and gave rise to exchange and commerce in which producers and merchants engaged (II, pp. 271–74, 316, 336–41), with the kind and the quantity of what was produced dependent upon the extent of demand and the realizable profit (II, pp. 301–02, 351–52, 367).[84] He did not suppose, however, that a price system alone might adequately organize a community's economy; for man lived in a Hobbesian world prone to strife and variation in level of civilization and always in need of strong governmental restraints (I, pp. 79, 84, 91–92, 284, 381; II, pp. 137–38, 300).

While it would be an exaggeration to say that Ibn Khaldūn was wholly aware of the price system as such and the composite role it did or might play, it is evident, as just indicated, that he was aware of the importance of prices and their bearing upon profit, the prospect of which was essential to the evocation of supply. He remarked also that the role played by prices was greater in capital or large cities than in outlying towns or in villages and thinly populated areas where civilization and hence the "quality and the number of crafts", together with science and other concomitants of advanced social organization, were not well developed (II, pp. 434–35, also 300–302, 347–52). Moreover, the supply and demand conditions prevailing in cities gave rise to urban price structures; the prices of necessities (e.g., foodstuffs) were low in large cities, there held down by the presence of large reserves, and high in small cities where reserves were small; in contrast, the prices of "conveniences or luxuries" were low in small cities whose inhabitants demanded little but high in large cities where demand was great in relation to supply, fed by the willingness of prosperous people to "pay exorbitant prices" (II, pp. 276–78). The services of crafts and labor were priced high in large cities since there demand was great in relation to supply which was kept down in part by the strong preference many workers, craftsmen, and professional people had for leisure (II, pp. 277–78). Costs were reflected in both urban and non-urban prices; duties and taxes incident only on goods sold in cities made urban prices higher than rural prices while increases in "the cost of agricultural labor" (due to the shift of cultivation to less fertile soil) gave rise to higher food prices everywhere (II, pp. 278–79).[85]

---

sumably) demand for such service were great enough. Craft specialization too gave rise to cumulating skill and sometimes also to skill- or knowledge-favoring spill-over effects. Acquisition of craft skills and of the habits underlying them made for "increase in intelligence" and apparently for behavior in conformity with more exacting "scientific norms" (II, pp. 406–07).

[84] Size of population appears to play a double role in the generation of prosperity. On the supply side it makes possible greater volume of output and, because of the effects of co-operation, greater output per worker; and on the demand side, it gives rise to a larger aggregate demand, in the absence of which there would be less or none at all of some goods and services produced. "Income and expenditure balance each other in every city" (II, p. 275). See II, pp. 272–74, 351–52, 434–35; III, pp. 149–50.

[85] Ibn Khaldūn is referring to the effect of the loss by Muslims of their better land to

Having outlined the significance of urban as distinguished from non-urban media for the conduct of economic activities, attention may be directed to his discussion of particular topics. At least six of these are of interest.

(1) *Population Growth*. Both natural increase and migration are touched upon. While Allah wanted the world settled "with human beings", they could not multiply outside "civilization", increase in number being almost commensurate with the growth and spread of civilization (I, pp. 91–92) and increase in the labor force being commensurate with increase in population (II, pp. 272–73). Numbers tended to grow where food was abundant and life was comfortable, though rich diets were less favorable than frugal diets to bodily and mental health (I, pp. 177–83; II, pp. 274–76). Similarly, "luxury" and "prosperity" were initially favorable to population growth, stimulating both natural increase and immigration (I, pp. 351–53; II, pp. 280–81), though in time a luxurious mode of life tended to be unfavorable, if only because it rendered a people meek, docile, and militarily weak (I, pp. 286–89, 297) and fostered homosexuality which was unfavorable to fertility and adultery which was conducive to child mortality (II, pp. 295–96). Within limits population growth was self-generating, numbers augmenting a people's strength and strength favoring increase in numbers, if, as was typically the case, there was more accessible territory than population to exploit it (I, pp. 327–32). Cities tended to draw population from rural areas, the prospect of higher incomes tending to attract migrants, though Bedouins often were unable to make a living in cities (I, pp. 252–53; II, pp. 235–37, 270, 274–75, 279–80). Mortality was higher in towns than elsewhere, sedentary life, urban crowding, and the richness of diets being relatively unfavorable to health (II, pp. 136–37, 244–45, 361–62, 376–77), though city planning could improve the physical environment (II, pp. 245 ff.). The destructiveness of famine and pestilence is noted (I, pp. 64–65; II, pp. 136–37), Variation in life span and life expectancy was not anticipated (I, pp. 343–44), and man's powers were said to be at their peak when he was forty (II, pp. 291–92). No reference to population forecasting appears in Ibn Khaldūn's comment on astrological and other forecasts (II, pp. 200–223). He did, however, associate population increase (decrease) with economic progress (retrogression) and assume that population growth (decline) made for the growth (decline) of "civilization" (II, pp. 104, 272 ff., 280–83, 290, 299, 314). "Civilization", as indicated earlier, fluctuated with the rise and fall of dynasties, dynasty being related to "civilization" as form to matter (II, pp. 104, 291, 300–01); and this fluctuation affected even population distribution in that a new dynasty usually transferred the population of the former capital city to a new one (II, pp. 299–301).

Spanish Christians; he does not distinguish between average and marginal cost, but refers instead to the greater labor and fertilizer inputs required on poor than on good soils (II, pp. 278–79).

298   JOSEPH J. SPENGLER

(2) *Supply, Demand, and Price.* The dependence of price and hence of gross profit upon conditions of supply and demand, each of which is implicitly conceived in a quasi-schedule sense, is explicitly recognized as is parallel dependence of wages though the rationing function of pricing is neglected.[86] Merchants could sell at profitable prices, given their costs, only if demand were great enough; and they would most likely be able so to sell if they handled goods desired by many rather than by only a few (since then, his statement implies, demand would be both more elastic and less likely to shift downward),[87] and if supply were inelastic at least in the short run (as was true of imports from relatively inaccessible foreign lands but not of domestic products whose supply might be increased rapidly if prices warranted) and hence goods were scarce (II, pp. 336–38). He implied, further, however, that the demand of the rich for luxury goods, even those in "short supply", was quite inelastic (II, p. 277) and that the elasticity of the monetary demand for goods in general was associated positively with their variety (II, p. 339). Inasmuch as supply-demand relations varied in time, merchants could hold goods until prices had improved (II, pp. 336–37), but (for reasons that are not entirely clear) Ibn Khaldūn supposed that considerable risk attached to storage (II, pp. 339–40, 341) and that the presence of reserves kept urban food prices down (II, pp. 276–77). He indicated that wages as well as returns to craftsmen depended upon demand-supply relations, with supply conditioned at any time by the desire of workers for leisure, together with the extent to which they felt able to afford it (II, pp. 277–78); indeed, whether any particular craft service would be supplied turned on whether the dynasty or the public demanded it at a price suppliers deemed sufficient (II, pp. 292, 311–12, 351–52). These prices, as noted, were higher, as a rule, in cities with sedentary culture (II, pp. 276–79, 292–94) than elsewhere.

He had less to say of costs and supply than of demand, though he indicated that supply would be forthcoming only if the price offered covered costs and was superior to alternatives open to the seller (II, pp. 276–78). Increases in costs (e.g., in wages, customs duties, taxes "on profits", etc.) are reflected in prices; thus whatever increases the cost of supplying foodstuffs enters "into the price of foodstuffs", and whatever swells the expenses of merchants enters into "the sales price" (II, pp. 278–79, 292–93, 314). Similarly, what increases the money cost of the worker's or the merchant's standard of life is or may be reflected in his supply price (II, pp. 278–79, 293, 314). Ibn Khaldūn's statements suggest, however, that it is usually demand rather than supply

[86] Ibn Khaldūn remarked that "whatever is obtained by one is denied to the other, unless he gives something in exchange (for it)" (II, p. 311).
[87] In a work supposedly written in the eighth or ninth century by Abū᾽ al-Fadl, the author advised merchants to invest in commodities for which there was a mass demand, not in expensive specialities, or items fancied by scholars. See Lopez, in Postan and Rich, *op. cit.*, p. 283. Whether this is the work cited above in note 49, I am not sure; it reflects Bryson's influence.

that fixes the price of labor which, though it ought at least to furnish the "necessities of life", often fails to do so in villages and hamlets where demand for labor is negligible (II, pp. 273–74, 277, 334–35); and he attributes the lowness of the pay received by religious officials and teachers in part to the fact that "the common people have no compelling need" for their services (II, p. 334). He was not concerned about the measurement of cost or price in real or numeraire terms, taking it for granted that Allah had provided gold and silver (the only stable form of wealth) to serve this purpose and facilitate exchange (II, pp. 59, 313; III, p. 277); and he did not consider the possible response of natural increase to infra- or supra-subsistence wages. He noted the dependence of elasticity of supply in any place (apparently) upon its size (II, pp. 271-79, 286–91) and upon its transport connections (together with their security) with other places (II, pp. 247, 337–38, 342), but not upon the technological attributes of industries and crafts.

(3) *Profits and Their Role.* The availability of profit to private enterprise was essential to its conduct and growth and hence to general economic prosperity. By profit, however, Ibn Khaldūn meant the income an individual got "through his own effort and strength" and whence came his "sustenance" (or "necessities and needs") and "capital accumulation" when "profits" exceeded "needs". "Labor", Ibn Khaldūn remarked, compatibly with his apparent emphasis on demand as the source of value, was desired because of "the value realized from it" in the form of output which men wanted and for the supply of which labor was entirely responsible, or (as in husbandry, mining, and some crafts) predominantly responsible, in that all or most of the ingredients of the price of output consisted in "the share of labor" (II, pp. 311–14, also 278). In the absence of labor, however, nothing was of use or value, though for technological reasons as well as lack of demand; and only in the presence of great supplies of labor (e.g., in large cities where incomes were relatively high) were productive conditions especially favorable, presumably because of the benefits of division of labor and collaboration (II, pp. 271–73, 280–81, 314–15, 325). "Sustenance and profit" were obtainable in three "natural" ways: in agriculture, man's primary and earliest and most humble livelihood; in crafts, to be found "only among sedentary peoples"; and in commerce, which "contains an element of gambling" and which legally employs "cunning" and "tricky" methods to "obtain the (profit) margin between purchase prices and sales prices" — a margin that yielded a very "small" profit "in relation to the (invested) capital" (II, pp. 315–17, 335–36, 342).[88] Sustenance and profit were obtainable also in a number of unnatural

[88] Commerce did not, of course, embrace interest-taking, or usury, which had Koranic disapproval (II, p. 293); while it involved cunning and trickery, it did not involve "taking away the property of others without giving anything in return" and so it was legal (II, p. 317, also pp. 110, 343) though "honest (traders) are few" and the "judiciary is of little use" in the prevention of fraud, deceit, etc. (II, p. 342). Because of the risks involved in commerce and the need of the merchant to be aggressive, disputatious, quarrel-

ways. Among these he included searching for buried treasure; serving others, especially the ruler, for wages, un unmanly form of occupation in which virtually no one, *both* trustworthy and capable, would engage (II, pp. 317–19); and the collection of "protection" or blackmail, or of imposts and taxes "according to a generally recognized norm", through the exercise of "political power (which) is not a natural way of making a living" (II, pp. 315–16, 327, also 19 ff.). Whatever the source of profit, if it is not forthcoming in adequate amount, activity or business slumps and the adversely affected craft or undertaking is contracted or abandoned. Ibn Khaldūn refers to the depressive influence of too low prices upon merchandising (II, pp. 340–41); to the destruction of private incentive occasioned by the ruler's engaging in profit-seeking commercial activity, especially when he or his agents employ unfair or oppressive methods (II, pp. 93–96, 109–111); to the destruction of "all hopes" (of profit) and hence of all incentive to earn and save by the imposition of unduly heavy and inequitable taxes (II, pp. 90–93), or by the seizure of property (I, p. 305; II, pp. 99–101, 103–07, 109–111, 123–24, 285–86, 297); and to the contraction of what had been an extensive market (II, pp. 103, 291, 293–95, 302, 351–52).

(4) *Rank, Obsequiousness, and Profit.* Profit, or the value one realized from his labor, was affected by one's rank and by one's capacity for obsequiousness as well as by the demand for one's labor.[89] Possession of "rank", based on relation to or connection with the ruler, or on "group feeling that the ruler will respect", is described as extremely useful in a pyramidal, hierarchical society of the sort Ibn Khaldūn saw about him (II, pp. 328–31). One who had accumulated property was constantly exposed to its seizure by amirs, etc. (as even Mohammed had anticipated) unless he had rank, or was protected by someone with rank (II, pp. 285–86). For affording such protection a person of rank would be rewarded. Indeed, rank permitted its possessor not only to share in the property income of others but also to extract surplus value out of all dependent upon him for protection against harm and for

---

some, cunning, etc., only persons with such qualities were suited to be merchants; but these qualities were "detrimental to and destructive of virtuousness and manliness" and affected the "soul" toward "evil". Merchants were inferior in character, therefore, to "noblemen and rulers"; for only most rarely was a merchant a man of rank who could leave all "business manipulations" to his agents and servants (II, pp. 342–45). Undoubtedly Ibn Khaldūn's experience as a judge as well as his strong disposition to look to his own interests (see I, pp. lxiii–iv) made him alert to the necessity the merchant was under to disguise his motives and behavior. E.g., see Levy, *op. cit.*, pp. 255–60, 340.

[89] "The value realized from one's labor corresponds to the value of one's labor and the value of (this labor) as compared to (the value of) other labor and the need of the people for it. The growth or decrease of one's profit, in turn, depends on that" (II, p. 328, also p. 330). "Most" merchants, farmers, and craftsmen, however, if without rank, "make only a bare living, somehow fending off the distress of poverty" (II, p. 330). Even today connection with persons of rank is deemed highly useful in parts of the Islamic world (as well as in other parts), particularly when such a person can be put under obligation.

ECONOMIC THOUGHT OF ISLAM   301

access to "advantages" (II, pp. 327–28).[90] Possession of rank was very desirable, therefore, and many a person was anxious to acquire it, by being "obsequious" and using "flattery, as powerful men and rulers require." It followed that men with this disposition tended to displace proud and haughty persons without it; they tended to become wealthy, or to replace older and relatively arrogant members of the ruler's entourage (II, pp. 329–34).[91]

(5) *Surplus, Luxury, and Capital Formation.* Both the development of crafts adapted to the supply of conveniences and luxuries and the formation of capital depended upon the emergence of a capacity to produce a surplus above a population's elementary needs. Ibn Khaldūn does not, however, explain the distribution of this surplus between capital formation and the satisfaction of demands for conveniences and luxuries, except to note conditions unfavorable to capital formation; nor does he explicitly account for the emergence of this capacity to produce a surplus in the first place. As has been suggested, however, he seems to have reasoned that, with the establishment of political order and security, population could conglomerate in cities and enable co-operation and civilization to flourish and with such conglomeration there would emerge division and collaboration of labor, specialization, improvement in both the proficiency of the population and the pool of skills at its disposal, and development of markets commensurate with the growing supply of output (I, pp. 308–10, 347; II, pp. 235–38, 270–83, 291–92, 301, 325, 329, 347, 351, 434–35).

[90] "People help him with their labor in all his needs, whether these are necessities, conveniences, or luxuries. The value realized from all such labor becomes part of his profit. For tasks that usually require giving some compensation (to the persons who perform them), he always employs people without giving anything in return. He realizes a very high value from their labor. It is (the difference) between the value he realizes from the (free) labor (products) and the prices he must pay for things he needs. He thus makes a very great (profit). A person of rank receives much (free) labor which makes him rich in a very short time. With the passing of days, his fortune and wealth increase. It is in this sense that (the possession of) political power (*imārah*) is one of the ways of making a living" (II, p. 327). For this reason merchants with rank were in a very favorable situation (II, pp. 327, 344–45). "Many jurists and religious scholars and pious persons" who had acquired "a good reputation" also enjoyed the benefits of rank, since the masses believe "they serve God" by giving these people presents (II, p. 327). He looked upon the advantages attaching to rank as an undesirable by-product of a prerequisite (i.e., rank or hierarchy) to orderly co-operation, an accidental evil associated with a source of good, illustrative of a type of association that frequently existed (II, pp. 329–30).
[91] "Obsequiousness and flattery are the reasons why a person may be able to obtain a rank that produces happiness and profit, and that most wealthy and happy people have the quality (of obsequiousness and use flattery). Thus, too, many people who are proud and supercilious have no use for rank. Their earnings, consequently, are restricted to (the results of) their own labors, and they are reduced to poverty and indigence" (II, p. 331). He suggests that some religious officials and teachers are poor in part because they answer to this description (II, pp. 334–35). "Obsequiousness and flattery toward the ruler, his entourage, and his family" finally win positions of rank for "many common people", often at the expense of those previously in this entourage who had become arrogant there (II, pp. 333–34).

302   JOSEPH J. SPENGLER

A surplus emerges with the progress of civilization and permits the consumption and importation of non-necessities, together with capital formation, population growth, and possibly a further enlargement of the surplus in consequence of population growth.

A great surplus of products remains after the necessities of the inhabitants have been satisfied. (This surplus) provides for a population far beyond the size and extent of the (actual one), and comes back to the people as profit that they can accumulate . . . Prosperity, thus, increases, and conditions become favorable. There is luxury and wealth. The tax revenues . . . increase on account of business prosperity (II, p. 281).[92]

When the city is organized and the (available) labor increases and pays for the necessities and is more than enough (for the inhabitants), the surplus is spent on luxuries (II, p. 347).

Or a part of the surplus could be devoted to "capital accumulation" as might happen when an individual's "profits" exceeded his "needs" (II, pp. 283–84, 311–12, 340, 341). Ibn Khaldūn himself condemned the wasteful use of property rather than its accumulation (I, pp. 354, 420–21), though his frequent emphasis upon otherworldly objectives (I, pp. 386–88, 415) and the role of Allah's will led him to play down the importance of the amassing of wealth.

His interpretation of the use to which an emerging surplus is put seems to have run as follows. (a) Individuals formed and preserved capital only if, having earned or otherwise acquired means beyond their needs, they had incentive to maintain it (e.g., see I, pp. 80–81; II, pp. 105, 110), or to utilize it for the support of their dependent children (II, pp. 284–85), and their property as well as "the divine rights of (private capital)" (II, p. 336) were secure against seizure by the dynasty and local rulers (II, pp. 103–08, 109–11, 285–86, 343). (b) As luxurious expenditure of private individuals rose, under the impact of urban development and dynastic example, there finally was less available for investment. (c) As the tax burden rose in response to mounting dynastic expenditure upon luxury, etc., the after-tax incomes of private individuals permitted less and less saving and even this was likely to be absorbed by increasing luxury consumption on the part of these individuals. In time, after the dynasty sought to collect more taxes than the economy could support and thereby initiated economic contraction, there would be no incentive and little or no capacity to form capital.[93]

[92] "If the labor of the inhabitants of a town or city is distributed in accordance with the necessities and needs of those inhabitants, a minimum of that labor will suffice. The labor (available) is more than is needed. Consequently, it is spent to provide the conditions and customs of luxury and to satisfy the needs of the inhabitants of other cities. They import (the things they need) from (people who have a surplus) through exchange or purchase" (II, p. 272). Inasmuch as the activities associated with a town usually embraced considerable agricultural activity, this statement may be interpreted to imply a capacity on the part of agriculturalists to produce a surplus of foodstuffs for urban consumption (I, p. lxxvii; II, pp. 283–84).

[93] The processes referred to under (b) and (c) have already been discussed and are

Ibn Khaldūn implied that the withdrawal of money from circulation through taxation and the accumulation of treasure (which could be very extensive; I, pp. 360–71) could depress the economy and its capacity to generate a surplus, but he apparently supposed that, as a rule, revenue would be soon expended (e.g., II, pp. 283, 291) though possibly at points other than those where it was collected (II, pp. 283, 325). He cited with approval the counsel given in the early ninth century by Tāhir (a general) to his son (a newly appointed governor): "property, once it is gathered and stored in treasuries, does not bear fruit, but if it is invested in the welfare of the subjects and used for giving them what is due them and to prevent them from need, then it grows and thrives" (II, p. 146, also pp. 149–53). Keeping treasure in circulation was indicated, therefore (cf. I, pp. 146, 291).

(6) *Consumption Patterns; Expenditure.* Ibn Khaldūn did not expect the standard of life to lag behind the capacity of an economy to provide for it, nor did he anticipate a constrictive dearth of expenditure. It was true that custom, man's "second nature" (II, p. 117), conditioned a people's wants, especially their nutritive wants, and that custom changed slowly (I, p. 181; II, pp. 117–18, 347); yet customs did change, and as men accepted "the yoke of the city" they added "conveniences and luxuries" to their consumption requirements which originally had embraced only "necessities" (I, p. 252). Men imitated both those victorious over them and those in superior situations (I, pp. 298, 338, 348, 351); as they moved into new and wealthier environments, their expectations rose, they progressed from "the necessities of life and a life of austerity . . . to the luxuries and a life of comfort and beauty", and their expectations rose further still (I, p. 338). He traced the expansion of wants and consumption through the stages of the dynasties (I, pp. 347, 353–55; II, pp. 297–98) and indicated that private expectations and the desire for luxuries increased in the wake of the increasing consumption of luxury products by the dynasty (I, pp. 340–42). Accordingly, while he implicitly acknowledged the possibility of a backward-sloping labor-supply curve (II, p. 277), he apparently supposed that increasing wants would increase the disposition of workers to exchange leisure and effort for conveniences and luxuries (e.g., see II, pp. 272–75). He took it for granted also that income and expenditure balanced, whether at high or low levels. "Income and expenditure balance each other in every city" (II, p. 275).

---

further discussed in (6) following. While taxes could be increased, there was a limit to such increase (II, pp. 297–98). "The amount of tax revenue, however, is a fixed one. It neither increases nor decreases. When it is increased by new customs duties, the amount to be collected as a result of the increase has fixed limits" (I, p. 340). Accordingly, if dynastic luxury is further increased, military expenditure must be decreased (I, p. 341; II, pp. 122–24).

304   JOSEPH J. SPENGLER

CONCLUSION

This review of the economic ideas of Ibn Khaldūn does not yield clear-cut conclusions. Only a much more detailed inquiry into economic thought in the world of Islam might do so. Several inferences follow, however. First, even though a number of Muslim authors were familiar with the economic ideas of the Neopythagorean Bryson, one can hardly look upon the content of this set of household-administration precepts as representing the extent of Muslim knowledge of man's economic behavior. Ibn Khaldūn's knowledge of this category of behavior greatly transcended that present in the work of Bryson and his followers; it extended far beyond the household, embracing market, price, monetary, supply, and demand phenomena, and hinting at some of the macro-economic relations stressed by Lord Keynes. Second, one is compelled to infer from a comparison of Ibn Khaldūn's economic ideas with those set down in Muslim moral-philosophical literature that the knowledge of economic behavior in some circles was very great indeed, having been acquired through contact with cumulating experience, and that one must turn to the writings of those with access to this knowledge and experience if one would know the actual state of Muslim economic knowledge. Undoubtedly Ibn Khaldūn must have acquired much of his quite solid understanding of economic behavior through his legal and administrative experience and through his contact with the pool of unwritten administrative knowledge. Indeed, a comparison of his ideas with those of similarly situated writers in early Indian, Chinese, and European societies suggests that there did exist a very considerable pool of economic knowledge or wisdom, even though, for a variety of reasons, this did not get set down in an orderly fashion in manuals or treatises. After all, even the work of Adam Smith did not appear until long after an extensive body of information had come into being.[94] It is the organized presentation of economic analysis that was slow to appear, therefore, not the emergence in urban and interurban markets of a considerable apprehension of economic behavior which was acted upon even in proto-étatistic economies. It is knowledge of this sort that is reflected in Ibn Khaldūn's work rather than precepts oriented to household management.

Ibn Khaldūn did not differentiate the economy from other analytically specifiable components of the Islamic societal system within which the economy was embraced. His primary concern was not the economy or economic analysis as such, but the development, illustration, and application of a general science of culture that was intended to explain the behavior over time of interrelated economic and non-economic phenomena. In consequence his economic analysis is never prominent. The resulting cost is compensated, in part, however, at least in respect to the economy Ibn Khaldūn knew, by

[94]   E.g., see my account of mercantilism in Bert F. Hoselitz, ed., *Theories of Economic Growth* (Glencoe, 1960), chap. 1 and appendix.

his implied stress upon the empirical interconnection of economic and non-economic phenomena, a connection that is especially important in simpler economies and in state-dominated economies. Despite this compensation, however, the cost may have been great, in that economic analysis was not carried forward and developed in the world of Islam after Ibn Khaldūn's death. Had his economic analysis not been so submerged in his more socio-logical analysis, it is possible that economic inquiry might have been carried forward effectively in the Muslim world, at least in the absence of oppressive governmental or ecclesiastical action.

Probably more responsible for what Toynbee calls the flash-in-the-pen impact of Ibn Khaldūn's work was the cut-and-dried character of Egyptian Arabic civilization and the inability of this civilization to render Islamic culture dynamic and fruitful within the framework of an Ottoman Empire that finally absorbed Egypt in 1517. Nor was Iran at this time very congenial to Arabic intellectual influences.[95] In the Ottoman state kingship was blended with the *Shari'a* which continued to express God's will and define right action, but the role of "group feeling" (*'aṣabiyah*) had been diminished. In time, however, interest in Ibn Khaldūn's work revived. For the political structure of the Ottoman state, fragile to begin with, was losing strength already in the seventeenth century. Whence there began to develop interest in the causes of the decline of nations. This interest re-enforced that of Turkish scholars in the *Muqaddimah*, manifested already in the sixteenth century, and resulted in a Turkish translation in 1730, published in Cairo along with an Arabic edition in the 1850's when there was much interest in progress and reform.[96] This work was not adapted, however, to generating elan in a society that lacked it,[97] nor, for the matter, could the ideas of Adam Smith and Ricardo[98] unleash much economic drive.*

JOSEPH J. SPENGLER
Duke University

---

[95] See Toynbee's account of events after Ibn Khaldūn's death in *op. cit.*, I, pp. 366–67, 379, 383–84, 387–88, 393–98.

[96] See F. Rosenthal's introduction to his translation, I, pp. lxvi–vii, cvii–viii; Albert Hourani, *Arabic Thought in the Liberal Age 1798–1939* (New York, 1962), pp. 41, 52, 71–72, 78–79, 88, 90, 152, 326, 328, 344.

[97] In the sixteenth and seventeenth centuries there was virtually no interest in European science, nor much manifestation of that desire to better one's condition by which classical economists set so much store. Indeed, a Turkish student in Paris in the late 1820's recorded as strange the fact that each Frenchman hoped to go further than his ancestors. *Ibid.*, pp. 41, 58, 77. See also A. Adnan (Adivar), *La science chez les Turcs Otomans*, Paris, 1939.

[98] Hourani, *op. cit.*, pp. 43–44, 105. More influential in Egypt were some of the followers of Saint-Simon, though his ideology never caught on. *Ibid.*, pp. 53, 76–77.

306 JOSEPH J. SPENGLER

* Much of the work done on this paper was carried out while I held a John Simon Guggenheim Memorial Fellowship. I am grateful to the officers of the Foundation for having made possible the research involved as well as to the Ford and the Rockefeller Foundations for having made assistance and materials available. I am very grateful also to Professor Gustav E. von Grunebaum for his valuable comments and suggestions. For the errors and misinterpretations I alone am responsible.

[7]

ON THE INTERPRETATION
OF THE JUST PRICE*

> *Carius vendere quam valeat*—here indeed is
> a very fine hare which, with no obvious
> asthmatic symptoms, is still gallantly
> breasting the uplands, pursued from afar
> by a great company of short-winded
> metaphysicians and economists.—Sir
> ALEXANDER GRAY.

At one time it was regarded almost as a truism that by the 'just price'
the schoolmen, including ST. THOMAS AQUINAS, were referring to a
'normal' price dependent upon costs of production, rather than a
fluctuating price dependent upon the chances of the market. Production costs, it was believed, were determined by a deserved standard
of living on behalf of the producers, and would not of course include
interest[1]. Recently, the debate has been re-opened and the circle has
made a complete turn. The idea that the just price was directly
related to costs is now denied by some authors. It is argued that the
just price was the going market price, and particular emphasis was
placed on demand and utility[2]. Others agree that the price determined in a competitive market was considered by the main stream
of scholastic thought to be the just price; however, passages exist
where it would seem that cost ratios play an important role. It is
therefore argued that 'beyond doubt ... he [Aquinas] considered the

* I am indebted to Professors K. F. HELLEINER, A. KRUGER, C. B. MACPHERSON,
and A. ROTSTEIN for very helpful comments. This paper was read at the meetings
of the Canadian Political Science Association in Vancouver, June 1965.

1. W. J. ASHLEY on the Just Price in *Dictionary of Political Economy*, ed. R. H. I.
PALGRAVE (London: Macmillan, First edition, 1896), Vol. II, p. 500. The idea of
a just price related to social hierarchy and a corresponding standard of living
related to status can be traced back to the interpretations of the German Historical
School, in particular to SOMBART and ROSCHER. See RAYMOND DE ROOVER, 'The
Concept of the Just Price: Theory and Economic Policy', *The Journal of Economic
History*, XVIII, Dec. 1958, pp. 418–34; and W. J. ASHLEY, *English Economic History*
(New York: G. P. Putnam's Sons; London: Longmans & Co., Second edition,
1893), Part II, p. 391 ff.

2. JOHN T. NOONAN, Jr., *The Scholastic Analysis of Usury* (Cambridge, Mass.:
Harvard University Press, 1957), pp. 84–6.

SAMUEL HOLLANDER

market price as just' but the market price would 'tend to coincide with cost or to oscillate around this point like the swing of a pendulum'[3].

These interpretations all appear to be based on the implied assumption that there is to be found in Aquinas a single version of the just price. In some cases it is further implied that one can expect to find consistent economic analysis reflected in his discussion of the issue. But it should always be remembered that the early writers were not primarily concerned with economic processes. To ignore this fact, given the natural desire to find predecessors, can lead to serious distortion.

In this note we shall argue that there is strong evidence to support the claim that the just price was in fact related to costs within the medieval context of social status. On the other hand it is also clear that Aquinas did at times define the just price as the market price. *Both versions are to be found depending upon the problem under investigation,* and statements made within one context need not be applicable to the other. Attempts to discern a single version of the just price even in the work of a single author may be misleading. We shall also argue that there is little evidence to show that AQUINAS related analytically the market price to production costs in the classical or neo-classical fashion.

As a preliminary it will be necessary to clarify the position on justice in exchange adopted by Aristotle and the comments thereon by Aquinas *(Section I)*. We shall then turn to the discussion of the issue in Aquinas' independent writings *(Section II)*. Finally, we shall consider the proposition that it is possible to interpret Aquinas in terms of a neo-classical theory of price determination *(Section III)*.

I

The Aristotelian comments in the *Nicomachean Ethics*[4] on just rates of exchange between craftsmen is the traditional starting-point for the

3. DE ROOVER, *op. cit.*, p. 422.
4. Volume I in the Library of Living Catholic Thought series (Chicago: Henry Regnery Company, 1964), contains St. Thomas Aquinas' *Commentary on the Nicomachean Ethics* and also the relevant passages from Aristotle. The new translations of Aquinas and Aristotle are by C. I. LITZINGER. Page references are to this translation.

ON THE INTERPRETATION OF THE JUST PRICE

analysis of the scholastic doctrine on just price. The context is the definition and analysis of commutative justice: 'Therefore, that which is just is an equal, a mean between more and less in such a way that gain is taken as more, and loss as less'[5]. The principle is applied to the exchange of products by specialist craftsmen.

This is true also in other arts, for they would be destroyed if the craftsman doing the quality and quantity of work which he should is not supported accordingly. (*Nic. Eth.*, V. Lecture VII, 1132 a 25, p. 414.)

ARISTOTLE then elaborates in passages which are of sufficient importance to our subject to be quoted in detail.

A conjunction by means of a diagonal shows how to make that compensation which is according to proportionality. Let *A* be a builder, *B* a shoemaker, *G* a house, and *D* a sandal. It is necessary that a builder should take from the shoemaker his product and in return give what he himself makes. If first an equality according to proportionality be found and then reciprocation be made, it will be as we have said. But if not, there will not be an equality—and the state would not continue to exist—because nothing hinders the work of one craftsman from being of more value than the work of another. Therefore, these things must be equated.

This is to be observed also in the other arts, for they would be destroyed if a workman did not receive according to the quantity and quality of what he produced. Between two doctors an exchange does not take place but between a doctor and a farmer who are altogether different and unequal. These then must be equated. (*Nic. Eth.*, V. Lecture VIII, 1132 b 21, pp. 418–19.)

Therefore all things capable of exchange ought to be compared in some way. For this purpose money was invented and became a kind of medium measuring everything including excess and deficit.

A certain number of sandals are equal in value to a house or to a quantity of food. Therefore, as many sandals must be exchanged for a house or a quantity of food in proportion as the builder contributes more than the shoemaker (or the farmer). If this is not observed, there will be neither exchange nor sharing. But this reciprocation will not be possible unless things are equated.

Therefore, it is reasonable to measure all things by one norm ... This norm in reality is demand which connects all things. If men were not in need there would be no exchange, or if they did not have a similar demand, exchange would not be the same. Money originated by agreement on account of necessary exchange ...

When things have been equated there will be reciprocation, so that as the farmer is to the shoemaker, the amount of the shoemaker's work is to the amount of the farmer's work. When things are to be exchanged they ought to be represented in a figure showing proportionality. If this is not done one extreme will have both

---

5. *Nic. Eth.*, Book V, Lecture VI, 1131 b 25, p. 409.

SAMUEL HOLLANDER

excesses, but when all have what is theirs they will be equal, and will do business with one another because this equality can be brought about for them.

... if there is no such reciprocation, there will not be any sharing of goods. (*Nic. Eth.*, V. Lecture IX, 1133 a 18, pp. 423–4.)

Conflicting versions of Aristotle's just price doctrine are to be found in the literature. Traditionally, the above passages have been taken as evidence that Aristotle maintained a cost theory of the just price. This view has been challenged: J. T. Noonan, for example, argues that Aristotle's example of commutative justice—'the builder's work in building the house equalling the shoemaker's work in making the shoes'—is 'not pressed, and it seems clear that Aristotle intended it only as an illustration, not an absolute affirmation that equality in exchange demanded an equality of labor being matched; a little after this passage, he explicitly says that value is determined by need'[6]. Similarly, J. J. Spengler concludes that 'Aristotle, with his emphasis upon demand and his neglect of costs, was a forerunner of the Austrian rather than the English classical school'[7]. It has also been argued that Aristotle assumed the *coincidence* of both criteria in the sense that 'that which is the more costly to supply (in terms of labor expended and skill exerted) will be that which is the more eagerly desired'[8].

Whether or not Aquinas adopted Aristotle's position in his *Commentary* is also a matter for debate. According to Noonan 'a repetition of Aristotle in a commentary on him cannot be taken as an expression of the commentator's view'[9].

It appears likely, however, that Aristotle did present a doctrine of just price based upon costs. Moreover, it is probable that Aquinas ascribed to this doctrine. For it is not quite true to say that he merely repeated Aristotle *verbatim*, as Noonan argues; at certain critical junctures he clarified serious ambiguities.

Several phrases included in the passages quoted earlier leave some room for uncertainty: 'nothing hinders the work of one craftsman

6. Noonan, *op. cit.*, p. 86.

7. Joseph J. Spengler, 'Aristotle on Economic Imputation and Related Matters', *Southern Economic Journal*, Vol. XXI, April, 1955, p. 388.

8. Barry J. Gordon, 'Aristotle and the Development of Value Theory', *Quarterly Journal of Economics*, Vol. LXXVIII, February 1964, pp. 115–28.

9. Noonan, *loc. cit.*

ON THE INTERPRETATION OF THE JUST PRICE

from being of more value than the work of another'[10]; 'as many sandals must be exchanged for a house ... in proportion as the builder contributes more than the shoemaker'; the arts 'would be destroyed if a workman did not receive according to the quantity and quality of what he produced'[11]. But according to the *Commentary* by Aquinas the 'superiority' of one craftsman over another—the proportion by which the one 'contributes' more than the other—refers to the *relative costs incurred in production:*

The arts would be destroyed if the craftsman, who works at some handicraft, would not be supported, i.e., would not receive for his workmanship, according to the quantity and quality of what he produced. (*Comm. on Nic. Eth.*, V. VII, p. 416.)

... proportionality must be employed in order to bring about an equality of things because the work of one craftsman is of more value than the work of another, e.g., the building of a house than the production of a penknife. (V. VIII, p. 420.)

... first an equality according to proportionality is found so that on one side a certain number of sandals be fixed as equal to one house (for a builder incurs more expense in building one house than a shoemaker in making one sandal: *nam plures expensas facit aedificator in una domo, quam coriarius in uno calceamento*) ... (V. VIII, p. 421.)

In order then to have just exchange, as many sandals must be exchanged for one house ... as the builder ... exceeds the shoemaker in his labor and costs *(in labore et in expensis)*. If this is not observed, there will be no exchange of things and men will not share their goods with one another. (V. IX, p. 426.)

This is done in such a manner that as the farmer ... excels the shoemaker ... in the same proportion the work of the shoemaker exceeds in number the work of the farmer, so that many sandals are exchanged for one bushel of wheat ... If this was not done ... if a farmer gave a bushel of wheat for a sandal, he would have a surplus of labour in his product and would have an excess of loss because he would be giving more than he would receive. But when all have what is theirs, they are in this way equal and do business with one another because the equality previously mentioned is possible for them[12]. (V. IX, pp. 426–7.)

---

10. The phrase has been translated by W. D. Ross as: 'for there is nothing to prevent the work of one from being better than that of the others'. Cf. Spengler, *op. cit.*, p. 384.

11. Alternatively rendered as 'they would be destroyed, if the effect upon the patient were not, in kind, quantity and quality, the same as the effort of the agent' in the translation by J. E. Welldon in: Arthur E. Monroe, *Early Economic Thought* (Cambridge, Mass.: Harvard University Press, 1951), pp. 27–8.

12. I have given the latin original of the key phrases found in *In Decem Libros Ethicorum Aristotelis ad Nicomachum*, ed. A. M. Pirotta and M. S. Gillet (Turin 1934), p. 326.

SAMUEL HOLLANDER

Aquinas interprets Aristotle's doctrine as one based on cost ratios and does not simply repeat him word for word. This would suggest that he was in agreement with the view that the just price must reflect relative costs. Moreover, in the questions on 'economic' matters in *Summa Theologica*, to be discussed presently, references to the Philosopher's *Ethics* are so frequent as to imply strongly such accord.

What role was played by 'demand' or 'need' in Aristotle's scheme? Immediately after the apparent definition of justice in terms of costs, Aristotle, as we have seen, writes 'it is reasonable to measure all things by one norm ... This norm in reality is demand which connects all things. If men were not in need there would be no exchange, or if they did not have a similar demand, exchange would not be the same. Money originated by agreement on account of necessary exchange'. These remarks are continued in the following passages:

That human demand connects everything as by a kind of measure is evident because when men are so mutually situated that both or at least one is not in need, they do not exchange their goods. But they engage in exchange when one needs what the other has, e.g., wine, and they give grain for it. An equation then must be made between these goods.

For future exchanges money is, as it were, a guarantee that a man, who has no present need, will be helped when he is in want later on. However, currency suffers like other things, for it is not always of the same value; although it tends to be more stable than other things.

Everything then must be evaluated in money, for in this way exchange will always take place and consequently association among men. Money equates goods making them commensurate after the manner of a measure ...

It is impossible that things so greatly different be made commensurate according to reality, but they agree sufficiently by comparison with the needs of man, and so there must be one measure determined by man. And this is called money, which makes all things commensurate inasmuch as they are measured in money.

Let *A* represent a house and *B* five minae. Let *G* represent a bed worth one mina. The bed then will be one fifth the value of the house ... Likewise it is obvious that barter took place before money existed. But it makes no difference whether five beds or the value of five beds are given. (*Nic. Eth.*, V. Lecture IX, 1133 a 18, pp. 424–5.)

It is apparent that Aristotle in the chapter on money was increasing the complexity of his 'model'. It will be noted, however, that these statements occur immediately after the establishment of the rule that the just price is determined by relative costs. Furthermore, the existence of money does not alter the 'real' situation: 'Like-

ON THE INTERPRETATION OF THE JUST PRICE

wise it is obvious that barter took place before money existed. But it makes no difference whether five beds or the value of five beds are given.' With these considerations in mind let us turn once more for clarification by Aquinas.

He says first, in order that the products of the different workmen be equated and thus become possible to exchange, it is necessary that all things capable of exchange should be comparable in some way with one another so that it can be known which of them has greater value and which less. It was for this purpose that money or currency was invented, to measure the price of such things. (*Comm. on Nic. Eth.*, V. IX, pp. 425–6.)

It is clear that no additional rules were introduced at this point to explain the determination of exchange ratios, for Aquinas then refers back to the original rule; the just price still depends upon relative costs:

In order then to have just exchange, as many sandals must be exchanged for one house ... as the builder ... exceeds the shoemaker in his labor and costs ... But what has been said, that a number of sandals are exchanged for one house, is not possible unless the sandals are equated with the house in some way. (V. IX, p. 426.)

This 'commensuration' is made by means of money. Money, however, is merely a 'convention'. Behind the creation of money lies the phenomenon of human need:

He states that for this reason it is possible to equate things because all things can be measured by some one standard ... But this one standard which truly measures all things is demand. This includes all commutable things inasmuch as everything has a reference to human need. Articles are not valued according to the dignity of their nature, otherwise a mouse ... should be of greater value than a pearl ... But they are priced according as man stands in need of them for his own use. (V. IX, p. 426.)

Considered in isolation this latter statement might suggest that (in Aquinas' view) Aristotle had stated a law of just exchange squarely based upon relative utility. Taken in the general context, however, it seems clear that this conclusion would be incorrect. For Aquinas continues:

An indication of this is that if men were not in need there would be no exchange, or if they did not have a similar need, i.e., of these things, exchange would not be the same because men would not exchange what they have for things they did not need.

621

SAMUEL HOLLANDER

What Aristotle seems to be indicating, and what Aquinas makes more explicit, is not that the just exchange ratios will be *determined* by the relative strength of 'needs', but that in the broadest sense *human* needs underly the system of specialization and exchange, and the convention 'money'. But the classical economists too were in full agreement with such propositions. Demand is clearly recognized as the binding force of society for specialization depends upon mutual demands. Moreover, the classics state explicitly that utility is 'absolutely essential' to exchange value. But they do not conclude that exchange value will, therefore, be determined thereby.

While relative costs appear to govern the just price Aristotle does not explain how the costs are determined. But it is probable that the position of the producer in the 'social hierarchy' would be relied upon to determine the weight attached to his 'effort'. Certainly the ranking of different occupations plays an important part in the work of Aristotle. If this is the case, then the absence of an *explanation* of cost determination is not a critical omission for relative costs would be largely *data*.

We have referred to the view that Aristotle assumed the *coincidence* of both relative cost and relative utility. In this interpretation by B.J.Gordon both cost and utility receive equal weight as determinants of Aristotle's exchange rate. Textual evidence is brought to suggest that the higher the cost of obtaining a good the greater the want-satisfying power thereof[13]. While it is probably correct to say

---

13. BARRY J. GORDON, *op. cit.*, p. 124. Examples of this relationship quoted by Gordon are the following statements:

'Thus gold is a better thing than iron; though less useful: it is harder to get, and therefore better worth the getting.'

'...we appreciate better the possession of things that cannot be easily acquired.'

'...all men love more what they have won by labour...' from the *Rhetoric, Topica*, and the *Ethics* respectively. In his paper, GORDON also emphasises the ranking of skills which is to be found in Aristotle; this ranking is 'non-economic' and based on criteria such as the extent to which 'the body must be deteriorated', and the element of chance involved (p. 126).

One possible approach to the relationship between cost and utility may be added here. Aristotle may not have been concerned, when he referred to 'demand' and 'need' in our texts, with the *individuals* concerned. But the ranking of each occupation (and consequently production costs) may partly be dependent upon the *social* demand for, or rather the importance attached by *society as a whole* to, the relevent products. In this case too, *both* costs and 'utility' play a role although once again it is the former which receives the emphasis, the latter being of indirect relevance.

ON THE INTERPRETATION OF THE JUST PRICE

that Aristotle did not envisage a potential divergence between relative costs and relative utility, it is important to bear in mind that in fact Aristotle did not emphasize relative utility. This would perhaps be of little relevance if his account of the 'determination' of the just price was analytical. But, as we shall try to show presently, Aristotle did not give an analytical explanation of the determination of price. His doctrine was an ethical 'prescription'. As far as the *influence* of such a doctrine is concerned the emphasis given to costs of production would appear to be of great consequence, for later authors may not adopt the strict relationship between the two 'variables'.

II

We have noted above the viewpoint that the comments on the *Nicomachean Ethics* should not be taken as an expression of Aquinas' opinion. Noonan points out that in Aquinas' own work we cannot find views similar to those expressed in his *Commentary*. In the case of Aquinas and other scholastic authors 'the just price is seen to be the price where demand and supply meet: in short, the market price'[14]. For the most part the scholastics assumed

... that any man engaged in an honest trade may and will charge enough to support himself and his family. But they do not believe that the just price on the seller's part will be determined by the cost of his labor alone. St. Thomas teaches explicitly that value may increase by a change in place or time alone without labor or risk by a good's owner; and the other writers... who teach that value changes with changes in demand or supply, show no disposition to assert that changes must reflect the cost of labor. Labor will influence cost and so the supply; but no scholastic teaches that it is the sole determinant of value[15].

On the other hand, in the previous section we argued that Aquinas in fact does appear to agree with the Aristotelian doctrine of justice in exchange and explicitly refers to cost ratios as the determinant of just prices. Older scholarship, moreover, placed great emphasis on production costs:

Knies and others have remarked that what the doctrine of just price aimed at may be described as a *normal* price, in accordance with *cost of production*, instead

14. NOONAN, *op. cit.*, p. 85.
15. *Ibid.*, p. 87.

SAMUEL HOLLANDER

of a fluctuating price dependent upon the changes of the market. This is an accurate description, if it be understood that cost of production was to be determined by a fixed standard of living on the part of the producers, and was not to include any element of *interest*.

In principle, according to this view of the matter, it would be possible for each individual producer to determine for himself the just price of his product 'by reckoning what he needed to support his rank'. This was explicitly argued by LANGENSTEIN but was probably 'assumed as a matter of course by Aquinas and other writers'[16].

We turn now to examine these interpretations. We shall argue that the assumption of a single criterion of justice is false. A different rule was adopted in different circumstances.

There is little doubt that at times St. Thomas referred in his discussion of just exchange to the market price. This is obviously the case in his *Summa Theologica*. Responding to the question 'Whether a seller is bound to declare a defect in a thing sold?', St. Thomas raises a possible analogy suggesting that the seller need not do so, and finally denies its relevance:

... if a man is bound to declare a defect in a thing sold, this is only in order that the price may be lowered. But sometimes the price may be lowered even apart from any defect in the thing sold, for some other reason; for example, if a seller, bringing wheat to a place where grain is dear, knows that many are following with more wheat, knowledge of which on the part of the buyers would cause them to pay less. This, however, the seller does not have to tell, apparently. Hence for analogous reasons, he does not have to declare defects in the thing sold ...

In reply ... it is to be said that a defect in a thing makes its present value less than it seems; but in this case the thing is expected to fall in value in the future through the arrival of merchants, which is not expected by the buyers; hence a seller who sells at the prevailing price does not seem to act contrary to justice, in not telling what is going to happen. If, however, he did tell, or lowered his price, he would act more virtuously; though he does not seem to be bound by the requirements of justice to do this[17].

Clearly to sell at the prevailing price is to act 'justly'. The just price in this context is simply the market price.

Similarly in answer to the question 'Whether in trading it is lawful to sell a thing for more than was paid for it?' Aquinas argues at one

16. Contribution by W. J. ASHLEY to PALGRAVE's *Dictionary, loc. cit.*

17. *Summa Theologica*, Question LXXVII, Article III, in: A. E. MONROE, *op. cit.*, pp. 60–2.

ON THE INTERPRETATION OF THE JUST PRICE

point that 'it can be done lawfully ... because the price has changed with a change of place or time'[18]. Elsewhere he is equally explicit:

For if the merchants of Tuscany, bringing cloth from the Fair of Lagny, to wait for it [payment?] until Easter, sell the cloth for more than it is worth in the general market, there is no doubt that this is usury[19].

What must not be forgotten, however, is that all these references apply *specifically to the merchant or trader*. The problems of conscience, with which Aquinas had to deal, apparently arose within the particular context of *trading* rather than within that of *production*. There is no *a priori* reason to generalize from the former to the latter problem.

The just price is frequently defined as that price which reflects 'the community's estimate' of the product. The market price may be considered 'lawful' simply because it is the most suitable indicator of the entire set of objective and subjective elements which forms the community estimate. But there is a less positive view that seems to be closer to the truth. Clearly, at least part of the reason for the adoption of the market price as the criterion lay in the desire to avoid monopolistic and monopsonistic exploitation. If this end could be achieved by means of the market then all well and good. But in some circumstances there may have existed equally satisfactory, if not preferable, criteria. To say that the essence of the matter is the avoidance of exploitation by *individual* sellers and buyers need not lead to the conclusion that exchange at competitive market prices is the only solution. There may be others. Thus, for example, it was generally accepted that the 'common estimate' may be determined by the civil authority.

Now the ideal, and perhaps typical, economic organization with which Aquinas was familiar has been described as one of 'non-competing groups', where complementary functions were carried on largely by guilds 'each of which was an organ for fulfilling some requisite of community life'.

Because social relations are governed by justice ... exchange must take place according to the community's estimate of the social utility of the two products,

18. *Summa Theologica*, Question LXXVII, Article IV, p. 64.
19. From a letter translated and analyzed by ALFRED O'RAHILLY, 'Notes on St. Thomas; III—St. Thomas on Credit', *Irish Ecclesiastical Record*, XXXI, February 1928, p. 165.

SAMUEL HOLLANDER

because the producer who expects sustenance from society in return for his labour, by performing his function in the social organism, has earned his right to a just return. The factors that will normally determine the community estimate of social utility are labour, cost of materials, risk, and carriage charges[20].

Competition was 'far from Aquinas' mind':

In the temporal commonwealth, peace departs because the individual citizens seek only their own good ... Rather through diversity of function and status is the peace of temporal commonwealths promoted inasmuch as thereby there are many who participate in public affairs[21].

The discussions of justice in exchange which turn to the market do not seem to be applicable to such a system. But in his independent work Aquinas does not treat the problem of justice within the stratified society based upon status and rank. It may be suggested that this was simply because the rules of justice were here self-evident. They had been laid down by Aristotle and were perfectly acceptable. The serious problems which had to be dealt with were those arising outside the 'traditional' sector.

In the trading market, and particularly the international fairs, the stratified social relationships had presumably far less meaning, and the Aristotelian principles would have been impractical to apply and, therefore, largely irrelevant. This may have also been true where production was discontinuous, or where there occurred commonly violent changes in output. In these instances the only solution would be to rely on the market price, if such a price existed. But this statement must be qualified, for the hesitancy with which Aquinas permits the adoption of this standard strongly implies that it was acceptable *faute de mieux*.

Consider the reply to the question already referred to 'Whether in trading it is lawful to sell a thing for more than was paid for it?'

Gain, however, which is the end of trading, though it does not logically involve anything honorable or necessary, does not logically involve anything sinful or contrary to virtue; hence there is no reason why gain may not be directed to some necessary or even honorable end; and so trading will be rendered lawful; as when a man uses moderate gains acquired in trade for the support of his household, or

---

20. BERNARD W. DEMPSEY, *The Functional Economy* (Englewood Cliffs: Prentice-Hall, Inc., 1958), p. 426.

21. Quoted, *ibid.*, p. 423.

ON THE INTERPRETATION OF THE JUST PRICE

even to help the needy; or even when a man devotes himself to trade for the public welfare, lest there be a lack of things necessary for the life of the country; and seeks gain, not as an end, but as a reward for his efforts.

In reply to the first argument, then, it is to be said that the words of CHRYSO-STOM [that gain is sinful] are to be understood as applying to trade insofar as gain is its ultimate end; and this seems to be the case chiefly when a man sells a thing at a higher price without making any change in it: for if he charges a higher price for a thing that has been improved, he seems to receive a reward for his efforts; though the gain itself may also be sought, not as an ultimate end, but for some other necessary or honorable end, as explained above.

In reply to the second argument, it is to be said that not everyone who sells for more than he paid is a trader, but only the one who buys for the express purpose of selling dearer. Now if he buys a thing, not for the purpose of selling it, but with the intention of keeping it, and later wishes to sell it, for some reason, it is not trading, though he sells at a higher price. For this can be done lawfully, either because he has improved the thing in some way, or because the price has changed with a change of place or time, or because of the risk he takes in transporting the thing from one place to another, or even in having it transported for him[22].

Clearly should it happen that the selling price exceeds the purchase price of the commodity a trader is in danger of sinful behaviour by relying on the market. He must be able to justify the excess which, incidently, should be 'moderate'. Moreover, either the use to which this moderate gain is put must be suitable, or it must be possible to view the 'gain' as a 'reward for his efforts'. Specifically, a return to labour, a return to risk-taking, and transportation costs are enumerated. The case where one is justified in earning the excess simply 'because the price of a thing has changed with the change of place or time' occurs in a particular context, namely where the individual had not originally purchased the commodity with the intention to resell it, that is where the individual is not strictly a trader at all. Such qualifications suggest that Aquinas accepted the market price as just most hesitantly, and would not have recommended its adoption as a general rule[23].

The case may be concluded as follows: there are to be found in Aquinas several distinct versions of justice in exchange. One was

22. *Summa Theologica*, Question LXXVII, Article IV, pp. 63–4.

23. Indeed, it has been argued that the very notion of commutative justice is superseded and contradicted by that of market price. This view is implicit in HOBBES. Cf. C. B. MACPHERSON, *The Political Theory of Possessive Individualism: Hobbes to Locke* (Oxford: Clarendon Press, 1962), p. 63.

SAMUEL HOLLANDER

based on an exchange determined by the hierarchies of producers. This version would appear to be relevant in a social system where rank is well determined. Another criterion was the prevailing market price and this would apply with qualification, in circumstances where status and rank were not clearly defined, and where market determination of price was the rule[24]. In the following section we will have occasion to consider in greater detail the conditions which should be satisfied for the market price to constitute a just price.

III

We turn finally to consider one further interpretation of the just price. An attempt has been made to reconcile the apparently divergent propositions to be found in the writings of Aquinas. Professor DE ROOVER recognizes both the references to cost ratios in the *Commentary* and the references to market prices elsewhere and combines them into a consistent whole by suggesting that according to Aquinas the 'arts and crafts would be doomed to destruction if the producer did not recover his outlays in the sale of his product. In other words, the market price could not fall permanently below cost', but would tend 'to coincide with cost or to oscillate around this point like the swing of a pendulum'[25]. Elsewhere DE ROOVER makes his point in even stronger terms: 'A vrai dire, c'est une théorie surprenante par sa modernité, et qui s'accorde entièrement avec les enseignements de l'économie politique suivant laquelle le prix courant tend à osciller autour du coût de production comme le balancier d'une pendule, bien entendu sous un régime de libre concurrence'[26].

24. We have also noted that the prices set by civil authority were acceptable. Moreover, there was considerable flexibility. For example, a seller of a thing who is 'injured if he is deprived of it' may allow for this. (Question LXXVII, Article I, p. 55.) But the discussion here pertains not to the case of specialist craftsmen or to traders, but rather to an 'occasional' exchange of objects.

25. DE ROOVER, *loc. cit.*

26. RAYMOND DE ROOVER, 'La Doctrine Scolastic en Matière de Monopole et Son Application à la Politique Economique des Communes Italiennes', in: *Studi in Onore di Amintore Fanfani* (Milan, Dott. A. Giuffrè, 1962), p. 154.

A somewhat similar view is taken by JOSEPH A. SCHUMPETER in his *History of Economic Analysis* (New York: Oxford University Press, 1954), p. 93. According to Schumpeter, Aquinas' just price was, as it was for Aristotle, 'simply normal

ON THE INTERPRETATION OF THE JUST PRICE

This view would appear to be unjustified. The only reason for offering the interpretation is apparently that there would otherwise be a 'contradiction' between Aquinas' argument that the just price is the market price and his comments on Aristotle's cost ratios. However, there is no reason to expect that it is necessary to avoid 'contradictions'. Aquinas was not an analyst of economic phenomena, and we cannot ascribe to him a full-fledged Marshallian theory of price determination involving a recognition of the relationship between supply curves of various 'runs'.

In support of this view let us turn back to Aristotle's treatment of justice in exchange and the comments thereon by Aquinas. It is tempting to see in the statement that without justice 'the arts would be destroyed' an argument to the effect that unless outlays are recovered the producer would be doomed to destruction, so that the market price could not fall permanently below costs. However, while it is certainly true that price cannot fall permanently below cost it is not by means of a classical or neo-classical mechanism that this fact is assured. It does not seem to be the case, in other words, that the price would tend to oscillate around costs 'like the swing of a pendulum'. Aristotle and Aquinas were treating a problem which did not concern the classical or later writers. They seem to be referring to the possibility that unless the exchange rate reflected relative costs of production the social structure, in particular the system of specialization, would collapse:

> ... as many sandals must be exchanged for one house ... as the builder ... exceeds the shoemaker in his labour and costs. If this is not observed, there will be no exchange of things and men will not share their goods with one another.

On the other hand, if the rules of justice are followed there will be mutual interchange between the specialist craftsmen:

> But when all have what is theirs, they are in this way equal and do business with one another because the quality previously mentioned is possible for them[27].

competitive price'. Some passages suggest 'that, by implication, at least, he did relate just price to cost'. But it was DUNS SCOTUS who must be credited with

"...having discovered the condition of competitive equilibrium which came to be known in the nineteenth century as the Law of Cost. This is not imputing too much: for if we identify the just price of a good with its competitive common value, as Duns Scotus certainly did, and if we further equate that just price to the cost of the good (taking account of risk, as he did not fail to observe), then we have ipso facto, at least by implication, stated the law of cost not only as a normative but also as an analytic proposition.'

27. Quoted above p. 619.

SAMUEL HOLLANDER

It is essential to recognize that neither Aristotle nor Aquinas in his *Commentary* explain how the exchange ratios will come to reflect costs of production. The topic under discussion was exchange between individual craftsmen, who were not to engage in any form of bargaining; the just rate was well defined *prior* to the act of exchange. One cannot find an argument to the effect that resources will move from one occupation to another in response to relative profitability. There is no indication of the manner in which an unprofitable trade will decline and a profitable trade expand. In short, there is no mechanism whereby current prices are related to production costs. Yet such a mechanism is essential if one wishes to explain a tendency to long-run equilibrium. It is evident that social opprobrium, or the 'self-interest' and above all the 'conscience' of the craftsmen must have been relied upon. There is no economic mechanism to explain the cost 'determination' of price.

When we consider the discussion by St. Thomas in *Summa Theologica*, and elsewhere, the conclusion must still be that he failed to relate the market price and production costs. Although it is clear that the mechanics of market price determination were understood, no consideration was given to the consequences of a failure to cover long-run costs. The extent to which the relationship between market price and costs was dealt with may be illustrated by the response made to an argument that traders should be permitted to charge for usurious payments they had undertaken. These individuals 'wish to recover that usury by selling the cloth at more than its worth':

Nor are they excused by the fact that they wish to indemnify themselves, for no one should indemnify himself by committing mortal sin. And although they can in selling the cloth lawfully recover other expenses lawfully contracted, for example, the cost of transporting the cloth, still they cannot recover the usury they paid, for this was an unjust payment; especially since by paying usury they sinned as giving the usurers an occasion for sinning, since the necessity which is urged—namely that they may live more respectably and do a bigger trade—is not such a necessity as suffices to excuse the aforesaid sin. This is clear by comparison; for a man could not in selling cloth recover expenses which he might have incurred carelessly and imprudently[28].

---

28. Quoted in O'Rahilly, *loc. cit.* It is evident from the context that the term 'its worth' refers to the going market price (see above p. 625). Considered in isolation, the statement that 'a man could not in selling cloth recover expenses which he might have incurred carelessly and imprudently', might be interpreted as a

ON THE INTERPRETATION OF THE JUST PRICE

We have seen earlier that to justify the 'gain' of a trader Aquinas insisted that a return to effort of some kind must be refected, although there are acceptable claims to the excess of purchase price over sales price based upon the *use* to which the excess is put. Now in the above passage Aquinas is considering the problem of 'loss'. If the going market price should fail to cover costs, the trader may legitimately charge a price higher than that ruling in the market, should an opportunity present itself, providing that his costs are legitimate claims. If the costs represent interest payments, or if they are 'abnormally' high because of his carelessness and imprudence, he must charge the going market price, and suffer the loss.

We can discern in this discussion a sense in which Aquinas may be said to be groping towards the idea of normal long-run competitive price. In the first place, it will be noted that the nature of 'costs' in the treatment of problems relating to trading is more sophisticated than is that to be found in the *Commentary*; for Aquinas no longer restricted himself to the simple labour costs of specialist craftsmen. Secondly, whereas a market price which permitted 'gain' was satisfactory if the seller's costs were reflected thereby, a market price which failed to cover his legitimate and 'normal' expenses was not obligatory. But this result, reflecting both an absence of pure profit and of loss, will be attained in the long run by the neo-classical competitive process. Our point, however, is that Aquinas did not reach his conclusions by means of analytical reasoning. He did not explain how the market price would come to reflect normal costs of production. In brief, he did not trace through the consequences of a failure to cover supply price; this problem did not concern him. St. Thomas was prescribing certain 'just' courses of action which suggest that he envisaged the market price as satisfactory provided that it did not permit pure profit on the one hand, and did not lead to losses on the

highly sophisticated recognition of the fact that the competitive market price will, in the long run, cover normal costs so that the individual seller—selling at the going price—would be *unable* to cover his abnormally high costs. However, Aquinas seems rather to have in mind the individual who has an opportunity to charge a price in excess of the current market price in a particular transaction. He was morally prohibited from so doing if his costs were carelessly incurred, but might do so if his costs were legitimate and normal claims. Furthermore, even if the former interpretation were in fact correct, there is still to be found no economic mechanism by which the result is assured.

SAMUEL HOLLANDER

other. This conclusion must of course be qualified, for a pure profit would in some cases be permissible if it were utilized in a satisfactory manner, and the seller must suffer losses due to his own carelessness. Thus cases can be found where the market price may be charged although the consequence would be profit, or must be charged despite the losses which would ensue.

IV

It has been argued that 'preoccupation with the ethics of pricing ... is precisely one of the strongest motives a man can possibly have for analyzing actual market mechanisms'[29]. It is true that the ethics of pricing *may* lead to analysis of economic phenomena, but the question is whether St. Thomas can be said to have taken the step from ethics to analysis.

It is probable that Aquinas by his own experience and observation would not have been led to recognize the influence of the current price on supply, and thereby the mechanism of adaptation of supply to demand which assures the long-run cost determination of price. Resource mobility would have been low even in the long run and any relationship between market price, the relative profitability of operations, and production costs would probably have been clouded[30].

It is clear that Aquinas was concerned with giving advice to individuals concerned with the morality of their actions. Certain charges can morally be made. By implication it may be argued that this is also a recognition that these functions (of labour, risk-taking, and transportation) have a *supply* price which, if not covered, would lead to the withdrawal of factors from the particular occupation. But this is no more than an implication; the full recognition was at no point made. What is implicit in a man's writings and what the man himself recognized in them are two distinct questions. The step from ethics to analysis was a task for the future.

University of Toronto   SAMUEL HOLLANDER

29. SCHUMPETER, *op. cit.*, p. 60.
30. See for example the discussion of supply elasticity in agriculture, in *The Cambridge Economic History of Europe*, Vol. II: *Trade and Industry in the Middle Ages*, ed. M. POSTAN and E. E. RICH (Cambridge 1952), pp. 166–7, 211.

ON THE INTERPRETATION OF THE JUST PRICE

SUMMARY

It was at one time believed that St. Thomas Aquinas meant by the 'just price' a normal price dependent upon production costs rather than a fluctuating market price. This view has recently been challenged and it is now argued that the just price was the going market price. In one instance an attempt has been made to reconcile apparently divergent statements by Aquinas into a consistent whole by suggesting that the market price was envisaged as oscillating around costs in the neo-classical manner.

In this paper we shall argue that the evidence suggests that the just price was related to production costs within the medieval context of social status. On the other hand, it is also clear that at times the just price was considered to be the market price. Both versions are to be found depending upon the problem at hand; attempts to discern a single critereon of justice, even in the works of one man, may be misleading. We shall also argue that there is little evidence to show that Aquinas related the market price to production costs in the neoclassical fashion.

ZUSAMMENFASSUNG

Thomas von Aquins «gerechter Preis» wurde früher als produktionskosten-orientierter Preis und nicht als fluktuierender Marktpreis interpretiert. Neuerdings wird jedoch der Marktpreis-These der Vorzug gegeben. Es wurde ferner auch der Versuch unternommen, aus offensichtlich divergierenden Aussagen Aquins ein konsistentes System zu entwickeln. Der Marktpreis sollte sich demnach entsprechend der neoklassischen Theorie an den Produktionskosten orientieren.

Im vorliegenden Artikel wird folgendermassen argumentiert: auf der einen Seite wird der gerechte Preis, im Rahmen der mittelalterlichen sozialen Verhältnisse, eindeutig auf die Produktionskosten bezogen. Aus Aquins Schriften ergibt sich jedoch ebenso deutlich, dass mit dem gerechten Preis manchmal auch der Marktpreis gemeint ist. Bei der Diskussion des Problems tauchen also beide Versionen auf. Ob es in diesem Falle sinnvoll ist, nur ein Kriterium als Grundlage der «Gerechtigkeit» anzunehmen, erscheint fragwürdig. Nach Ansicht des Autors lässt sich zudem auch nur schlecht nachweisen, dass Aquin den Marktpreis in «neoklassischer» Weise auf die Produktionskosten bezogen hat.

RÉSUMÉ

Jadis on interprétait «le prix juste» de St. Thomas d'Aquin comme un prix normal dépendant des coûts de production, et non comme un prix du marché fluctuant. On changea d'opinion récemment, et à présent, on est d'avis que le prix juste correspond au prix du marché. On a fait l'essai, de réconcilier des énonciations apparemment divergentes de St. Thomas d'Aquin en un système consistant, en

SAMUEL HOLLANDER

présumant, que le prix du marché oscillait autour des coûts de production selon la théorie néoclassique.

L'argumentation de l'auteur est la suivante: d'une part, le prix juste se réfère aux coûts de production dans le contexte des conditions sociales du Moyen Age; d'autre part, on constate, que de temps en temps le prix juste était identique au prix du marché. Nous avons donc deux versions; l'essai de discerner un critère de «justice» semble peu approprié. En plus on ne peut démontrer, que St. Thomas d'Aquin rapportait le prix du marché sous la forme néo-classique aux coûts de production.

[8]

SOME FURTHER REASSESSMENT OF THE SCHOLASTIC DOCTRINE OF USURY*

Following the Second World War, BERNARD DEMPSEY [10] and JOSEPH SCHUMPETER [24] presented the Scholastic doctrine of usury as a major advance in interest theory, thus breaking with a long tradition of mostly abusive or apologetic treatment. A more recent work by JOHN T. NOONAN [22], covering the entire period from the early Christian era to the present, canonists and theologians alike, offers perhaps the first opportunity for a balanced judgment on the question by a non-medievalist. I propose to take advantage of the many fresh insights that NOONAN has afforded us into the usury doctrine to reassess this doctrine. My main emphasis will be analytical. With regard to the scholastic sources, I shall rely mostly on NOONAN, DEMPSEY, GABRIEL LE BRAS [18], T. P. McLAUGHLIN [20], and RAYMOND DE ROOVER [11], [12], [13], [14], [15]. The evidence, I believe, is highly unfavorable to the DEMPSEY-SCHUMPETER argument. Also, NOONAN's verdict that 'the [Scholastic usury] theory is formally perfect' (p. 360) is very dubious. In fact, I shall argue, along with DE ROOVER, that the usury doctrine was an especially backward element of Scholastic economics.

I. A DOCTRINAL SUMMARY

A brief statement of the rudiments of the usury doctrine follows, exclusive of the 'natural law' arguments. Most important, the Scholastic doctrine condemns all payments above principal on loans of *fungibles* calling for repayment of different fungibles of the same class, not the originals. The primary example of such a loan is that of money repayable in money[1]. In the case of the relevant loans, *ceteris paribus*—that is, in the absence of extrinsic titles (to be set forth shortly)—any positive interest rate, however low, is usurious, regard-

---

* The exposition of this article has benefited from comments by my former colleague in the History Department at Tulane University, CHARLES T. DAVIS, and an earlier basic misunderstanding with RAYMOND DE ROOVER.

1. We shall examine the general meaning of fungibles and the 'natural law' arguments in a subsequent section.

473

JACQUES MELITZ

less of the form of payment. With respect to other loans, usury is not an issue except so far as the loan is a deliberate attempt to circumvent the usury ban.

Honest intentions are important because of the narrow scholastic construction of the usury problem, which offers much scope for evasion of the usury ban. 'A usurious will makes the usurer', admonishes WILLIAM OF AUXERRE (French, 1160–1229) ([22], p. 33); and according to NOONAN's paraphrase of Pope ALEXANDRE III (d. 1181): 'God will judge beyond the form of contract' (p. 19)[2]. Yet, however much the Scholastics may have wished to avoid resting the ethical question of the absence of usury on the form of contract, a theory of licit credit transactions was essential, if nothing else because Christian rulers needed advice as to which forms of contracts they could allow.

Among the licit interest-bearing credit contracts, the least controversial were the rental or lease of a durable good, like an apartment (that is, the *locatio*), and the investment in a partnership. Every other licit credit contract encountered important opposition at some time. By the end of the sixteenth century, widely endorsed credit contracts bearing interest included the credit sale (and the corresponding late delivery), the bank deposit, the low-interest-bearing bond *(contractus trinus)*, the loan of one currency in return for payment in another, the mortgage (a form of *census*), the annuity (another form of *census*), and increasingly, the ordinary loan of money where the interest could be viewed as a part of the fruits of the durable property which the lender had enabled the borrower to employ (still another form of *census*)[3].

2. For further evidence of Church emphasis on intentions, see NOONAN and MCLAUGHLIN, *passim*, and LE BRAS [18], col. 2348. The extent to which the Scholastics permitted usury to depend on the particular form of contract is sometimes exaggerated. According to some accounts, if only the contract does not conform to a *mutuum*, or the loan of a fungible repaid in kind, usury is ruled out. However, prior to 1450, usurious contracts included the resale agreement, the guaranteed *census*, the *census* redeemable at the option of the buyer, the personal *census*, and the saving deposit, in addition to the interest-bearing *mutuum*. Even when the balance of opinion finally shifted in favor of all of these contracts, the contracts were not commonly treated as inherently non-usurious, even as late as 1700. Rather it was largely supposed that if usury were an issue, the *extrinsic titles* to interest would apply.

3. A *census* may be generally understood as a loan contract requiring the borrower to make periodic payments based on some fruitful property.

SCHOLASTIC DOCTRINE OF USURY

Various factors, in addition, compelled the Scholastics to make concessions in regard to illicit contracts. The major extenuating circumstances were failure of borrowers always to repay on time, and recurrent use of force by governments (especially in the Italian city-states) in order to obtain loans from citizens. The Scholastics essentially approved of compensations to lenders in these cases. This led them by successive steps to the formulation of a theory of *extrinsic titles*. The extrinsic nature of the titles resulted from the assumption that the titles were restitutions for special costs *separable from the loan itself*.

Various *extrinsic titles* were proposed; but three found a fundamental place in the usury doctrine: (1) *lucrum cessans*, (2) *damnum emergens*, and (3) the *poena conventionalis*. The first two refer, respectively, to a possible opportunity cost and emergent loss attributable to a loan, in accord with the Latin terms. *Lucrum cessans* ordinarily could only be claimed by men of business, as others would lack the necessary evidence. *Damnum emergens* was virtually unavailable to anyone because the Church conceded the title only if the lender could show that he was forced to borrow at interest as a result of his lending. The *poena conventionalis* was a clause in the loan contract stipulating damages for failure to repay a gratuitous loan by a certain date. The clause was an accepted title to interest, as such, provided that the lender had not lent in anticipation of gaining the penalty, and that the penalty was within reasonable bounds and not strictly proportional to the duration of delay. It is important to observe that licit credit transactions had much greater currency than *extrinsic titles* prior to the sixteenth century.

II. ON THE ISSUE OF CHURCH MOTIVES

One important traditional defense of the Scholastic usury theory explains the Church position on the basis of a desire to help the needy borrower. Advocates of this defense forever point to the few alternative sources of loans to borrowers in 500–1300, and the marked tendency for poor to borrow from rich at the time[4]. One basic outcome of NOONAN's book, though not by the author's design, is to put

4. An arch example is W.J. ASHLEY [1], I, pp. 155–7, and II, pp. 434–9.

JACQUES MELITZ

this defense in proper perspective. As is easily inferred from this work, the charitable intentions of the Church could have been effectively promoted without any regard to the usury doctrine by relying on the biblical, patristic and early canonical writings, which emphasized Christian behavior and previous religious authority[5]. By contrast, the usury doctrine, dating mainly to 1150–1350, appeals not to authority and charity, but to 'natural law', therefore to reason and commutative justice. Accordingly, the whole thrust of the doctrine was to promote usury as a sin independent of the borrower's circumstances and his allocation of credit. Practically speaking, the doctrine treated the sin of usury as equally urgent in the case of the poor widow lending to the MEDICI as in the reverse[6].

Because of this severity, the usury doctrine often came into conflict with charitable Church designs. The most striking example is the *mons pietatis*, an ecclesiastical experiment in charitable lending which produced acute embarrassment to the Church because of the necessity for a mild interest charge. Furthermore, the intellectual development of the theory of licit credit transactions and the theory of extrinsic titles evidently owed something to a desire to accommodate the credit demands of the needy in spite of the general inhibitions to lending imposed by the usury doctrine. Ironically, the two preceding theoretical developments eventually brought the whole usury doctrine as much, or more, under attack by zealous supporters of low interest charges to the masses, like JOHN CALVIN (1509–64), as by commercial interests.

Even though, therefore, the usury *prohibition* may never have ceased to be largely inspired by charitable designs, the *doctrine* of usury cannot be traced to these designs. To suppose differently would be to think that the Scholastics were guilty of poor reasoning, and failed to recognize their mistake in the face of persistent mani-

5. The same inference can also be drawn from A. BERNARD [2], cols. 2323–9; OVIDIO CAPITANI [7]; BENJAMIN NELSON [21]; and A. VERMEERSCH [28].

6. In his review of NOONAN, CAPITANI tries to blur the distinction between the usury doctrine and the general Scholastic opposition to usury, claiming that the motives which underlay the latter also motivated the former. Yet the distinctness of the usury *doctrine*, as such, is extremely clear in NOONAN, McLAUGHLIN, DE ROOVER, DEMPSEY, SCHUMPETER, and many of the major Scholastics whom the previous writers quote.

SCHOLASTIC DOCTRINE OF USURY

festations over centuries. Rather than exonerating the Church on account of benign motives, therefore, sympathizers would do better to recognize the late medieval Church's abundant authoritative and moral ground for condemning uncharitable lending activity, and to represent the usury doctrine as part of a major twelfth- and thirteenth-century attempt (belonging to a general intellectual revival inside the Church) to free as much religious doctrine as possible from the roof of the authority of biblical texts, patristic writtings, and papal and conciliar decrees.

III. THE NOONAN VIEW

With this basic perspective in mind, we may now turn to Noonan's book, the predominant emphasis in which is on the suppleness of the usury doctrine, or the willingness and ability of adherents to accommodate a large variety of credit transactions. In line with this emphasis, Noonan argues that, apart from any laxity of enforcement, the usury doctrine was not a serious handicap to economic development in the middle ages and renaissance[7]. While thus minimizing the practical significance of the doctrine, he also maintains that 'the theory is formally perfect' (p. 360); and that 'along with the foolish arguments there developed a sound analysis of usury and valid, if narrow and technical, case against it' (p. 4)[8]. This thesis of the essential validity of the doctrine, even if only in some 'narrow and technical' context, will be our main concern in this section.

Noonan rests his view entirely on the Thomistic argument (Thomas Aquinas, 1225–74), which although very important, never

7. For a somewhat different outlook, see Le Bras [19], pp. 564–7.

8. Because of this effort to defend the logic of the 'natural law' case against usury, while yet also supporting the principal Scholastic arguments against the application of the usury ban, Noonan becomes entwined in considerable hairsplitting and some inconsistency. I refer, for example, to his sundry passages on the doctrine of intentions or 'mental usury' (read pp. 32–33, 158–9, 259–61, 265–6, and 336–7 in succession), and his diverse commentaries on the Scholastic notion of the constant value of money, where somehow he manages to find merit in the view that the political authorities can establish the value of money by fixing the legal price, though he recognizes that the value of money is market-determined and nominal and real value can differ.

JACQUES MELITZ

dominated Scholastic thinking. As NOONAN himself clearly shows, AQUINAS' argument was frequently ignored, not only by most Franciscans and many later Jesuits, but also numerous prominent canonists and even AQUINAS' own pupil, GILES OF LESSINUS, in a tract entirely devoted to usury (and for a long time mistakenly attributed to AQUINAS, by BÖHM-BAWERK among others). Furthermore, even during the peak of Thomistic influence, in the fourteenth and fifteenth centuries, many of those who relied on the Thomistic argument leaned heavily on other distinct arguments as well.

The Thomistic argument grew out of some Scholastic reasoning related to Roman law. The Scholastics accepted the Roman *mutuum* as the prototype of the loan. The *mutuum* was a contract pertaining to the loan of an article in return for a promise to repay an exact replica later on, *not the original*, and nothing more. The contract applied only to a class of goods styled as fungibles, which is still defined today by the ancient formula as goods 'counted by number, weight, or measure'. The Romans did not view the *mutuum* with any exclusive favor, encomium, as may be partly witnessed by the fact that Roman law admitted the contract of the *foenus*, relating to loans of fungibles bearing an interest clause.

Roman law provided that in a *mutuum* ownership of the article passes to the borrower. This view was perfectly sensible since, according to the contract, the lender would never regain dominion over the relevant article. The previous Roman law provision served as the basis for one of the Scholastics' central 'natural law' arguments against usury at the time AQUINAS wrote. They reasoned that because of the passage of ownership to the borrower, any payment above principal, or any usury, would be a receipt for the use of something that the lender does not own[9]. It is quite revealing of the rigor of Scholastic logic that the churchmen admitted a charge over and above repairs and depreciation in the case of a lease or rental, since in this case as opposed to that of a *mutuum*, the recipient of the charge retains possession.

AQUINAS tried to improve on the previous argument by strengthening the ground for the transfer of ownership in a loan. In this

9. NOONAN observes an important difficulty in this argument because of the lack of any 'natural law' foundation for private property in Catholic thought, where private property is seen as a consequence of the 'fall' of man (pp. 28–9).

SCHOLASTIC DOCTRINE OF USURY

effort, he presented his famous argument, pertaining to *consumptibles*, that ownership must pass in a loan because use involves destruction. The argument supposedly applied not only to perishables—clearly a kind of consumptible—but also to money, a type of durable capital. The idea was that the use of coins, without destroying them, involved alienation of the goods from the holder, a type of destruction from the borrower's viewpoint. This argument led AQUINAS to conclude, as in the Roman-law case, that any payment above principal would be a charge for something the lender does not own. *I shall contend, first, that the Scholastic theory really cannot be pinned on AQUINAS' argument; second, that the argument does not properly apply to money; and third, that even on its own grounds, the argument is incorrect.*

The difficulty in founding the Scholastic position on AQUINAS lies in the strict application of the usury doctrine to the conditions of the Roman-law *mutuum*, and therefore to fungibles, not consumptibles. The issue escaped adequate attention only because of the medievalist tendency, never since sufficiently repaired, to cite genuine or supposed consumptibles as examples of fungibles: notably, money, wine, grain, oil and corn[10]. But other basic Roman examples of fungibles, like brass and silver, are obviously not necessarily destroyed or even alienated through use: A craftsman can use borrowed silver without surrendering it to someone else, say, in making a preliminary model or for his pleasure[11]. In general, Roman-law usage would suggest interpreting fungibles broadly as perfectly substitutable, hence perfectly homogeneous, goods. The prominent Roman-law examples may suggest economic divisibility as a subordinate requirement, but this

---

10. The modern confusion on the subject among the experts is alarming. O'BRIEN [23] totally ignores the distinction between consumptibles and fungibles (p. 178); ELIO DEGANO [9] (col. 937) identifies the two; SCHUMPETER [24] supposes the usury doctrine to apply to consumptibles (pp. 104–5), while the historian ASHLEY goes so far as to insist that the Scholastic usury ban does *not* apply to fungibles but *only* consumptibles. To make matters worse, ASHLEY egregiously defines fungibles as goods 'such as a house, which is not consumed by use' [1], I, p. 152, and II, p. 395. In fact, the house is a standard Scholastic example of a non-fungible. ASHLEY was evidently misled by his central focus on the Thomistic argument, as were DEGANO and SCHUMPETER.

11. DE ROOVER thus errs in saying: '[The *mutuum*] applied only to fungible goods of which the use could not be separated from the substance or, in different words, which could not be used without being consumed' [14], p. 29.

JACQUES MELITZ

feature plays no part in the medieval reasoning[12]. The Cardinal JOHN DE LUGO (1593–1660) even included building materials as a non-Roman example of a fungible non-consumptible; NOONAN similarly cites paper clips (p.57). But even these examples do not adequately indicate the theoretical breadth of fungible non-consumptibles; for the whole class of durable mass-produced goods of modern technology is a case in point. There being no scarcity of fungible non-consumptibles, the Scholastic usury doctrine applies in numerous cases where the Thomistic argument does not.

Consumptible non-fungibles are even more of a problem than fungible non-consumptibles. For in these cases, there is no usury issue despite the application of the Thomistic argument. Given any meaningful difference between the item returned and the one lent, usury is clearly absent in the Scholastic sense. Major examples of consumptible non-fungibles are foodstuffs such as apples or lobsters, any one of which chosen at random cannot be supposed perfectly to substitute for any other even if the two belong to the same grade. Consider also the whole class of personal services, consisting of goods destroyed through use but generally incapable of return in kind in a loan.

The question of the application of the Thomistic argument to money turns on whether money is really a consumptible. The unhesitating positive answer of the Scholastics to this question is one of the most difficult elements to reconcile with favorable modern appraisals of their economics. Hardly any mistake in monetary thinking is more telling than the notion of money as useful in spending, not in inventory. It needs no emphasis now that a stock of money can serve in reducing transaction costs apart from any rate of turnover. Interestingly enough, AQUINAS may have perceived the problem in one subordinate context, relating to money lent *ad pompam* or for display. In these cases, he views a charge above principal as non-usurious. Had he therefore observed the possibility that a medieval merchant would use some of his money simply to reduce hired help, AQUINAS might have scrapped his entire argument for the Church

12. The Roman tendency to refer to economically divisible fungibles may be largely a reflection of the primitive state of the manufacturing arts in ancient Rome. That is, possibly the best examples of perfectly homogeneous goods in ancient Rome were goods which were highly economically divisble.

SCHOLASTIC DOCTRINE OF USURY

position[13]. However, there is an alternative interpretation of AQUINAS. Rather than any services of idle money, he may have had in mind the mere fact that in the case of a loan of money *ad pompam*, the lender does not surrender ownership over the lent goods. The two interpretations are not inconsistent; and in either case, AQUINAS concedes that money is not inherently a consumptible[14,15].

The most important theoretical question in connection with AQUINAS' argument is whether if we restrict ourselves to consumptibles, properly speaking, his logic is perfect. Clearly AQUINAS is right that if the use of a good entails destruction, ownership must pass to the borrower in a loan. Furthermore, he cannot be gainsaid

13. The relation of money to hired labor can be easily explained. With more money, the merchant can manage his business with less synchronization of receipts and expenditures; therefore he can afford to buy less often in bigger lots, which requires less use of labor on shopping errands. He can also manage with less record-keeping and less careful scheduling of payments and expenditures.

14. In his formal attempt to reconcile his position with the usury doctrine, AQUINAS observes that a loan of money *ad pompam* is a bailment, not a *mutuum*. If we ignore the Thomistic framework, it is important that the doctrinal ground for excluding money lent *ad pompam* from the usury prohibition is clear-cut. For the good returned is the identical one previously lent in the contract, and therefore the proper conditions for a *mutuum* are not met. From a doctrinal standpoint, all difficulty in endorsing interest on money lent *ad pompam* stems from the Thomistic notion of the inseparability of the ownership and use of money. AQUINAS compromises his view of this inseparability at another point, as NOONAN correctly notes: in defending *societas* (partnerships) on the ground that even a silent partner retains ownership over his money investment in the contract.

15. Altogether apart from the Thomistic stand, there is also some genuine doubt as to whether the Scholastics ought to have accepted money as a fungible. Through most of the middle ages, many individual coins of the same issue differed substantially in weight and fineness. In fact, prior to the thirteenth century, coinage methods hardly permitted less than a .05 to .10 variation in weight between individual coins struck from the same plate. As late as the seventeenth century, the accounting prices of different coins of the same issue often varied. In addition, coins from different political sources, bearing different names, often circulated side by side, especially on the continent. These sometimes changed in relative value. Thus, contrary to the Scholastics, two collections of coins considered identical at one time possibly would not be considered as such at a later time. See MARC BLOCH [3]; CARLO CIPOLLA [8], ch. 4; A. E. FEAVEARYEAR [16], ch. 1; P. SPUFFORD [26]; ABBOTT P. USHER [27], ch. 7; and MAX WEBER [29], ch. 19. I must emphasize again that this point about the fungibility of money is irrelevant to the Thomistic argument.

JACQUES MELITZ

in holding that the lender has no claim over and above the present
capital value of the good he lends—nor would the market grant him
any under ordinary competitive assumptions. In modern terms
(anticipated by at least one Scholastic writer)[16], the present capital
value of the good lent includes full allowance for the present dis-
counted value of all of the future services on the good. Any additional
return constitutes pure profit, both in the pejorative and the technical
sense of the term. However, this does not answer the question why
the present value of the loan of the good, entailing future payment,
is fixed independently of the date of contractual payment. Why
should a lender have no special claim to compensation for deferred
payment; or still, why should permission of delay in payment not in
itself constitute a service justifying a return[17]? If the Scholastics were
pressed on this issue, NOONAN implies that they would have proffered
the pious notion that time is no man's to sell. But since NOONAN
himself recognizes this notion as trite, it is not clear why he considers
AQUINAS the author of a valid case against usury, 'narrow and
technical' or otherwise[18]. We shall now pursue the problem of the
logical basis for the schoolmen's case against usury in connection
with DEMPSEY and SCHUMPETER.

IV. THE DEMPSEY-SCHUMPETER STAND

DEMPSEY and SCHUMPETER suggest a way in which the essential Scholastic position possibly could be salvaged. They claim to find in the
writings of certain late Scholastics, whom they consider representative
of mature Scholastic though in 1500–1700, an acceptable argument
for the unproductivity of time. In their view, the late Scholastics anticipated the fundamental theorem—largely associated with IRVING

16. See a remarkable quotation from the Cardinal LUGO in DEMPSEY [10],
p. 166.

17. The same criticism, in essence, was raised by CONRAD SUMMENHART
(German, ca. 1455–1502) in 1499—the same SUMMENHART who bore the brunt
of the civilian MOLINAEUS' (French, 1500–66) attack against the rigorous Church
doctrine (see NOONAN, pp. 340–2). Thus BÖHM-BAWERK [4], [5] was hardly the
first to perceive the issue.

18. NOONAN's effort to answer SUMMENHART at one point (pp. 359–60) misses
the present objection to the Thomistic argument.

SCHOLASTIC DOCTRINE OF USURY

FISHER and SCHUMPETER himself—about the tendency toward a zero interest rate in a stationary state. Although he rather guardedly states this thesis[19], DEMPSEY provides the essential groundwork for it in his book, *Interest and Usury*, which contains a glowing introduction from SCHUMPETER. Though with only implicit reference to a stationary state, SCHUMPETER later put forward the position boldly in his *History of Economic Analysis* (p. 105).

DEMPSEY, in his work, focuses almost exclusively on three late Jesuits—LUIS MOLINA (Spanish, 1535–1600), LEONARD LESSIUS (Belgian, 1554–1623), and JOHN DE LUGO (Italian, 1593–1660). These three authors clearly perceived the strategic importance of the unproductivity of time in opposing usury. They also attempted to defend this unproductivity apart from theology, arguing that the productivity of time, at least, in certain instances of credit, resolves to zero if we fully abstract from all yield on capital, returns to risk, and costs of lending activity. In harmony with this view, they placed heavy emphasis on the title of *lucrum cessans*, involving the notion of opportunity cost. Furthermore, they recognized credit risk as a valid title to interest, apart from *lucrum cessans* and the other two basic *extrinsic titles (damnum emergens* and *poena conventionalis)*.

Although NOONAN does not address himself to DEMPSEY's historical analysis, his work shows that the three Jesuits were not really representative of Scholastic thinking in 1500–1700. Rather, the vigor of their emphasis on the unproductivity of time, and their strenuous reliance on 'natural law', was extreme. NOONAN especially calls into question DEMPSEY's contention that by the time the three wrote, 'the position was almost universal... that usury was forbidden by natural law, and by this alone' (p. 165). According to NOONAN, MOLINA's contemporary, the canonist NAVARRUS (Spanish, 1493 to

19. To quote the most apt passage in DEMPSEY: 'If the underlying relationship of productive factors is such that the person already possessed of money in hand could not employ it in any way that would yield "increment" or value surplus, then on Scholastic grounds there would be no interest permissible; and on the ground of the moderns there would be neither the motive to borrow nor, on a business loan, a source from which to pay interest. The basic position from which the older and earlier writers proceed is the same. The conditions in which the one would allow moral existence of interest are broadly those in which the other would recognize its emergence on economic grounds' (pp. 193–4). Another very pertinent statement is on p. 197.

JACQUES MELITZ

1586), had 'several centuries of usage to support his sense of outrage' in attacking Dominic Soto (Spanish, 1495–1560), another contemporary, for asserting the exclusive 'natural law' foundation of the case for the usury ban (p. 346). Furthermore, Noonan refers to a general 'weakness of the natural-law case in the seventeenth and eighteenth century' (p. 355). This weakness apparently stemmed from increasing embarrassment over the inconsistencies and over-subtleties of the 'natural law' arguments. Already in 1499, Conrad Summenhart had presented a strong attack on the whole 'natural law' case against usury, which was destined to acquire much influence after a lapse of a century.

Based on Noonan, the three Jesuits' warm embrace and extension of the *lucrum cessans* title also was hardly representative. It is true that this title gained considerable importance following 1450. But the three Jesuits were extreme in advocating the use of this title as a substitute for some leading recognized licit contracts, including the money-yielding *census* and the low-interest bond or *contractus trinus*. Dempsey is equally misleading, it seems, in proposing credit risk as a widely recognized title to interest among the late Scholastics. The firm position before 1450 was that the bearing of credit risk was implicit in the obligation to lend without usury[20]. In regard to the late Scholastics, Noonan judges: 'Although by 1750 a complete rational case had been made out by the Scholastics for risk interest, it is the least warmly accepted of all the titles to gain from credit extension' (p. 293). In this climate of lukewarm acceptance of the risk titles, Noonan notably considers Molina, Lessius, and Lugo as the 'chief champions' of the risk titles from 1450 to 1750.

These historical objections, however, do not touch on the important question of the tenability of the Schumpeter-Dempsey interpretation of Molina, Lessius, and Lugo, as such. One basic difficulty with Schumpeter and Dempsey's position is that, as emerges in Dempsey, the three Jesuits faithfully adhered to the Scholastic restriction of the usury problem to loans of fungibles repaid in kind. While they may have stretched the significance of these loans and accordingly narrowed the application of licit contracts (relying more heavily than other schoolmen on *extrinsic titles* in order to justify

20. Noonan traces the admission of the 'risk' title to John Medina (Spanish, 1419–1516).

SCHOLASTIC DOCTRINE OF USURY

interest), they still recognized many licit contracts. In their view, the *societas*, the *locatio*, the credit sale of merchandise, and the *census* bearing payments in kind, all fell outside the pale of the usury question provided usurious intentions were absent. Their arguments for the unproductivity of time, therefore, could not concern time in all credit transactions, much less in all uses of 'roundabout' methods of production. For this reason, MOLINA, LESSIUS, and LUGO could hardly have had any genuine apprehension of the FISHER-SCHUMPETER theorem. The mere focus on a special type of credit repaid in a certain manner is entirely inimical to a grasp of the FISHER-SCHUMPETER argument: A general-equilibrium proposition completely submerging all distinction between money and non-money lending, lender or borrower legal possession of lent goods, and interest payments in money or in kind.

It is also difficult to follow SCHUMPETER and DEMPSEY in relating the three Jesuits' position, if only implicitly, to equilibrium in a stationary state. DEMPSEY himself makes it clear that there is not the vaguest allusion to assumptions of equilibrium or constant tastes, technology, and population in any of the three writers. Moreover, any limitation to such conditions would imply a possible positive yield to time for borrowers, in opposition to their writing and the whole tenor of Scholastic thought. There is no reason for treating these three authors, or any other major Scholastics, as advocating the sinfulness of usury, in the strict sense, only under ideal conditions. In so far as the Scholastics held that time, as such, *does not*, as well as *should not*, yield a product to borrowers, they clearly meant time in general.

SCHUMPETER and DEMPSEY also overlook the extent of disagreement between the usury idea and the *extrinsic title* of *lucrum cessans*. The concept of usury asserts that anyone supplying a *mutuum* has no claim to a charge for time, while the idea of *lucrum cessans* grants anyone the possibility of an opportunity cost of lending. The two thoughts might be reconciled if a person with a valid claim of *lucrum cessans* thereby also would be considered to have a valid claim to a charge for time. But that certainly is not the case, as the notion of *lucrum cessans* as an *extrinsic title* makes clear. Thus, to whatever extent the Scholastics conceived of a zero yield to time, they regarded this zero yield as consistent with a positive return to capital. Austrian economics may have taught us to understand the yield to capital as

JACQUES MELITZ

a yield to time under special assumptions. But we know as yet no way to make sense of the allegation of a zero marginal product to time while the marginal product of capital is positive.

The previous inconsistency in Scholasticism is especially pregnant in DEMPSEY, who wishes to praise the Scholastics for the notion that the interest rate must be zero apart from any risk or transaction costs, while also giving them credit for anticipating the modern theory of interest in their treatment of *lucrum cessans*. As seen, these two views are incompatible. I am, of course, identifying the Scholastics' interest theory with their stand on usury and not *lucrum cessans*.

It is also dubious that the Scholastic theory of *lucrum cessans* may be viewed as a close parallel to modern interest theory. *Lucrum cessans* is a title varying with each individual in every circumstance. Thus, for example, a banker able to prove opportunities for a higher rate of profit than his colleagues in the industry could claim a larger title of *lucrum cessans* per unit of credit (in livres, groats, *etc.*) than the rest. It would appear, therefore, that the Scholastic notion of *lucrum cessans* is more closely allied to the modern concept of a producers' surplus than any idea of a market price[21]. Admittedly, the issue is somewhat obscured by the Scholastic habit of relying on market prices to gauge the proper level of *lucrum cessans*.

Still, there can be little question that the Scholastic treatment of *extrinsic titles* generally involved far better interest theory than their discussion of usury. In fact, rather than anticipating modern interest theory, the central Scholastic usury doctrine entailed a failure to grasp the entire interest rate problem. The basic clue is the Scholastic emphasis on the case of loans repaid in the same form as the original. This emphasis may have initially derived from the influence of the Roman law *mutuum*. But eventually the factor acquired independent significance. The Scholastics clearly came to view the case of a loan repaid in the same form as the original as one where market pricing ceased to matter. Costs and public estimations (or all aspects of the 'just price' doctrine) could be ignored, and the question of ethical pricing securely pinned on abstract logic. The relevant principle of abstract logic was the fixed value of all fungibles, an argument

21. I say producers' not consumers' surplus, because by and large, the Scholastics recognized *lucrum cessans* as a title to compensation for producer, not consumer, losses.

SCHOLASTIC DOCTRINE OF USURY

that NOONAN traces especially to the canonist JOANNES ANDREA (Italian, 1270–1348). This Andrean principle, as NOONAN terms it, is indeed a truism, saying that the value of any fungible *in terms of itself* is always the same. This must have been the argument since the Scholastics recognized that the value of a fungible in terms of anything other than itself can change.

The Andrean principle was limited to fungibles, we can infer, because in other instances, no objective yardstick of the identity of goods was available, and therefore two goods could not be termed identical apart from the market place. The Scholastics especially reinforced their view of the fixed value of fungibles in the case of money, their main preoccupation in regard to loans. They held that the value of money as a standard of value is necessarily invariant, and that secular authorities assure the constancy of value of this good in some way.

These ideas now can be fitted together as follows, adding some important provision for risk. If a person receives Y at time $t + 1$ in return for lending X at time t, 'natural law' cannot determine how much Y he should charge, since the value of Y relative to X is subject to market factors, and can change. The lender thus faces a genuine risk of an adverse movement in the value of Y relative to X. Therefore, he may justly charge interest. Two influential twelfth- and thirteenth-century papal decretals concerned with credit sales and late deliveries (see Chapter IV in NOONAN, especially in regard to *venditio sub dubio*) strongly indicate this reasoning. The same logic also is found in some Scholastic discussions of interest-bearing loans repaid in foreign currency (rather indulgently styled *cambium* or exchange).

If, however, payment for lending X at t is received at $t + 1$ in the form of a different X, then the Andrean principle says that the receipt of the same amount of X ('in number, weight, or measure') as the original quantity lent totally discharges all obligation to the lender. Any payment above principal therefore is usurious[22].

22. It may be added that in many cases of apparent loans of X requiring future payments of X, the Scholastics would insist on the absence of a loan, but the presence of a spot or future sale instead. Thus, for example, the Scholatics interpret the lease (either a *commodatum* or *locatio*, depending on the presence of an interest charge) and the *census* as futures sales and often treat the postdated bill of exchange as a spot sale (mainly of transportation services).

JACQUES MELITZ

I do not pretend that the previous thinking, related to the Andrean Argument, encompasses all of the Scholastic reasoning—far from it. It does, however, manage the essential task of honoring the boundaries of the *mutuum* while pushing the logic of the usury opposition considerably beyond the Roman-law case. By contrast, the Thomistic argument deviates from, and partly opposes, the Roman-law case (as it centers on consumptibles and not fungibles). The Scholastic arguments for the sterility of time also do not fit comfortably in the preceding framework, where they play no essential role. But as seen, these arguments are generally very difficult to integrate satisfactorily in the usury doctrine, as they are crippled by the restriction of the doctrine to the *mutuum* and the late-Scholastic endorsement of *lucrum cessans*. Despite the attachment of MOLINA, LESSIUS, and LUGO to the unproductivity of time, the three clearly agree with every element of the previous conception. To quote LUGO in a reference to Andrean logic: 'If you gave ten and [later] receive back ten, you have already received as much as what you gave was worth' (DEMPSEY, p. 165).

If we now turn from exposition to assessment, the conclusion must be that there is little merit to the above Andrean reasoning against usury. The necessary unity of the value of every good in terms of itself at all times has no practical significance (except possibly in implying the constancy of the *accounting* price of a commodity unit of account)[23]. In terms of the only relevant considerations—purchasing power and procurement cost—the value of any good at any two points in time (including a commodity unit of account) can change[24]. More import-

23. Note that money is not inherently a commodity unit of account. In fact, as evident from n. 15 above, the view of money as such was hardly plausible in 1150–1700. Dempsey conveys the impression that Molina, Lessius, and Lugo were especially enlightened on the question of money, rejecting the aforementioned special scholastic arguments for the constant value of money (see DEMPSEY, pp. 156–7). But Noonan offers contradictory material (pp. 321–7, esp. 325). In addition there is no indication anywhere in the secondary literature, including DEMPSEY, of any disaffection by the three Jesuits from the basic proposition that a lender gets full value when he receives the same amount as he lent in the same physical form, though not the original. (See also the quote from LUGO in the preceding paragraph in the text.)

24. It may be observed, in this connection, as generally did not escape the secular writers, that the Scholastic stand implied the justice of a negative rate of return on an ordinary money loan under inflation.

SCHOLASTIC DOCTRINE OF USURY

ant, even if the value of a good stays constant, the return of the same amount as originally borrowed need not cancel all rightful claims by the lender. Here we come back to our earlier accusation that the Scholastics missed the entire interest rate problem in treating usury. For the whole issue of interest largely centers precisely on the question why a promise of one X tomorrow could be worth either less or more than the payment of one X today even if the value of X stays the same.

In light of the preceding factors, we can only marvel at the extent of DEMPSEY and SCHUMPETER's praise[25]. True, DEMPSEY's three Jesuits perceived some important general distinctions and the problem of condemning usury if time is productive. But they stayed within a framework where the issue of interest is confined to the intertemporal exchange of perfectly substitutable goods through credit (the usury problem), or else, in regard to the *extrinsic titles*, where interest is necessarily independent of any 'waiting' as such. I conclude, as presaged at the start, that there is no possible basis for a favorable verdict regarding the Scholastic interest theory, or the interest theory of any major Scholastic writers.

Tulane University and   JACQUES MELITZ
Ministère des Finances, France

25. Another effort to find some scientific significance in the usury doctrine, by H. SOMERVILLE [25] in 1932, supposes that the Scholastics anticipated JOHN MAYNARD KEYNES' view that individual saving may not correspond to real social investment, and therefore may be damaging. In a subsequent symposium, J. M. KEYNES spoke very kindly of SOMERVILLE's suggestion, as he did again in his *General Theory of Employment, Interest, and Money* ([17], pp. 351–2). Yet the Scholastics saw nothing but good in private saving involving moneylending at a *zero* interest rate. So far as interestbearing loans were concerned, also, their doubts about private saving never extended far beyond the *mutuum*. In addition, they never cared much whether usurious actions would enhance or diminish aggregate output and employment. From their perspective, the issue was basically one of equitable relations between *individual* borrower and *individual* lender. They were concerned about saving the lender's soul. The participants in the relevant symposium (EDWIN CANNAN, *et. al.* [6]) were remarkably indifferent concerning the authentic Scholastic doctrine.

489

JACQUES MELITZ

REFERENCES

[1] ASHLEY, W.J.: *An Introduction to English Economic History and Theory*, 1st ed., 1888 (London, Longmans, Green and Co., 4th ed., 1909), I, ch. 3, and II, ch. 6.

[2] BERNARD, A.: 'Usure: I. La Formation de la Doctrine Écclésiastique sur l'Usure', in: É. AMANN, Ed., *Dictionnaire de Théologie Catholique*, XV, 2 (Paris, Librairie Letouzey et Ané), cols. 2316–36.

[3] BLOCH, MARC: *Esquisse d'une Histoire Monétaire de l'Europe* (Paris, Librairie Armand Colin, 1954).

[4] BÖHM-BAWERK, EUGEN: *Capital and Interest: A Critical History of Economical Theory*, 1st German ed., 1884; 1st English trans. with Preface and Analysis by William Smart, 1890 (New York, Kelley and Millman, reprint, 1957).

[5] BÖHM-BAWERK, EUGEN: *The Positive Theory of Capital*, 1st German ed., 1889, 1st English trans. 1891 with Preface and Analysis by WILLIAM SMART (New York, G. E. Stechert and Co., reprint, 1923).

[6] CANNAN, EDWIN, B. P. ADARKAR, B. K. SANDWELL, and J. M. KEYNES, 'Saving and Usury: A Symposium', *Economic Journal* 42 (1932), pp. 123–37.

[7] CAPITANI, OVIDIO: 'Sulla Questione dell'Usura nel Medio Evo (A Proposito del Volume di J. T. NOONAN)', *Bulletino dell'Istituto Storico Italiano per il Medio Evo* 70 (1958), pp. 537–66.

[8] CIPOLLA, CARLO: *Money, Prices, and Civilization in the Mediterranean World* (Princeton, Princeton University Press, 1956).

[9] DEGANO, ELIO: 'Usura', in: *Enciclopedia Cattolica*, XV (Florence, G. C. Sansoni, 1954), cols. 937–41.

[10] DEMPSEY, BERNARD W.: *Interest and Usury* (London, Dennis Dobson Ltd., 1948).

[11] DE ROOVER, RAYMOND: 'Monopoly Theory Prior to Adam Smith: A Revision', *Quarterly Journal of Economics*, 65 (1951), pp. 492–524.

[12] DE ROOVER, RAYMOND: 'Scholastic Economics: Survival and Lasting Influence from the Sixteenth Century to Adam Smith', *Quarterly Journal of Economics*, 69 (1955), pp. 161–90.

[13] DE ROOVER, RAYMOND: 'J. A. Schumpeter and Scholastic Economics', *Kyklos*, 10 (1957), pp. 115–46.

[14] DE ROOVER, RAYMOND: *San Bernardino of Siena and Sant'Antonino of Florence: The Two Great Economic Thinkers of the Middle Ages* (Boston, Kress Library Series, Harvard University, 1967).

[15] DE ROOVER, RAYMOND: 'Economic Thought: Ancient and Medieval Thought', in: DAVID SILLS, Ed., *International Encyclopedia of the Social Sciences*, 10 (1968), pp. 430–5.

[16] FEAVEARYEAR, A. E.: *The Pound Sterling: A History of English Money*, 1st ed., 1931; 2n ed., revised by E. VICTOR MORGAN (Oxford, Clarendon Press, 1963).

[17] KEYNES, JOHN MAYNARD: *The General Theory of Employment, Interest, and Money* (New York, Harcourt, Brace and Co., 1936).

SCHOLASTIC DOCTRINE OF USURY

[18] LE BRAS, GABRIEL: 'Usure: La Doctrine Écclésiastique de l'Usure à l'Époque Classique (XIIe–XVe siècle)', in: É. AMANN, *Dictionnaire de Théologie Catholique*, XV, 2 (Paris, Librairie Letouzey et Ané, 1950), cols. 2336–72.

[19] LE BRAS, GABRIEL: 'Conceptions of Economy and Society', in: M. M. POSTAN, E. E. RICH, and EDWARD MILLER, Eds., *Cambridge Economic History of Europe*, III (Cambridge, England, Cambridge University Press, 1963), pp. 554–75.

[20] McLAUGHLIN, T. P.: 'The Teaching of the Canonists on Usury (XII, XIII and XIV Centuries)', *Mediaeval Studies*, 1 (1939), pp. 81–147 (Part I), and 2 (1940), pp. 1–22 (Part II).

[21] NELSON, BENJAMIN: *The Idea of Usury: From Tribal Brotherhood to Universal Otherhood*, 1st ed., 1949; 2d ed., 1969 (Chicago, University of Chicago Press).

[22] NOONAN, JOHN T.: *The Scholastic Analysis of Usury* (Cambridge, Harvard University Press, 1957).

[23] O'BRIEN, GEORGE: *An Essay on Medieval Economic Teaching*, 1st ed., 1920 (New York, Augustus M. Kelley, reprint, 1967).

[24] SCHUMPETER, JOSEPH A.: *A History of Economic Analysis* (New York, Oxford University Press, 1954).

[25] SOMERVILLE, H.: 'Interest and Usury in a New Light', *Economic Journal*, 41 (Dec. 1931), pp. 646–9.

[26] SPUFFORD, P.: 'Coin and Currency', in: M. M. POSTAN, E. E. RICH, and EDWARD MILLER, Eds., *Cambridge Economic History of Europe*, III (Cambridge, England, Cambridge University Press, 1963), pp. 576–602.

[27] USHER, ABBOTT P.: *The Early History of Deposit Banking in Medieval Europe* (Cambridge, Harvard University Press, 1943).

[28] VERMEERSCH, A.: 'Usury', in: CHARLES G. HERBERMANN and others, Eds., *The Catholic Encyclopedia*, XV (New York, Robert Appleton Co., 1912), pp. 235–8.

[29] WEBER, MAX: *General Economic History*, 1st German ed., 1923; 1st English trans. by FRANK H. KNIGHT, 1927 (New York, Collier-Macmillan, reprint, 1961).

SUMMARY

This article offers a systematic criticism of the Scholastic usury doctrine from the standpoint of modern economics. There is also an effort to examine the conformity of the Scholastics' various major arguments against usury with their narrow conception of the usury problem. DEMPSEY and SCHUMPETER's claims of important Scholastic contributions to interest theory receive special attention. With regard to medieval sources, the article relies mainly on the post-1938 writings of NOONAN, DEMPSEY, LE BRAS, and DE ROOVER.

ZUSAMMENFASSUNG

Vom Standpunkt der modernen Ökonomie aus bietet dieser Artikel eine systematische Kritik der scholastischen Lehre über den Wucher. Auch wird versucht,

JACQUES MELITZ

die verschiedenen Argumente der Scholastiker gegen den Wucher und ihre enge Definition des Wucherproblems auf ihre Vereinbarkeit zu prüfen. Besondere Aufmerksamkeit wird der Auffassung DEMPSEYS und SCHUMPETERS gewidmet, die Scholastiker hätten bedeutend zur Zinstheorie beigetragen. Für die mittelalterlichen Quellen verlässt sich der Autor hauptsächlich auf die nach 1938 erschienenen Schriften von NOONAN, DEMPSEY, LE BRAS, McLAUGHLIN, and DE ROOVER.

RÉSUMÉ

L'auteur du présent article fait, du point de vue de l'économie moderne, une critique systématique de la doctrine Scholastique de l'usure. Il essaie d'étudier la conformité des divers arguments majeurs des Scholastiques relatifs à l'usure avec leur conception étroite du problème de l'usure. L'auteur porte un intérêt particulier aux affirmations de DEMPSEY et de SCHUMPETER en ce qui concerne l'apport important des Scholastiques dans le domaine de la théorie de l'intérêt. Quant aux sources médiévales, l'auteur se réfère tout spécialement aux écrits de NOONAN, DEMPSEY, LE BRAS, McLAUGHLIN et DE ROOVER, postérieurs à 1938.

[9]

Ibn Khaldûn: A Fourteenth-Century Economist

Jean David C. Boulakia

Louisiana State University in New Orleans

Ibn Khaldûn was a fourteenth-century thinker who found a large number of economic mechanisms which were rediscovered by modern economists. Also, he used these concepts to build a coherent dynamic system. By quoting Ibn Khaldûn's *Muqaddimah*, this article tries to explain how Ibn Khaldûn reached economic conclusions and how he organized them into an extremely coherent model.

Ibn Khaldûn, Abu Zayd, was born in Tunis on May 27, 1332. His given name was Abd ar Rahmân, and his ethnic denomination was al-Hadramî. His family was connected with the Hafsid dynasty, then ruling North Africa, and, because of that connection, had settled in Tunisia, after having emigrated from Hadramawt to Spain, and remained there one century. In Tunis, although members of his family held high ranks in the civil services, they remained attached to the Spanish culture and considered themselves as being part of a foreign elite.

Consequently, as a member of this aristocratic family, Ibn Khaldûn was destined to occupy the highest ranks in the administration of the state and to take part in most of the political quarrels of North Africa. But because of his Spanish background, he never became a full member of his society and remained an exterior observer of his world.

At this time, the oriental world was ruled by an aristocratic international technocracy which cultivated the arts and sciences. When people were, by birth or by education, members of that elite, they were offered high ranks and important technical positions by the kings and the sultans, who rented their services. According to the revolutions and the wars, the

---

In my study, all the quoted passages are from the beautiful translation by Franz Rosenthal, and I use the original numeration (Ibn Khaldun, *"The Muquaddimah": An Introduction to History*, trans. from Arabic by Franz Rosenthal, 3 vols., Bollingen series no. 43 [New York: Pantheon, 1958]). Numbers in parentheses and brackets following quotations refer to volume and page numbers.

salary offered, and the personal connection, they traveled from one city to the other, following a conqueror or escaping condemnation.

Ibn Khaldûn was, by birth and by education, part of this elite. He studied under the direction of famous scholars. In 1352, only twenty years old, he became master of the seal and started a political career which would last until 1375. His fortunes were diverse, but whether in a jail or in a palace, rich or poor, a fugitive or a minister, he always took part in the political events of his time, always remained in touch with other scholars, Muslims as well as Christians or Jews, and above all, he never stopped studying.

From 1375 to 1378, he retired to Gal'at Ibn Salâmah, a castle in the province of Oran, and started to write his history of the world, of which the *Muqaddimah* constitutes volume 1.

In 1378, because he wanted to consult books in large libraries, he obtained the permission of the Hafsid ruler to go back to Tunis. There, until 1382, when he left for Alexandria, he was professor of jurisprudence. He spent the rest of his life in Cairo, where he died on March 17, 1406.

The major work of Ibn Khaldûn is his world history, but he wrote many other books, an autobiography, and a treatise on logic. His world history (*Kitâb al Ibar*) is a general history of the Arabs, but also of the Jews, the Greeks, the Romans, the Byzantines, the Persians, the Goths, and all the people known at that time. Like most of the authors of the fourteenth century, Ibn Khaldûn mixes philosophical, sociological, ethical, and economical considerations in his writings. From time to time, a poem enlightens the text. However, Ibn Khaldûn is remarkably well organized and always follows an extremely logical pattern.

In his short introduction (*Muqaddimah*) and the first of his seven books, Ibn Khaldûn, after having praised history, tries to demonstrate that historical mistakes occur when the historian neglects the environment. Ibn Khaldûn tries to find the influence that the physical, nonphysical, social, institutional, and economical environment has on history.

Consequently, the *Muqaddimah* is mainly a book of history. However, Ibn Khaldûn elaborates a theory of production, a theory of value, a theory of distribution, and a theory of cycles, which combine into a coherent general economic theory which constitutes the framework for his history.

I. The Theory of Production

For Ibn Khaldûn, production is a human activity which is organized socially and internationally.

A. Human Nature of Production

On the one hand, man is an economic animal. His end is production. He can be defined in terms of production: "Man is distinguished from the

other living beings by . . . [his] efforts to make a living and his concern
with the various ways of obtaining and acquiring the means [of life]"
(1:67).

On the other hand, the main factor of production is human labor:
"Profit [production] is the main value realized from human labour"
(2:272). "[Man] obtains [production] through no efforts of his own as,
for instance, through rain that makes the fields thrive, and similar things.
However, these things are only contributory. His own efforts must be combined with them" (2:273). "Human labor is necessary for every profit
and capital accumulation. When [the source of production] is work as
such, as for instance [the exercise of] a craft, this is obvious. When the
source of gain is animals, plants or minerals, human labour is still necessary, as one can see. Without [human labor], no gain will be obtained,
and there will be no useful [result]" (2:274). Consequently, man has to
produce in order to fulfill himself, and production results from his labor.

B.   Social Organization of the Production

To produce is also vital for man. If he wants to live and subsist, man is
obliged to eat. And he must produce his food. Only his labor will allow
him to eat: "Everything comes from God. But human labour is necessary
for . . . [man's livelihood]" (2:274).

However, man cannot produce enough food to live by himself. If he
wants to subsist, he is obliged to organize his labor. Through capital or
through skill, the most simple operation of production requires the collaboration of many men and the technical background of an entire civilization:
"The power of the individual human being is not sufficient for him to
obtain [the food] he needs, and does not provide him with as much food
as he requires to live" (1:69).

Each food requires a number of operations and each operation requires
a number of tools and crafts. This social organization of labor must be
done through a higher specialization of the workers. Only through specialization and repetition of simple operations do people become skilled
and able to produce goods and services of good quality at a good speed:
"Each particular kind of craft needs persons to be in charge of it and
skilled in it. The more numerous the various subdivisions of a craft are,
the larger the number of the people who [have to] practice that craft.
The particular group [practicing that craft] is coloured by it. As the days
follow one upon the other, and one professional colouring comes after the
other, the craftsmen become experienced in their various crafts and skilled
in the knowledge of them. Long periods of time and the repetition of
similar [experiences] add to establishing the crafts and to causing them to
be firmly rooted" (2:250).

Moreover, through specialization and social cooperation, man's efforts are multiplied. The aggregate production made by men working in co-operation is larger than the sum total of the individual production of each one working alone and larger than the amount that they need to subsist. A surplus is left which can be used for trade: "What is obtained through the co-operation of a group of human beings satisfies the need of a number many times greater [than themselves]" (2:235). "The combined labour produces more than the needs and necessities of the workers" (2:235). "Through co-operation, the needs of a number of persons, many times greater than their own [number] can be satisfied" (1:69).

Consequently, Ibn Khaldûn advocates a social organization of production in the form of a specialization of labor. Only specialization allows the high productivity which is necessary for the earning of an adequate livelihood. Only division of labor allows the production of a surplus and trade between the producers.

C. International Organization of Production

Just as there is a division of labor inside the country, there is an international division of labor. This international division of labor is not based on the natural resources of the countries, but on the skill of their inhabitants, for labor is, for Ibn Khaldûn, the most important factor of production: "Certain cities have crafts that others lack" (2:265). Consequently, the more numerous the active population, the greater the production: "With regard to the amount of prosperity and business activity, cities and towns differ in accordance with the different size of their civilization [population]" (2:234).

A surplus of goods is produced which can be exported, thus increasing the prosperity of the city. "A great surplus of products remains after the necessities of the inhabitants have been satisfied. [This surplus] provides for a population far beyond the size and extent of the [actual one], and comes back to the people as profit that they can accumulate. . . . Prosperity, thus, increases" (2:244).

On the other hand, the greater the prosperity, the greater the demand of its inhabitants for goods and services: "Luxury again increases in correspondence with the increasing profit, and the customs and needs of luxury increase. Crafts are created to obtain [luxury products]. The value realized from them increases, and, as a result, profits are again multiplied "Crafts and labour also are expensive in cities with an abundant civilization (population) in a city, the more luxurious is the life of its inhabitants" (2:236). This increased demand for goods and services brings a rise in their prices and an increase in the salaries paid to the skilled laborers: "Crafts and labour also are expensive in cities with an abundant civilization. There are three reasons for this. First, there is much need [of them] because of the place luxury occupies in the city. . . . Second, industrial workers place a high value on their services and employment. . . . Third, the number of people with money to waste is great and these people have many needs."

Thus, Ibn Khaldûn elaborates a theory showing the interaction between supply and demand, the demand creating its own supply which in its turn creates an accrued demand. Furthermore, he tries to show the cumulative process of development due to the intellectual infrastructure of the country. The more developed a country is, the greater is its intellectual capital and the organization of its intellectual infrastructure. Skilled people are attracted by this infrastructure and come to live in the country, thus increasing its intellectual capital and infrastructure.

Because, for Ibn Khaldûn, the main factor of production is labor and the only bottleneck to development is an insufficient supply of skilled labor, this cumulative process is, in fact, an economic theory of development: "The crafts require teachers" (2:306). "The crafts are perfected only if there exists a large and perfect sedentary civilization" (2:307). "The crafts are firmly rooted in a city [only] when sedentary culture is firmly rooted and of long duration" (2:309). "Crafts can improve and increase only when many people demand them" (2:311).

Consequently, Ibn Khaldûn elaborates a theory of economic development based on the interaction of supply and demand and, moreover, on the utilization and constitution of human capital. The premises of this theory are a social and international division which results in a cumulative process making the wealthy countries wealthier and impoverishing the poor.

His theory constitutes the embryo of an international trade theory, with analyses of the terms of exchange between rich and poor countries, of the propensity to import and export, of the influence of economic structures on development, and of the importance of intellectual capital in the process of growth. His theory of production, based on human labor, leads Ibn Khaldûn to theories of value, of money, and of prices.

II. The Theories of Value, Money, and Prices

Ibn Khaldûn, in his *Muqaddimah*, elaborates a theory of value, a theory of money, and a theory of prices.

A. A Theory of Value

For him, the value of any product is equal to the quantity of labor which has been incorporated in it: "The profit human beings make is the value realized from their labour" (2:289). Also, the wealth of nations does not consist of the quantity of money that the nations have, but of their production of goods and services and a favorable balance of payments. And, we saw, these two elements are linked together, this favorable balance of payments being the natural consequence of a high level of production.

> The question has been asked: Where is the property of the nations . . . ? [In reply], it should be known that treasures of gold, silver, precious stones, and utensils are no different from [other] minerals and acquired [capital]. . . . . It is civilization that causes them to appear, with the help of human labour, and that makes them increase or decrease. [2:285]
>
> The common people . . . think that the prosperity of these people is the result of the greater amount of property owned by them, or of the existence of gold and silver mines in their country in larger number [than elsewhere], or of the fact that they, to the exclusion of others, appropriated the gold of the ancient nations. This is not so. . . . A large civilization yields large profits because of the large amount of [available] labour, which is the cause of [profit]. [2:245, 246]

Ibn Khaldûn thereby elaborates a theory of labor value.

B. A Theory of Money

However, an economic measure of the value of the goods and services is necessary to man if he wants to trade them. This measure of value must possess a certain number of qualities: It must be accepted by all as legal tender, and its issue must be independent of all subjective influences.

For Ibn Khaldûn, two metals, gold and silver, are the measures of value. These metals are naturally accepted by all as money; their issue is not submitted to subjective fluctuations: "God created the two mineral 'stones,' gold and silver, as the [measure of] value for all capital accumulations. [Gold and silver are what] the inhabitants of the world, by preference, consider treasure and property [to consist of]" (2:274).

Consequently, Ibn Khaldûn advocates the use of gold and silver as monetary standards. For him, coinage is only the guarantee given by the ruler that a coin contains a certain quantity of gold and silver. The mint is a religious office and, consequently, is not submitted to temporal rules. The quantity of gold and silver included in a coin cannot be modified once the series has started: "The office of the mint is concerned with the coins used by Muslims in [commercial] transactions, with guarding against possible falsification or substandard quality [clipping] when the number of coins [and not the weight of their metal] is used in transactions" (1:407). "[The metal standard] is not something rigidly fixed but depends upon independent judgment. Once the inhabitants of a particular part or region have decided upon a standard of purity, they hold to it"

IBN KHALDÛN   IIII

(1:407). "[The office] is a religious office and falls under the caliphate" (1:407).

Consequently, Ibn Khaldûn advocates a metallic standard and a constant price of gold and of silver: "All other things are subject to market fluctuations, from which gold and silver are exempt" (2:274). So, metallic money is not only a measure of value but can also be used as a reserve of value.

C. A Theory of Prices

For Ibn Khaldûn, prices result from the law of supply and demand. The only exception to this rule is the price of gold and silver, which are the monetary standards. All other goods are submitted to price fluctuations which depend on the market. When a good is scarce and in demand, its price is high. When a good is abundant, its price is low: "The inhabitants of a city have more food than they need. Consequently, the price of food is low, as a rule, except when misfortunes occur due to celestial conditions that may affect [the supply of] food" (2:240).

Consequently, Ibn Khaldûn elaborates a theory of value based on labor, a theory of money which is quantitative, and a theory of prices determined by the law of supply and demand. This theory of prices leads him to analyze the phenomena of distribution.

III. The Theory of Distribution

The price of a product consists of three elements: salary, profit, and taxes. Each one of these elements constitutes the remuneration of a class of the population: salary is the remuneration of the producer; profit is the remuneration of the tradesman; and tax is the remuneration of the civil servant and the ruler. Consequently, Ibn Khaldûn divides the economy into three sectors: production, exchange, and public services.

A. Fixation of the Remuneration of these Elements

The price of each one of these elements is itself determined by the law of supply and demand.

1. Salary

As the value of a product is equal to the quantity of labor which is incorporated in it, salary is the major constituent of the price of goods. The price of labor is the basis of the price of an article: "Their treatment [of the land] required expensive labor and materials. . . . Thus, their

1112   JOURNAL OF POLITICAL ECONOMY

agricultural activities required considerable expenditures. They calculated these expenditures in fixing their prices" (2:242).

But the price of labor is itself determined by the law of supply and demand: "Crafts and labour also are expensive in cities with an abundant civilization. There are three reasons for this. First, there is much need [of them], because of the place luxury occupies in the city on account of the [city's] large civilization. Second, industrial workers place a high value on their services and employment, [for they do not have to work] since life is easy in a town because of the abundance of food there. Third, the number of people with money to waste is great, and these people have many needs for which they have to employ the services of others" (2:241).

2. Profit

Profit results from the difference which the tradesman acquires between the buying price and his selling price. But this difference depends on the law of supply and demand, which determines the buying price through salaries and the selling price through market: "Commerce means the attempt to make a profit by increasing capital, through buying goods at a low price and selling them at a high price" (2:297).

Ibn Khaldûn defines the two principal functions of trade, which are the translation of a product in time and space: "The attempt to make such a profit may be undertaken by storing goods and holding them until the market has fluctuated from low prices to high prices. . . . Or the merchant may transport his good to another country where they are more in demand than in his own, where he brought them" (2:297).

And, for Ibn Khaldûn, "the truth about commerce" is to "buy cheap and sell dear" (2:297).

3. Taxes

Taxes vary according to the wealth of the ruler and the subjects. Consequently, the amount of taxes is determined by the supply and demand of products, which in turn determine the income of the citizens and their readiness to pay.

B. *Existence of an Optimum Distribution*

Consequently, the level of these three categories of income is determined by the law of supply and demand. For Ibn Khaldûn, it has an optimum value.

1. Salary

If salaries are too low, the market is depressed and production is not promoted: "Little business is done [and] the prices . . . become particularly low" (2:241).

If salaries are too high, inflationary pressures occur and the producers lose their will to work: "Workers, craftsmen and professional people become arrogant" (2:241).

2. Profit

If profits are too low, the merchants are obliged to liquidate their stocks and cannot renew them because of the absence of capital: "When the prices of any type of goods . . . remain low . . . the merchants lose their capital" (2:301).

If profits are too high, the merchants also liquidate their stocks and cannot renew them because of the inflationary pressures: "The same [destruction of the livelihood of the merchant] applies to prices which are too high. . . . It is medium prices and rapid fluctuations of the market that provide people with their livelihood and profit" (2:302).

3. Taxes

If taxes are too low, the government cannot assume its functions: "The owner of property and conspicuous wealth in a given civilization needs a protective force to defend him" (2:250).

If taxes are too high, the fiscal pressure becomes too strong, the profits of the merchants and producers decrease, and their incentive to work disappears:

"[When] the taxes are too heavy, and the profits anticipated fail to materialize, . . . the incentive for cultural activity is gone" (2:81).

Consequently, Ibn Khaldûn divides the national income into three categories: salary, profit, and taxes, with an optimum level for each one of these categories. However, these optimum levels cannot exist in the long run, and cycles of the economic activity must occur.

IV. The Theory of Cycles

For Ibn Khaldûn, production depends on the supply and demand of products. But the supply itself depends upon the number of producers and their desire to work, as well as the demand upon the number of buyers and their desire to buy. The producers are the active population. The will to produce is the result of psychological and financial motives, determined by a high demand and a distribution favoring the producers and the merchants and, consequently, low taxes and high salaries and profits. The buyers are the population and the state. The power to buy is determined by a high income, which means a high supply and, for the state, a large amount of taxes.

Consequently, the determining variables of production are the population and the income and spending of the state, the public finances. But, according to Ibn Khaldûn, population and public finances must obey inexorable laws and fluctuate.

A. The Population Cycle

Production is determined by population. The larger the population, the greater the production. Also, the larger the population, the larger its demand upon the market and the greater the production.

But the population itself is determined by production. The greater the production, the greater is the demand for laborers on the market, the higher are salaries, the more workers are interested in moving into the area, and the more the population increases. Consequently, there is a cumulative process of growth of population and of production, the economic growth determining population growth and vice versa.

This cumulative process is due also to sociological and psychological causes. The workers want to live in a good intellectual environment and are the product of a good intellectual infrastructure. But the intellectual infrastructure of a city is itself determined by the number of skilled laborers and their income. Consequently, the richer and the more populated a city, the better its intellectual infrastructure and the more it attracts and creates new skilled laborers.

So, according to these mechanisms, there should be a cumulative process of development and of underdevelopment, the richest city attracting more producers, thus making these cities richer, and the poorest cities discouraging their producers and becoming poorer through their emigration.

However, the theory of Ibn Khaldûn is dynamic, and cycles must occur. According to him, fluctuations happen because of the existence of bottlenecks. On the one hand, there is a physical limit to the size of a city. When the inhabitants become too numerous, the streets become too narrow, the supply of water insufficient, and the buildings too old. Of course, through good town planning, this physical bottleneck can be avoided momentarily, but a good plan can increase the population optimum of a city, but cannot suppress it. The same problem occurs when the new optimum is passed.

On the other hand, an increase in population requires an increase in agricultural production. But an increase in city population brings an increase in manufactured production and an absolute as well as relative decrease in agricultural production. The number of peasants decreases compared with the number of citizens. Also, the increase in the level of living of the urban laborers brings an increase in the price of manufactured goods. Consequently, profits become much higher in the industrial sector than in the agricultural one, and the farmer's incentive to produce decreases. Finally, the inhabitants of the city cannot be fed if their number becomes too high. Famines and pestilences occur: "In the later [years] of dynasties, famines and pestilences become numerous. As far as famines are concerned, the reason is that most people at that time refrain from cultivating the soil. . . . The large number of pestilences has its reason in the large number of famines just mentioned. . . . The principal reason for the latter is the corruption of the air through [too] large a civilization [population]. . . . This also is the reason why pestilences occur much more frequently in densely settled cities than elsewhere" (2:125, 126).

Consequently, there is a population cycle in the cities. The population grows and, in its growth, brings an increase in demand and in production which, in turn, brings new immigrants. But this growth becomes too large for the geographical possibilities of the city and for the agricultural production, and the population naturally decreases. This population cycle determines an economic cycle, as population is the major factor of production.

B. The Public Finance Cycle

The state is also an important factor of production. By its spending it promotes production, and by its taxation it discourages production.

1. Government Spending

For Ibn Khaldûn, the spending side of public finance is extremely important. On the one hand, some of the expenditures are necessary to economic activity. Without an infrastructure set by the state, it is impossible to have a large population. Without political stability and order, the producers have no incentive to produce. They are afraid of losing their savings and their profits because of disorders and wars: "Royal authority calls for urban settlements" (2:201).

On the other hand, the government performs a function on the demand side of the market. By its demand, it promotes production: "The only reason [for the wealth of the cities] is that the government is near them and pours its money into them, like the water [of a river] that makes green everything around it, and fertilizes the soil adjacent to it, while in the distance everything remains dry" (2:251).

If the government stops spending, a crisis must occur: "Thus [when the ruler and his entourage stop spending], business slumps and commercial profits decline because of the shortage of capital" (2:92).

Consequently, the more the government spends, the better it is for the economy.

2. Taxation

However, the government cannot create money. Money is issued by a religious office according to a metallic standard. Consequently, if it drains money out of the economy, the economic activity must slow down. Money comes from the economy and must go back to the economy: "Money circulates between subjects and ruler, moving back and forth. Now, if the ruler keeps it to himself, it is lost to the subjects" (2:93).

The money spent by the government comes from the subjects through taxation. The government can increase its expenditures only if it increases its taxes, but too high a fiscal pressure discourages people from working. Consequently, there is a fiscal cycle. The government levies small taxes and the subjects have high profits. They are encouraged to work. But the needs of the government, as well as the fiscal pressure, increase. The profit of the producers and the merchants decreases, and they lose their will to produce. Production decreases. But the government cannot reduce its spending and its taxes. Consequently, the fiscal pressure increases. Finally, the government is obliged to nationalize enterprises, because producers have no profit incentives to run them. Then, because of its financial resources, the government exercises an effect of domination on the market and eliminates the other producers, who cannot compete with it. Profit decreases, fiscal revenue decreases, and the government becomes poorer and is obliged to nationalize more enterprises. The productive people leave the country, and the civilization collapses:

> It should be known that at the beginning of the dynasty, taxation yields a large revenue from small assessments. At the end of the dynasty, taxation yields a small revenue from large assessments. . . .
>
> [At the beginning] the tax revenues are low. When tax assessments and imposts upon the subjects are low, the latter have the energy and desire to do things. Cultural enterprises grow and increase, because the low taxes bring satisfaction. When cultural enterprises grow, the number of individual imposts and assessments mounts. In consequence, the tax revenue increases.
>
> When the dynasty continues in power . . . , [it becomes] sophisticated. . . . Every individual impost and assessment is greatly increased, in order to obtain a higher tax revenue . . . in correspondence with the gradual increase in the luxury customs and many needs of the dynasty. . . .
>
> The assessments increase beyond the limits of equity. The

> result is that the interest of the subjects in cultural enterprises
> disappears, since when they compare expenditures and taxes with
> their income and gain and see the little profit they make, they
> lose all hope. Therefore, many of them refrain from all cultural
> activity. The result is that the total tax revenue goes down, as
> the individual assessment goes down. . . . Finally, civilization is
> destroyed, because the incentive for cultural activity is gone.
> [2:80, 81]
>
> Commercial activity on the part of the ruler is harmful to his
> subjects and ruinous to the tax revenue. . . .
>
> Competition between them [the subjects] already exhausts . . .
> their financial resources. Now, when the ruler, who has so much
> more money than they, competes with them, scarcely a single
> one of them will be able to obtain the things he wants. . . . [The
> subject] thus exhausts his capital and has to go out of business.
> [2:83, 84, 85]

Consequently, for Ibn Khaldûn, there is a fiscal optimum but also an
irreversible mechanism which forces the government to spend more and
to levy more taxes, bringing about production cycles.

Thus, Ibn Khaldûn elaborated a dynamic theory based on a law of
population and a law of public finances. According to these inexorable
laws, a country must necessarily pass through cycles of economic development and depression.

V. Conclusion

Ibn Khaldûn discovered a great number of fundamental economic notions
a few centuries before their official births. He discovered the virtues and
the necessity of a division of labor before Smith and the principle of
labor value before Ricardo. He elaborated a theory of population before
Malthus and insisted on the role of the state on the economy before
Keynes. The economists who rediscovered mechanisms that he had already found are too many to be named.

But, much more than that, Ibn Khaldûn used these concepts to build
a coherent dynamic system in which economic mechanisms inexorably lead
economic activity to long-term fluctuations. Because of the coherence of
his system, the criticisms which can be formulated against most economic
constructions using the same notions do not apply here.

Should we retire the fatherhood of these economic concepts from the
authors to whom they are attributed in our histories of thought? Ibn
Khaldûn has been claimed the forerunner of a great number of European
thinkers, mostly sociologists, historians, and philosophers. However,
although his ideas were known in Europe since the seventeenth century,

1118   JOURNAL OF POLITICAL ECONOMY

and his works translated since the nineteenth century, it does not seem that his successors were familiar with his economic ideas. Consequently, although Ibn Khaldûn is the forerunner of many economists, he is an accident of history and has had no consequence on the evolution of economic thought. He is alone, without predecessors and without successors. Without tools, without preexisting concepts, he elaborated a genial economic explanation of the world. His name should figure among the fathers of economic science.

Additional References

Andic, S. "A Fourteenth Century Sociologist of Public Finance." *Public Finance* 20, nos. 1–2 (1965): 20–44.
Bouthoul, G. *Ibn Khaldoun: sa philosophie sociale.* Paris, 1930.
Fishel, W. *Ibn Khaldûn in Egypt.* Berkeley: Univ. Calif. Press, 1967.
Ibn Khaldoun. *Les prolegomènes.* Translated by William MacGuckin, baron de Slane. Paris: Imprimerie Imperiale, 1862–68.
———. *Les textes sociologiques et économiques de la "Mouquaddima," 1375–1379.* Classified, translated, and annotated by G. H. Bousquet. Paris: Rivière, 1965.
Lacoste, Y. *Ibn Khaldoun, naissance de l'histoire, passé du tiers monde.* Paris: Maspero, 1966.
Rabi, M. M. *The Political Theory of Ibn Khaldûn.* Leiden: Brill, 1967.
Warren, E. G. "The Spread of Ibn Khaldûn's Ideas on Climate and Culture." *J. Hist. Ideas* 28, no. 3 (July/September 1967): 415–22.

[10]

The economics of the just price

George W. Wilson

It is astonishing the amount of controversy that has occurred among economists concerning the "just price." Innumerable authors, some eminent, others mere toilers in the academic vineyard, have sought to explain what Aquinas or Aristotle "really meant." The fact that the latter are delightfully vague and terse on this point, as on all others pertaining to economics, provides an endless series of re-interpretations following the latest interpretation or misrepresentation.

But why should economists, of all people, be so engrossed in what Aquinas and Aristotle "really meant"? Because, aside from a natural interest in precursors in any discipline, economists have a special concern as far as value theory is involved. Value theory—the explanation of how prices are formed in a market economy, how the system is held together by interlocking markets and the normative properties of such a system—has long been central to economic analysis qua analysis. Thus the pedigree of the "ultimate" determinants of supply and demand becomes a matter of general interest to many economists and of consuming passion to some.

At a more fundamental level both Aristotle and Aquinas were attempting to come to grips with the problem of achieving stability in a disintegrating environment and the related problem of nonmarket regulation of varying degrees of monopoly power. We, in our times, can scarcely afford to ignore whatever insights Aristotle and Aquinas might provide in either context. All market-oriented economies are groping toward some workable "incomes policy." The recent spate of phases and freezes in the United States highlights the need for some clearer conception of justice in exchange. As the traditional tools of monetary and fiscal policy appear less and less effective in the control of inflation without creating unacceptably high levels of unemployment, partly because of market imperfections (the cost push and demand shift explanations of inflationary pressures), society feels compelled to "intervene" more in particular markets. The growing gap between private and social costs as evident in the problems of pollution leads to similar

GEORGE WILSON *is Professor of Economics and Business Administration in the Graduate School of Business at Indiana University.*

interventions. Of course, it is obvious that neither Aristotle nor Aquinas was much concerned with these types of problems. Yet, to the extent that they were concerned with just exchanges in noncompetitive markets, some of their views may be of interest and possibly relevance today.

In addition, the relationship of thought in general, and economic thought in particular, to environment is a study of some importance, especially as it may shed light on current thinking. The economic thought of Aristotle and Aquinas may have suited their times in the sense of being directly relevant to the plight of the Greek city-state on the one hand and the status of the medieval economy on the other. Thus, while one may not learn much in the way of economics as we now think of it, simply because the market *system* was then absent, one may achieve a better perspective of the relativity of economic analysis. As Alfred Marshall was later to assert, "though economic analysis and general reasoning are of wide application, yet every age and every country has its own problems; and every change in social conditions is likely to require a new development of economic doctrine."[1]

In scrounging around in the Aristotelian or Thomistic attic in search of economic fragments and tidbits regarding value, assuming that Aquinas' notion of justice in exchange is straight Aristotle (even this is doubtful, as noted below), economists have reached every possible conclusion.

Some even contend that there is no economic analysis whatsoever in Aristotle: Schumpeter argues that "Aristotle's performance is . . . decorous, pedestrian, slightly mediocre and more than slightly pompous common sense."[2] Polanyi, on the other hand, believes that Aristotle attacked "the problem of man's livelihood with a radicalism of which no later writer on the subject was capable—none has ever penetrated deeper into the material organization of man's life."[3]

No one, not even Aristotle's staunchest admirers among the economics fraternity, believes that it makes any difference whatsoever to an understanding of contemporary economics what Aristotle or Aquinas had to say—nor did economic analysis derive much, if any, benefit from Book I of the *Politics* or Book V of the *Nicomachean Ethics* or the *Summa Theologica*. Yet, as noted above, we may derive something of value from another examination and, hopefully, resolve some of the conflicting interpretations. The present article has this as its goal.

The central issue is value theory. On the one hand various inter-

1. A. Marshall, *Principles*, book 1, chap. 3, sec. 5.
2. Joseph A. Schumpeter, *History of Economic Analysis* (Oxford, 1954), p. 57.
3. George Dalton, ed., *Primitive, Archaic and Modern Economics: Essays of Karl Polanyi*, Anchor Books (New York, 1968), pp. 79–80.

pretations stress the role of utility or want satisfaction as the ultimate determinant not only of the *act* of exchange but as the *measure of true, natural,* or desirable exchange value. For example, Haney asserts that Aristotle's "notion of value is clearly subjective and is based upon the usefulness of the commodity exchanged. . . . An exchange is just, when each gets exactly as much as he gives the other; yet this equality does not mean equal costs but equal wants."[4] On the other hand, some argue that Aristotle and Aquinas had an *objective cost* theory of value or even a labor theory of value.[5] On the latter interpretation Aquinas is the philosophical forerunner of Marx, or alternatively Marx, as has been said, was the last of the Schoolmen.

The problem of the role of cost vs. utility in determining exchange value is an interesting one in the development of economic analysis. After Adam Smith scrubbed utility as a measure of value, because, among other reasons, he failed to distinguish between total and marginal utility, value theory became essentially cost of production through Ricardo, J. S. Mill, Marx, to the 1870's, when the so-called marginal utility revolution occurred which argued for utility as the ultimate determinant not only of exchange per se but also of the measurement of exchange value.

Thus, some economists see Aristotle and Aquinas as forerunners of the Austrian school of economics of the 1870's, and others see them as predecessors of the cost-of-production theorists. A few see them as predecessors of both! Nor has the surprisingly large number of more recent discussions done much to clarify this longstanding debate.

For example, Spengler has argued that "Aristotle, with his emphasis upon demand and his neglect of costs, was a forerunner of the Austrian . . . School."[6] Lowry asserts that Aristotle was "dealing with the problem of dual subjective estimates of value between two exchanging parties" and that there is "no room for doubt."[7] Soudek concludes that for Aristotle, "the ratio of exchange of two products is the reciprocal of the ratio of the utilities of what A gives away to what he receives and conversely to what B gives away to what he receives."[8] Soudek even

4. Lewis H. Haney, *History of Economic Thought* (New York, 1949), p. 65. Alexander Gray, in *The Development of Economic Doctrine* (London, 1931), pp. 27–30, expresses a similar view. See also A. A. Trever, *A History of Greek Economic Thought* (Chicago, 1916), p. 109.

5. See, for example, Schumpeter, pp. 61–62.

6. J. J. Spengler, "Aristotle on Economic Imputation and Related Matters," *Southern Economic Journal,* April 1955, p. 388.

7. S. Todd Lowry, "Aristotle's Mathematical Analysis of Exchange," *History of Political Economy* 1 (1969):47.

8. Josef Soudek, "Aristotle's Theory of Exchange: An Inquiry Into the Origin

goes so far as to suggest that Jevons' "ideas as presented in his *Theory of Political Economy* read like a modern paraphrase of the fifth book of the *Ethics*."[9]

On the other hand, Hollander suggests that "relative costs appear to govern the just price,"[10] and de Roover argues that "beyond doubt . . . [Aquinas] considered the market price as 'just' " but the market would "tend to coincide with cost or to oscillate around this point."[11]

Others see strong elements both of cost and utility in determining "just" exchange ratios. Thus, Gordon states that "there is a labor element in the value thinking of Aquinas . . . [and] there are a number of passages in Aristotle's writings which can be interpreted as indicating that he also thought that labor cost was connected with the process of value determination."[12] De Roover, while arguing that utility was, for Aquinas, "the principal source of value," modifies this by noting that "cost, however, is an important adjunct, because it affects value to the extent that it affects supply."[13]

There are others who believe that it is necessary to distinguish between Aquinas and Aristotle in their theories of just exchange. The cost side, it is argued, was grafted on Aristotle by medieval writers. Thus, Baldwin concludes that "for Aristotle the value of economic goods was based on the 'subjective' factor of need or want. It was not until the rehabilitation of Aristotle . . . in the thirteenth century that the so-called 'objective' factors of labor and expense were added to the Aristotelian analysis."[14]

It is perhaps surprising that so many conflicting opinions exist among rather diligent scholars who are, presumably, interpreting the same brief statements. The obvious answer is that both Aquinas and Aristotle were singularly obscure in their writings and hence subject to varying interpretations. Furthermore, any intelligent person can read almost anything he chooses into statements that have elements of ambiguity. There is, of course, some of that in the above set of viewpoints. However, it

---

of Economic Analysis," *Proceedings of the American Philosophical Society* 96, no. 1 (Feb. 1952):74.

9. Ibid., p. 73.

10. S. Hollander, "On the Interpretation of the Just Price," *Kyklos* 18 (1965): 622.

11. R. de Roover, "The Concept of the Just Price: Theory and Economic Policy," *Journal of Economic History,* Dec. 1958, p. 422.

12. Barry J. Gordon, "Aristotle and the Development of Value Theory," *Quarterly Journal of Economics,* Feb. 1964, p. 115.

13. R. de Roover, "Schumpeter and Scholastic Economics," *Kyklos* 10 (1957): 130.

14. J. W. Baldwin, *The Medieval Theories of the Just Price, Transactions of the American Philosophical Society* 49, part 4 (July 1959):12.

60   *History of Political Economy*

is possible to develop an interpretation that renders the foregoing differences somewhat more comprehensible and understandable.

In the first place Aristotle appears to have been "preoccupied with the isolated exchange between individuals."[15] All of the ratios and turgid discussion thereof in Aristotle suggest this kind of interpretation. Furthermore, although this is less apparent, Aristotle gives the impression that he is referring to the exchange of existing stocks of two commodities rather than production flows. The references to the "justice which distributes common possessions"[16] and to rectificatory justice imply isolated exchange of stocks of commodities, although other passages referring to the "work" of the builder and shoemaker suggest some concept of production flows or rates. Nevertheless, if this is the interpretation of Aristotle's viewpoint, then the analogy with Jevons is, in fact, very close, as Soudek argues.[17] Under the assumptions of isolated exchange of existing stocks, it is perfectly legitimate to ignore production in terms of rates and costs of output per time period of alternative commodities. If so, then there is little wonder that Aristotle ignored production costs. Aristotle was, therefore, led to emphasize some other factor in exchange, namely, utility. Now this type of analysis is largely irrelevant if one is talking in terms of maintaining a viable and hierarchical economic and political system over time. Yet this is precisely how Soudek interprets Aristotle. In fact, Soudek's rather turgid representation of the equating of four ratios to achieve proportionate reciprocity ignores completely the quantities that people may have to exchange and rates of output per time period. Thus, to obtain an exchange ratio, Soudek—and possibly also Aristotle—had to revert to some other units of measure which an economist might define as units of utility or utils. Without some

15. Soudek, p. 46.

16. *Nicomachean Ethics* 5.1131b, 25–30. All quotations from Aristotle are from the W. D. Ross translation as they appear in Richard McKeon, ed., *Introduction to Aristotle*, Modern Library (New York, 1947).

17. As Jevons puts it, "Imagine that there is one trading body possessing only corn, and another possessing only beef. . . . Let us now suppose that the first body, A, originally possessed the quantity a of corn, and that the second body, B, possessed the quantity b of beef. As the exchange consists in giving x of corn for y of beef, the state of things after exchange will be as follows:

A holds $a - x$ of corn, and y of beef
B holds x of corn and $b - y$ of beef."

W. S. Jevons, *The Theory of Political Economy* as reprinted in George W. Wilson, ed., *Classics of Economic Theory* (Bloomington, Ind., 1964), pp. 551–52. The analogy with Aristotle's statement "Let A be a farmer, C food, B a shoemaker, D his product equated to C, etc." is obvious; hence Soudek's conclusion noted earlier. However, since Aristotle ignored the *quantities to be exchanged*, no determinate ratio or price is possible.

notion of relative quantities to be exchanged, either in terms of existing stocks or rates of output using normal or traditional production techniques, there is no way to establish an exchange ratio. Even here, however, Gordon has argued that Aristotle did not neglect the cost element and points out that "exchange is to take place mainly by direct association of varieties of producers. The typical exchange transaction is an association between two persons who are simultaneously both buyers and sellers. Each exchanges his surplus produce with the other. Justice is done and hence exchange will occur where the ratio of exchange between the two goods concerned is such as to equate the two persons both as sellers [hence the cost factor] and as buyers [hence the utility element]."[18] To the extent that Soudek is correct in asserting that Aristotle dealt with isolated exchange of stocks of goods between two individuals, there is little wonder that he and others can find no production cost element in the Aristotelian analysis. On the other hand, to the extent that Gordon's interpretation is valid, it is clear that Aristotle had elements of production cost as well as of utility.

When, however, we look at Aquinas, there is more specification of production costs even as far as particular items of cost—wages, transport costs, raw-materials prices, etc.—are concerned. It is, therefore, clearer in Aquinas that he was dealing with flows, not stocks, of goods and that, therefore, if society wants to maintain a preexisting flow of goods, one must insure that the producers of the goods are recompensed by an amount equivalent to that required to keep them producing at the current level of efficiency and at the current rates of output. There is also evidence to support this general view. As Baldwin notes, "both Albert and Thomas stated . . . explicitly that a just exchange must be an equal exchange of labor and expenses so that society can continue to exist. . . . [W]ithout equivalence of value exchange will not take place. In other words, goods will not be produced permanently below cost."[19] O'Brien has also concluded that medieval economic teaching "aimed at extended production"[20] and thus dealt with an ongoing process. In other words, the apparent differences noted above seem to emerge from interpreting Aristotle in terms of stocks of goods while at the same time interpreting Aquinas largely in terms of production flows. Furthermore, as argued below, Aquinas was more self-consciously con-

18. Gordon, p. 123.
19. Baldwin, p. 77. Baldwin, however, does not attribute an objective cost theory of value to Aquinas, mainly because Aquinas only referred to "labor and expenses" in his earlier *Commentary to the Ethics* and did not make similar references in the later *Summa* (p. 77).
20. George O'Brien, *An Essay on Mediaeval Economic Teaching* (London, 1920), p. 223.

cerned with maintaining a given and specified status quo (as far as feudal society was concerned) than Aristotle was.

Now I do not wish to belabor further the already belabored economic fragments in Aristotle and Aquinas. Nor do I profess to know what they "really" meant by reinterpreting once again the translations of their few words having economic content. Rather, I wish to interpret the just price in terms of what it must probably have meant to an observant scholar given the economic conditions of the times and the objectives of society as seen by the analysts.

At the risk of considerable oversimplification, the economic conditions of the Athens of Aristotle and the medieval system of Aquinas may be dubbed low-level chronic stagnation.[21] The possibility of economic expansion was generally not envisioned except through conquest; growth through productive use of the economic surplus and technological change was not seen as either possible or especially desirable. Satisfactions could be raised by decreasing wants rather than assuming them to be urgent and boundless. Thus, Greeks were told that "to have few wants is godlike." Now just as in the poor countries at present, the fact of low-level stagnation itself breeds attitudes and beliefs inconsistent with economic progress, so in the economies of Aristotle and Aquinas. In fact, however, both were concerned with instability, the demise of the city state and the manorial systems as viable economic and political forms. Thus both were concerned with the preservation of these forms of economic organization, which had performed so effectively in earlier centuries.

Clearly, the economics of preservation is necessarily different from the economics of growth. To preserve a society along traditional lines implies that people perform their tasks in the same general fashion as their ancestors. This means that where exchange of goods for money takes place, this must leave both buyer and seller in their traditional positions and able to perform traditional functions in the usual way. Thus while commodity exchange is necessary, and money as well to facilitate such exchange, the terms of exchange become crucial. In no sense can the market be allowed to decide these terms unless it is a

21. Some details of the Athenian economy appear in C. G. Starr, "Overdose of Slavery," *Journal of Economic History*, March 1958, pp. 17–32, and A. H. Jones, "The Social Structure of Athens in the Fourth Century, B.C.," *Economic History Review*, Dec. 1955, pp. 141–55; see also H. Mickel, *The Economics of Ancient Greece*, 2d ed. (Cambridge, 1957). There are innumerable studies of the medieval economy. The recently published works of M. M. Postan, *Essays on Medieval Agriculture and General Problems of the Medieval Economy* and his *Medieval Trade and Finance*, both published by the Cambridge Univ. Press, 1973, provide much information and interpretation.

"free" market and unless the pattern of income distribution is deemed acceptable. But a free market implies not only large numbers of suppliers but also the unbridled pursuit of gain. In a stagnant or declining economy, one man's gain is another's loss. In a low-level stagnant economy, differential loss or gain is apt to be fatal to the society as a whole if it leads to the extinction of people whose role it was to perform an "essential" function. The terms of exchange must therefore be watched to guard against such substantial gains or losses that people are induced either to ignore their traditional obligations or cannot pursue them because of excessive loss. In individual acts of exchange there is plenty of latitude between "acceptable" gains and losses and unacceptable, and there was never any hint that exchange ratios were to be fixed and immutable, although some interpretations deny this. Rather, the emphasis was always on justice and equity and, in Aristotle, the "mean."

The meaning of justice and equity in exchange: the just price

In the context of preservation, maintenance of the status quo, justice and equity in economic matters must obviously mean a set of exchange ratios that leaves buyer and seller in a position that enables both of them to fulfill their "necessary" functions, however these may be defined.

In the Middle Ages the necessary functions become part of the system of mutual rights and obligations. As Tawney puts it:

> The facts of class status and inequality were rationalized in the Middle Ages by a functional theory of society, as the facts of competition were rationalized in the eighteenth by the theory of economic harmonies; and the former took the same delight in contemplating the moral purpose revealed in social organization as the latter in proving that to the curious mechanism of human society a moral purpose was superfluous or disturbing. Society, like the human body, is an organism composed of different members. Each member has its own function, prayer, or defense, or merchandise, or tilling the soil. Each must receive the means suited to its station, and must claim no more. Within classes there must be equality. . . . Between classes there must be inequality; for otherwise a class cannot perform its function or—a strange thought to us—enjoy its rights. . . . Society was interpreted, in short, not as the expression of economic self interest, but as held together by a system of mutual, though varying obligations. Social well-being exists, it was thought, insofar as each class performs its functions and enjoys the rights proportioned thereto.[22]

22. R. H. Tawney, *Religion and the Rise of Capitalism* (New York, 1950), pp. 27, 29.

64   *History of Political Economy*

Thus, given a pattern of needs or wants imposed, not by self-interest or the acquisitive instinct, but by tradition, reinforced by Church sanctions and civil authorities, it is possible to determine the resource needs of each class. Or, alternatively, given traditional occupations and techniques of production, it is possible to determine the number of persons (plus dependents) who would be needed to perform given functions. For a given set of "classes" or "occupations" there will be an amount of income necessary to each in order to perform its functions. The just "price," in those areas of the society where goods are bought and sold, when combined with quantities bought and sold, is one that ensures an income adequate to each class's functions.

Thus, we have Aristotle's oft-quoted statement to the effect that justice in exchange occurs when the "terms have been equated so that as farmer is to shoemaker, the amount of the shoemaker's work is to that of the farmer's work for which it exchanges." Albertus Magnus (1193–1280) reasserted the same thing when he wrote that

> the carpenter ought to receive the product of the tanner and in turn the tanner that which according to a just exchange is his. . . . And when this equality is not preserved, the community is not maintained, for labor and expenses are not repaid. . . . The state cannot be built up of one type of workers alone. Properly, therefore, these things are exchanged not absolutely but with a certain comparison to their value according to use and need.[23]

Finally, Aquinas states that for exchange to be just,

> as many shoes should be exchanged for a house or for a man's food, as the labor and expense of the builder or farmer is greater than that of the tanner because, if this be not observed there will be no exchange. . . . This one thing which measures all other things is in truth the *need* which embraces all exchangeable goods. . . . This is manifest because if men had no needs, there would be no exchange. . . . In other words, insofar as a farmer . . . is more necessary than the tanner . . . by that amount in numerical proportion must the work of the tanner exceed that of the farmer so that many shoes are exchanged for one measure of grain. . . . If reciprocity is absent, there will be no equality of things exchanged and these men are no longer able to dwell together.[24]

How do we interpret these statements in terms of the true measure

23. *Opera omnia* (Paris, 1891), vol. 7, chap. 7, no. 31.
24. *In decem libros ethicorum*, Liber V, Lecture 9.

of exchange value? I believe the proper interpretation is relatively straightforward. For each occupation (or even individual) there is a "socially determined" ranking so that if, let us say, a builder is "worth" or "esteemed" or "needs" twice as much as a cobbler, then, on the average over a period of time, the value created by the builder must be twice the value created by the cobbler. If on the average the builder constructs one house during a time period while the cobbler makes 500 pairs of shoes during a similar time period, then one house equals 1,000 pairs of shoes. Thus, if one house is valued at $10,000, one pair of shoes will be worth $10.

In a more general sense, if we have two kinds of labor (or occupation), L_1 and L_2 socially valued or esteemed as A_1 and A_2, where $A_1 + A_2 = 1$, and if the average output per period is X_1 units of commodity M for L_1 and X_2 units of commodity N for L_2, the exchange ratio between M and N is not X_1/X_2, but rather the exchange ratio is weighted such that $A_1/A_2 = X_1/X_2$. The preceding example of the builder and cobbler is a specific illustration of this weighting system, where $A_1 = \frac{2}{3}$ and $A_2 = \frac{1}{3}$.

The crucial question is the weighting system, to which I now turn.

The weighting system

As with the various interpretations of value in exchange, there are differences with respect to the meaning and determination of the weights. Spengler argues that "Aristotle's analysis implies that if some men are more skilled than others, they will produce more want-satisfaction per time period and hence will command more want-satisfaction or money per time period. Thus if A is four times as skilled as B, and A's product C is equal in money value to B's product D, then the proportion A : B :: C : D implies that A gives up only one-fourth as much work (or work time) as does B, or that A commands a time-rate four times that of B when each is paid according to his merit or his contribution of want satisfaction."[25]

Soudek argues that the way the equality of subjective utility is achieved is through bargaining and suggests that Adam Smith's discussion in book 1, chapter 5, of *The Wealth of Nations* is what "Aristotle's idea must have been."[26] Now Smith's discussion of the relative weights to be accorded different kinds of labor in chapter 5 was an unsuccessful attempt to rescue his labor theory of value from one of the two aspects of circularity. His assertion that different "sorts of labor" come to be

25. Spengler, "Aristotle on Economic Imputation," p. 387.
26. Soudek, p. 63.

66   *History of Political Economy*

"adjusted . . . not by any accurate measure but by the higgling and bargaining of the market"[27] was later followed up by Ricardo's cryptic comment that "the scale, when once formed, is liable to little variation"[28] and Marx's assertion that the "different proportions . . . are established by a social process that goes on behind the backs of the producers. . . ."[29]

27. Adam Smith, *The Wealth of Nations*, Modern Library (New York, 1937), p. 31.

28. David Ricardo, *Principles of Political Economy and Taxation* (London, 1911), p. 11.

29. Karl Marx, *Capital*, Modern Library (New York, n.d.), 1:52. It may be worth noting here that the obvious circularity in the above assertions *could* have been removed in Smith had he incorporated his discussion in book 1, chapter 10, as part of his value theory. In chapter 10 the differences among various sorts of labor are made to depend upon occupational differences which determine the net relative disutilities of the various kinds of productive effort. Within particular occupational categories Smith assumes comparable disutility but not among them. Chapter 10 thus implies that the basic numéraire be construed in terms of common, unskilled labor, with all other occupations weighted in terms of this basic unit by a disutility premium. This disutility depends, according to Smith, upon five factors: (1) agreeableness of the employment, (2) cost of learning the business, (3) constancy of employment, (4) the trust reposed, and (5) the probability of success. Regardless of the merits of this particular list of conditions and its more proper use as the basis for developing the principle of net equal advantage to explain equalizing wage differentials, it nevertheless provides a basis for evaluating different sorts of labor prior to the market process which itself is to be explained.

That is, if we let r_i represent the disutility premium to be added to the basic value unit for occupation i ($i = 1, \ldots, n$) then the relative value of different sorts of labor per man hour is simply determined. Thus knowing the amount of labor of each type k_i and k_{i+s} required to produce one unit of product (and assuming constant costs), the relative commodity exchange ratio between A and B could be expressed as follows:

$$\frac{k_i(1 + r_i)}{k_{i+s}(1 + r_{i+s})} = \frac{A}{B}$$

assuming one sort of labor produced both A and B respectively.

There is no difficulty in principle if several sorts of labor are required to produce one unit of product so long as the proportions are constant and we know the r_i's.

The disutility function exists independently of the market. The market process merely gives a pecuniary representation of it: in this sense this aspect of circularity disappears.

Now the determinants of the r_i's are (1) individual psychology and (2) the nature of the employments. But there would clearly be problems in an impersonal labor market if all people were psychologically different, for then, even within a given occupation, the r's would differ. Thus, Smith's *tabula rasa* assumption and his insistence upon individual similarities at birth make it reasonable to presume that the r_i's are solely a function of particular employments. Within occupations, there is comparable disutility insofar as each occupation differs from every other in terms of Smith's five factors but not among them. It is clear then

It is difficult to believe that Aristotle had any such notion, especially in view of his emphasis upon a *prior* determination of just prices. The market was not to be invoked to establish the relative merits of particular occupations. On the contrary, the differences among people were, in the main, noneconomic for Aristotle. Indeed, he refers explicitly to "freedom, wealth, noble birth, general excellence" (*Politics* 3.1280a and 1281a); he asserts that slaves are wanting in virtue and deliberative faculties (*Politics* 3.1255a, b, 1259b, 1260a) and argues that defects of nature may render some unfit for full membership in a state (*Politics* 3.1327b–1330a). Finally, in a delightfully terse and ambiguous statement he notes that "all men agree that what is just in distribution must be according to merit in some sense."[30] This is not only a set of noneconomic criteria which were clearly neither market-determined nor established by any higgling and bargaining but also much more of an individualistic interpretation which presumably applies not to builders and cobblers in general but to specific builders and cobblers. It is as if, for Aristotle, builder A *ought* to get more than builder B if he is, let us say, more virtuous or in some way contributes more to society than B does, over and above their respective abilities as producers. This interpretation is consistent with the view of Aristotle's value theory that treats it in terms of isolated exchange. However, this view of his economics does not fit very well with the notion that Aristotle was concerned with social cohesion and the perpetuation of the city state. Of course, all of this is pretty fuzzy in Aristotle's writings, but the meaning of the weighting system implies a sort of objective labor-cost theory of relative exchange value where the kinds of labor are weighted, not in terms of marginal productivity or necessarily in terms of skills, but in a socially predetermined fashion prior to the act of exchange, and in a fashion designed to preserve the hierarchical structure. That this is inconsistent with the notion of justice involved in isolated exchange

---

that $r_i = f_i O_j$ where O_j refers to occupational differences and $j = 1, \ldots, 5$ (Smith's five factors).

Thus the exchange ratio between the products of industry 1 and industry $1 + s$ would be:

$$\frac{k_1(1 + f_1 O_j)}{k_{1+s}(1 + f_{1+s} O_j)}$$

where k_1 and k_{1+s} are the number of man hours of a particular grade of labor required to produce one unit in industries 1 and $1 + s$, respectively.

In short, Smith's analysis in chapter 10 could have been used to establish a scale of different sorts of labor based upon disutility instead of the higgling and bargaining of the market. In this way the disutility and labor theories of value are closely linked, and one aspect of circularity is removed.

30. *Nicomachean Ethics* 5.1131a, 25–30.

68   *History of Political Economy*

of existing stocks is also obvious. This suggests that Gordon's "reconciliation," cited above, may be more appropriate.

For Aquinas the weighting system was much more closely oriented to maintenance of the economic status quo and hence much less individualistic than for Aristotle. Spengler suggests that for Aquinas, "If the persons belong to the same category . . . and work for the same amount of time they must be paid the same amount. If one person belongs to a higher category than the other . . . he must be paid at a proportionally higher rate."[31] The frequent references to the "common estimate" in medieval writings indicate more of a social than an individual concern. In short, the weighting system for Aquinas differs sharply from that of Aristotle. Thus, if we interpret the just price as one which yields an income to the producer adequate to maintain his traditional volume of production, this income must cover (i) his production costs—raw materials, maintenance and repairs, and transport, and (ii) his own profits or wages adequate to maintain his family's status.[32] But all production costs, including his own inputs, involve a social weighting, not an individual weighting, to maintain the status quo. It is this which distinguishes the just price from long-run market price; the costs in the latter are not related to status quo, because costs change in a market economy in response to (i) technological change and (ii) shifts in consumer demand. But in the Middle Ages, both (i) and (ii) were disparaged. Economic progress was not an important goal to be sought after, nor was consumer sovereignty to be the guiding principle for resource allocation, largely because of their disruptive properties.

It is, however, interesting to note that a static, purely competitive economy accepting the existing distribution of income with constant tastes and preferences would yield the same results as Aquinas' just price, except that the Church or State would and, in the medieval view, should condition the patterns of consumer demand by minimizing material wants, emphasizing charity, noble works, the golden rule, excellence, the mean, and so on.[33] It is not unlike the contemporary concern

31. J. J. Spengler, "Hierarchy vs. Equality: Persisting Conflict," *Kyklos* 21 (1968):226.
32. As O'Brien puts it: "Langenstein lays down that everyone can determine for himself the just price of the wares he has to sell by reckoning what he needs to support himself in the status he occupies. According to the *Catholic Encyclopedia*, the just price of an article included enough to pay fair wages to the worker —that is, enough to enable him to maintain the standard of living of his class." George O'Brien, *An Essay on Mediaeval Economic Teaching* (London, 1920), pp. 111–12.
33. Curiously, Baldwin (p. 12) agrees that Aristotle's "justice of exchange was probably nothing more mysterious than the normal competitive price."

with the *quality* of our wants, the stress on the composition of GNP, and the erosion of the connection between rewards and efforts.

In short, Aquinas' theory of justice in exchange involves prices which cover the "costs" of production where these are weighted by the social estimate of the "worth" of the laborer in a particular class.[34]

The problem of utility

The foregoing interpretation of the just price in terms of socially weighted production costs is contrary to the interpretation of those who have stressed the utility explanation, especially as far as Aristotle is concerned, although there is less disagreement with respect to Aquinas. We may therefore concentrate on Aristotle.

The argument that subjective utilities are equated in a just transaction is rooted in the interpretation that Aristotle referred to or was preoccupied by isolated exchange between two individuals. If we also view exchange not only as between two individuals but also as involving existing stocks, as noted earlier, there can be no interpretation of Aristotle's meaning other than one stressing utility.

It is obvious, for example, that for exchange to take place at all following the division of labor, there must be reciprocal need or demand. Aristotle is perfectly clear on this point—"for if men did not need one another's goods at all, or did not need them equally, there would be either no exchange or not the same exchange."[35] And again, "when men do not need one another, i.e., when neither needs the other or one does not need the other, they do not exchange."[36] In addition, the division of labor is natural since it forms the basis of the state— " . . . the state comes into existence for the sake of the good life."[37] Thus exchange is natural and desirable. However, it is one thing to assert that reciprocal demand is essential for exchange; it is quite another to assert that demand, need, or utility *measures* exchange in a just transaction. To be sure Aristotle asserts that "all goods must . . . be measured by some one thing . . . now this unit is in truth demand. . . ."[38] This has been interpreted to mean that the utility given up equals the utility received and is based upon the statement that "the just is intermediate between a sort of gain and a sort of loss. . . . it consists in

34. For a lucid supporting view, see Bernard W. Dempsey, "Just Price in a Functional Economy," *American Economic Review*, Sept. 1935, pp. 471–86.
35. *Nicomachean Ethics* 5.1133a, 26–29.
36. Ibid., 1133b, 7–9.
37. *Politics* 1.2.1252b, 28–30.
38. *Nicomachean Ethics* 5.1133a, 25–28.

70   *History of Political Economy*

having an equal amount before and after the transaction."[39] Lowry even refers to a "fund of mutual benefit" (=satisfaction or utility?)[40] whereas Soudek, who has most carefully and fully elaborated the utility interpretation, believes that this means "a real equality of want satisfaction is accomplished (in a just exchange)" and that this involves "the comparison by each individual of the relative utilities of the goods involved in exchange—the utility of what one gives and what one receives. Equal ratios of both utilities to each party to the exchange means 'exchange of equivalents.' "[41] Without some notion of diminishing marginal utility of the goods involved, this does not permit establishing an exchange *ratio* between two goods. It merely states that for an equilibrium of satisfaction, the utility to A of a given amount of D acquired relative to the loss of utility to A of a given amount of C given up should equal a similar ratio for B. But unless one makes interpersonal utility comparisons and at the same time postulates diminishing utility, this in no way permits establishing a ratio of *quantities* exchanged. Trever seems to make such an interpersonal comparison when he states that "each shall receive an equal quantum of economic satisfaction,"[42] and Gordon believes that Aristotle has a notion of diminishing utility.[43] However, with Aristotle's emphasis upon individual differences, interpersonal utility comparisons would seem even more far-fetched than use of Adam Smith's *tabula rasa* notion. Contemporary analysis of course rejects the whole notion of interpersonal utility comparisons. Furthermore, Gordon's attribution to Aristotle of diminishing marginal utility stems from Aristotle's isolated comments in a noneconomic context. In fact, Gordon carefully avoids the adjective "marginal" and concludes that at most "there was only a bare foreshadowing of the principle of diminishing utility."[44]

Nevertheless, since no one has argued that Aristotle's theory of exchange was any more than normative or prescriptive, the above views seem to be imparting far more than is, in fact, in any of his writings. It is likely that Aristotle meant nothing more than that in isolated exchange of stocks, justice occurred when each was satisfied with the bargain. The tortured attempt by Soudek to interpret Aristotle's notion of "proportionate reciprocity" as a proportion involving *four* ratios and as ultimately implying a utility measure cannot be sustained. It is based

39. Ibid., 1132b, 15–20.
40. Lowry, p. 47.
41. Soudek, p. 46.
42. Trever, p. 109.
43. Gordon, p. 117.
44. Ibid., p. 119.

upon the assumption that the Euclidian notion of proportionate reciprocity means that "two magnitudes are said to be reciprocally proportional to two others when one of the first is to one of the other magnitudes as the remaining one of the last two is to the remaining one of the first" and that this means that,

$$\frac{A}{C} : \frac{B}{D} :: \frac{A}{D} : \frac{B}{C}.^{45}$$

This, however, implies that $C = D$, and without some notion of the units in which C and D are measured (i.e., is C one or more houses and D, 1, 100, or more pairs of shoes?) the amounts of C and D exchanged for one another remain indeterminate and thus also the "just price." In short, we need to know the quantities available for exchange. In isolated exchange between two people these can be highly variable over time and are dependent upon the particular circumstances of the two individuals (or Jevons' "trading bodies"). Thus, interpreted as isolated exchange of existing stocks, justice may imply a wide range of exchange ratios.

On the other hand, interpreting exchange as attempting to find ratios among goods in accordance with their rates of output per period, assuming normal or traditional techniques of production and assuming the desirability of maintaining the status quo, leads to the determination of the just price that I have already noted. Now it is easy to interpret the cryptic remarks of ·Aristotle either way. My own belief is that he intermingled various notions within excessively brief paragraphs and that in attempting to "explain" the several kinds of particular justice, namely, distributive, rectificatory or corrective (voluntary and involuntary),[46] he thoroughly fudged them, at least as far as the fragments and translations currently at our disposal are concerned.

Furthermore, *subjective individual* utility is an inappropriate technique for evaluating production in a "functional society" where the aim is not to maximize utility but to preserve the status quo. However, if the utility view is interpreted as relating to individual "needs" within

45. Soudek, p. 55.
46. Baldwin (p. 11) argues that there is a third type of justice, reciprocation in Aristotle, and that the three types correspond to the three mathematical ratios then current in Greek thought, such that corrective justice refers to the arithmetic ratio, distributive justice to the geometric ratio, and reciprocal to the harmonic ratio. I can find no basis for this whatsoever. There is no way in which Aristotle's four variables can be related to these ratios and their presumedly respective types of justice. To be sure, Aristotle illustrates rectificatory justice in a simplistic and, as Schumpeter would say, pedestrian fashion, but one is pushed to the limits of interpretation to arrive at Baldwin's conclusion although, as he admits, "the actual text of the *Ethics* will never be completely free from ambiguity"(!).

72   *History of Political Economy*

the context of status quo, then the "needs" reflect "costs" (socially weighted production costs) and the two versions coalesce so far as the weighting system may be "subjective."

It may be objected, however, that a nonsocialist society does not determine any specific weighting system. That is, there was no secret ballot or central determination of such a weighting system as I have outlined. Rather, the price that was deemed to be just in practice was at best a reflection of a general estimate. In fact, in the Middle Ages it became a conventional price acquiesced in, the current or going price, or one established by the ruler of the guilds or town authorities on a similar basis.[47] But construed in the sense of maintaining stability it can be no other than a weighted cost-of-production theory of value. As such it is a normative theory. The fact that actual practice did not always conform to precept does not deny the normative theory. Nor was all the analysis normative. Both Aristotle and Aquinas knew something of monopoly price and generally condemned it, although for Aquinas much depended on how the excess profits were used.

In any event, a just price once formed, even if it is the resultant of a mass of subjective judgments or common estimates, becomes wholly objective in individual transactions. But because of the possibility of injustice even at a just price in specific transactions, these may take place at a price other than the common estimate or going price. If the seller, owing to a particular circumstance, would be seriously disadvantaged by exchange at the just price, a premium may be paid. So the just price of the Middle Ages lay within a range: i.e.,

P = socially weighted costs of production ± excessive loss or gain in any individual transaction + a risk payment (later!) under certain circumstances.

As Saint Antoninus (1389–1459) put it:

The third thing to be considered regarding the value of an object is that we can hardly ever determine it except conjecturally and with probability, and this not at a mathematical point but within a certain range respecting times, places, and persons. . . . With regard to the second principle division, namely, that there is an appropriate range within the limits of which prices may vary, it should be observed that this may be known in three ways; from law, from custom, and from practical judgment. . . . This same proper range is known also in a second way. For as Scotus says in his commentary referred to above, experience shows clearly enough that the

47. See O'Brien, pp. 115 ff. and Baldwin, p. 29.

matter is ordinarily left to those making the exchange so that, having due regard for each other's wants, they judge themselves to give and receive equivalents. . . . Thus a certain real gift or concession commonly accompanies contracts. It is therefore probable enough that when the contracting parties are mutually satisfied, they wish to concede something to each other as long as they do not too grossly depart from perfect justice.

This same appropriate range of price is known, in the third place, from practical judgment. For practical judgment dictates that when a thing, which in itself is worth ten, is as dear to the owner as though worth twelve, if I propose to own it, I must give not only ten but as much as it is worth to him according to his desire of retaining it. One reason why things are worth more or less is the shortage or abundance of money among the townspeople. When they have money, they buy and then things sell dearer, but when those who have power in the community need money, things are bought and sold for less.[48]

Conclusion

The notion of the just price was rooted in the quest for stability at a time when existing social forms were changing. But it was also a product of low per capita levels of output and, as such, was a social and prescriptive device that attempted to have the needed goods and services produced and distributed in accordance with prevailing views of equity. In the absence of competitive markets, justice in exchange required some special social constraints. The attempt to integrate and preserve a functional society was not, of course, successful. But the aim to create a society in which men "stand united by what they do, not divided by what they have or have not"[49] is surely a matter of much interest to us all, as the events of the past decade so loudly proclaim. The market mechanism is a highly efficient way to organize productive activity, but it is clear that we need to go well beyond the market to ensure justice in the distribution of income. Although our definition of justice differs sharply from that of the Middle Ages, we can still accept the aim of a society where, to repeat, men stand united by what they do—not divided by what they have.

I do not believe that the study of either Aristotle or Aquinas provides much detailed guidance for contemporary forms of an "incomes"

---

48. Cited in Dempsey. Aristotle's view of *corrective* justice coincides with this in the sense of a mean relative to specific individuals rather than a mean "which is one and the same for all men." Soudek, p. 51.

49. Dempsey, p. 486.

74   *History of Political Economy*

policy. Nor do I believe it is worth while reinterpreting their economic judgments much more, disconnected, confused, inconsistent, and normative as they are. However, the view that what is justice in exchange depends upon a society's goals and the refusal or inability to rely upon even competitive market forces as determining just exchange ratios may be something worth reiterating as the world's economies grope towards the twin goals of rapid growth *and* greater social and economic justice.

[11]

Justum pretium: one more round in an "endless series"

Stephen T. Worland

In a recent article in this journal, George Wilson calls attention to the "astonishing . . . controversy" and "endless series of re-interpretations" deriving from Aristotle's and Aquinas' teaching on the just price.[1] So far as the treatment of Aquinas is concerned, Wilson's main thesis amounts to restatement of an interpretation of the just price which, originating among the romanticist and historicist critics of Classical economics, was once taken for granted as correctly epitomizing an irreconcilable clash between medieval economic doctrine and capitalism. Over the past few years, this traditional reading of Aquinas has come to be rejected as inaccurate by several scholars.[2] Whereas one writer concludes that the traditional interpretation of the just price doctrine is "a historical myth,"[3] Wilson surveys the literature, reinterprets the sources yet one more time, and finds that there is truth in the myth after all. This is not to say that he serves old wine from old bottles. For it is the use of a special interpretive tool—the sociology of knowledge—that leads Wilson to differ with contemporary scholarship and to reaffirm the traditional interpretation of Aquinas. What is more important, Wilson not only provides new interpretive support for a traditional conclusion. The very precision (with arithmetic illustration) of his restatement brings to light an unresolved ambiguity found in both the traditional interpre-

STEPHEN T. WORLAND *is an Associate Professor of Economics at the University of Notre Dame.*

1. George W. Wilson, "The Economics of the Just Price," *History of Political Economy* 7 (1975): 56–74.

2. For a brief summary of the debate on this point and for citation of the relevant literature, cf. J. Gilchrist, *The Church and Economic Activity in the Middle Ages* (New York, 1969), pp. 58–62. For a conspicuous exception to the now common view that the medieval just price should be understood as the equivalent of competitive market price, cf. Samuel Hollander, "On the Interpretation of the Just Price," *Kyklos* 18 (1965): 615–32. Hollander argues that the attempt to find a single, internally consistent theory of the just price in Aquinas is mistaken.

3. Mark Blaug, *Economic Theory in Retrospect*, rev. ed. (Homewood, Ill. 1968), p. 31.

tation of the just price doctrine and in latter-day efforts to replace that interpretation with an alternative based on Neoclassical economics.

The question can be introduced with Jevons' well-known statement of the relationship between cost and value:

> Cost of production determines supply.
> Supply determines final degree of utility.
> Final degree of utility determines value.[4]

As Wilson interprets Aquinas, whether the above statement expresses the just price doctrine depends upon how the first proposition is understood. For a Ricardian, cost of production (given constant input-output coefficients) would be determined by biological forces which fix the subsistence wage. For a Neoclassical marginalist, costs are determined by factor marginal productivity in alternative uses. According to Wilson's reading, cost is determined in Aquinas' view by the position of the producer in the social hierarchy: "justice in exchange involves prices which cover the 'costs' of production where these are weighted by the social estimate of the 'worth' of the laborer."[5] For each occupation in the economy, society establishes a relative ranking—for example, that a builder is "worth" twice as much as a cobbler. This relative ranking, in conjunction with technological data, then determines the exchange ratio between commodities. The cost of a commodity is thus made to depend upon, or is weighted by, society's estimate of an occupation's relative "worth."[6]

Wilson's reading of Aquinas thus parallels that once employed by economic historians, particularly the immensely influential Sir William Ashley.[7] However, whereas Ashley derived such an understanding of the just price from Sir Henry Maine's thesis that social development follows a pattern of evolution from status to contract,[8]

4. Quoted in G. W. Wilson, *Classics of Economic Theory* (Bloomington, Ind., 1964), p. 556.

5. Wilson, "Economics of the Just Price," p. 69.

6. Ibid., p. 65.

7. Sir William Ashley explains Aquinas' reference to the golden rule (*Summa Theologica*, II-II, q. 77, a. 1.) as follows: "If price therefore was to be determined by the rule of doing to others as we would wish them to do to us, then the maker (of a product) should receive what . . . would permit him to live a decent life according to the standard of comfort which public opinion recognized as appropriate to his class." Cf. *English Economic History and Theory*, 3d ed. (London, 1894), 1: 138. Cf. also "Justum Pretium" in *Palgrave's Dictionary of Political Economy* (London, 1923), 2: 500 ff. Wilson's understanding of the just price also coincides with that implied in some versions of Catholic teaching on the "living wage." Cf. John A. Ryan, *Distributive Justice*, 3d ed. (New York, 1942), pp. 258 ff.

8. Cf. Sir Henry Maine, *Ancient Law*, World's Classics edition (London, 1931), esp. p. 141. An interpretation similar to Ashley's underlies Tawney's oft-quoted con-

Wilson reaches a similar interpretation by a different and novel route. For it is his belief that scholastic teaching on justice evolved out of a concern, more pronounced in Aquinas than in Aristotle, for forestalling breakdown of a traditional, hierarchical social structure. Aquinas (so Wilson believes) tried to lay down rules of exchange justice that would prevent extreme gains and losses and thus permit each class in the social hierarchy to continue fulfilling its allotted function. Thus, Aquinas was led to define as "just" that "set of exchange ratios that leaves buyer and seller in a position . . . to fulfill their 'necessary' functions."[9] Each class or occupation requires an income sufficient to let it perform its function, and the just price "is one that ensures an income adequate to each class's functions."[10] Less individualistic than Aristotle, Aquinas defines the just price as that which will allow the producer to maintain a given rate of output, cover his production costs, and allow him to earn "profits or wages adequate to maintain his family's status."[11] Thus, according to Wilson's interpretation, Aquinas began from the value judgment that the existing hierarchical social structure should be maintained, saw that the maintenance of such a structure required a given pattern of income distribution, and thus was led to define as "just" that price which when multiplied by a standard rate of output would provide the producer with the requisite level of income.

Ever since Marx made the famous statement that "it is not the consciousness of men that determines their existence, but . . . their social existence which determines their consciousness,"[12] students of economic thought have had to face the possibility that what passes for knowledge may be the result of a more or less subconscious reaction to the demands of a particular social system. The sociology of knowledge reminds the historian that explanation for the characteristic features of a system of thought may be found, not in the demands of abstract reason, but in social stresses generated by a particular historical situation. According to such a viewpoint, the growth of economic knowledge is "relativist" rather than "immanent,"[13] or to

clusion, "the last of the Schoolmen was Karl Marx." *Religion and the Rise of Capitalism*, Mentor paperback ed. (New York, 1947), p. 39. Whereas later commentators were to reinterpret the just price doctrine in terms of Neoclassical marginal utility theory, Ashley's and Tawney's views reflect adherence to the older labor theory of value.

9. Wilson, "Economics of the Just Price," p. 63.

10. Ibid., p. 64.

11. Ibid., p. 68.

12. Quoted in W. Stark, *The Sociology of Knowledge* (Glencoe, Ill., 1958), p. 12.

13. Cf. A. F. Chalk, "Relativist and Absolutist Approaches to the History of Economic Theory," *Southwestern Social Science Quarterly* 48 (1967): 5–12.

use Joseph Spengler's terminology, it is "exogenous" factors, rather than the "endogenous" demands of the discipline, that explain the key developments in economic thought.[14] Though Wilson does not explicitly refer to the sociology of knowledge, his assertion that Aquinas lived in a society characterized by "low-level chronic stagnation," that this fact gave rise to his concern for maintaining the status quo and thus controlled his formulation of the just price doctrine, falls into the sociological pattern.[15] It is this resort to a sociological explanation, rather than appeal to philosophic principle, which distinguishes Wilson's view of the just price from that of the Historical School.

There is no need to question that social factors conditioned the economic thought of Aquinas, especially since he wrote at a time when economics had not yet differentiated itself from other disciplines nor created for itself a basic core that would render economic thought immune to exogenous influences.[16] However, granted that economic doctrine is subject to exogenous causal influences, it is important to keep in mind that those causal influences may include not only social conditions but also intellectual developments in cognate fields.[17] And in the case of Aquinas, there was one such exogenous intellectual development that is of crucial importance for understanding his economic thought.

Writing in an age thrown into intellectual turmoil by the recent discovery of highly unsettling philosophic sources,[18] Aquinas tried to meet the challenge offered by the new doctrine by attempting a massive synthesis of Judeo-Christian revelation with the naturalistic philosophy of Aristotle. The effort required Aquinas to submit the work of his predecessors, especially the immensely influential Augus-

14. J. J. Spengler, "Exogenous and Endogenous Influences in the Formation of Post-1870 Economic Thought," in *Events, Ideology, and Economic Theory*, ed. R. V. Eagly (Detroit, 1968), pp. 159–87.

15. Wilson, "Economics of the Just Price," p. 62. For deliberate application of the sociology of knowledge to the understanding of Aquinas, cf. W. Stark, *The Contained Economy* (London, 1956). After carefully outlining Aquinas' theory of usury, Stark argues that the opposition to interest-taking derives, not from the explicitly avowed "formal" reasons cited by Aquinas, but from an exogenous factor—the fact that the dynamism of capitalism threatened the social order. Cf. ibid., pp. 17–20. Stark's analysis of usury thus parallels Wilson's views on the just price.

16. Cf. Spengler, pp. 166, 187.

17. Ibid., pp. 173–77.

18. For a description of the impact of Aristotle on medieval intellectual life, of the various attempts to suppress the newly discovered doctrine, and of the ruthless academic politicking which the controversy called forth in medieval universities, cf. Friedrich Heer, "The Hour of Aquinas (1225–1274)," in *The Intellectual History of Europe*, trans. Jonathan Steinberg (New York, 1953), pp. 141–58.

tine, to a searching and critical reexamination.[19] And at one point the attempt to integrate the revolutionary new ideas into Christian theology led to Aquinas' dismissal from his university and to the condemnation of his views by ecclesiastical authorities.[20] So far as economic thought is concerned, one feature of the Aristotelian doctrine that Aquinas tried to assimilate is of critical significance.

As one authority puts it, "one of the most conspicuous features of Aristotle's view of the universe is his thorough-going teleology." In the world of Aristotle, "all that happens . . . happens for an end."[21] Scientific knowledge in the Aristotelian schema requires that one discern the causes of things, and the causes include the end or final cause of the event or phenomenon in question.[22] The teleological conception of natural processes is linked up with the basic notion that nature is characterized by qualitative, "formal" differences between kinds of things.[23] Or as the point is frequently put, whereas the predominant world view since Newton tends to explanation in terms of quantity and mechanism, Aristotle's explanation of natural processes was "qualitative, not mathematical . . . teleological and functional, not mechanical."[24] Such an Aristotelian view of the universe as structured and purposeful had a decisive impact on medieval social thought.[25] Taking Aristotle to be "a witness of the very best that the natural reason of man can do,"[26] Aquinas took over such a view of the universe, gave it a theological reinterpretation, and allowed it to control an important dimension of his economic thought.

For Aquinas, as for Aristotle, nature is marked both by qualitative distinctions and by teleological purpose. And the scheme of natural

19. Cf. E. Gilson, *The Elements of Christian Philosophy* (New York, 1960), p. 15.

20. Cf. Heer, p. 148; and J. A. Weisheipl, O.P., *Friar Thomas D'Aquino* (New York, 1974), pp. 333–39.

21. Sir David Ross, *Aristotle*, 5th ed. (London, 1949), p. 185.

22. J. H. Randall, Jr., *Aristotle* (New York, 1960), p. 124.

23. For an explanation of how the scale of being—i.e., the formal distinction between inorganic matter and plants, animals and man—fits into the Aristotelian notion of the structure of the universe, cf. F. Copleston, S.J., *A History of Philosophy*, Image Books edition (1962; Westminster, Md., 1946), vol. 1, part II, pp. 68–71. For an indication of how Aristotle's view of nature as qualitative and purposeful related to economic activity, cf. J. J. Spengler, "Aristotle on Economic Imputation and Related Matters," *Southern Economic Journal* 31 (1955): 371–89, esp. p. 374 n. 15.

24. Randall, p. 165. Cf. the chart depicting the difference between the medieval and post-Galileo, scientific world views in E. A. Burtt, *The Metaphysical Foundations of Modern Science*, Doubleday Anchor Books ed. (New York, 1954), p. 100, and the discussion of the difference between the teleological and mechanical conceptions of the universe, ibid., p. 113.

25. Thomas Gilby, *The Political Thought of Thomas Aquinas* (Chicago, 1958), pp. 73–78.

26. Gilson, p. 15.

purposes requires that those objects (mineral, plant, and animal) holding a lower place on the scale of being be subordinated to, and serve
the purposes of, the higher type of being—i.e., man. Stressing final
causality, medieval philosophy employed "the teleological hierarchy
of Aristotelian forms," placed man in an intermediate position between God and the material world, and held that "events in the latter
could be explained mainly in terms of their use to man."[27] Thus a
discussion of how the various productive crafts (*ars possessiva*) relate
to the moral purposes of the household leads Aquinas to the observation that, since nature does nothing in vain, "it is manifest that nature
has made animals and plants for the sustenance of man."[28] The same
conception of man's command over nature is repeated in a theological
context, Aquinas holding that it is in accord with nature "plants make
use of the earth . . . , animals make use of plants, and man makes use
of both plants and animals."[29] Applied to economic activity and exchange, this Aristotelian conception of the basic structure and working of the universe carries a very important implication for the interpretation of the just price doctrine. For if all activity (including
economic) is teleological and if the rest of nature is to be subordinated
to the needs of man, it follows that economic goods are to be valued,
in the last analysis, in terms of their usefulness to man—i.e., in terms
of their utility.

Thus, in the Commentary on Book V of Aristotle's *Ethics*, where
he outlines the factors that determine the value of goods, Aquinas
first extends the thought of Aristotle by indicating that the exchange
ratio between commodities should be determined by a comparison of
relative labor and expense. After listing these cost factors, he goes on
to explain how establishing such a proportion between commodities
involves measurement of the commodities against one common standard. The conventional standard is money. But this man-made conventional standard presupposes a more fundamental natural standard.
This natural standard is human need. Combining Christian theological
tradition with Greek naturalism, he then uses an example borrowed
from St. Augustine to explain Aristotle. He observes that "articles
are not valued according to the dignity of their nature, otherwise a
mouse, an animal endowed with sense, should be of greater value

27. Burtt, p. 98.
28. *Politicorum*, Liber I, Lectio VI, in *Opera Omnia Sancti Thomae Aquinatis*,
Parmae ed., photographic reimpression (New York, 1949), 21:385.
29. *Summa Theologica*, trans. Fathers of the English Dominican Province (New
York, 1947), I, q. 96, a.l. The justification for private property and explanation of
why such property should be "common as to use" are derived by Aquinas from the
same Aristotelian view of nature. Cf. ibid., II-II, q. 66, a. 1, a. 2.

than a pearl, a thing without life. But they are priced according as
man stands in need of them for his own use."[30] With this reference to
the difference between value measured according to the dignity of
nature and value measured in terms of human need, Aquinas reminds
his readers that his economic reasoning must be understood within
the architectonic framework of the Aristotelian view of nature. And
when the place of his economic reasoning within such a cosmic frame
of reference is allowed for, it becomes clear that in Aquinas' view
utility must be a major determinant of economic value and hence of
the just price.[31]

The reference to utility as a determinant of value brings up what is
a perennial problem for those who would understand the economic
thought of Aquinas. How does the assertion that value is determined
by utility relate to the principle, which Wilson takes to be the correct
interpretation of the just price doctrine, that value is determined by
society's estimate of the "worth" of the producer? Wilson finds
strong textual evidence to support the latter interpretation in Book V,
Lectio VIII, of the Commentary on the *Ethics*.[32] In his Commentary,
Aquinas tried to clarify Aristotle's complicated treatment of reciprocation or reciprocal justice as a principle governing social relationships. Reciprocal justice does not govern the distribution of common
goods among members of a community; nor does it provide the appropriate rule for dealing with "involuntary commutations" such as
theft or assault. However, reciprocal justice does come into play in
acts of exchange—for example, between a builder and a shoemaker.

As Wilson has shown,[33] Aquinas requires that a proportion be
established—so many shoes for one house—and exchange must take

30. *Ethicorum*, Liber V, Lectio IX, p. 172. The same point is made with another
example in the discussion of the just price in the *Summa*, II-II, q. 77, a. 2. Cf. Stark,
The Contained Economy, p. 6.

31. The connection between teleology, utility, and value is made quite explicit in
the thought of a later scholastic: "The value of objects is estimated according to
human need. . . . This is proved as follows: the goodness or value of a thing depends
upon the end for which it is produced. . . . *Nothing* is good except through final
causes; but the natural end to which commutative justice orders external commodities
is the fulfillment of human need. Therefore, the fulfillment of human need is the true
measure of commodities. But the fulfillment is seen to be measured by the need; for
the fulfillment is of greater value which fulfills a greater need." Jean Buridan, *Ethica*,
V, 14, 16, quoted in Stark, *The Contained Economy*, p. 6. Value derives from the
purpose to which commodities are ordained—i.e., the fulfillment of human need. But
the end to be attained can be achieved by different combinations of commodities, so
that substitution is possible within the means-end chain that subordinates goods to
men. Cf. A. Sandoz, "La notion du juste prix," *Revue Thomiste* 23 (1939): 285–305,
esp. 286–88.

32. *Opera Omnia*, 21: 169–71.

33. Wilson, pp. 64 f.

place according to this proportion if the demands of justice are to be fulfilled. And it is Wilson's understanding of Aquinas that the appropriate proportion would be determined by society's estimate of the relative "worth" of the two occupations. It is also interesting to note that, following Aristotle closely, Aquinas goes on to explain what would happen if justice in exchange is violated. He observes that all exchange between crafts must follow the rule illustrated by the case of the builder and shoemaker and then adds: "Indeed the crafts would be destroyed if a workman did not receive according to the quantity and quality of what he produced."[34] The assertion that injustice would lead to destruction of the crafts lends strong support to Wilson's belief that the just price doctrine derived from Aquinas' concern for maintaining a given social structure. If a stable social order is to be preserved, terms of exchange must be established, or a just price defined, that will not allow destruction of the crafts to occur.

However, the assertion that exchange at less than the just price would cause the crafts to be destroyed has also suggested to several commentators how utility as a determinant of value would, in the mind of Aquinas, be related to cost factors operating from the supply side. Briefly, the argument consists of utilizing the Neoclassical distinction between short-run market price and long-run normal price. Thus, Raymond de Roover once argued that the just price "was nothing more mysterious than the competitive price . . . set by the free valuation of buyers and sellers, . . . by the interplay of supply and demand."[35] In later work he uses the reference to destruction of the crafts to show that Aquinas understood that the market price could not fall permanently below cost but would "tend to coincide with cost or to oscillate around this point like the swing of a pendulum."[36] Another commentator, while insisting that "there is no doubt that Thomas considered need as the fundamental determinant of value," points out that the just price has both short-run and long-run aspects and suggests that "it is not unreasonable to assume that [Aquinas] believed in the tendency of prices to equal production costs in the long run."[37] And in his exhaustive study of the just price,

34. *Opera Omnia*, 21: 171.
35. "Monopoly Theory Prior to Adam Smith: A Revision," *Quarterly Journal of Economics* 65 (1951): 492–524, esp. p. 496.
36. "The Concept of the Just Price: Theory and Economic Policy," *Journal of Economic History* 18 (1958): 419–31, esp. pp. 421 f. Cf. the passage quoted by Hollander, p. 628.
37. Désiré Barath, "The Just Price and Costs of Production According to St. Thomas Aquinas," *New Scholasticism* 34 (1960): 412–30, esp. 416, 422. Barath, how-

Baldwin concludes that although Aquinas did not clearly connect market price and cost of production, he was close to a reconciliation of the two views whereby "value emphatically depends on utility" on the one hand, and "goods will not be produced below cost" on the other.[38]

Wilson recognizes that his interpretation of the just price "is contrary to the interpretation of those who have stressed the utility explanation."[39] Though he considers the role of utility in the thought of Aristotle, he does not attempt to reconcile the utility and cost explanations in Aquinas and insists that the just price, in his view, must be distinguished from long-run market price.[40] Various passages suggest that he shares Hollander's belief that trying to find a Neoclassical adjustment mechanism in the thought of Aquinas is to read history backwards.[41] In any case, Wilson's systematic restatement of the traditional interpretation of the just price brings to light a basic ambiguity in the attempt to systematize Aquinas by way of the Neoclassical synthesis of utility and cost.

The crucial role of the Aristotelian reading of nature in the system of Aquinas suggests very strongly that, in the latter's view, the value of a commodity is determined by its relative utility. Interpreting the texts rather freely, one might agree with de Roover that the just price theory implies that market price, based on utility, tends to coincide in the long run with average cost. However, such an interpretation leaves a crucial question unanswered. What is there to guarantee that exchange at such a price would provide producers with an income proportionate to what the community decides is their social "worth"? Neoclassical micro theory suggests one answer to this question. If the value of a commodity is determined by its utility, and if society's estimate of the "worth" of a craft is determined exclusively by economic considerations, it follows that the social rank of a craftsman is determined by the value of what he produces. The "worth" of the producer and "value" of his product are, as in standard marginal productivity theory, mutually determined, so that value based on rank of the producer and value based on utility coincide neatly.

ever, emphatically rejects the notion that the "worth" of the producer determines the just price. "A status theory of the just price has no foundation in Thomas' concept of valuation." Ibid., p. 428.

38. J. W. Baldwin, "The Medieval Theories of the Just Price," *Transactions of the American Philosophical Society,* n.s. 49, part 4 (1959): p. 73.

39. Wilson, "Economics of the Just Price," p. 69.

40. Ibid., pp. 68, 69–72.

41. "Aquinas was not an analyst of economic phenomena, and we cannot ascribe to him a full-fledged Marshallian theory of price determination involving a recognition of the relationship between supply curves of various 'runs.'" Hollander, p. 629.

There is some evidence to suggest that, for Aquinas, the "worth" or *dignitas* of a member of the community depends upon what he produces. In one place, he uses a hypothetical wage example to illustrate Aristotle's views on justice and says that if Socrates works two days and Plato one, then Socrates should be paid twice as much as Plato.[42] The claim to income of a worker—which would reflect his "worth" in the community—seems to be determined by the time he works and thus by the amount he produces. And Spengler takes Aquinas' view of the social hierarchy to imply that a craftsman who produces more, or belongs to a higher category supplying a superior product, deserves a higher income.[43] Also, Wilson's illustration of the connection between the "worth" of the producer and value of his product could be reversed to show that the cobbler is entitled to half as much income as the builder because the value of the latter's product (one house priced at $10,000 to reflect its relative utility) is twice that of the cobbler's output (500 pairs of shoes at $10 per pair).[44] However, Wilson explicitly rejects the notion that in Aristotle's scheme the social weighting of a producer is determined by his marginal productivity.[45] And when he asserts that the just price must cover not only production costs but also provide an income sufficient to maintain the status of a producer's family,[46] he seems to imply that status (as viewed by Aquinas) is a factor somehow independent of the craftsman's contribution to production. In other words, Wilson espouses the traditional view that the just price must provide the producer an income commensurate with his socially determined "worth" or status, but he does not take Aquinas to mean that status is determined by the income receiver's contribution to production.

Concerning the latter point, there is rather conclusive evidence in the commentary on the *Politics* to suggest that Wilson is correct.[47] Justice in distribution, Aquinas says, requires that goods be shared according to the relative *dignitas* of the community's members. However, if the estimate of *dignitas* is not made with respect to the proper scheme of values or ends, then the community which distributes in proportion to *dignitas* will establish justice of a sort (*justum secundum quid*) but not thoroughgoing or complete justice (*justum*

42. *Ethicorum*, Liber V, Lectio V, in *Opera Omnia*, 21: 164.
43. J. J. Spengler, "Hierarchy vs. Equality: Persisting Conflict," *Kyklos* 21 (1968): 217–36, esp. pp. 225 f.
44. Wilson, "Economics of the Just Price," p. 65.
45. Ibid., p. 67.
46. Ibid., p. 68.
47. *Politicorum*, Liber III, Lectio VII, in *Opera Omnia*, 21: 468–70.

514   *History of Political Economy 9:4 (1977)*

simpliciter). If the civil community were nothing more than a business venture organized for the sake of acquiring wealth, the *dignitas* of a person and his share in common goods would depend upon his contribution to production. But wealth is not the highest good, and the civil community is not organized for the sake of wealth. Rather the true purpose or final cause of the civil community is *felicitas*, the good life for its members. And in such a community, organized for the sake of true good, *dignitas* would be judged, not in terms of contribution to production, but in terms of contribution to the common life of virtue.[48] Thus whereas it may be appropriate to distribute goods in proportion to productivity in a private business venture—as in the Socrates-and-Plato wage example noted above—to apply the same rule of distribution in civil society would imply failure to take account of the true purpose of civil life.

But if status or *dignitas* depends upon contribution to the civic life of virtue, rather than on contribution to production, one cannot apply Neoclassical marginal productivity theory to explain how exchange at the just price would provide an income proportionate to one's status. *Dignitas* in the full sense depends upon fulfilling a social function other than the production of wealth, and income must be distributed in proportion to such *dignitas*, or in such a manner as to allow the income recipient to continue fulfilling his social function. For the proper understanding of Aquinas, the question is acute—what is the rule or procedure which guarantees that, while goods exchange at their just prices, income will be distributed in proportion to the relative *dignitas* of society's members?[49]

In this connection, it is important to keep in mind the fundamental distinction Aquinas makes between two kinds of justice—distributive

48. "... finis propter quem instituta est civitas bene ordinata, est secundum virtutem perfectam vivere ... et communicatio politica consistit in hujusmodi actionibus; manifestum est quod illi qui plus addunt ad talem communionem plus addunt ad civilitatem ... si justum est aequale aliquarum rerum aliquibus personis secundum dignitatem in ordine ad finem ... politia illa in qua ponitur rectus finis, est justum simpliciter. ... In politia autem in quo ponitur finis non rectus, non est justum simpliciter." Ibid., p. 470.

49. Hollander argues (pp. 639 f.) that Aquinas had no conception of the allocation mechanism which brings market price to equality with cost in the long run and that the statement that "the crafts would be destroyed" refers to the possibility that the "social structure ... would collapse." If resources are immobile, as perhaps might be the case in a guild system, factor payments would consist largely of rent (i.e., exceed opportunity cost). If so, a fall of price below costs would not "destroy the crafts" in the sense of forcing a suspension of production, but could cause "collapse" of the "social structure" by depriving the producer and resource owner of the income required to fulfill a noneconomic social function.

and commutative.[50] The first has to do with the distribution of common goods (income, honors, "offices") among members of the community. The second provides the moral principles that should be adhered to in transactions between private individuals. Furthermore, the two kinds of justice follow different rules, or seek a different kind of mean—distributive justice seeking to establish a geometric proportion, while commutative justice adheres to arithmetic proportion or seeks an arithmetic mean. In distributive justice

> a person receives all the more of the common goods, according as he holds a more prominent position in the community . . . the mean is observed, not according to equality of thing and thing, but according to the proportion between things and persons;

whereas in commutative justice, which governs exchange, the rule is different:

> in commutations . . . it is necessary to equalize thing with thing so that one person should pay back to the other just so much as he has become richer out of that which belonged to the other.[51]

The key to a clear understanding of the difference between the two kinds of justice is to be found in the phrase "equality of thing and thing" (aequalitas rei ad rem). This formula emerges in the commentary on the Ethics and crops up repeatedly in Aquinas' discussion of justice.[52] In the case of barter, justice in exchange requires that there be an arithmetic equality of thing and thing in the sense that the two parties should give and receive equal values—a number of sandals equal in value to one house or to one bushel of wheat.[53] In the case of monetary exchange, equality of thing and thing requires that the price be equal to "the quantity of the thing's worth."[54] The references to labor, to labor plus expense, and to need in the commentary

50. Cf. Josef Pieper, Justice (New York, 1955), p. 50, and the "schematic representation," p. 121.

51. Summa Theologica, II-II, q. 61, a. 2. The critical distinction Aquinas makes between the two species of justice, and his insistence that each presupposes different criteria, coincides very closely with the distinction between two levels of contract—a basic "social" contract that assigns rights, and subsequent contracts covering exchange—employed by James Buchanan in his recent book, Limits of Liberty (Chicago, 1975), pp. 28–32, 51 n. 13, 183.

52. "Dicendum est autem, quod circa justitiam commutativam semper quidem oportet esse aequalitatem rei ad rem. . . ." Ethicorum, Liber V, Lectio VIII, in Opera Omnia, 21: 170. Cf. Summa Theologica, II-II, q. 61, a. 2; q. 61, a. 4; q. 77, a. 1.

53. Ethicorum, Liber V, Lectio VIII, Lectio IX, in Opera Omnia, 21: 171, 172.

54. Summa Theologica, II-II, q. 77, a. 1.

516   *History of Political Economy 9:4 (1977)*

on *Ethics* V show that, in Aquinas' thought, these are the factors which would determine the number of sandals that must be exchanged for one house in order to achieve the necessary equality of thing and thing. Furthermore, Aquinas carefully distinguishes the proportion between commodities which must be established in order to achieve arithmetic equality in values exchanged, from the *geometric proportion* which is the concern of distributive justice.

Aristotle's assertion that justice in exchange requires proportionality, Aquinas notes, seems to contradict the previous statement to the effect that

> in commutative justice the mean is taken not according to geometric proportionality . . . but according to arithmetic proportionality which consists in quantitative equality.

And he goes on to resolve the difficulty:

> in the case of commutative justice it is always required that there be equality of thing to thing. . . . And in this case it is necessary to adhere to proportionality to establish equality of things since the work of one craftsman is greater than the work of another, as the building of a house and the making of knives.[55]

Thus a *proportion* must be established because, owing to differences in the value of the different commodities, a unit-for-unit exchange would not achieve the arithmetic equality required by commutative justice. Furthermore, the *proportion* between commodities required for justice in exchange is not the same as the *proportion* (between one's position in the community and one's share of the common goods) which is to be established by distributive justice. Nor is the first proportion, according to the thought of Aquinas, derived from the second.

For as a matter of fact, the equality-of-thing-and-thing formula seems to have been introduced by Aquinas for the express purpose of establishing the principle that the social rank or standing of a person, while of decisive significance for justice in distribution, is

---

55. "Videtur autem hoc esse contra id quod supra dictum est quod scilicet in commutativa justitia, medium accipitur non quidem secundum geometricam proportionalitatem, quae consistit in aequalitate proportionis, sed secundum arithmeticam, quae consistit in aequalitate quantitatis . . . circa justitiam commutativam, semper quidem oportet esse aequalitatem rei ad rem. . . . Sed in hoc oportet adhiberi proportionalitatem ad hoc, quod fiat aequalitas rerum, eo quo actio unius artificis major est quam actio alterius, sicut aedificatio domus, quam fabricatio cultelli. . . ." *Ethicorum*, Liber V, Lectio VIII, in *Opera Omnia*, 21: 170.

not a relevant consideration in matters having to do with commutative justice. Following Aristotle closely, Aquinas distinguishes between distributive and commutative justice, and then further divides the latter according as transactions are voluntary (buying and selling) or involuntary (theft and assault).[56] Explaining how the mean of commutative justice differs from the geometrical proportion of distributive justice, he observes at one point that "in commutative justice the equal is observed according to arithmetic proportion. This is clear from the fact that here the different proportion of persons is not considered."[57] And with his usual concern for logical precision, he takes pains to point out that there can be, in a highly special case, an indirect connection between a person's rank and the demands of commutative justice. In the case of assault, the gravity of the offense and hence the severity of the requisite punishment (a matter for "rectificatory" or communtative justice) do depend upon the rank of the person offended.[58] As those familiar with scholastic procedures will recognize, this exceptional case, though a logical extension of the main argument, is not introduced merely to clarify an obscure text of Aristotle. Rather, the exception is introduced in order to clarify the general rule. And according to the general rule, the social standing of the two parties to a voluntary transaction does not determine what the just terms of the transaction should be.[59]

Thus, the *aequalitas rei ad rem* formula indicates that, in the mind of Aquinas, there must be an arithmetic equality in exchange between the value of the goods given up and the value of those received. Whereas the relative social position of different persons is the explicit concern of distributive justice, commutative justice—the moral virtue which controls the act of exchange—considers only a relationship between things. On such a reading, the value of a commodity is *not* a function of the social position of the craftsman producing it.[60] An interpretation of the just price doctrine which asserts

---

56. *Ethicorum*, Liber V, Lectio IV, in *Opera Omnia*, 21: 162.

57. ". . . . in commutativa justitia attendatur aequale secundum arithmeticam proportionem, manifestat per hoc, quod non consideratur ibi diversa proportio personarum. . . ." *Ethicorum*, Liber V, Lectio VI, in *Opera Omnia*, 21: 167.

58. Ibid., p. 170. The argument is repeated with clarification in the *Summa Theologica*, II-II, q. 61, a. 4.

59. In explaining how the kinds of justice relate to Aquinas' conception of a social hierarchy, Spengler notes (p. 225): "Disorder ensues . . . when rank is not taken into account in . . . distributive justice or when it is taken into account in commutative justice."

60. In the words of a commentator: "In commutative justice . . . A just price can be determined without reference to the person of the buyer or the seller, simply by taking into consideration the market value of the object that is to be sold. In this case

518   *History of Political Economy 9:4 (1977)*

the contrary—e.g., as offered by Sir William Ashley and reaffirmed by Wilson—stands in need of amendment.

However, Wilson does make it clear that, in the thought of Aquinas, exchange of goods at the just price must provide each member of the community with an income proportionate to his "worth" or *dignitas*—i.e., with an income that would allow him to fulfill his social function. But if the just price is determined by the want-satisfying quality of *things*, and not by the relative "worth" of the producer, how can exchange at such prices provide the pattern of income distribution required by consideration of the *dignitas* of society's members? Replacing the traditional interpretation of Aquinas with a Neoclassical reading, which takes the *justum pretium* to be a market price tending in the long run to equality with cost, does not provide an answer to this question. For, as noted above, the concept of *dignitas* which figures in Aquinas' exposition of distributive justice cannot be considered the equivalent of the Neoclassical notion of producer's value productivity.

In this connection, further consideration might be given to that Aristotelian world view which, as has been noted, played such a critical role in the economic thought of Aquinas. According to such a view, nature is marked by qualitative, formal differences between kinds of things; by teleological movement towards ends or final causes; and—what is of particular importance in the present context—by the subordination of mineral, animal, and plant to man. This schema provides Aquinas with the philosophic justification for his belief that man has a natural dominion over external things—i.e., a natural right to use the resources of nature for his own benefit.[61] Moreover, adopting Aristotle's pragmatic criticism of communism,[62] he believes that the institution of private property must be established if man's natural right of dominion over nature is to be exercised

---

justice and equity consist in the *aequalitas rei ad rem*. . . ." Cf. Pieper, p. 66. After a careful examination of the texts, Barath reaches a similar conclusion (pp. 426 f.). At one point, Aquinas makes the statement that "as the farmer exceeds the shoemaker . . . in the same proportion the work of the shoemaker exceeds in number the work of the farmer, so that many sandals are exchanged for one bushel of wheat" (quod quantum agricola . . . excedit coriarium . . . in tanta proportione excedat, secundum numerum, opus coriarii opus agricolae, ut scilicet calceamenta multa dentur pro uno modio tritici). *Ethicorum*, Liber V, Lectio IX, in *Opera Omnia*, 21: 173. If this passage is to be consistent with Aquinas' careful distinction between the two kinds of justice, the assertion that the farmer "exceeds" the shoemaker must refer, not to a difference in social rank, but to a quantitative difference in per unit costs of production (labor and expenses).

61. *Summa Theologica*, II-II, q. 66, a. 1.
62. Cf. Gilby, p. 295.

effectively. Thus, by man-made agreement acting as a supplement to the natural law, resources which by nature are common must be divided up and made the private property of the members of the community.[63]

And according to the system of Aquinas, it is at this point in the social process—when resources common by nature are by human agreement to be made the private property of particular individuals—that *distributive justice* first begins to operate. It is because of the difference between the essence of man and that of animals, plants, or minerals, that man has the moral right to bend nature to human purpose. And since all men are in essence equal, each member of a social community has a natural right to *a* share in the benefits derived from the community's resources. But so far as social function is concerned, individuals are not equal, some having a greater social "worth" or *dignitas* than others. And the *amount* of an individual's share is determined, according to Aquinas, not by his nature as a member of the human species, but by his place or function in the social hierarchy.[64] The work of distributive justice consists in first ascertaining how the community ranks its various members—i.e., discovering how the *dignitas* of one man compares with that of another. Having done so, distributive justice then divides up resources in a proportion which matches the ratio of one man's social standing to that of another. Thus, distributive justice establishes among the stock of resources "the proportion that it discovers in the arrangement of persons"[65] so that, in Aquinas' words, "a person receives all the more of the common goods according as he holds a more prominent position in the community."[66]

According to this view, the social decision whereby resources are distributed in proportion to relative social standing is fundamental, the policymaker's first step in the design of a just economic system.

63. *Summa Theologica*. II-II, q. 66, a. 2.

64. As Spengler (p. 224) interprets Aquinas, "hierarchical structure had its origin, not in variation in the substantial natures of men, but in differences in the functions individuals performed and hence in the relative importance of the services they rendered." Another commentator points out that according to the scholastic theory of distributive justice, the social hierarchy will shift as historical circumstances evolve so that the distribution of common goods must adapt to the changing social order. Cf. P.-D. Dognin, "La justice distributive," *Revue des Sciences Philosophique et Théologique* 39 (1955): 18–37, esp. 28. Among economists, there seems to have been some misunderstanding of Aquinas on this point. Cf. A. F. Chalk "Natural Law and the Rise of Economic Individualism in England," *Journal of Political Economy* 59 (1951): 332–47, esp. 332.

65. Dognin, p. 28.

66. *Summa Theologica*, II-II, q. 66, a. 2.

520   *History of Political Economy 9:4 (1977)*

Once a just distribution of resource ownership has been established, the process of production, division of labor, and exchange can then begin to operate. The exchange of goods—governed by commutative justice which requires exchange at the *just price*—thus presupposes the anterior establishment of an equitable distribution of resources. Or, in the words of a commentator, distributive justice "prepares the field for commutative justice."[67]

If the preceding interpretation of Aquinas is correct, then it is apparent how, in his view, justice in exchange is to be related to the relative dignity of society's members. The "worth" of a producer does not determine the value of his product; such is determined by relative cost and utility. Nor does the value of the product, as in Neoclassical marginal productivity theory, determine the "worth" of the producer. Rather, as Wilson correctly indicates, society through its common estimate establishes a social ranking, or decides how the *dignitas* of one man compares with that of another. Distributive justice then takes over and establishes, not the exchange ratios between goods, but a pattern of factor ownership which, with some receiving more and others less, reflects society's decision as to the relative "worth" of its members.[68] In a market economy, the value of resources will reflect the value (measured at the just price) of the goods produced by those resources. Thus when production and exchange take place, each member of the community will receive a rental income

---

67. Dognin, p. 18.

68. Wilson's assertion ("Economics of the Just Price," p. 74) that "justice in exchange depends upon a society's goals" touches on a characteristic and profound aspect of scholastic economic thought. However, if the above outline of the connection between distributive and commutative justice is correct, the connection between society's ideals and the exchange value of goods is indirect. The distinctive goals that differentiate one society from another would first of all be reflected in the community's estimate of the relative "worth" of its members. Such an estimate would then control the distribution of resources and income. And the distribution of income would have an effect on the pattern of demand and hence on the exchange value of commodities. Thus, for Aquinas, the value of goods is dependent not only upon their "utility" but also upon the community's commitment to a pattern of transcendent ideals. With the reference to the role of "society's goals" in the system of Aquinas, Wilson also brings out a characteristic difference between scholastic thought and the kind of individualism sometimes presupposed in contemporary discussions of welfare economics and social contract. As indicated above (n. 51), there is a close parallel between Buchanan's view that social life is based upon a two-stage contractual process and the distinction Aquinas makes between *distributive* and *commutative* justice. However, the initial basis for distribution in Buchanan's scheme (pp. 56–59, 79) depends upon and shifts with the balance of power in a state of nature. In the scholastic view, the basis for distribution is to be found in the community's common commitment to shared cultural ideals, translated into an estimate of the relative *dignitas* (social function) of society's members.

from his property sufficient to maintain himself in his relative social position.[69] While commutative justice requires *aequalitas rei ad rem* in exchange, distributive justice requires *geometric proportionality* in the pattern of factor ownership.[70] And the two together provide each member of the community with an income adapted to his *dignitas*, or social function, in the community.

Finally and in conclusion, Wilson's bold generalization—"a static competitive economy accepting the existing distribution of income . . . would yield the same results as Aquinas' just price"[71]—is refreshing in its clarity and freedom from ideological bias. However, if the analysis offered above is correct, Wilson's statement can be taken as an accurate summary of the thought of Aquinas only if (i) the competitive price is taken to reflect, not the position of persons, but the value of things; and (ii) "accepting the existing distribution of income" is meant to indicate that the pattern of factor ownership matches the relative *dignitas* of society's members.

69. Distributive justice, trying to match income with social function would also have to take wage income into account. There seems to be no indication in the texts as to how Aquinas would relate wage and property income. In the wage example noted above (n. 42) he seems to base wages on productivity. However, no mention is made of the relative social position or function of the wage earners. If they were charged with a particular social function—such as the support of a family—then Aquinas' analysis indicates that they would be entitled in distributive justice to a share of society's property income sufficient to permit them to perform such a function. Aquinas also does not raise the question what kind of institutional procedure (property and inheritance laws) society might use to establish the match between factor ownership and social function required by distributive justice.

70. Dognin points out (p. 26) that in the system of Aquinas an impersonal, mechanical equating of thing and thing is said to satisfy commutative justice precisely because distributive justice has previously taken the relative positions of persons into account.

71. "Economics of the Just Price," p. 58.

[12]

KYKLOS, Vol. 30 – 1977 – Fasc. 2, 195–213

A FOURTEENTH-CENTURY THEORY OF ECONOMIC GROWTH AND DEVELOPMENT

L. Haddad*

I

Two recent studies of the economic thought of IBN KHALDUN, the celebrated fourteenth-century Arab historian, show quite convincingly that not only did he have quite a deep insight into the nature of economics, but also his ideas were advanced compared with contemporary European economic thought[1]. What is even more impressive and refreshing and what has not so far received sufficient attention, is his method. This is astonishingly 'modern': it is empirically orientated, analytical, comprehensive and above all 'dynamic'. SHACKLE describes this kind of approach as 'constructive' or 'transformational', that is, showing the historical succession of stages and events[2]. This inductive and dynamic approach which was rather rare and revolutionary in the fourteenth century[3], ideally suited his

---

* University of Sydney.

1. See JEAN DAVID C. BOULAKIA, 'IBN KHALDUN: A Fourteenth-century economist', *Journal of Political Economy*, Vol. 79 (1971), 5; S. ANDIC, 'A Fourteenth-century Sociology of Public Finance', *Public Finance*, Vol. 20 (1965), 1,2. SCHUMPETER, who is generally generous to early writers on economics, mentions IBN KHALDUN twice: once in a footnote as being an influence on VICO and once in connection with development in historical sociology. See J. A. S. SCHUMPETER, *History of Economic Analysis*, George Allen and Unwin, London, 1955, pp. 136, 788.

2. G. L. S. SHACKLE, *Epistemics and Economics*, Cambridge University Press, 1972, pp. 55–57.

3. The muslim legal and economic literature of this period was dominated by speculative and normative discussions; practical economic and financial matters were apparently deemed too mundane and unworthy of being treated in learned books. See IBN KHALDUN, *The Muqaddimah: An Introduction to History*, translated from the Arabic by FRANZ ROSENTHAL in 3 volumes, Routledge and Kegan Paul, London, 1958, pp. 82–83.

L. HADDAD

objective of developing a 'new science', a science of history or a science of culture (ilm al-umran)[4], to explain the origins, rise and decline of civilisations. At the same time he wanted to correct the erroneous views of previous and contemporary historians and their tendency towards sensationalism and exaggeration which he believed to be partly or mainly the result of their ignorance of the ever-changing nature of social, economic and political phenomena. He was convinced that such phenomena are determined by and subject to certain universal laws and rules, and that it is essential to discover these laws in order to explain the past and present and anticipate the future. He himself explained his great historical work – *The Muqaddimah* – in the following terms:

'When I had read the work of others and probed into the recesses of yesterday and to-day, I shook myself out of that drowsy complacency and sleepiness. Although not much of a writer [...] [I] composed a book on history. In this book I lifted the veils from conditions as they arise in the various generations. I arranged it in an orderly way in chapters dealing with historical facts and reflections. In it I showed how and why dynasties and civilisation originate.

I followed an unusual method of arrangement and division into chapters. From the various possibilities, I chose a remarkable and original method. In the work, I commented on civilisation, on urbanization and on the essential characteristics of human social organization, in a way that explains to the reader how and why things are as they are, and shows him how the men who constituted a dynasty first came upon the historical scene. As a result, he will wash his hands of any blind trust in tradition. He will become aware of the conditions of periods and races that were before his time and that will be after it[5].'

This grand scheme to find a new science of society makes him the forerunner of many of the eighteenth and nineteenth centuries system-builders such as VICO, COMTE and MARX. What is perhaps most interesting and striking to the economist about IBN KHALDUN's work, is that long before those writers, he realized and analysed the importance of economic factors in history, especially the role of labour in economic growth and development. As one of the early founders of

4. The Arabic word *'umran'* has been variously translated as 'civilisation', 'society', 'human association' and 'culture'. However, for the purpose of this paper and from the point of view of an economist, it may be conveniently translated as 'development'. On the difficulty of translating this term see M. MAHDI, *Ibn Khaldun's Philosophy of History*, The University of Chicago Press, Chicago 1964, pp. 184–186.

5. IBN KHALDUN, *op. cit.*, Vol. 1, pp. 10–11.

A FOURTEENTH-CENTURY THEORY

the social sciences he saw very clearly the interdependence and continuous interplay of economic and sociological factors and political power in the evolution and collapse of civilisations, and gave them a fairly modern treatment.

Earlier studies of the economics of IBN KHALDUN have tended to be either too general or too narrow[6], and to give too little stress to his preoccupation with economic development and growth. Consequently such studies do not give an accurate assessment of his contribution and place in the evolution of economic thought.

The primary purposes of this paper are (i) to elicit from IBN KHALDUN's wider and more complicated theory of the evolution of civilisation his theory of economic growth and development and (ii) to show how he geared together the economic and non-economic factors to produce a coherent and constructive theory of the development of society from the subsistence of the affluent stage.

II

Unlike most modern theorists of economic growth and development, IBN KHALDUN assumes very little. He starts from square one with a description of the natural environment and geographical factors and discusses their influences upon the behaviour and characteristics of the population. These are his postulates and prerequisites of civilisation. He shows how the natural environment, especially the climate affects man's physical appearance, his colour, character, temperament, wants, customs, political life and economic activity. Thus, for example, because of the warm climate

'The Egyptians are dominated by joyfulness, levity and disregard for the future. They store no provision of food neither for a month nor a year ahead [...]. Fez in the Maghrab on the other hand, lies inland and is surrounded by cold hills. Its inhabitants can be observed to look sad and gloomy and to be too much concerned for the future. Although a man in Fez might have provisions of wheat stored sufficient to last him for years, he always goes to the market early to buy his food, because he is afraid to consume any of his hoarded food[7].'

The physical environment imposes severe constraints on human activities. Civilisations cannot emerge in those regions of extreme

6. See, for example, the references cited in *footnote 1*.
7. IBN KHALDUN, *op. cit.*, Vol. 1, p. 175.

L. HADDAD

climatic conditions. In such regions man is closer to animals for he spends all his time hunting for food in order to subsist[8]. To the influence of the climate on economic development IBN KHALDUN adds the effect of the fertility of the soil on the supply of food. A temperate climate is necessary but not sufficient for abundance of food and population and comfortable living[9]. The importance of the physical environment, the characteristics of land and climate are stressed by IBN KHALDUN because of their influence on economic behaviour. Natural resources vary from place to place and human physical wants are very much conditioned by the differences in climate. Without taking these factors into account it would have been difficult for him to explain the variety of human civilisations and why some societies are more developed than others.

Having described the natural environment and its consequences, IBN KHALDUN begins his analysis of the first stage of civilisation which consists of primitive societies living at subsistence level and takes place as soon as men get together and co-operate. Prior to this stage man is hardly distinguishable from other animals, living a precarious existence. But besides the exogeneous factors of climate and soil, the socioeconomic organization, or the way of making a living, also governs men's attitudes and activities. All this is discussed and explained in great detail in Chapter 2 of Book 1 which begins with this statement:

'It should be known that differences of conditions among people are the result of the different ways of making a living. Social organization enables them to co-operate toward that end and to start with the simple necessity of life before they get to conveniences and luxuries[10].'

IBN KHALDUN goes on to make an important economic distinction between two modes of living or two kinds of culture: '*badawa*' and '*hadara*' which may be broadly translated as primitive and civilised, or rural and urban[11]. The former is characterised by the production and satisfaction of the most simple and basic needs: food, clothes, shelter, defence, sexual intercourse and reproduction. These needs

8. IBN KHALDUN, *op. cit.*, Vol. 1, pp. 167–169.
9. *Ibid*, Vol. 1, p. 177.
10. *Ibid*, Vol. 1, p. 249.
11. *Ibid*, Vol. 1, pp. 249–250. Cf. M. Mahdi, *op cit.*, pp. 193–194.

A FOURTEENTH-CENTURY THEORY

are inherent in human nature and tend to be more or less constant, and when they vary from place to place the variation is due to climatic factors. The economic activity of primitive people (bedwins) consists of farming, animal husbandry, and hunting. They do hard physical labour and employ the most primitive and necessary tools; their foods are simple and consumed with little or no preparation; their clothes consist of animal skins and hand-woven materials; and they live in caves, tents or huts. Money is not used and there are no taxation, market institutions and state. The size of groups is normally small and self-supporting. Primitive groups are at once both simple, courageous, independent, rough, backward and undisciplined. But such cultural characteristics change with a change in their economic way of life.

Civilised groups, on the other hand, live in towns and cities: 'they build mansions and castles, provide them with running water and compete in furnishing them most elaborately[12].' They engage in the production of luxury goods and services of the most intricate and complex kind, and their economic activity is characterised by the use of money and trade, industry and elaborate technology. Moreover, having unlimited desires, they strive to create more and more efficient ways of satisfying them. This is the first attribute of civilisation – its progressive and dynamic nature.

Both groups are natural and necessary, but the primitive precedes in time and is logically necessary to the development of the civilised:

'We have mentioned that the Bedwins restrict themselves to the [bare] necessities in their conditions of life and are unable to go beyond them, while sedentary people concern themselves with conveniences and luxuries in their conditions and customs. The [bare] necessities are no doubt prior to the conveniences and luxuries. [Bare] necessities, in a way, are basic and luxuries second and an outgrowth of necessities. Bedwins are thus the basis of and prior to the cities and sedentary people. Man seeks first the [bare] necessities. Only after he has obtained the [bare] necessities does he get to comfort and luxuries. The toughness of desert life precedes the softness of sedentary life. Therefore, urbanization is found to be the goal of the Bedwin. He aspires to [that goal]. Through his own efforts, he achieves what he proposes to achieve in this respect. When he has obtained enough to be ready for the conditions and customs of luxury, he enters upon a life of ease and submits himself to the yoke of the city[13].'

12. Ibn Khaldun, *op. cit.*, Vol. 1, pp. 250.
13. *Ibid*, Vol. 1, pp. 252–253.

L. HADDAD

The transition from the stationary state of subsistence to the dynamic stage of affluence is explained both by a change in taste, by the desire for goods of convenience and luxury among primitive people, and by a change in the production system, through economic co-operation and specialisation. Like ADAM SMITH some four hundred years later, IBN KHALDUN emphasised the tremendous importance of the principle of division of labour and gave it a prominent place in his work. It is in fact placed at the forefront. Chapter 1, Book 1 begins with this statement:

'Human social organization is something necessary [...]. The power of the individual human being is not sufficient for him to obtain the food he needs and does not provide him with as much food as he requires to live [...]. Through co-operation the needs of a number of persons many times greater than their own number can be satisfied.'

What is significant about IBN KHALDUN's treatment of the division of labour is that he stressed the increase in productivity which results from specialisation *per se* unlike some of his predecessors, *e. g.* PLATO, who emphasised the increase in productivity from allowing everyone to specialise in what he is naturally best suited for. This is fairly evident from the following passage:

'As is well known and well established the individual human being cannot by himself obtain all the necessities of life. All human beings must co-operate to that end in their civilisation. But what is obtained through the co-operation of a group of human beings satisfies the need of a number many times greater [than themselves]. For instance, no one by himself can obtain the share of the wheat he needs for food. But when six other persons, including a smith, a carpenter to make the tools, and others who are in charge of the oxen, the ploughing of the soil, the harvesting of the ripe grain and all other agricultural activities undertaken to obtain their food and work towards that purpose either separately or collectively and thus obtain through labour a certain amount of food, [that amount] will be food for a number of people many times their own. The combined labour produces more than the needs, necessities of the workers[14].'

Moreover, IBN KHALDUN, like ADAM SMITH, linked the division of labour to the size of the local market and to external trade. The division of labour raises productivity and creates a surplus over and above the necessities. This surplus may be used either as wages for additional labour to be employed in the production of non-essential

14. IBN KHALDUN, *op. cit.*, Vol. 2, pp. 272.

A FOURTEENTH-CENTURY THEORY

goods, or may be exchanged for such goods produced in other towns and cities. In this way the division of labour is linked to trade, and the surplus labour is used to provide the conditions and customs of luxury. Thus, a community which has surplus labour gets a good deal of wealth. For IBN KHALDUN wealth does not consist merely of gold, silver and precious stones or money. These he regarded as part of wealth only:

'It should be known that treasures of gold, silver and precious stones and utensils are not different from other minerals and acquired [capital], from iron, copper lead and any other real property or ordinary minerals. It is civilisation that causes them to appear with the help of human labour and that makes them increase or decrease[15].'

'Civilization and its well-being as well as business prosperity depend on productivity and people's efforts in all directions in their own interest and profits[16].'

As the community becomes more prosperous and the standard of living rises, the division of labour is extended further to meet the growing demand for luxury goods. In turn more specialisation leads to higher incomes and profits. Clearly this is a typical cumulative process of mutual causation: the division of labour depends on the extent of the market and the extent of the market on the division of labour[17]. More specifically, the demand for luxury goods raises their price and specialisation lowers the cost of production. Profits increase and entrepreneurs are encouraged to invest their capital in the production of luxury goods and services[18]. The higher the investment, the greater is the profit, for 'gains correspond to capital invested'[19].

It is quite clear that in IBN KHALDUN's scheme of things economic progress takes place mainly in the urban sector, as it depends on the

15. IBN KHALDUN, *op. cit.*, Vol. 2, p. 325. It is interesting to note that the confusion of wealth with money and precious metals in the mercantalist literature, at least up to the middle of the 17th century, hindered the progress of economics. It was not until a concept of real wealth had been adopted that we begin to see a decisive shift of emphasis from commerce to production – a movement that culminated in the rise of classical political economy.

16. *Ibid*, Vol. 2, p. 104.

17. Cf. ALLYN YOUNG, 'Increasing Returns and Economic Progress', *The Economic Journal*, (1928), December.

18. IBN KHALDUN, *op. cit.*, Vol. 2, pp. 276–277, 348.

19. *Ibid*, Vol. 2, pp. 93, 342.

L. HADDAD

development of luxury goods and the size of the population. The demand for essential goods such as food is relatively static and depends on the growth of population, while the increase in aggregate demand is mainly centred on non-essential goods. Consequently, the profit rate on the latter is higher than on the necessities of life, and labour moves out of primary production in the rural sector, into industry and trade located in towns and cities[20]. There is again a dynamic process of cause and effect between economic growth and population. As the city becomes more prosperous its population expands which, in turn, increases the demand for luxury goods:

'When civilization [population] increases, the [available] labor again increases. In turn, luxury again increases in correspondence with the increasing profit, and the customs and needs of luxury increase. Crafts are created to obtain [luxury products]. The value realized from them increases, and, as a result, profits are again multiplied in the town. Production there is thriving even more than before. And so it goes with the second and third increase. All the additional labor serves luxury and wealth, in contrast to the original labor that served [the necessities of] life. The city that is superior to another in one [aspect of] civilization [that is, in population], becomes superior to it also by its increased profit and prosperity and by its customs of luxury which are not found in the other city. The more numerous and the more abundant the civilization [population] in a city, the more luxurious is the life of its inhabitants in comparison with that [of the inhabitants] of a lesser city. This applies equally to all levels of the population, to the judges [of the one city] compared with the judges [of the other city], to the merchants of the are city compared with merchants of the other city, and, as with the judges and merchants, so with the artisans, the small businessmen, amirs, and policemen[21].'

Moreover, there is a fine balance between income and expenditure which must be maintained for the sake of continued stability and prosperity:

'Income and expenditure balance each other in every city. If the income is large, the expenditure is large, and *vice versa*. And if both income and expenditure are large the inhabitants become more favourably situated and the city grows[22].'

The highest stage of growth is reached when the labour force is large enough to permit the production of pure luxury and the devel-

20. The dependence of the urban sector on the rural sector is not confined to the initial stage. The city relies constantly on the rural surroundings for fresh supplies of manpower and foodstuffs in exchange for some non-essential goods.

21. IBN KHALDUN, *op. cit.*, Vol. 2, pp. 272–273.

22. *Ibid*, Vol. 2, p. 275.

A FOURTEENTH-CENTURY THEORY

opment of the sciences. But it is not a stationary or a permanent state of the kind postulated by the classical political economists. For beyond this stage the city ceases to grow and begins to decline. The development towards luxury and 'the good life' carries with it its own seed of destruction. As society becomes more and more affluent, certain habits of consumption and attitudes are generated which weaken the driving forces behind economic development. The consumption of luxury goods becomes a necessity[23], and when their prices rise, due to an increase in demand and high taxations, people continue to consume them until they impoverish themselves. They cease to save: their expenditure increases at a faster rate than their income and they eventually end up in poverty. At first demand falls and causes unemployment in crafts producing luxury goods and services. People begin to leave the city to seek employment elsewhere. This in turn causes a further decline in business activity until finally the city is weakened and reduced to a small size:

'The expenditures of sedentary people, therefore, grow and are no longer reasonable but extravagant. The people cannot escape [this development] because they are dominated by and subservient to their customs. All their profits go into their expenditures. One person after another becomes reduced in circumstances and indigent. Poverty takes hold of them. Few persons bid for the available goods. Business decreases and the situation of the town deteriorates. All this is caused by excessive sedentary culture and luxury. Corruption of the individual inhabitants is the result of painful and trying efforts to satisfy the needs caused by their [luxury] customs; [the result] of the bad qualities they have acquired in the process of obtaining [those needs][24].'

However, the decline of towns and cities is not necessarily the final stage of economic growth, but may be only a temporary setback until the next round, when a new dynasty emerges and starts reconstructing old cities or building new ones. As will be seen more clearly below, IBN KHALDUN saw the growth process not in terms of a steady state but rather in cyclical terms.

With his understanding of economic growth and the way it is generated, it is not surprising that IBN KHALDUN emphasised production rather than commerce, the role of population and labour, and especially the principle of division of labour – points that were

23. IBN KHALDUN, *op. cit.*, Vol. 1, p. 338, Vol. 2, p. 279.
24. *Ibid*, Vol. 2, p. 293.

L. HADDAD

stressed so much by the classical economists. For him labour is the chief factor of production, the source of wealth and profit: 'labour is the cause of profit' and 'profit is the value realized from labour products'[25]. The importance of production and the role of labour in it is further stressed by his distinction between two notions of profit: *ribh* and *kasb*[26]. The former is a mercantile concept, being the difference between buying cheap and selling dear, while the latter is a more general term denoting the gains from productive labour. (It is rather unfortunate that the English translation of his work inaccurately uses profit for both terms, which may explain why this significant distinction was not noticed by previous writers on IBN KHALDUN's economic ideas).

Although IBN KHALDUN emphasised time and time again the importance of man power in the development of cities and towns he did not neglect the role of machinery and technology especially in the construction of large projects. This is made abundantly clear in the following passage:

'The construction of cities can be achieved only by united effort, great numbers, and the co-operation of workers. When the dynasty is large and far-flung, workers are brought together from all regions, and their labor is employed in a common effort. Often, the work involves the help of machines, which multiply the power and strength needed to carry the loads required in building. [Unaided] human strength would be insufficient. Among such machines are pulleys and others.

Many people who view the great monuments and constructions of the ancients [...] think that the ancients erected them by their own [unaided] powers, whether they worked as individuals or in groups. They imagine that the ancients had bodies proportionate to [those monuments] and that their bodies, consequently, were much taller, wider, and heavier than [our bodies], so that there was the right proportion between [their bodies] and the physical strength from which such buildings resulted. They forget the importance of machines and pulleys and engineering skill implied in this connection[27].'

Finally IBN KHALDUN pays considerable attention to the location of cities, the importance of clean air and the need for town planning for the progress of civilisation[28]. In particular, he links pollution

25. IBN KHALDUN, *op. cit.*, Vol. 2, pp. 280, 334.
26. *Ibid*, Vol. 2, p. 340.
27. *Ibid*, Vol. 2, pp. 238–239.
28. *Ibid*, Vol. 2, pp. 243–249.

A FOURTEENTH-CENTURY THEORY

which leads to the outbreak of plagues and disease, to overpopulation. The following passage has indeed a modern ring:

'There, much unrest, bloodshed and plagues occur. The principal reason for the latter is the corruption of the air [climate] through [too] large a civilization population [...]. [Such civilization] is the result of the good government, the kindness, the safety, and the light taxation that existed at the beginning of the dynasty. This is obvious. Therefore, it has been clarified by science in the proper place that it is necessary to have empty spaces and waste regions interspersed between civilized areas[29].

Thus far we have discussed only the economic aspects of IBN KHALDUN's theory of growth and development. Although it is a plausible theory, it is far from complete. The critical points of passing from the static to the growing stage and from the growing to the declining phase are explained inadequately by economic factors alone. For a more satisfactory account of these points we must now introduce the non-economic factors which interact with the economic ones to re-inforce the evolutionary process from primitive to civilised living.

III

The driving forces underlying economic co-operation in the early primitive stage are the fundamental instincts in man – the instinct of survival and the desire for affiliation with blood relations. According to IBN KHALDUN these are the basic needs which lead to the formation of human society; they compel men to co-operate with one another and defend themselves against the hostile natural environment and attacks of other groups[30]. At this early stage, men possess the most simple and strongest form of social solidarity or group loyalty (asabiyya)[31]. This is both natural and necessary; without 'asabiyya' society would not come into existence. But when survival is assured and the community starts to become prosperous, following economic co-operation and specialisation, new elements emerge which disturb the static character of the primitive community. The

29. IBN KHALDUN, op. cit., Vol. 2, pp. 136–137.
30. Ibid, Vol. 1, pp. 262–265.
31. 'Asabiyya' plays a crucial role in IBN KHALDUN's work and has been the subject of a number of thorough studies. Cf. M. M. RABI, The Political Theory of Ibn Khaldun, E. J. BRILL, Leiden, 1967, Chs. 1 & 3.

L. HADDAD

increase in population resulting from increased prosperity weakens the natural family ties and creates conflict[32]. Dissention replaces co-operation and the livelihood of the community is once more endangered. At the same time, a struggle for leadership takes place, and the leader of the group with stronger *asabiyya* imposes his will on the rest of the community and forces men to live together and co-operate[33]. Thus in the absence of the primitive conditions for co-operation, a political force is needed to ensure the survival of the community. Further, in order to retain his leadership and satisfy the newly reunited group the new ruler turns to the conquest of other weaker and isolated groups[34].

This constitutes the second phase in the development of civilisation. It is a long and gradual process of expansion and unification, requiring an additional force to strengthen social solidarity. This force is religion, which springs from the group with strong *asabiyya*, and is propagated among other groups either by force or persuasion[35]. But once religion is adopted it becomes a second powerful force in the development of civilisation by uniting isolated groups into one large group. The leader of such a group may then succeed in establishing a new dynasty or a state. Thus, when re-inforced by religion, *asabiyya* becomes more effective than before in strengthening its unifying power, by eliminating rivalry and jealousy and by persuading the people to obey the ruler more willingly[36].

The state, in turn, becomes necessary for the development of a civilised society and is responsible for the building of cities and towns:

'Dynasties are prior to towns and cities. Towns and cities are secondary [products of royal authority] [...]. As a matter of fact [human beings] must be forced and driven to [build cities]. The stick of royal authority is what compels them, or they may be stimulated by promise of reward and compensation. [Such reward] amounts to so large a sum that only royal authority and dynasty can pay for it. Thus, dynasties and royal authority are absolutely necessary for the building of cities and the planning of towns[37].'

32. IBN KHALDUN, *op. cit.*, Vol. 1, pp. 91–92.
33. *Ibid*, Vol. 2, p. 329.
34. *Ibid*, Vol. 1, pp. 284–285.
35. *Ibid*, Vol. 1, pp. 319–326.
36. *Ibid*, Vol. 1, pp. 305–306.
37. *Ibid*, Vol. 2, p. 235.

A FOURTEENTH-CENTURY THEORY

The transition from primitive to civilised living is explained by *asabiyya* (aided by religion) which plays a co-ordinating function both within and between groups. It is not reactionary force rendering a group self-sufficient and isolated, but is, on the contrary, a dynamic and constructive force necessary for the development of civilisation. Indeed, it is 'the vehicle of change from primitive to civilised life and is the fundamental condition and dynamic force in history and the development of the state'[38]. It provides motivation for co-operation and division of labour, resulting in a surplus which in turn is employed to satisfy the higher wants of the community. *Asabiyya* in the social and political sphere is the counterpart to the division of labour in the economic sphere.

Since the founding of a dynasty requires large numbers of people, and this is necessary for civilisation, the state is thus linked to the higher stage of civilisation. Once more a process of interaction takes place:

'One cannot imagine a dynasty without civilisation, while a civilisation without a dynasty and royal authority is impossible, because human beings must by nature co-operate, and that calls for a restraining influence [...]. Since the two cannot be separated, the disintegration of one of them must influence the other, just as its non-existence would entail the non-existence of the other[39].'

IBN KHALDUN shows that there is also a reciprocal relationship between politics and economics. In the initial period the state possesses an austere attitude towards expenditure. An extensive bureaucracy and paid army are hardly needed, since *asabiyya* based on communal sentiment is still strong. The state levies little taxation and respects private property; its expenditures are not yet large:

'It should be known that at the beginning the dynasty has a desert attitude, as we mentioned before. It has the qualities of kindness to subjects, planned moderation in expenditures, and respect for other people's property. It avoids onerous taxation and the display of cunning or shrewdness in the collection of money and the accounting [required] from officials. Nothing at this time calls for extravagant expenditures. Therefore, the dynasty does not need much money[40].'

Consequently, there is much incentive for investment. Further, this incentive is strengthened when the state begins to develop legal,

38. M. RABI, *op. cit.*, p. 13.
39. IBN KHALDUN, *op. cit.*, Vol. 2, pp. 300–301.
40. *Ibid*, Vol. 2, pp. 122–123.

L. HADDAD

social and economic institutions such as the mint, the control of weights and measures, just commercial laws and protection of private property[41]. These institutions ensure economic stability, facilitate exchange and encourage cultural and entrepreneurial activities. Production increases and the population grows:

> 'A kind and benevolent rule serves as an incentive to the subjects and gives them energies for cultural activities. [Civilization] will be abundant, and procreation will be vigorous. All this takes place gradually, the effects will be noticeable after one or two generation at best. At the end of two generations, the dynastie approaches the limits of its natural life. At that time civilization has reached the limit of its abundance and growth[42].'

As a result of increased prosperity, the total taxes levied by the state increase. The state in turn starts to engage in public works, e.g. construction of roads, public baths, mosques, hospitals, schools, monuments and the establishment of scientific institutions, which cause further growth of the city and state revenue. As time goes on the state becomes the biggest spender through the development of infrastructures. It creates a demand for luxury goods. Prices rise and expectations of high profits attract skilled artisans and traders to the city. They develop efficient techniques of producing these articles and supply the services demanded[43]. The increase in the population of the city, and the increase in their wages and profits, lead to a further rise in demand which in turn leads to more production.

Eventually the state attains absolute power, coinciding with the highest stage of economic development – the affluent stage, a period of rest, self-indulgence in luxury and comforts of life. But a life of ease and comfort leads to physical weaknesses and corruption. Religious commands lose their force and a process of secularisation begins[44]. A period of decay then sets in and the dynamic process is reversed, leading ultimately to the downfall of the dynasty and decline of the city. If not attacked from the outside the city will slowly disintegrate. The same interrelated factors that produced the growth process are responsible for the decline. Absolute power attained by the state has to be preserved by coercion and continuous

41. IBN KHALDUN, op. cit., Vol. 2, Ch. 3.
42. Ibid, Vol. 2, p. 135.
43. Ibid, Vol. 2, pp. 348.
44. Ibid, Vol. 1, p. 260.

A FOURTEENTH-CENTURY THEORY

expenditure on luxuries and indulgence in the conventional way of life[45]. This has a two-fold effect; it causes financial difficulties and weakens feelings of communal loyalty. Consequently, the dynasty relies more heavily on mercenaries to enforce its commands and defend itself against foreign aggression. The danger of external aggression is induced internally by the strained relation between the ruler and the population caused by his excessive controls over sources of power and wealth. In these times of trouble foreign groups are tempted to invade the city and overthrow the dynasty[46]. To raise the necessary funds the ruler must increase taxation or find some other means of raising revenue. But high taxation and fear of invasion reduce investment and discourage people from making long-range plans. Economic opportunities decline, skills in building and luxury articles are lost, public works are ruined and the birth rate and population begin to fall[47]. In turn this leads to a fall in the total revenue of the state. The ruler then resorts to more drastic measures of raising revenue including confiscation of private property and direct intervention in economic activity. This destroys the competitive process and incentives to private enterprise. Entrepreneurs cease to make normal profits and go out of business:

'Sometimes, the ruler himself may engage in commerce and agriculture, from desire to increase [his] revenues. [He sees] that merchants and farmers make great profits and have plenty of property. He sees that their gains correspond to the capital they invest. Therefore, he starts to acquire livestocks and fields in order to cultivate them for profit, purchase goods and [enter business and] expose himself to fluctuations of the market. He thinks that this will improve his revenues and increase his profits. However, this is a great error. It causes harm to the subjects in many ways [...]. Competition between them already exhausts, or comes close to exhausting, their financial resources. Now, where the ruler, who has so much money than they, competes with them, scarcely a single one of them will [any longer] be able to obtain the things he wants [...]. The trouble and financial difficulties and the loss of profits which it causes the subjects, takes away from them all incentives. Thus, when the farmer gives up agriculture and the merchant goes out of business, the revenue from taxes vanishes altogether or becomes dangerously low[48].'

45. IBN KHALDUN, *op. cit.*, Vol. 1, pp. 257–261, vol. 2, pp. 291–297.
46. *Ibid*, Vol. 2, p. 126.
47. *Ibid*, Vol. 1, pp. 300–301.
48. *Ibid*, Vol. 2, pp. 93–95.

L. HADDAD

The destruction of incentive which is regarded as an act of injustice on the part of the state, leads to the collapse of the dynasty and the decay of urban civilisation: 'civilisation is ruined when people have lost all incentive'[49]. However, IBN KHALDUN is careful to point out that the fall of a dynasty does not always spell the final end of civilization and economic progress. It may simply lead to the interruption of the long-term development process by causing people to move out of towns and cities. But when a new dynasty establishes itself the people return and the growth process starts again:

'The dynasty that has built a certain town may be destroyed. Now the mountainous and flat areas surrounding the city are a desert that constantly provides for [influx of] civilization [population]. This [fact], then, will preserve the existence of [the town], and [the town] will continue to live after the dynasty is dead[50].'

Thus, for sustained economic progress it is not necessary that towns and cities be governed by the same dynasty, though it is important that successive dynasties should not interrupt for long the advance in science and technology since these are the product of a long and gradual cumulative process of development[51]. IBN KHALDUN shows that a new dynasty does not necessarily start from the very beginning but builds on the gains of previous dynasties:

'Frequently it happens that after the destruction of the original builders of [a town, that town] is used by another realm and dynasty as its capital and residence. This then makes it unnecessary for [the new dynasty] to build [another] town for itself as a settlement. In this case, the [new] dynasty will protect the town. Its building and constructions will increase in proportion to the improved circumstances and the luxury of the new dynasty. The life [of the new dynasty] gives the [town] another life[52].'

Thus economic growth and development may be sustained from one dynasty to another and the achievements of older civilizations are preserved and passed on. In this way IBN KHALDUN explains the development of higher civilizations.

49. IBN KHALDUN, *op. cit.*, Vol. 2, p. 107.
50. *Ibid*, Vol. 2, p. 236.
51. *Ibid*, Vol. 2, pp. 424–435.
52. *Ibid*, Vol. 2, p. 237.

A FOURTEENTH-CENTURY THEORY

IV

Judged by the standards of present day economic studies of the growth and development process, IBN KHALDUN's theory suffers from some serious technical drawbacks: it lacks rigour, precision and quantification. But in the fourteenth century such standards were not yet attained even in the natural sciences. Further, today's standards are very often obtained at the cost of realism and totality of the growth process. Interestingly, IBN KHALDUN warns against excessive abstraction, misuse of mathematics and preoccupation with 'unusual and rare cases'[53]. Admittedly, his theory is not very rigorous nor a thorough-going explanation, but it does provide a plausible picture of the evolution of pre-industrial societies from the stationary state of subsistence to the state of affluence.

This evolutionary process is by no means simple. It involves, among other things, the evolution of the state, religion, towns and cities, large population, division of production, trade, accumulation of wealth, social and economic institutions including money, bureaucracy and development of the sciences. IBN KHALDUN's theory dealt with all these both in terms of the facts about the physical environment and in terms of universal laws or behavioural constants. Such constants include the desire for survival, wealth, power, status, blood ties and group loyalty. In a changing society these laws influence and causally determine one another. They are intimately and inevitably interrelated. There is no sharp and artificial distinction between economic and non-economic factors and between causes and consequences. IBN KHALDUN showed how the economic and non-economic factors interact to produce a civilization which is changing constantly. Unlike his contemporaries, he regarded change as the rule rather than the exception and perceived that once a society breaks through the primitive state in which wants and resources are unchanging, it gets on a dynamic path.

The dynamic complications of the growth process are indeed very great. IBN KHALDUN's theory is perhaps too primitive to cope with these complications, but nevertheless remains a very interesting one, viable and basically sound in its approach. It does not map out the

53. IBN KHALDUN, *op. cit.*, Vol. 3, pp. 21–22.

L. HADDAD

path to prosperity in narrow economic terms; it is not divorced from sociology, politics and demography. These factors appeared to him to be continually re-inforcing one another in a cumulative process of circular causation so that it would be futile to treat them separately. IBN KHALDUN showed how it is possible for economists to analyse the growth process not simply in terms of economic motivation but also in terms of other human motivations. Because of this, and despite its technical deficiencies, his theory goes a long way to explain the economic history of those economies which started on the growth path, got far along it, and then slipped back. It is in fact a 'model' of the economic history of Islamic countries and other oriental civilizations.

SUMMARY

Earlier studies of the economics of IBN KHALDUN, the celebrated fourteenth-century thinker, have failed to stress his preoccupation with economic development and growth. Consequently, such studies do not give an accurate assessment of his contribution and place in the evolution of economic thought. This paper attempts first to elicit his theory of economic growth and development from his wider and more complicated account of the evolution of civilizations, and secondly it shows how he geared together the economic and non-economic factors to produce a coherent and constructive theory of the development of society from the substance to the affluent stage. IBN KHALDUN's theory, which suffers from a number of technical drawbacks, remains relevant today, in that it illustrates the value of a multidisciplinary approach to a very complicated process.

ZUSAMMENFASSUNG

Frühere Untersuchungen der volkswirtschaftlichen Theorien von IBN KHALDUN, dem berühmten Denker des 14. Jahrhunderts, haben es versäumt, hervorzuheben, wie sehr er sich mit wirtschaftlichen Entwicklungs- und Wachstumsprozessen befasst hatte. Darum können diese Untersuchungen weder über seinen Beitrag zur Entwicklung des volkswirtschaftlichen Denkens noch über seine Rolle in der Entwicklung dieses Denkens ein vollständiges Urteil abgeben. In diesem Artikel wird als erstes seine Theorie des Wachstums und der Entwicklung der Volkswirtschaft aus seinem breiten und umfassenden Verständnis der Entwicklung der Kulturen abgeleitet. Zweitens wird gezeigt, wie er unter Verwendung von ökonomischen und nicht-ökonomischen Faktoren eine zusammenhängende und konstruktive Theorie für die Entwicklung der Gesellschaft vom Steinzeitalter zur Überflussgesellschaft entwickelte. IBN KHALDUNS Theorie weist zwar einige

A FOURTEENTH-CENTURY THEORY

technische Mängel auf, aber sie ist auch heute noch von Bedeutung, denn sie beweist, wie wertvoll ein interdisziplinärer Ansatz für die Untersuchung eines komplexen Phänomens ist.

RÉSUMÉ

Les études antérieures portant sur les doctrines économiques du célèbre penseur du XIVᵉ siècle, IBN KHALDUN, n'ont pas suffisamment mis en valeur l'intérêt qu'il portait aux problèmes de développement et de croissance économiques. Par conséquent ces études ne fournissent une évaluation correcte ni de sa contribution à la pensée économique ni de sa place dans l'évolution de cette pensée.

La présente étude tente premièrement de retracer sa théorie du développement et de la croissance économiques d'après son analyse plus vaste et plus complexe de l'évolution des civilisations, et deuxièmement de montrer comment il a fait appel à un ensemble de facteurs économiques et non économiques pour construire une théorie à la fois cohérente et constructive du développement de la société du stade de la subsistance à celui de l'abondance. La théorie d'IBN KHALDUN, bien qu'elle souffre d'un certain nombre de défauts techniques, reste pertinente aujourd'hui en ce qu'elle illustre la valeur d'une méthode pluridisciplinaire appliquée à un processus fort compliqué.

[13]

History of Political Economy 12:2
© 1980 by Duke University Press

In defense of Thomas Aquinas and the just price

David D. Friedman, Virginia Polytechnic Institute and
State University

There is a sharp division in medieval economic theory between teachers of canon and Roman law, who, with some qualifications,[1] considered a sale legitimate provided only that the price was acceptable to both parties, and Scholastic writers, who taught that it was sinful to sell a good for more or buy it for less than its just price.[2] The former doctrine corresponds to both current legal practice and conventional economic views on the desirability of freedom of contract. The latter appears, from the point of view of modern economics, to be an undesirable interference with the market process.[3] I shall argue that both the medieval legal doctrine of freedom of contract and the Scholastic ethical doctrine of just price may have been desirable institutions, and that the latter in particular may have served an important and non-obvious function in the medieval economy.

What determined the just price?

> The other way in which we can look at a contract of sale is in so far as it happens to bring benefit to one party at the expense of the other, as in the case where one badly needs to get hold of something and the other is put out by not having it. In such a case the estimation of the just price will have to take into account not merely the commodity to be sold but also the loss which the seller incurs in selling it. The commodity can here be sold for more than it is worth in itself though not for more than it is worth to the possessor.
>
> If, on the other hand, a buyer derives great benefit from a transaction without the seller suffering any loss as a result of relinquishing his property, then the latter is not entitled to charge

---

1. In particular the doctrine of *laesio enormis*, discussed below.
2. For an extensive discussion see Baldwin 1959.
3. To some extent the bad reputation of the doctrine of just price comes from its supposed connection with the prohibition on usury. The connection is actually very tenuous; see Noonan 1957, pp. 82–91. I do not intend to argue that the prohibition served any useful purpose, although the ingenuity of medieval bankers in finding ways around it may have made it less damaging than one might otherwise expect. See Baldwin 1959, p. 7; Noonan 1957, pp. 181–89; and de Roover 1974, pp. 183–99.

more. This is because the surplus value that accrues to the other is due not to the seller but to the buyer's situation: nobody is entitled to sell another what is not his own though he is justified in charging for any loss he may suffer.[4]

This seems to mean that the just price was either the intrinsic value of the commodity or its value to the seller, whichever was higher.[5] This leads us to the question of what the Scholastic writers meant by the intrinsic value of the commodity, a subject of some controversy.

It appears, from the arguments of de Roover and others,[6] that most of the Scholastic writers meant by the value of a commodity simply its market value, although Duns Scotus and some of his followers interpreted value as meaning cost of production.[7] The former interpretation appears at first to make the doctrine of the just price superfluous; since the market value of a good is the highest price for which the seller can sell it and the lowest for which the buyer can buy it, it hardly seems necessary to instruct sellers not to charge more than the good's value and buyers not to buy for less.

But a market price is only well defined when there are many buyers and sellers. Such a situation was far from universal in the medieval

4. Aquinas 1975, 2a 2ae, 77, pp. 215–16.
5. The doctrine that a price above the value of a good is licit if the seller suffers a loss in selling is familiar in discussions of usury as *damnum emergens*. Whether opportunity cost (*lucrum cessans*) deserved the same treatment was a subject of debate. See Schumpeter 1954, p. 103; Baldwin 1959, p. 79; and Noonan 1957, p. 88.
6. For arguments in favor of this position, see de Roover 1951, p. 496, 1958, and 1967, pp. 17–21; Gordon 1975, pp. 174–76; Baldwin 1959; Barath 1960, pp. 420–30; Worland 1967, pp. 16–18, 222, 233; Noonan 1957, pp. 82–99; and Schumpeter 1954, pp. 61–62, 98–99. Cahn (1969) gives an extensive discussion of the development of the doctrine, leading to the same conclusion. Hollander (1965) argues that Aquinas's views were inconsistent. For the older position, according to which the just price was that required to maintain the social status of the producer, see references in the above. Bartell (1962, pp. 369–81) rejects both positions, suggesting, if I understand him correctly, that for Aquinas the just price is what the market price would be if the tastes of those participating in the market were virtuous. Where the price was controlled by government, the Scholastics accepted the legal price (if enforced) instead of the (nonexistent) market price. See de Roover 1958, pp. 425–26; Baldwin 1959, p. 79; Cahn 1969, p. 48; and Noonan 1957, p. 89. For an interesting exchange on this subject in the recent literature see Wilson 1975 and Worland 1977. The former defends the older position, arguing that Aquinas was concerned with maintaining social stability. The latter argues that income according to status is a feature of *distributive justice*, which ought to determine the initial allocation of factor endowments, while price is a feature of *commutative justice* and consequently depends on the qualities of the objects, not the status of their producers.
7. Whether Duns Scotus recognized the connection between cost of production and market price is a matter of debate. De Roover (1958, p. 422) and Barath (1960, pp. 421–22) argue that Aquinas did, but Gordon (1965) and Hollander (1965, pp. 628–32) argue the contrary. De Roover (1951, p. 487) also claims that Sant' Antonino of Florence recognized the connection. For general discussions see Noonan 1957, pp. 82–87; Bartell 1962, pp. 364–68; and Worland 1967, pp. 210–33.

economy. Both the writers in the Scholastic tradition and Aristotle,[8] their primary source, were largely concerned with exchanges involving small numbers of buyers and sellers. As the situation approaches closer and closer to the pure case of bilateral monopoly—one buyer and one seller—the price at which a good can be bought or sold becomes increasingly less determinate. The purpose of the doctrine of just price was to determine the price in such non-competitive situations,[9] and I will argue that in doing so it may have served a useful economic purpose.[10]

Consider a bilateral monopoly. I own the only horse in the village; you are the only one in the village who wants to buy a horse. I value the horse at 10 pennies, you at 20. Conventional economic analysis says only that we will agree on some price between 10 and 20. But suppose further that each of us can influence the price by various costly means. For instance, I can overstate the value of the horse to me, you can understate its value to you. The cost here is the risk that if both of us misstate our values too much—if I persuade you that the horse is worth 21 pence to me, and you persuade me that it is worth 9 to you—I may sell you a line but fail to sell you a horse. Alternatively, you may try to prove that the horse is not worth much to you by making a low offer and trying to wait me out—while crops rot in your field. This is a common situation in union-management bargaining, a familiar example of bilateral monopoly.

While there is no satisfactory theory to tell us how much of the 10-penny profit will be eaten up by bargaining costs, much of it may be.[11] If so, it might be in our joint interest to accept some less costly way of deciding on a price. Suppose, for instance, that a neutral arbi-

---

8. "[Aristotle] was preoccupied with the isolated exchange between individuals and not with the exchange of goods by many sellers and buyers competing with each other" (J. Soudek 1952, p. 46). This position is attacked by M. I. Finley (1970, p. 36) in an essay which argues the nonexistence of Aristotle's economic theory. See on the other hand Lowry (1969), who argues that Aristotle may have had a sophisticated theory obscured, perhaps irrecoverably, by errors in the transmission of his ideas.

9. "Goods sold outside of the marketplace were to be sold at the price then prevailing in the market place" (Cahn 1969, p. 3). The reference is to Pope Gregory IX's Decretals, published in 1234. Wilson (1975, p. 56), discussing the just price doctrine, refers to the "problems of non-market regulation of varying degrees of monopoly power."

10. The doctrine was also used to condemn non-market prices produced by fraud; the argument that this might lead to, in modern terms, inefficient transactions (in which the good was worth more to the seller than the buyer) was made explicitly; see Baldwin 1959, pp. 54–57, 67–68. Aquinas did not, however, consider it unjust for a merchant to withhold knowledge of market conditions that would have lowered the price for which he could sell his goods; in this case the question is only one of distributional transfers, not inefficient transactions (Baldwin 1959, p. 78).

11. For general discussions of this sort of problem see Tullock 1967 and Krueger 1974. Oliver Williamson (1975) has constructed a theory of organization based largely on the attempt to avoid costs of this sort.

trator with a lie detector agrees to ask each of us how much he really
values the horse, then set a price halfway between. Although I might
expect to do better than that on some bargains, I would do worse on
others; if bargaining costs were substantial, the arbitrator's decision
might be more attractive than my *ex ante* value for bargaining.

The doctrine of the just price may be interpreted as just such an arbitration procedure, designed for an economy containing both competitive and non-competitive markets. The value of a good—its market
price when it was sold on a competitive market—would be a price at
which the merchants in the competitive market could afford to sell it.
In the normal non-competitive case the merchant's costs would be the
same as those of a merchant in the competitive market; hence the market value of the good would be within the bargaining range and would
provide a reasonable arbitrated price. In the exceptional case in which
a good was worth more than its market price to the seller, the just price
would be adjusted upward accordingly, as Aquinas explained in the
passage quoted above.[12]

Before going on to discuss the evidence for this view, two points
are worth making. The first is that the particular arbitrated price
imposed by the doctrine of the just price has the great advantage of being relatively easy to determine, simplifying enforcement, whether by
legal, social, or moral means. In situations where the buyer was willing
to pay much more than the market price and the seller had no reason to
accept less (goods that could easily be stored until more purchasers appeared, for instance), the doctrine would allocate virtually all of the
surplus to the buyer. In other situations, where the seller was stuck
with a good he had to get rid of and faced by a buyer prepared to bargain the price down to almost nothing, the arbitrated price would be favorable to the seller.[13] On average, both buyer and seller might be better off than if they were free to engage in unrestricted bargaining.

The second point is that in any arbitration scheme a perfect arbitrated price—one guaranteed to be within the bargaining range
—depends on knowledge of the subjective values of the bargainers. In
my hypothetical case, that knowlege was provided by a lie detector. In
the actual medieval case, the competitive market price gave a first approximation to the subjective values, and the provision allowing a
higher price where the cost to the seller was higher gave a second approximation. This latter was far more practical for a rule enforced by

12. In addition to the sort of implicit "arbitration" discussed here, both Romanists
and Scholastics frequently suggested the use of real, 'fair-minded' arbitrators to settle
disputes and determine what was just (Cahn 1969, p. 46).

13. The possibility of monopsony was discussed by Lessius; see de Roover 1951,
p. 500.

238   *History of Political Economy 12:2 (1980)*

moral sanctions than it would have been for one enforced by law.[14] To the extent that those sanctions were effective (and there is evidence that they often were[15]) the seller only needed to know his own opportunities and preferences in order to decide whether a particular price was licit. This suggests that the system of combining legal freedom of contract with a morally enforced arbitration procedure for imperfect markets may have been an efficient use of the available instruments of control.

The plausibility of this interpretation of the role of the just price depends, first, on the medieval economy being characterized by a mixture of competitive and non-competitive markets, and second, on medieval writers having been aware of the problems of imperfect competition. The first condition is quite generally conceded;[16] the second is shown by the extensive discussion of problems of imperfect competition in medieval writing.

One case discussed by early medieval writers was that of a stranger entering a village whose inhabitants could and would charge him cartel prices. According to a Carolingian capitulary of 884, later incorporated into canon law, a priest or bishop was entitled to arbitrate in order to guarantee that the stranger was charged no more than local market prices.[17]

The possibility of discriminatory pricing, a typical symptom of imperfect competition, was recognized in Roman times,[18] and the practice was repeatedly condemned during the Middle Ages.[19]

Medieval writers were also concerned about attempts to deliberately create monopoly situations. "Everywhere measures were taken against engrossers (*accapareurs*), forestallers (*recoupeurs*), and regraters (*regrattiers*) who tried to accumulate stocks, to prevent supplies from reaching the market, or to form corners in order to drive prices

14. There were some cases in which the just price could be enforced in the courts (de Roover 1951, 500–508). For the general distinction between *forum internum* (confessional) and *forum externum* (the courts) see Baldwin 1959, pp. 10, 57–58.

15. De Roover 1951, p. 498: "There are countless examples of restitution of usury and ill-gotten gains in medieval wills, so that there can be no doubt that the code of social ethics was actually enforced by the Church, chiefly *in foro conscientiae*, that is, through the sacrament of confession.

16. For the existence of both competitive and imperfect markets see Cipolla 1967, pp. 10–12, 53–57; de Roover 1951, p. 502; and Roll 1953, p. 47. For the prevalence of bargaining, which suggests the existence of imperfect markets, see Baldwin 1959, pp. 21–22, and the sources he cites.

17. The canon "Placuit" was incorporated into canon law in the thirteenth century; see de Roover 1958, p. 421, and Baldwin 1959, p. 33.

18. De Roover 1951, p. 493; Baldwin 1959, p. 80.

19. De Roover 1951, p. 497, 1958, p. 426. The term used for a discriminating price was *pretium affectionis*. See also Cahn 1969, pp. 40–42.

up."[20] To a modern economist familiar with the difficulties of maintaining a successful monopoly their concern seems if anything excessive,[21] but that may be a reflection of improvements in the market, not in economic wisdom, over the intervening centuries.[22]

As a final piece of evidence on the medieval concern with bargaining ranges and imperfect markets, it is worth examining briefly the doctrine of *laesio enormis*, as it developed in the Middle Ages. Originally, *laesio enormis* was a provision in Byzantine law under which the seller of land could cancel the sale if he could show that the land had been sold for less than half its true value. This rule was an exception to the general principle of Roman, Byzantine, and canon law, under which any price freely agreed to by the buyer and seller was legally binding.[23] As the principle developed in medieval law, it was generalized to apply to all goods, and extended to permit the buyer to cancel the sale if the price was more than one and a half times, or in some interpretations twice, the value of the goods.[24]

The doctrine of *laesio enormis* shows that medieval writers recognized the possibility of a freely bargained price other than the market price, and the existence of a range of such prices within which both buyer and seller might be satisfied.[25] The bounds of half the market price to one-and-a-half times the market price provided some sort of rough approximation of that range.[26]

Conclusion

I have tried to show in this article that the medieval economy was characterized by frequent but not universal imperfect competition, that

20. De Roover 1958, p. 429. See also de Roover 1951 and 1967, p. 22; Noonan 1957, p. 88; and Gordon 1976, pp. 143–44, 220, 266–67.

21. For a specific case see McGee 1958; the general arguments are discussed in Stigler 1964 and Friedman 1973, pp. 39–50.

22. A friend who has lived for some time in a city in India describes non-competitive behavior that seems extraordinary, including successful discriminatory pricing in a market with a considerable number of sellers.

23. Baldwin 1959, pp. 16–21.

24. Baldwin 1959, pp. 22–27, 43–46. Cahn (1969, pp. 12–29) argues that the medieval law may have developed from a misreading of a Byzantine law intended to apply either exclusively to minors or perhaps to cases where less than half of the agreed-upon price had been actually paid out.

25. "We should therefore bear in mind the possibility that, at least for some Scholastics, 'just price' may have meant the zone of possible prices inherent within the 'natural' preconditions of trade" (Lowry 1969, p. 49). As evidence that Scholastics perceived the existence of a bargaining range, this conjecture supports my argument; as a definition of the just price it is inconsistent with it. See also Wilson 1975, p. 72–73.

26. *Laesio enormis* was less of a restriction on freedom of contract than it at first appears, since formulas by which the seller could renounce its remedies in advance were developed and accepted as legally binding within medieval Roman law (Baldwin 1959, pp. 24–27).

this was a problem of which medieval writers on economics were intensely conscious, and that the doctrine of just price can be interpreted as a useful device to minimize the (bargaining) costs resulting from imperfect competition by providing an arbitrated price enforced by moral sanctions. I have given reasons for the relative superiority of moral over legal sanctions for this purpose and thus provided a possible explanation of the division between the Roman and canonist lawyers, who supported freedom of contract, and the Scholastics, who argued for the doctrine of the just price.

I close by pointing out what I have not done. I have not shown that the doctrine of just price was sufficiently well enforced to serve the purpose I suggest, although I have given reasons why one may believe moral sanctions to have had force in medieval society. I have not shown that the advantages of the just price as an arbitrated solution to the bargaining problem make up for its disadvantages as a constraint on price flexibility; in particular I have not dealt with the possibility that the just price might be above the bargaining range in a situation in which the merchant was stuck with goods which were worth less than their market price to the only buyer. It is worth noting that the most notorious Scholastic doctrine related to price (although not derived from the just price doctrine), the prohibition on usury, set the price of credit at zero,[27] outside the bargaining range, and so, insofar as it was enforced, prevented transactions from occurring. Lastly, I have made no attempt to show that the Scholastic writers were themselves concerned with the economic (as opposed to the moral) costs of imperfect competition.[28] Indeed, by suggesting that the doctrine of the just price served a useful economic function I do not intend to imply that that was the principal reason why particular philosophers believed in it. I do intend to suggest that its economic function was one of the reasons why the doctrine, even if adopted for wholly different reasons, survived and spread. This essay is thus at least intended as a contribution not only to the history of economic thought, but to the economic history of thought as well.

27. But see references in note 3 above for discussion of the exceptions by which Scholastics justified interest.

28. It is worth noting that according to Schumpeter (1954, pp. 96–97) the economic sociology of the Scholastics "continued to treat temporal institutions as utilitarian devices that were to be explained—or justified—by considerations of social expedience centering in the concept of the Public Good" and "the scholastics' idea of what is 'unjust' was associated—though never identified with—their idea of what is contrary to public welfare." Similarly, Worland (1967, p. 17) cites Aquinas (commenting on Book V of Aristotle's *Ethics*) as defending justice in exchange by arguing that "if this is not observed—if goods do not exchange in proportion to the labor and expense of their producers—there would be no exchange of goods, nor will men share their goods with one another." For a contrasting view see Bartell 1962. Readers may wish to compare my argument with the very different defense of the just price doctrine in Lowry 1974.

Friedman   ·   Aquinas and the just price   241

REFERENCES

St. Thomas Aquinas. *Summa Theologiae*. Translated and edited by Marcus Lefebure, O.P. New York, 1975.

John W. Baldwin. "The Medieval Theories of the Just Price." *Transactions of the American Philosophical Society*, n.s. 49, pt. 4 (1959), reprinted in *Pre-Capitalist Economic Thought* (New York, 1972).

Désiré Barath. "The Just Price and the Costs of Production According to St. Thomas Aquinas." *New Scholasticism* 34 (1960): 413–30.

Ernest Bartell. "Value, Price and St. Thomas." *Thomist* 25 (1962): 325–81.

Kenneth S. Cahn. "The Roman and Frankish Roots of the Just Price of Medieval Canon Law." *Studies in Medieval and Renaissance History* 6 (1969): 1–52.

C. Cipolla. *Money, Prices, and Civilization in the Mediterranean World*. New York, 1967.

M. I. Finley. "Aristotle and Economic Analysis." In *Studies in Ancient Society*, M. I. Finley, ed. (London, 1974).

David Friedman. *The Machinery of Freedom: Guide to a Radical Capitalism*. New York, 1978.

Barry J. Gordon. "Aristotle and the Development of Value Theory." *Quarterly Journal of Economics* 78 (Feb. 1964): 115–28.

—— *Economic Analysis Before Adam Smith*. New York, 1975.

Samuel Hollander. "On the Interpretation of the Just Price." *Kyklos* 18 (1965): 615–32.

Ann Krueger. "The Political Economy of the Rent-Seeking Society." *American Economic Review*, June 1974.

S. Todd Lowry. "Aristotle's 'Natural Limit' and the Economics of Price Regulation." *Greek, Roman and Byzantine Studies* 15 (1974): 57–63.

—— "Aristotle's Mathematical Theory of Exchange." *History of Political Economy* 1 (1969): 44–66.

John S. McGee. "Predatory Price Cutting: The Standard Oil (N.J.) Case." *Journal of Law and Economics* 1 (1958): 137–69.

John T. Noonan, Jr. *The Scholastic Analysis of Usury*. Cambridge, Mass., 1957.

Eric Roll. *A History of Economic Thought*. Englewood Cliffs, N.J., 1953.

Raymond de Roover. "Monopoly Theory Prior to Adam Smith: A Revision." *Quarterly Journal of Economics* 65, no. 4 (1951): 492–524.

——. "Joseph A. Schumpeter and Scholastic Economics." *Kyklos* 10 (1957): 115–43.

——. "The Concept of the Just Price: Theory and Economic Policy." *Journal of Economic History* 18, no. 4 (1958): 418–34.

——. *San Bernardino of Siena and Sant' Antonino of Florence*. Cambridge, Mass., 1967.

——. *Business, Banking and Economic Thought*. Chicago, 1974.

Joseph A. Schumpeter. *History of Economic Analysis*. New York, 1954.

J. Soudek. "Aristotle's Theory of Exchange." *Proceedings of the American Philosophical Society* 96 (1952): 45–75.

George J. Stigler. "A Theory of Oligopoly." *Journal of Political Economy* 72 (1964): 44–61.

Gordon Tullock. "The Welfare Costs of Tariffs, Monopolies, and Theft." *Western Economic Journal* 5 (1967): 224–32.

242   *History of Political Economy 12:2 (1980)*

Oliver E. Williamson. *Markets and Hierarchies: Analysis and Antitrust Implications*. New York, 1975.
George W. Wilson. "The Economics of the Just Price." *History of Political Economy* 7 (1975): 56–74.
Stephen T. Worland. *Scholasticism and Welfare Economics*. Notre Dame, Ind., 1967.
———. *"Justum pretium*: One More Round in an 'Endless Series,' " *History of Political Economy* 9 (1977): 504–21.

[14]

History of Political Economy 14:2
© 1982 by Duke University Press

Economic freedom in Scholastic thought

Odd Langholm

I. Benchmarks of Liberalism

When natural law philosophers in the seventeenth century prepared
some of the ideological basis of classical economics, it is well known
that they drew some support from the liberalistic principles of Roman
law. Historians will not agree as to whether merchants make law or law
makes merchants, but in European history from the Middle Ages the
parallel ascent of Roman law and capitalism is indisputable. What may
be less well known, however, is that some of the legal principles in
question had been for centuries the objects of criticism by Scholastic
economists who sought to reconcile them with patristic teaching. The
question whether natural law philosophy broke with late Scholasticism
or rather took up existing threads of thought is not one to be answered
in generalities. It depends on what happened to single identifiable
threads. This study is concerned with a limited number of specific maxims coined in the Middle Ages on the basis of the Code and Digest of
Justinian and serving for the Scholastic moralists as benchmarks of
economic liberalism from which they could measure their own positions. Fastening on these maxims, authors like Hugo Grotius and Samuel Pufendorf, to a large extent, and an author like Thomas Hobbes
seemingly completely, set aside the Scholastic efforts at reconciliation.
It is for the historians of later periods to fully assess the instability thus
built into the bedrock of the new economics and for those who seek the
longer perspective to identify Scholastic antecedents to the subsequent
reaction against the classical ideology. The task I have set myself here
is mainly to trace the Scholastic dispute itself. But it is useful, in order
to define and appreciate its terms, to review them first as they emerged
in natural law writing.

"Among those who live in natural liberty," says Pufendorf, "each
man is allowed to fix the price of an article of his at his own pleasure,
since every man in such a state is the final arbiter of his possessions
and actions."[1] In Hobbes's blunt language, "every man may dispose

Correspondence for the author may be sent to Professor Odd Langholm, The Norwegian
School of Economics, Helleveien 30, N-5035 Bergen/Sandviken, NORWAY.

1. *De iure naturae et gentium*, V, i, 8.

of his own, and transfer the same at his pleasure."[2] Property rights are cornerstones of economic liberalism resting on Roman law. Pufendorf's phrases echo a medieval maxim derived from the Code and frequently cited in Scholastic discourse: "Everyone is the moderator and arbiter of his own thing."[3] Justice in the exchange of property is assured by consent. To pick up Pufendorf again a few lines further down, "others who feel my price too high," he says, "have the very simple course left them of leaving me in possession of what is mine." Grotius calls on the strange support of the Greek author he believed to be Andronicus of Rhodes, a paraphrast on Aristotle's *Nicomachean Ethics*, who states: "A gain, which is made with the consent of the contracting parties, is neither unjust nor subject to suit."[4] In Hobbes this idea is absolutely central: "forasmuch as both the buyer and the seller are made judges of the value, and are thereby both satisfied: there can be no injury done on either side."[5] Elsewhere he quotes "an old saying, 'volenti non fit injuria,' the willing man receives no injury."[6] It is in fact a Scholastic saying, based on suggestions in the Digest.

Applied to economic exchange, these two principles absorb the ethical premise in such a way that the conventional concept of a just price becomes meaningless. If both parties to the exchange negotiate to the best of their abilities to further their own advantages in the disposal of their property, to which they have a right, the just price will be the one they can finally agree upon and this will be (to the seller) the highest at which it is possible to conclude a sale.[7] I do not injure the buyer "if I sell my goods for as much as I can get for them," says Hobbes;[8] the just "value of all things contracted for" is what the contractors "be contented to give."[9] Grotius (and through him Pufendorf) quotes Seneca: "Though you have well praised your wares, they are worth only the highest price at which they can be sold."[10] Now to say that is to

2. *The Elements of Law*, II, iii, 5.

3. "Quisque suae rei est moderator et arbiter." "Arbiter" in Pufendorf is the Carnegie edition's rendering of his Latin *moderator*.

4. *De iure belli ac pacis*, II, xii, 26 (translation of the Carnegie edition). The Greek paraphrase, of uncertain authorship, was published in Latin by Heinsius. The translation (Leiden 1607, revised 1617 and closer to Grotius's Latin version) is faithful to the original, which is, however, an overinterpretation of Aristotle at *EN*, V, 4 (1132b).

5. *Elements*, I, xvi, 5.

6. *Philosophical Rudiments*, III, 7; cp. its Latin version, *De Cive*, as well as *Elements*, II, ii, 3.

7. The Scholastics normally thought of the seller as having the upper hand and thus being the one to be preached to about restraint. I adopt this convention for simplicity, though the moral problem is of course in principle symmetrical.

8. *Rudiments*, III, 6; cp. *De Cive*: "si res nostras vendamus quanti possumus."

9. *Leviathan*, XV.

10. *De beneficiis*, VI, xv, 4 (Loeb translation); cp. Grotius, II, xii, 14; Pufendorf, V, i, 9.

bypass the *Corpus iuris civilis*, but the Stoic moralist is certainly one of the writers of Roman antiquity who best express the spirit of its economic tenets. Throughout the Digest as received by the medieval commentators the idea is indicated in a number of phrases recalling Seneca and crystallized in the maxim which embodies the very essence of a free-exchange economy: "A thing is worth as much as it can be sold for."[11]

While the supporting statements are not, this is explicitly an economic statement. It defines exchange value exactly as it came to be defined in nineteenth-century textbooks. Value is what can be obtained, with an emphasis on 'can.' Value is power, said Ricardo.[12] On its long road to triumph this concept met with a certain amount of opposition from moral philosophers who had different ideas about value and subjected these three maxims to word by word scrutiny. Freedom is a momentous issue and Scholastic economic thought is a large and still unexplored field. The kind of literary exercise conducted in the present essay can hardly do full justice to its title. But it provides something definite—a distinct path through the field.

II. Scholastic Interpreters

A preliminary survey of Scholastic sources will simplify references and serve to identify the leading protagonists. The body of law compiled under the sponsorship of the emperor Justinian I in the sixth century consists of the Code (in twelve books), the Digest (in fifty books), and supplementary material. The earliest medieval comments to be consulted are marginal glosses by members of the legal school of Bologna, extant in old manuscripts of the Digest. Prominent among the later glossators are Azo and his pupil Accursius (d. c.1260), who compiled the authoritative Ordinary Gloss on the basis of this tradition. The civilians (Roman lawyers) now took to writing longer commentaries on the Digest. The towering figure is Bartolus (d. 1357). He studied and taught at Perugia, a city whose fame in the field of law is due to him as well as to his teacher Cinus and his most competent pupils like the brothers Baldus and Angelus de Ubaldis. The following are some of the 'Bartolists', i.e. jurists who carried on his tradition in the fifteenth century: Raphael Fulgosius, Johannes de Imola, Paulus Castrensis,

---

11. "Res tantum valet quantum vendi potest"; cp. Hobbes's Latin wording in n. 8 above.

12. "By exchangeable value is meant the power which a commodity has of commanding any given quantity of another commodity" (*Works*, ed. Sraffa, IV, 398; cp. Böhm-Bawerk on the analogy between value and power, *Grundzüge*, Introd.). In English (e.g. in Marshall's value definition in *Principles*, II, ii, 6) the analogy is less obvious than in the Latin languages where the word 'can' is itself indicative of it; cp. Say's definition: "qu'on *peut* obtenir" (*Traité*, II, 1; my emphasis).

Langholm · Economic freedom in Scholastic thought   263

Ludovicus Pontanus, Alexander Tartagnus, Jason Maynus.[13] Most of these savants spent parts of their academic careers at Bologna, as did Bartolus himself. Some of them also wrote on canon law.

Starting in the late twelfth century, a series of five compilations were made of the canons and decretals of recent popes along with related older material. Each of these compilations is in five books, and several of them include a title on buying and selling in Book III and a title on usury in Book V. Interesting legislation pertaining to economics is to be found in the first compilation, on which there are glosses by Laurentius Hispanus and Tancredus. But the preliminary compilations were soon superseded as much of their material went into the definitive collection of Decretals promulgated by Pope Gregory IX in 1234, also in five books. Under Boniface VIII a sixth book, the Sextum, was added. Vincentius Hispanus and others annotated Gregory's Decretals. Previous glossatory material was utilized by Bernardus Botone for his Ordinary Gloss. A slightly later Gloss is due to the greatest of the early canonists, Henry of Susa, known as Hostiensis (d. 1271), who also wrote a *Summa* on the Decretals, initiating a comprehensive commentary literature by authors of the Bolognese school. Most important in the fourteenth century is Johannes Andreae. Then there is a marked (and in medieval economics highly characteristic) literary gap following the Black Death, until the tradition picks up again with Petrus de Ancharano, Franciscus Zabarella, Antonius de Butrio, Johannes de Imola (who also commented on the Digest), Johannes de Anania and, crowning these efforts, Nicolaus Tudeschis, known as Panormitanus (d. 1445).[14]

The canonists were instrumental in transmitting civilian ideas to those who wrote in the older traditions of moral philosophy, reaching even teachers like William of Auxerre, Thomas Aquinas, Johannes Duns Scotus, and Henry of Ghent.[15] The latter is a key name here,

13. Early editions of the Digest and commentaries were conventionally divided into the Old Digest (through Book 24,2), the Infortiatum (through Book 38) and the New Digest, each segment frequently in two parts with separate paginations (omitted here in reference to places in the law). Editions used: Accursius (Digest with Gloss), Paris 1559; Bartolus, Basel 1588; Baldus, Venice 1599; Angelus, Venice 1579–80; Fulgosius, Lyon 1554; Imola, Bologna 1580; Castrensis, Venice 1593; Pontanus, Venice 1580; Tartagnus, Venice 1595; Maynus, Venice 1598. Commentaries on the Code: Cinus, Venice 1493; Baldus, Venice 1615.

14. Editions used of commentaries on Decretals: Botone, Mainz 1473; Hostiensis (Gloss), Venice 1581: id. (*Summa*), Basel 1573; Andreae, Trino 1512; Ancharano, Bologna 1581; Zabarella, Lyon 1557; Butrio, Venice 1578; Imola, Lyon 1517; Anania, Lyon 1553; Panormitanus, Lyon 1550.

15. Auxerre's *Summa* is quoted at f.225ᵛ of the Paris 1500 edition; Scotus on the *Sentences* of Petrus Lombardus, IV,15,2, *Opera*, 18 (Paris 1894) at p. 324; and Aquinas in the *Summa theologiae*, II-II,77 and 78 (on buying and selling and on usury) as well as in *De malo*, XIII,4, *Opera*, 8 (Parma 1856), pp. 372–76. Three of Ghent's questions are rele-

264   *History of Political Economy 14:2 (1982)*

partly because some of his chosen questions (*quodlibeta*) on economic subjects seem to have inspired an author whose dominant influence on the best of Scholastic economic thought is only gradually becoming apparent to historians, namely Petrus Johannis Olivi, a Franciscan who taught in Southern France and Italy and died at Narbonne in 1298. He wrote a treatise in the form of a set of questions on economic contracts. It was read by Geraldus Odonis (d. 1349), another Franciscan, who took Olivi's ideas into the commentary tradition concerning Aristotle's *Ethics*, an important vehicle for part of the argument on economic freedom. An earlier tradition on the *Ethics*, that of the Paris Averroists, helped, along with Odonis, to influence the great Aristotelian Johannes Buridanus.[16] Odonis also wrote a treatise on contracts himself, paraphrasing Olivi. Bridging the post-Plague gap, Bernardino of Siena, yet another Franciscan (d. 1444), utilized both works in his economic sermons and passed them on to Antonino of Florence and subsequent traditions.[17]

This portion of Bernardino's sermons came in fact to be printed separately and thus belongs by accident to one important economic genre. Treatises on contracts were composed by Henry of Hassia, Henry of Oyta, Johannes Gerson, Bartholomaeus Caepolla (d. 1477), and Conrad of Summenhart (d. 1502). A pamphlet by Martin Luther owes something to this tradition as well as to the voluminous usury literature, of which it suffices to mention here the treatise by the early Thomist Giles of Lessines.[18] Books of a rather different type but drawing on the same sources are the summaries for confessors. These handbooks explain, often in alphabetical order, important canon law titles

---

vant, viz. *Quodl*. I,40 (ed. Paris 1518), ff. 26ʳ–27ᵛ—also in *Opera*, 5 (Leiden/Louvain 1979), pp. 219–30—III,28, ff. 87ᵛ–89ᵛ, and XIV,14, f. 570ᵛ.

16. The Averroists are represented by an unprinted commentary, Vat.Lat.2173, in a question of f. 40ᵛ, and Buridan in the corresponding question, V,23, ed. Paris 1489, ff. 139ᵛ–140ᵛ. Odonis is quoted on *EN*, IV (Venice 1500) at f. 73ʳ⁻ᵛ, and *EN*, V, at f. 113ʳ.

17. Olivi's treatise has only recently been edited by A. Spicciani, Rome (Accademia Nazionale dei Lincei) 1977; quotations here are from his first question (pp. 253–57). The work is extant in several manuscripts, of which Bernardino is known to have used Siena BCom U.V.6 (first question on ff. 295ʳᵃ–296ʳᵇ). Odonis's treatise (still unprinted) is in U.V.8 of the same collection (corresponding question on f. 81ʳ⁻ᵛ). Bernardino used the same material mainly in his Sermon 35, Article I (pp. 190–95) and briefly in Sermon 33 (at p. 157), *Opera*, vol. 4, Florence 1956; cp. Antonino, *Summa*, II, i, 16, 3–4, Verona 1740, vol. 2, col. 254–61.

18. Lessines's treatise on usury used to be ascribed to Aquinas and is in his *Opera*, vol. 17, Parma 1864 (quoted at p. 424). Hassia and Oyta on contracts were both printed in Gerson's *Opera*, vol. 4, Cologne 1484. Hassia is cited at f. 191ᵛ (in Section VI below) and at f. 220ᵛ (in Section VII below), Oyta at f. 234ᵛ and 242ʳ. Gerson's own treatise was studied in a more recent *Opera* edition, Antwerp 1706, vol. 3,1 (reference to col. 179–80). Caepolla is in *Tractatus illustrium iurisconsultorum*, vol. 7, Venice 1584, ff. 2ʳ–15ʳ; the issues recorded here are discussed on ff. 5ᵛ–6ʳ. The best edition of Summenhart is Venice 1580, where the relevant Question 57 is on pp. 267–74. The Weimar edition of Luther's works includes his *Von Kaufshandlung und Wucher* in vol. 15 (1899); it is quoted at p. 295 (in my translation).

and topics. They typically include brief articles on buying and selling and on usury. The earliest of them are less relevant here; the genre assumes importance as it picks up strains of argument from Olivi through Bernardino and from some of the later jurists. Mention must be made of the fourteenth-century *Summa Pisanella* by Bartholomaeus Pisanus only because of a later Supplement to it by the Franciscan Nicolaus de Ausmo. Absolutely essential to our discussion are the *Summa Rosella* by Baptista Trovamala and the *Summa Angelica* by Angelus Carletus, both fifteenth-century Franciscans, and the *Summa Silvestrina* by Silvester Mazzolini, a Dominican and Luther's opponent.[19] All these summarists were Italians.

After the break-up of the Scholastic community it is neither in Luther's Germany nor in Italy that we most profitably may seek a significant extension of these traditions, however, but rather in Spain, with the celebrated School of Salamanca, and this is worth doing in view of the persistent attempts to relate the classical ideology through natural law philosophy to post-Tridentine Spanish Scholasticism. It is imperative that the School be approached via the work of its true founder, Francisco de Vitoria (d. 1546), the Dominican whose comments on Aquinas set its course. An important cofounder and almost exact contemporary is Johannes de Medina, of Alcala rather than Salamanca. They used Mazzolini, Summenhart, and earlier Scholastics. A high point of the tradition is Domingo de Soto on Justice and Law. Later exponents, continuing in all the genres recorded above, and writing in the late sixteenth century, were Martin de Azpilcueta, Petrus de Navarra, Ludovicus Lopez, Franciscus Toletus, Michael Bartholomaeus Salon, and Petrus de Aragon, to mention only some of those who wrote in Latin and addressed the present issue.[20]

III. Power and Obligation

No ancient jurist seems to have said in so many words that a thing is worth as much as it can be sold for, but a number of places in the

19. Ausmo, *Supplementum Summae Pisanellae*, Venice 1473 (quoted in the article on *Usura*—no pagination); Trovamala, Strasbourg 1516 (quoted at f. 75^r in the article on *Emptio et venditio* [Buying and selling] and at f. 255^r, on *Usura*); Carletus, Rouen 1513 (f. 97^r) and Mazzolini, Antwerp 1581 (ff. 293–95), both summarists on Buying and selling.

20. Vitoria, *Comentarios a la Secunda secundae de Santo Tomás*, Tom. IV, *De iustitia*, in *Biblioteca de Téologos Españoles*, vol. 5, Salamanca 1934. The comments on Question 77, Article 1 are on pp. 116–30. Medina, *De restitutione et contractibus*, Cologne 1607 (quoted at pp. 198–99); Soto, *De iustitia et iure*, Salamanca 1559 (pp. 531–34); Azpilcueta, *Manuale sive enchiridion confessariorium*, Mainz 1603 (p. 667); Navarra, *De ablatorum restitutione*, III (vol. 2), Toledo 1585 (pp. 147–48); Ludovicus Lopez, *Instructorium negotiantium*, Salamanca 1589 (p. 40); Franciscus Toletus, *Summa casuum conscientiae*, Cologne 1599 (p. 725); Michael Bartholomaeus Salon, *De iustitia et iure*, Venice 1608 (vol. 2, pp. 17–18); Petrus de Aragon, *De iustitia et iure*, Lyon 1596 (p. 438)—the latter two commenting on Aquinas.

Digest openly invite the maxim. Six references are needed to fully explain its medieval history. Three of them (Digest 9,2,33; 35,2,62; and 39,6,18,3) are better postponed, for they also add elements of interpretation to be discussed later on. At three other places the Gloss of Accursius takes note of the maxim in its standard Latin form, "Res tantum valet quantum vendi potest." It is occasionally ascribed to Accursius, but sporadic manuscript evidence suggests that it may be older. At Digest 13,1,14 and 47,2,52,29 a related phrase—what one may get—is suggested in the text of the law as a principle of estimation; at Digest 36,1,1,16 the text itself uses the expression "what it can be sold for." In one of the few extant manuscripts of this segment of the Digest with pre-Accursian glosses, the maxim appears in the margin at this paragraph in only a slightly different grammatical form. The gloss is initialed in color in the manner of the copied text itself, thus indicating an original in a parent codex of unknown age.[21] In the manuscript in question no fewer than ten early glossators have been identified by ascription,[22] but the value maxim is unfortunately anonymous. There are some further pointers to its origin to be mentioned below. Suffice it to say here that it was mainly by the insistence of Accursius that students of the Digest were made to understand that a thing is worth what it can be sold for.

As knowledge of law spread in the Schools, one can picture upholders of conventional patristic ethics being asked to comment on this provocative new principle. Legal statements are by their nature prescriptive. The word 'worth,' and even more the Latin verb *valere*, are of course inherently prescriptive, but when a word like that appears in a legal gloss, prescription is open and intended within the domain of the law. To say that a thing is worth as much as it can be sold for would therefore mean that it may, in the appropriate domain, be so priced, and if this were to extend to the moral law it must mean that one may, without compunction, sell a thing for as much as one can get for it. Now Roman law principles would not immediately apply in the forum of conscience, but the great prestige of the legal backing made it absolutely imperative for teachers of moral law to explain the difference very carefully. The first to meet this challenge openly was Henry of Ghent, but he may have been influenced by an earlier writer. William of Auxerre touches upon economic transactions in his theological *Summa* and examines the objection that "a thing is worth as much as can be had for it"—this was written about 1220, before the maxim began to spread in the Accursian wording. True enough, says the summa-

21. Bamberg SB Jur. 15, f. 136ᵛᵃ: "Rem tantum valere quantum vendi potest." (The colorist has actually miscopied an initial T for an R.)
22. Savigny, *Geschichte des römischen Rechts im Mittelalter*, vol. 4.

rist, but what a thing can be sold for does not depend on craft but on charity. This is to give 'can' a new meaning, which is what Henry of Ghent did explicitly.

In his first *quodlibet*, disputed at Paris in 1276, Henry asks whether buying cheaper and immediately selling dearer is a sin. How can it be, if a thing is simply worth what it can be sold for? Because, says Henry, 'can' is not to be understood here in a factual but in a juridical sense, with reference to natural law. "As much as it can be sold for" (*quantum vendi potest*) should really be taken to mean "as much as it ought to be sold for" (*quantum vendi debet*). Many years later in his fourteenth *quodlibet* he asks whether it is permitted to sell dearer on account of a buyer's need. It would seem so; is not a thing worth what it can be sold for? No, not if 'can' is taken in an absolute or factual sense; only if it is taken, as it should be, in a moral sense. We "can," says Henry of Ghent, only what we can *de iure*. Quoting or paraphrasing these lines, a succession of later Scholastics stood firm against economic liberalism in this position. A thing is worth what it can be sold for under the moral law where we can only what we ought. Value is not a question of economic power as it came to be in the classical definition. It had always been, and was to remain, a question of obligation. When we presently proceed to other arguments made by these doctors, it should be kept in mind that this was still their basic assumption. Even in the sixteenth century, as Medina was about to bring Henry of Ghent's literal phrases into the Spanish tradition, Luther reproaches the German merchants: "It should not be thus, 'I may sell my wares as dear as I can or will', but thus, 'I may sell my wares as dear as I ought or as is right and fair.' For your sale ought not to be an activity freely in your power and will without any law or measure, as though you were a god, obliged to no one." As a preacher, Luther speaks for them all.

But there is a fine balance to be observed between sermon and syllogism in the teaching of ethics. It is doubtful whether the moral position could have been maintained if no attempt had been made to explain *why* the absolute 'can' does not apply and *how* it is to be modified so as to apply as a moral 'can'. It is well known, wrote Soto, professor at Salamanca, that the rule "A thing is worth as much as it can be sold for" is not to be taken as broadly as it sounds. Still, if it is moderated to mean (paraphrasing Ghent) "as much as it can justly be sold for, for we can only what we can *de iure*," it becomes empty. For if you were to answer someone who asks you what price he may sell for, "What justice will bear," you would have told him nothing that he did not know already. But Soto did not leave the matter there, nor did Henry of Ghent. From Ghent to Soto there is also an analytical tradition on the liberalistic value maxim. Running along several converging lines, it became one of the cores of Scholastic economic ethics. To make the legal maxim into an operational moral rule, the Scholastics modified and conditioned it on the basis of generally accepted principles and preferably by extending principles originating in the Roman law itself.

IV.   *Knowledge, Understanding, and Consent*

Nor were the jurists, of course, likely to take 'can' without question. The Roman law of sale observed strict conditions of valid contract, some of which might be taken for granted in any given point of commentary, and some of which were stated. The Scholastic moralists fastened on one line of modification of the value maxim which goes back to the glossators but was brought out by Bartolus. At Digest 39,6,18,3 it is suggested that a thing held by a man (as a kind of donation) is to be estimated at what it might have been sold for—assuming, says the Ordinary Gloss, that the man knows (*homini scienti*) its condition. I cannot trace this remark to an earlier glossator and must assume that it is due to Accursius.[23] Bartolus picked it up and tied it to the literal value maxim here and in a number of other places in the law. And his pupils repeated it. It is indeed hard to find a Bartolist who failed to add this stipulation. Through them it spread to canon law and into the economic texts. This is what they all said: A thing is worth what it can be sold for provided the buyer *knows* what he is buying.[24] Quite late on, Alexander Tartagnus in comment on Digest 36,1,1,16 made an addition to this: A thing is worth what it can be sold for provided the buyer *knows and understands* what he buys.[25] Bartolus's stipulation rules out fraud. Fraud was certainly not an unambiguous concept. The word was used differently and sometimes sloppily by the Scholastics, though less so by those trained in law. For the present purpose it is sufficiently precise to say that fraud meant wilful misrepresentation—of the objects and conditions of exchange. Tartagnus's addition can be said to rule out ignorance in one sense of the word, assuming that it can mean both insufficient received information and insufficient capacity for receiving information, as in children and the mentally retarded, the latter being then what is primarily intended here.

These conditions had long since been brought to bear on the value maxim by the moral philosophers. Giles of Lessines stated explicitly

---

23. Thus ascribed in Paris BN lat. 4483; 4486; 4486A.

24. Cp. at 13,1,14, Bartolus, Baldus, Fulgosius; at 35,2,63, Bartolus, Angelus, Tartagnus; at 36,1,1,16, Bartolus, Angelus, Imola, Pontanus; at 39,6,18,3, Bartolus, Imola, Castrensis, Pontanus; at 47,2,52,29, Bartolus, Angelus; furthermore, Baldus on Code 6, 20, 20; Anania on Decretals 3,17,1 and 5,19,6 (see below), etc., etc.

25. "homini scienti et intelligenti conditionem et rei qualitatem." This was repeated by Maynus on the same paragraph, by Caepolla, and by Trovamala on usury.

that a thing is justly worth what it can be sold for without fraud, and this was often repeated in the Thomist tradition, including its Spanish extension.[26] The tradition from Henry of Ghent made the conditioning less easy but rather more interesting. Henry himself said, in his first *quodlibet*, that a thing is *not* worth what it can be sold for due to *inscientia*, a word which can be taken several ways and may mean either 'ignorance' or 'inexperience.' Olivi makes exceptions for fraud and *levitas*, also a difficult word which may be rendered as 'frivolity' but was probably intended to convey a certain mental 'lightness' of a less obnoxious kind. On the bottom of the page in the manuscript of Olivi utilized by Bernardino an addition is indicated, reading *ignorantia*, and the two conditions appear together in his version. They were taken from there into the confessional literature through the intermediacy of Caepolla, who records nearly all traditions on the value maxim. Carletus and Mazzolini rule out fraud, but disagree as to whether *levitas* pertains to ignorance or not. Vitoria knew these texts and makes a great point of rejecting any kind of frivolity as an excuse.

Conceding some difference of wording and some disagreement about the meaning of certain words, it is clear that the moral philosophers could begin to modify the liberalistic value maxim by bringing to bear on it a set of conditions conceded by the civilians themselves. So far this is not troublesome. But why did they all agree on this? Clearly because, in the European legal tradition, justice of contract presumes consent. The positive principle that a willing party is not injured is stated in the Digest at 39,3,9,1 and at 47,10,1,5. The canonists included it in their list of general rules at the close of the Sextum: "No injury or deceit is done to him who knows and consents" (Rule 27—"Scienti et consentienti non fit iniuria neque dolus." This combination with the type of conditioning discussed above indicates the justification of the latter and points beyond it. No one can be said to consent to terms of exchange which he does not know or understand. But there is a condition which takes precedence here over both knowledge and understanding. When Soto confirms the positive rule, having criticized what he took to be an empty moral admonition, its meaning is, he says, that a thing is worth what it can be sold for "in the absence of force, fraud and deceit (*seclusa vi, fraude et dolo*) by which voluntariness is removed in the buyer." Consent cannot be forced! Restriction of information and restrictions within the mind which is to use information can both be said in different ways to restrict the operation of free will and to preclude consent. But prior to any of these conditions is restriction by way of positive compulsion.

26. Cp. Soto and Azpilcueta as quoted below, followed by Navarra, Lopez, Toletus, Salon.

270   *History of Political Economy 14:2 (1982)*

In its primary sense this was presumably too obvious to the Roman law commentators even to be mentioned in an economic context. A commodity is clearly not worth what it can be sold for only when physical coercion is exercised on the buyer to make him take it at that price. This case is trivial to the economist; it belongs in criminal law. So do blackmail and various forms of moral coercion. Other forms may pass legal but not moral criteria without pertaining to economics as such. What the Scholastic moral philosophers insisted on, however, was a possible extension of the concept of coercion to economic variables. This is the approach indicated by Soto's reference to *vis* (force). Vitoria had spoken similarly of *violentia* (violence). What *economic* factors can operate in those terms? What does consent mean in the face of those personal and impersonal economic influences at work in the exchange situation which determine the range and quality of choice?

V.   Aristotle on the Voluntary

As so often when they needed to get their bearings, the Scholastics took counsel with Aristotle. Towards the end of Book V of the *Nicomachean Ethics* where some loose ends are being tied up (in a passage not far below the analysis of justice in exchange) there occurs a remark to the effect that though suicide is unjust, it must be so towards the state, not towards the suicide himself, for he suffers voluntarily and "no one suffers injustice voluntarily."[27] The common origin in Graeco-Roman legal thought of this and the canon law rule derived from the Digest is evident.[28] It enabled the medieval economists to discuss the issue raised by the civilians in an Aristotelian setting. When it came to clarifying this, Aristotle provided the concept of *conditional consent*. These elements are drawn together in the treatise on contracts written by Johannes Gerson in 1421 and brought into the late Scholastic discussion by Vitoria. It is the first work I can find in which the two maxims about value and about justice and the voluntary are combined in a statement of the conditions of just exchange, and since it proved an influential little book, it impressed this combination on the ensuing tradition. Besides the absence of fraud and ignorance, says Gerson, it is required that consent be absolute and not only conditional, as Aristotle

27. "iniustum autem patitur nullus volens" reads the medieval translation (1138a12). Hobbes's form as quoted above, which is in fact exactly that of Vitoria, somewhat resembles a fifteenth-century translation of Aristotle, by Aretinus, "nulli autem volenti iniuria fit"; but the subcontemporary and more influential translator Argyropulus has "nemo vero sponte iniuriam patitur," and *sponte* (with the occasional variant *lubens*) was retained by the numerous sixteenth-century Latin translators, so Hobbes may not have associated this saying with Aristotle. On these translators and other authors quoted in this section, cp. my *Price and Value in the Aristotelian Tradition*, Oslo 1979.

28. This is pointed out by S. Todd Lowry, "Aristotle's Mathematical Analysis of Exchange," *HOPE* 1 (1969): 44–66 at p. 51.

says about goods abandoned at sea and about consent extorted by fear.

Moral judgment about a man's actions depends on his responsibility for them and what determines it; accordingly, in the opening of Book III of the *Ethics*, Aristotle discusses what 'voluntary' means. Very briefly summarized, what he says is that ignorance and external compulsion make actions involuntary; compulsion may be impersonal (as when a man is being carried away by the wind) or personal (as when a man is in another man's power). 'Compulsion' is the standard English translation here of Aristotle's *bia*, which is exactly the Latin *vis*. With regard to actions performed in fear it is open to dispute, Aristotle proceeds, whether they are voluntary or not. Abandoning cargo to save himself and his crew in a storm is a voluntary action on the part of a ship's captain, but apart from that circumstance no one throws away his goods voluntarily. Such actions are mixed, but they tend more to the voluntary because they are chosen at the time. In the abstract they are perhaps involuntary.[29]

Intended by Aristotle for the analysis of man's moral responsibility for his actions in the face of terms imposed on his freedom of choice from without, the concept of conditional consent was adopted by the Latin commentators for the analysis of the justness of economic terms from the point of view rather of the moral responsibility of the one who imposes them upon another. It is of the first importance to note that the Aristotelian model lacks the distinction between (impersonal) compulsion and (personal) coercion on which modern libertarians rely.[30] The distinction is irrelevant from the point of view of Aristotle's own application here and it would not be conceded by the Scholastics on the basis of the conventional patristic view of economic relations. The idea that terms of exchange are determined by suprapersonal forces which extenuate moral blame on the individual level was essentially foreign to ethical thinking at least until well into the sixteenth century. The patristic focus, even in the case of issues carrying broad social implications, was on immediate personal relations. You met another person in the context of exchange and offered him terms which were yours to choose and should be just, no matter what his predicament. The question invited by the Aristotelian concept was therefore how to decide when such terms meet only conditional consent and are therefore not just. Obviously the distinction does not stand up to abstract logical scrutiny. In a certain relative sense the price taker can always claim that he is losing. Terms accepted might always have been rejected if better terms were offered, and consent is therefore always conditional. To avoid

29. *EN*, III,1; 1110a.
30. Cp. F. A. Hayek, *The Constitution of Liberty* (1960; London 1976), p. 133.

reducing the problem to absurdity, operational criteria had to be established. The Scholastics looked at cases.

The question whether anyone may suffer injustice voluntarily first appeared in some of the late-thirteenth-century Averroist commentaries on the *Ethics*. The semi-obscure group behind this body of writing represents a countercurrent to patristic ethics. In an anonymous Averroist commentary preserved in the Vatican Library there is an argument against Aristotle's proposition in Book V which takes this question into the economic sphere. Suppose two men trade in a certain commodity ("duo mercantur aliquas res") and one willingly sells and the other willingly buys it for more than it is worth; then the one who buys suffers injustice voluntarily. Not so, says the commentator, pushing a characteristic distinction. He may suffer "what is unjust" but not "in such a way that it is unjust," for he buys because he hopes later to gain by doing so; hence the argument does not apply. Johannes Buridanus concludes a similar question in much the same way: No one exchanges except to get as much or more than he gives. This position looks amazingly familiar and modern. In that relative sense you always gain. Range of choice makes no difference. The fact that you have chosen between alternatives is prima facie evidence that you have achieved your preference and hence suffered no injustice. But although Buridan's version of Aristotle may represent an early root of liberalism, it seems that the conclusion recorded here permits of a different interpretation. Both the commentators mentioned use the verb *lucrari* ('to gain') to designate motive. It can be understood as relative to the rejected choice (not to buy), but gain may also be measured by some real economic standard. The Averroist's description of the exchange situation suggests professional merchants. If the buyer is a merchant expecting lucre from resale, why should not the original seller reap some of it in the first place? This puts another complexion on the case and raises a further question: What about exchanges where the buyer's consent is motivated by something more pressing than business profit?

In the Aristotelian sources there is also an early tradition which invokes the concept of conditional consent to counter an objection to the prohibition of usury. It was taken from the context of the *Politics* into that of the *Ethics*, where it appears in Book IV (on the virtue of liberality) as well as in Book V. In both places Buridanus copies the Franciscan commentator Geraldus Odonis, who was not an Averroist but transmitted a number of other influences and was very well informed. Discussing voluntary injustice he calls on Digest 39,3,9 and 47,10,1,5 to support Aristotle. How, then, can usury be sinful, seeing that it is consented to by the borrower? Answer: It is not absolutely, only conditionally, consented to. The borrower would have taken money without paying usury if he could have had it, says Odonis on Book V, but since he needs money and cannot have it otherwise, he consents to usury. Though he does in fact have a choice, his preference (to take money after all) is not represented as a gain relative to not taking money but as a loss (''damnum usurarum'') relative to being offered a better choice. Now what made the Aristotelians decide this case differently? The conclusion against usury would seem to be a foregone one in a fourteenth-century author, but some of the argument points beyond the case.

VI. The Nature of Economic Compulsion

When the great Franciscan teacher Johannes Duns Scotus discussed usury some decades earlier, he remarked at one point that the borrower pays it voluntarily, for nobody compels him (''nullus cogit eum''). Not so, according to Odonis on *EN*, IV: ''need (or necessity) compels him'' (''necessitas cogit eum''). But the translation of *necessitas* is a problem. It can signify a formal or a substantive condition. Odonis was a disciple (though at times oppositional) of Thomas Aquinas, who applied the Aristotelian concepts to the question of usury both in the *Summa theologiae* (in his first article on this subject) and in *De malo*. He who pays usury does not do so simply voluntarily, says Aquinas in the *Summa*, but under a certain necessity (''cum quadam necessitate''). It is certainly possible to interpret these words to mean no more than that there is compulsion; the borrower pays usury ''as it were coerced'' (''quasi coactus''), as he says in *De malo*. On this formal interpretation, ''need compels him'' would be a pleonasm, much as one might say in English that the borrower 'must needs pay' usury. There would be a classification of the case but no reason would be given for this classification in substantive economic terms. But while 'need' need not be then, so to speak, a substantive concept, there is no question but that Aquinas meant it to be just that. In *De malo* there is in fact an explicit appeal to Aristotle's distinction in Book V of the *Metaphysics* between 'necessary' in two substantive senses (i.e. the requisites either of life or of comfort) and in a formal sense (compulsion).[31] It is one or the other of the former which applies here according to Aquinas.

If this is how Odonis understood him, the statement that ''need compels him'' means that the borrower is forced, in order to fend off starvation or utter discomfort, to accept terms he would not otherwise have consented to. Need is not compulsion as such; need is a particular kind of *economic* compulsion, different from but on a par with physical

31. *Metaphysics*, V, 5; 1015a 20–27.

or moral compulsion. If we now turn from usury back to value in commodity exchange, it is quite clear that this is how Odonis and the tradition to which he belonged understood economic compulsion as modifying the liberalistic maxim. Odonis was a disciple also of Olivi and through him of Henry of Ghent. Explaining the value maxim, Henry rules out contracts based on ignorance, as we saw, and then adds those based on the buyer's need ("necessitas ementis"). Later authors who knew Ghent read this in substantive terms. Henry of Hassia speaks of "a poor man coerced by need," Henry of Oyta of someone "restricted by penury." Oyta and Olivi both use the word *egestas* (want, poverty). Justice in exchange is violated, says the latter, if one party "is compelled by such poverty or other need" ("ex tanta egestate vel alia necessitate compulsus") that the terms cannot be said to have issued freely. This was copied by Odonis in his treatise on contracts and by Bernardino of Siena and through him by Caepolla. What a thing can be sold for, says the latter, must be understood in the value formula to mean, "(sold for) to someone not in poverty or some other need." Trovamala (on usury), Carletus, and Mazzolini, in their several versions of the rule, carried this stipulation and brought it into the sixteenth century.

A thing is not worth what it can be sold for to a buyer who does not know or understand what he buys—or to one in need; for a buyer in need does not consent unconditionally to the terms of exchange offered him, he is compelled by his need to accept them. In the case of such uneven exchange, moral stricture must rather be placed on the party not so compelled (normally the seller) to make him forgo his bargaining advantage. As we know, this case is sometimes decided differently, also in the name of freedom. But reciprocal freedom is not possible. The Scholastics hardly envisaged the full ramifications of this basic dilemma. A very different solution from theirs had to be tried out before it dawned on economic legislators of a later age. But they were in a unique position to recognize the two voices of Janus at the city gates. It is a Roman voice that warns against restricting the profit motive and a patristic voice that warns against restriction by poverty. It was yet a while before the latter fell silent. And the Scholastics did not much appreciate the profit motive. Their concerns were for the seller's soul and for the buyer's body. It came to the same thing.

Like some post-classical systems, the Scholastic system of economic ethics recognized a moral distinction between need and other economic motives. In the classical tradition the basis of explanation was to be moved one step up, to effective demand, which all motives jointly determine and into which they all disappear. This was an analytical triumph in that it bypassed a difficult problem of measurement. It was a moral tragedy to the extent that it confused existence and measurability. The Scholastics, however, were saddled with the task of providing rules of thumb—if not for exact measurement, then at least for identifying those in need in order to know when to restrict free bargaining. They tried to solve this by distinguishing (i) commodities for which there was likely to be need and (ii) situations in which need was likely to arise. To these further traditions we must now address ourselves.

VII.   Necessaries and Luxuries

The idea that a seller could be blamed for taking what a sane and fully informed buyer agrees to pay for a commodity, just because he needs it particularly, would seem to run directly counter to the Roman law of property. This is not far wrong. Nevertheless, by adopting a certain canonist tradition the economic moralists managed to establish a mode of legal authority for their notion of economic compulsion. While the main Roman legal principle was that the right to use and disposal of property is coextensive with ownership, the law did recognize the responsibility involved in the public function of merchants and was prepared to regulate public supply of necessaries. The medieval legal maxim that everyone is the moderator and arbiter of his own thing is based primarily on Code 4,35,21, supported by Code 4,38,14. The later Scholastics took it mainly from the canonist Panormitanus, whose form is close to that of Baldus in comment on Code 1,4,1: "unusquisque in re sua est moderator et arbiter." The principle began to worry the moralists at about that time. It is interesting to note that the first attempt to tackle it may have been that of Henry of Hassia, who had read Henry of Ghent's transformation of 'can' to 'ought'. Summenhart knew them both and applied Ghent on the value maxim and Hassia on the property maxim. An arbiter is not simply any arbiter; a *just* arbiter must be assumed. A moderator is not simply any such, but one who prices his goods "moderately." This is in the Scholastic spirit, though again the legal challenge could not be countered by this kind of verbal sleight of hand, but must be met on its own terms.

Instrumental in ensuring this was Antonino of Florence, writing in the tradition of Olivi. The Franciscan had examined the objection that exchange is a voluntary thing: no law forces me to sell at a price which does not please me, just as no law forces the buyer to buy at a price which does not please him. True enough, concedes Olivi, but if I do sell I must observe the rules of law and justice in exchange, for once the goods are actually in exchange they are no longer simply mine to evaluate. This idea would not be foreign to the civilians. Bernardino borrowed the objection and the answer to it, and from there they passed to

276   History of Political Economy 14:2 (1982)

Antonino, who introduces the objection by quoting the property maxim from the Code and proceeds to state and counter it following Olivi. But then Antonino backs this up by citing a modification of the seller's rights founded in the Roman law itself. He receives it via the *Summa* of Hostiensis, explaining the opening canon in the title about buying and selling (3,17,1) in the Decretals. The canonist says almost exactly what Olivi was to say later (and the latter may well have consulted the *Summa*): No one can initially be compelled to sell his goods (referring to Code 4,38,14), but if goods are put up for sale and the seller will not accept the just price, he can be compelled to do so. Reference on this doctrine is to Digest 1,12,1,11. This is one of several places in the law providing authority for price regulation. But it is not general. As pointed out by Johannes Andreae on the same canon, the paragraph in question concerns the regulation of foodstuffs, and he makes a point of restricting its support to commodities like meat, grain, wine. In the case of non-necessary goods, says Andreae, the seller himself is moderator and arbiter.[32]

The right to impose a just price on dealers in victuals was taught by Cinus at Code 1,4,1, in fact countering an early version of the property maxim.[33] It was confirmed by Baldus and in the canon law context by Panormitanus. He states the basic rule, a thing is worth what it can commonly be sold for; then he repeats Hostiensis with Andreae's emphasis: he who offers foodstuffs for sale may be forced to sell at the just price. Panormitanus even suggests that he may be prepared to go back on Hostiensis on the point which Antonino had emphasized and tied to Olivi, namely the restriction of the principle to goods actually put up for sale. The law cannot be understood so narrowly; the important distinction is between necessaries, whether on sale or not, and luxuries. No informed teacher of economic ethics could easily pass over Panormitanus. His analysis is repeated almost verbatim by Mazzolini and at least echoed by Summenhart, who does not, however, concede the latter extension. Trovamala does, in his article on buying and selling, and his description there is the most explicit and vivid; the seller is moderator and arbiter only in the case of jewels and gems and similar articles not necessary for life but rather for pomp and ornament. Carletus also made the distinction and brought it to bear on the value formula. A thing may be sold for what it will bring under the conditions stated before as well as the condition that there is not such necessity as

32. In the line from Hostiensis and Andreae on this canon are also Ancharano, Zabarella, Butrio, Imola, Anania.

33. For some further references to the early legal tradition on this point, cp. John F. McGovern, "The Rise of New Economic Attitudes in Canon and Civil Law, A.D. 1200–1500," *The Jurist* 32 (1972): 39–50 at pp. 48 f.

to exclude voluntary choice. How to judge whether it is non-voluntary? Consider whether the commodity pertains to the necessities of life, such as grain, wine, clothes. A thing is worth what it can be sold for, said Mazzolini, but not if there is necessity, as when a starving man sells a choice horse for a pittance to buy bread. This is what the School of Salamanca inherited. It has been claimed that Vitoria was the first to distinguish between necessaries and luxuries in price analysis.[34] This is not quite so, but he gave much attention to the distinction and impressed it on his large following. With reference to one or the other or both of these legal maxims, limitation of free bargaining and valuation to luxuries is to be found in Medina, Soto, Navarra, Lopez, Toletus, Salon, Aragon.

The distinction is important not only for what it forbids but for what it permits. The list of luxuries compiled by these austere Iberians extends to a veritable catalogue of conspicuous consumption. It is beyond the immediate scope of this study to identify the spirit which turned back on Scholasticism, but it is worth recalling that it has sometimes been searched for in Spanish soil, and I believe it is fair to say that the School of Salamanca sometimes envisaged an interest in luxuries which goes somewhat beyond what is required for moral demarcation. Luxury articles according to Marx's definition were those exchanged for spent surplus value.[35] In neoclassical textbook examples there is a predilection for luxuries, on which economic forces can play freely without the stigma of exploitation. There is an analogy there to late Scholastic teaching. It is the oppression of the needy that is sinful. The moralist does not care to arbitrate the division of the spoils, but such arbitration provides a neutral field of analysis, and a growing interest in analysis at the cost of ethics means that the Scholastic matrix is fading.

VIII. The Common Estimate

Need is subjective and cannot be exactly classified against morally neutral or objectionable 'appetites,' but it has one dimension which can be identified by reference to the objects and services by which it is relieved. The idea that such objects and services, insofar as they are commodities, ought to be supplied to the needy below exchange value is at the basis of patristic alms teaching and of modern socialism. To decide what is necessary and what is not was less of a problem in a sur-

34. Demetrio Iparraguirre, "Las fuentes del pensamiento económico en España en los siglos XIII al XVI," *Estudios de Deusto*, 2a época, II,3 (1954), pp. 79–113 at p. 103.
35. *Capital* II,xx,4. It was not a new idea; cp. Montesquieu, *De l'esprit des lois*, VII,1: "le luxe . . . n'est fondé que sur les commodités qu'on se donne par le travail des autres."

278   *History of Political Economy 14:2 (1982)*

vival society than it is in the welfare state. The problem was enforcement. Henry of Hassia made a name for himself in the history of economics by advocating official price regulation of all necessaries, and it was certainly favored by many Scholastics. But in the unruly societies of the Middle Ages exchangers were mostly left to their own devices, and moralists had to rely on precepts about just pricing enforceable only in the internal forum. Simple positive rules were needed to guide the conscience in cases where free bargaining could not be allowed. These rules have been the objects of endless disputes about the nature of 'the medieval just price.' I submit that they might be less controversial if stricter reference were maintained to the type of negative conditioning discussed above, and in particular to the Scholastic teaching on economic freedom and compulsion, which determines the field of application and the moral purpose of these rules.

In the literal history of the liberalistic value maxim, one positive rule of just pricing takes absolute precedence. Its legal support is a piece of text which for some reason had found its way twice into the Digest, at 9,2,33 and at 35,2,63. It states that the prices of things do not work on the basis of singular affection or utility, but commonly ("sed communiter"). In both places the Ordinary Gloss applies this interpretation to the value maxim: A thing is worth as much as it can be sold for—commonly, that is ("intellige communiter" at 9,2,33; "scilicet communiter" at 35,2,63). The remark, which channels the legal tradition in the direction of central economic categories, is routinely ascribed to Accursius, but it can in fact be traced to earlier sources and is frequently signed *Az.* for Azo in the manuscripts.[36] An early dating is confirmed in canon law material. In the title on usury in the Decretals there is a canon (5,19,6) taken from the first compilation (5,15,8) which discusses present and future valuation. This is the cue to the following gloss, extant in numerous manuscripts: A thing is worth what it can be sold for, for the price of things is not to be estimated on the basis of the affection of singular individuals, but commonly. Now this is exactly the juxtaposition of the simple value maxim with the text of the Digest and 9,2,33 and 35,2,63. It is always signed *l.*, *la.* or *laur.* for Laurentius Hispanus, a student of Azo who annotated the first compilation before 1215, which in all likelihood makes the gloss independent of Accur-

---

36. As appearing in the Ordinary Gloss, it is thus signed in Paris BN lat. 4458; 4460; 4465; and 4466; and in Bamberg SB Jur. 13. There is a problem in that a family of manuscripts with pre-Accursian glosses, represented by Paris 4451; 4463; and Bamberg Jur. 11, have the gloss, signed *Azo*, but reading *firmiter* rather than *communiter*. If this is the original version, the early history of the value maxim has to be reconsidered, but the remark seems uncalled for by the text and may be due to a corruption. Further paleographical research is beyond my competence and present purpose.

sius.[37] It spread far and wide in the Scholastic world. Bernard Botone and Hostiensis in their Glosses both copied Laurentius (not quite verbatim), as did Henry of Ghent in his third *quodlibet*. Even more frequent is the extended value formula in the version of the Digest. Azo's "commonly"—if it is indeed to be ascribed to him—became universal. This is not to say that the medieval "common estimate" derived entirely from Roman law. It appeared early in theological texts. In the tradition of the *Ethics*, where Aristotle was taken to make value dependent on need, the Averroists interpreted this as 'common need.' These several traditions are interdependent. In some way they converged to build a familiar consensus.

However, while all agreed that value should be understood *communiter*, it remained to be explained what this meant in everyday economic terms. In the legal tradition it was Bartolus who took the concept literally out of the study and into the marketplace. In one of the places in the Digest (13,1,14) where the simple value maxim is stated in the Ordinary Gloss, Bartolus comments: A thing is worth what it can be sold for, that is, commonly and in a public place, to many people, over several days.[38] These are, of course, the characteristics of the regular market. A thing is worth as much as it can be sold for in the public market ("in foro publico"), said Ludovicus Pontanus at Digest 39,6,18,3. Now it took some time for the Bartolists to spell this out. Considering again the role of the canonists in Scholastic economics in general, it is curious to note that they seem to have been instrumental in developing Bartolus's hint and may in fact have brought their own reading back to the civilians. Pontanus and Tartagnus, who explained the value maxim in terms of the market at Digest 35,2,63, had both studied at Bologna under Johannes de Imola, a 'doctor of both laws.' He was in turn a student of the canonist Antonius de Butrio. Both cite the value maxim in comment on the Decretals. The text is the canon (3,17,1) on which we have already quoted a line of commentators concerning necessaries. It is actually an injunction against overpricing strangers: Merchants are not to charge those who pass through a region more for local commodities than they can sell

37. The gloss is known only as appearing in later collections, e.g. in that of Tancredus in Paris BN lat. 3931A; 14321; BMaz 1292; Bamberg SB Can. 19; 21; and in that of Vincentius Hispanus in Paris 3967; 3968. For some of the early canon law references I am indebted to John W. Baldwin, "The Medieval Theories of the Just Price," *Transactions of the American Philosophical Society* 49, no. 4 (1959).—From Endemann (1883—who discovered Caepolla) and Brants (1895—who located Ghent's key position), historians made only sporadic reference to the legal value maxim until serious textual research was initiated by Baldwin.

38. There are similar stipulations in Baldus and Fulgosius on the same law; cp. also Angelus on 35,2,63.

280   History of Political Economy 14:2 (1982)

them for in the marketplace ("quam in mercato vendere possunt").
Butrio applies that phrase to the value maxim: A thing is worth what it
can be sold for *in mercato*. Imola copied this, and Pontanus and
Tartagnus may have got the idea through him. From a twin faucet in
Roman and canon law the market interpretation saturated late Scholastic economics, tying the value maxim to a rule of pricing which goes
back to the thirteenth century.

IX.   Compulsion and the Market

So our investigation of the legal formula seems in the end to have
taken us, by some twists and turns, into the mainstream of current
opinion about the medieval just price. It was simply the common estimate as made by the market. This is in a sense true, but I should be
most reluctant to leave the matter there. In order to relate this last tradition to those discussed earlier, it is necessary to ask what 'common'
actually means in this context. In what ethically significant sense is a
market price common? Let us recall that the English word (as well as
the Latin *communis*) can mean 'usual' (that which commonly is done
or happens) as well as 'joint' (that which we have in common). These
meanings are not contradictory but emphasis on one or the other can
make a lot of difference to the formula. It was inspired by a text which
contrasts 'common' and 'singular'; so the latter meaning ('joint') is obviously present and perhaps dominant in the legal tradition in general,
though it should be noted that 'singular' sometimes means 'unusual'. A
thing is worth as much as it can be sold for, said Nicolaus de Ausmo,
"in the common course not in the singular event." This element of
meaning ('usual') is clearly signaled by Bartolus's stipulation that an
average or norm over a period of time be considered. Some of those
who speak of the medieval just price as the market price fail to make
this kind of stipulation, and I presume that this is so because it is taken
more or less for granted that the Scholastics considered the market
price just because it is common in the sense of joint rather than because
it is common in the sense of usual. But there is a danger there of reading too much of the present into the past. It is one of the characteristics
of markets to impose the same price on all. But it is surely anachronis-
tic to imagine that such a joint price in a medieval marketplace would
be justified in the eyes of a Scholastic observer the way the abstract
price mechanism is justified (in some eyes) today, namely as a guide to
social equilibrium and efficient allocation of joint resources. If the joint
price was justified, it would be so because it was jointly imposed, much
as a price *usually* imposed would be justified: not as a guide to
achieving the common good but as a guide to preventing singular evil.

There is a revolution in scientific economics when price comes to

Langholm · Economic freedom in Scholastic thought 281

be considered as an instrument in the social system and is seen to work in a certain way, carrying reward and information. Authors in the classical tradition argued that the price instrument, if left alone, would tend to optimize the social system in a certain sense, and *therefore* the free market price was, for them, in a sense a just price. In Scholastic authors this instrumental attitude to economic variables is rare. Though its thin voice speaks in Olivi (and even earlier, for instance in Albertus Magnus), it made itself definitely heard only much later and then grew slowly toward its breakthrough in the *Wealth of Nations*. The development of the attitude is particularly fascinating in the case of price because it does not appear readily on the surface where a body of teaching was inherited from the Scholastics. The market price was all along considered a just price. What changed, subtly and even unnoticeably from one author to the next, was the nature of its justification. This makes for a hidden ideological tension which tends to confuse accounts of early modern price theory. Justification would not originally rely on social considerations largely beyond the limited analytical horizon of the Scholastics and even running counter to their basic moral preferences. When they recommended the common estimate of the market, it was for different reasons—reasons which support all the arguments on value recorded in this study and tie them together.

Throughout the Scholastic centuries, a patristic core of ethics kept holding out against the social dimension of Greek thought. What must be stressed again is its personalistic orientation. If the seller is in a position to supply the buyer's need, this is nearly all there is to it from a moral point of view; duly considering his own needs as well, he should so do and not take undue advantage of his neighbor. To profit from the condition of the buyer, said Aquinas, is a kind of theft. Retracing our steps, the market rule follows from this position. Need is a kind of compulsion. As such it is limited to classes of commodities; some are luxuries and deserve no protection. Necessaries require no protection either, when supply is plentiful. In a dearth of necessaries it is a duty to share. But moral admonition is no less directed at those who wield the awful power of controlling supply—the merchants who can take advantage of scarcity or (worst of all economic sins) create scarcity. There is no essential difference here between extortion from a single buyer in need and extortion from a community by the monopolist withholding supply. Buyers may compete for what little is released and so determine a monopoly market price which is a joint price but includes profit from the unusual conditions of the buyers and is sinful. A thing is worth what it can be sold for, said Azpilcueta in his manual for confessors, "in the absence of monopoly, fraud, and deceit." When exchange takes place in a competitive market under normal conditions, no single

282   *History of Political Economy 14:2 (1982)*

buyer or group of buyers can be thus taken advantage of. All pay a joint and usual price. The market rule of just pricing is then redundant. It works only by hypothesis, as when market conditions are unusual or when exchange takes place out of reach of any market. Then the seller can be admonished by reference to what might be thought to be a usual market price, in the assurance that normal supply and competing sellers would rule out profit on the basis of the singular condition of the buyer. This was, on my reading, the simple justification of the rule in the sources we have studied here: Where there is a market, there is no compulsion.

If, that is, you can pay the market price. The beggar who lacks the price of bread is under the greatest compulsion of all, but his need was at best relieved by the puny powers of charity. In the end the usual is justified only by social convention. There would seem to us to be a point where concern for individual need must question distribution and leave value alone. But that meant social readjustments unthought-of by the Scholastics. When society did change, and social philosophy with it, it was not in the first instance to favor (as Aquinas saw them) the conditions of the buyers, but rather the conditions of the sellers.

X. *"Respect to Particular Good"*

In recent studies of the ideological bases of classical economics much of the emphasis has been on the idea usually associated in England with the name of Mandeville, namely that individual self-seeking may entail unintended social benefits and can be so justified. This way of thinking was not foreign to the natural law philosophers nor to some of the late Scholastics. Its importance is not in dispute, but it may be wise not to let it overshadow the idea of natural right discussed initially. It is not as though the two oppose one another; "there is no question," said Hume, discussing property laws, "but the regard to general good is much enforced by the respect to particular."[39] This sums up very nicely the constitution of classical economic liberalism as well. When individual self-seeking is justified by social benefits, *and* certain less pleasant consequences must be tolerated because individuals just do what they have a priori a right to do, there is a tremendous reinforcement effect building up in the system. It may explain some of the system's strength and longevity.

Perhaps it may also help answer a question which is beyond the scope of this study but naturally presents itself at its close, namely how the Scholastic efforts to modify Roman legal liberalism could be so easily swept aside in the seventeenth century when material opportunities

39. *An Enquiry concerning the Principles of Morals*, Appendix III, in *Philosophical Works*, 4 (London 1882), at p. 278.

Langholm　·　Economic freedom in Scholastic thought　　283

called for it. There is no denying that my quotation from the natural law philosophers is somewhat selective. Grotius appeals to the common estimate, quoting the Digest;[40] Pufendorf deplores terms of exchange that show "inhumanity toward the needy."[41] But though the teaching of the Schools can be heard in these authors, it sounds rather feebly. What came through was a proclamation of the rights, as against the obligations, of the property holder and the existence of the state for his purpose. There is a long tradition which sees this as a main root of liberalism. "For *right* is *liberty*," says Hobbes in *Leviathan*.[42] In the Christian ethic, liberty is duty, but after Mandeville it was no longer so obvious where one's duty lay. Value, as Joan Robinson reminds us, is "just a word."[43] But it is an evaluative word and tends to commend certain attitudes to the facts which it describes. Owing to a confluence of evaluative potential from the individual and the social sphere its inherent prescriptive content is many times multiplied. Value in exchange tells the owner how society evaluates his property while at the same time directing his obligation to social efficiency. Right and duty claim freedom in one voice.

But the guardian of freedom warns in a double voice after all. John Stuart Mill also took exception to fraud and force in advocating freedom of bargaining for the common good.[44] But he belonged to a tradition of social philosophers who had shut their eyes to the fact, once recognized, that when there is need, the bargain is not free on the part of the needy. "Necessity never made a good bargain," reads one of the aphorisms of homely wisdom adorning *Poor Richard's Almanac*.[45] "My poverty, but not my will consents," wrote the greatest domestic philosopher of them all.[46] It may be that the deeper strata of the European moral consciousness never really unlearnt that lesson. And so, perhaps, in this present age of welfare, our renewed insistence on the "particular good"—with a different address from that of Hume and *against* all considerations of social efficiency—is a measure of the extent to which our economics is once again, for better and for worse, Scholastic.

40. II, xii, 14.
41. VI, i, 8.
42. Ch. 26.
43. *Economic Philosophy* (London 1962), p. 46.
44. *On Liberty*, in *Collected Works*, 18 (Toronto 1977), at p. 293.
45. Year 1735.
46. *Romeo and Juliet*, Act V, i.

Name Index

Al-Dawwani 126, 127
Al-Farabi 125
Al-Ghazali 126
Althaus, J. 55, 56, 57, 58
Althusius *see* Althaus J.
Andrea, J. 187
Antonino, San 71, 72, 110, 223
Aristotle 155, 158, 160, 167, 218, 220, 221, 223, 230, 231, 238
Ashley, W. 72, 227
Augustinus, A. 4
Auxerre. W. of 174
Avicenna 126
Azpilcueta, M. de *see* Navarrus

Bacon, F. 49
Baldwin, J. W. 212, 234
Baxter, R. 50, 51, 106
Beaumanoir 44
Becher, J. J. 22, 61, 62, 63, 86
Becker, C. 24
Bernardino of Siena, San 41, 43, 70, 71, 102, 105
Biel, G. 73
Bodin, J. 45, 75
Bohm-Bawerk, E. 178
Bois, F. du *see* Sylvius, F.
Boisguilbert 87
Boulakia, J. D. C. 193–206
Brandini, C. 112
Bras, G. le 173
Bryson 124, 125, 126, 127
Buoninsegni, T. 102
Buridan, J. 39, 69, 70
Burke 23

Cajetan, Cardinal 90, 102
Calvin, J. 176
Cantillon, R. 81
Cecil, R. 43
Child, J. 86
Chivasso, A. C. da 106
Clark, J. M. 107
Cohn, E. J. 33
Coke, E. 49
Colbert 54
Condillac, E. B. de 81, 95

Cossa, L. 67
Cotton, J. 51, 107
Cotton, R. 24
Cournot, A. 65
Court, P. de la 59, 60, 87
Culpeper, T. 86

Damhoudere, J. de 42
Davenant, C. 85
Dempsey, B. W. 1–16, 173, 182, 183, 184, 185, 189

Endemann, W. 36

Fisher, I. 30, 31, 182–3
Friedman, D. D. 263–71

Galiani, F. 88, 95
Gerson, J. 104
Gordon, B. J. 160, 210, 212, 221
Gras, N. S. B. 2
Gresham, T. 49
Grice-Hutchinson, M. 95
Groot, H. de *see* Grotius, H. de
Grotius, H. 2, 63, 64, 87, 273, 295

Haddad, L. 244–62
Haney, L. H. 2, 209
Heckscher, E. F. 44, 51, 86
Hobbes, T. 272, 273, 295
Hollander, S. 153–72, 210, 234
Hubbard, W. 24
Hume 294
Hutcheson, F. 94

Jafar al-Dimashqi 128
Jevons 227
Johnson, E. A. J. 17–33, 86

Khaldun, I. 114–52, 193–206, 245–61
King, G. 85

Langenstein, H. of 98, 99, 162
Langholm, O. 272–95
Lessinus, G. of 178, 280
Lessius, L. 41, 42, 73, 106, 183, 184, 185
Leys, L. de *see* Lessius, L.

Leyva, D. de C. y 73
Lowry, S. T. 209, 221
Luca, G. de 77
Lugo, J. de 77, 180, 183, 184, 185, 188
Luther, M. 50

McLaughlin, T. P. 173
Maffei, S. 81
Magnus, B. A. 6, 7, 8, 100, 101, 215
Maine, H. 227
Malderus, J. 73
Malynes, G. de 23, 50, 84, 89
Marshall, A. 208
Marx, K. 100, 217, 228
Melitz, J. 173–91
Mercado, T. de 75
Mill, J. S. 295
Misselden, E. 52, 54, 75, 84
Molina, L. de 41, 74, 104, 111, 183, 184, 185
Moulin, C. de 80
Mun, T. 50, 84, 85

Nasir, al-Din Tusi 126
Navarrus 73, 105, 183
Noonan, J. T. 156, 161, 173, 174, 175, 177,
     178, 180, 182, 184, 187

O'Brien, G. 212
Odonis, G. 276
Oresme, N. 40

Pascal, B. 80
Peri, G. D. 58, 59
Petty, W. 85
Peutinger, C. 46, 47, 48
Plessner 129
Polanyi, K. 208
Pliny 35
Pufendorf, S. 63, 64, 272, 273, 295

Quincey, T. de 71

Ricardo, D. 217, 274
Ridolfi, L. di A. 70, 83
Robinson, J. 295

Rogers, T. 51
Roover, R. de 34–66, 67–96, 97–123, 166,
     173–91, 210, 233, 234
Roscher, W. 98
Rosenthal, E. I. J. 133

Salin, E. 70
Scaccia, S. 77
Schreiber, E. 36
Schumpeter, J. 173–91, 182, 183, 184, 185, 208
Scotus, J. D. 12, 13, 105
Seneca 273
Serra, A. 88
Shackle, G. L. S. 244
Smith, A. 34, 37, 60, 63, 65, 94, 95, 216
Sombart, W. 98
Soto, D. de 73, 75, 78, 184, 279, 281
Soudek 211, 216, 221
Spengler, J. J. 114–52, 156, 209, 216, 219, 229
Summenhart, C. 184
Sylvius, F. 73

Tawney, R. H. 32, 214
Thompson, J. W. 2
Toynbee 151
Turgot 80
Turri, R. de 77

Usury 86

Van den Hove, P. see Court, P. de la
Van Werkeke, H. 108
Vauban 87
Viner, J. 89
Vitoria, F. de 73

Weber, M. 50, 97
Wheeler, J. 52, 84
Wilson, G. W. 207–25, 226, 227, 228, 232,
     235, 240, 242, 243
Wilson, T. 23, 89
Worland, S. T. 226–43
Wycliffe, J. 110

Pioneers in Economics

Section I: The Forerunners of Classical Economics

1. The Historiography of Economics

2. Aristotle (384–322 B.C.)

3. St Thomas Aquinas (1225–1274)

4. The Early Mercantilists
   Thomas Mun (1571–1641), Edward Misselden (1608–1634), Gerard de Malynes (1586–1623)

5. The Later Mercantilists
   Josiah Child (1603–1699) and John Locke (1632–1704)

6. Pre-Classical Economists Volume I
   Charles Davenant (1656–1714) and William Petty (1623–1687)

7. Pre-Classical Economists Volume II
   Pierre le Pesant Boisguilbert (1645–1714), George Berkeley (1685–1753), Baron de Montesquieu (1689–1755), Ferdinando Galiani (1727–1787), James Anderson (1739–1808), Dugald Stewart (1753–1828)

8. Pre-Classical Economists Volume III
   John Law (1671–1729) and Bernard Mandeville (1660–1733)

9. Richard Cantillon (1680–1734) and Jacques Turgot (1727–1781)

10. François Quesnay (1694–1774), Volumes I and II

11. David Hume (1711–1776) and James Steuart (1712–1780)

Section II: The Golden Age of Classical Economics

12. Adam Smith (1723–1790) Volumes I and II

13. Henry Thornton (1760–1815), Jeremy Bentham (1748–1832), James Lauderdale (1759–1839), Simonde de Sismondi (1773–1842)

14. David Ricardo (1772–1823)

15. Jean-Baptiste Say (1776–1832)

16. Thomas Malthus (1766–1834) and John Stuart Mill (1806–1873)

17. Ramsay McCulloch (1789–1864), Nassau Senior (1790–1864), Robert Torrens (1780–1864)

18. Thomas Tooke (1774–1858), Samuel Longfield (1802–1884), Richard Jones (1790–1855)

19. William Whewell (1794–1866), Dionysius Lardner (1793–1859), William Lloyd (1795–1852), Charles Babbage (1792–1871)

20. George Scrope (1797–1876), Thomas Attwood (1783–1856), Edwin Chadwick (1800–1890), John Cairnes (1823–1875)

21. James Mill (1773–1836), John Rae (1796–1872), Edward West (1782–1828), Thomas Joplin (1790–1847)

22. James Wilson (1805–1860), Issac Butt (1813–1879), T E Cliffe Leslie (1827–1882)

23. Karl Marx (1818–1883)

Section III: Neoclassical Economics and its Critics

24. Johann von Thuenen (1783–1850)

25. Antoine Cournot (1801–1877 and Jules Dupuit (1804–1866)

26. Leon Walras (1834–1910) Volumes I and II

27. Carl Menger (1840–1921)

28. Eugen von Boehm-Bawerk (1851–1914) and Friedrich von Wieser (1851–1926)

29. Knut Wicksell (1851–1926) Volumes I and II

30. Alfred Marshall (1842–1924) and Francis Edgeworth (1845–1926)

31. Gustav Schmoller (1838–1917) and Werner Sombart (1863–1941)

32. Dissenters
    Charles Fourier (1772–1837), Henri de St Simon (1760–1825), Pierre-Joseph Proudhon (1809–1865), John A. Hobson (1858–1940)

33. Thorstein Veblen (1857–1929)

34. Wesley Mitchell (1874–1948), John Commons (1862–1945), Clarence Ayres (1891–1972)

35. Henry George (1839–1897) Volumes I and II

36. Vilfredo Pareto (1848–1923) Volumes I and II

Section IV: Twentieth Century Economics

37. Arthur Pigou (1877–1959)

38. Frank Knight (1885–1972) and Henry Simons (1899–1946)

39. Joseph Schumpeter (1883–1950)

40. Edward Chamberlin (1899–1967)

41. Michael Kalecki (1899–1970)

42. Harold Hotelling (1895–1973), Lionel Robbins (1898–1984), Clark Warburton (1896–1979), John Bates Clark (1847–1938), Ludwig von Mises (1881–1973)

43. Irving Fisher (1867–1947), Arthur Hadley (1856–1930), Ragnar Frisch (1895–1973), Friedrich Hayek (1899––), Allyn Young (1876–1929), Ugo Mazzola (1863–1899)

44. Harry Johnson (1923–1977)

45. Bertin Ohlin (1899–1979)

46. Pierro Sraffa (1898–1983)

47. Joan Robinson (1903–1983) and George Shackle (1903––)

48. John Maynard Keynes (1883–1946) Volumes I, II, III and IV